T0284751

S.T.A.R. Chess

Paul Motwani

First published in the UK by Gambit Publications Ltd 1998
Copyright © Paul Motwani 1998

A copy of the British Library Cataloguing in Publication data is available from
the British Library

ISBN 1 901983 03 X

DISTRIBUTION:
Worldwide (except USA): Biblios Distribution Services, Star Rd, Partridge
Green, West Sussex, RH13 8LD, England.
USA: BHB International, Inc, 994 Riverview Drive, Totowa, New Jersey 07511,
USA.

For all other enquiries (including a full list of all Gambit Chess titles) please
contact the publishers, Gambit Publications Ltd, 69 Masbro Rd, Kensington,
London W14 0LS.
Fax +44 (0)171 371 1477. E-mail 100561.3121@compuserve.com.

Edited by Graham Burgess
Typeset by Petra Nunn
Printed in Great Britain by Redwood Books, Trowbridge, Wilts.

10 9 8 7 6 5 4 3 2 1

Gambit Publications Ltd
Managing Director: GM Murray Chandler
Chess Director: GM John Nunn
Editorial Director: FM Graham Burgess
Assistant Editor: GM John Emms
German Editor: WFM Petra Nunn

Contents

Symbols

+	check
++	double check
#	checkmate
x	captures

!!	brilliant move
!	good move
!?	interesting move
?!	dubious move
?	bad move
??	blunder

Ch	championship

1-0	the game ends in a win for White
½-½	the game ends in a draw
0-1	the game ends in a win for Black

(*n*)	nth match game
(*D*)	diagram follows

Introduction

Welcome to the wonderland of *S.T.A.R. Chess*, my favourite adventure in the trilogy of journeys into original thinking that began with *H.O.T. Chess* and *C.O.O.L. Chess* (published in October 1996 and May 1997 respectively). Just as a star-bound rocket would kick off with a big blast, the forthcoming coded message is designed to propel our brains into a new excited level, and will reveal a statement which can be our motto as we aim higher and higher.

SJLZL XE RC VDR AXWXRQ PJC XER'S YDIDMAL CT FCXRQ VCZL SJDR JL SJXRNE JL YDR FC.

JLRZH TCZF.

Each letter must be replaced by a *different* letter (of the English alphabet) to discover the true message. The final two 'words' represent the name and surname of the man who made the statement.

It may be tempting to look at the solutions section near the end of this book, but I'm betting instead that you will not deny yourself the chance to find a **strategy** with which to **attack** the coded message. A bit like spotting **tactics**, isn't there some part of the message that you can hit first, just as you might focus on some prominent weakness in an opponent's position on the chessboard? It will take time though to crack this tough adversary, and fighting it may almost seem to induce a **reaction**, as if it were becoming more difficult and deliberately trying to stop you from succeeding! However, no fear. With *S.T.A.R. Chess*, let's boldly go where no one has gone before.

I think you are entitled to enjoy a high-level chess adventure in which we encounter lots of thought-provoking situations. Then we will feel like *stimulated, tested and refreshed* (S.T.A.R.!) people, and maximum learning and fun will be derived. The main requirement is that we start our journey together with open minds and a willingness to give the imagination some freedom to expand. Film fans like myself might compare it to wanting to see a movie in 3D and/or on an extra-large screen rather than in a plainer way. For example, the IMAX screen at Brussels's huge Kinepolis cinema is a real treat that has the edge over any of the other 28 screens. Incidentally, the 15 letters in *purer IMAX action* can be rearranged to give *Proxima Centauri*, the name of the nearest star to our Solar System. However, already our minds must be in star mode to cope with the distance meant by the word 'nearest', since light travelling from Proxima Centauri at the incredible speed of 300,000,000 metres per second still takes 4.24 years to reach

Earth, and so (provided we have a sufficiently powerful telescope) we are always seeing the star as it looked four years and three months ago!

Time is one of the most significant factors that influences the outcome of many over-the-board chess games, and we will examine it more later in the book, but at the moment I am reminded of two sayings that relate to time.

1) 'Yesterday is experience, tomorrow is hope; today is getting from one to the other.'

2) 'Today's special moments are tomorrow's happy memories.'

Well, as I write right now, my 'yesterday', 'today' and (hopefully!) 'tomorrow' are all part of 1997, and what a special year it is. That is emphasized by many details throughout the next few pages, but this introductory part of the book also lays the foundations on which later sections are built, and sets the scene properly to give an appropriate background before the action really takes off.

I find it inspiring that on Sunday 13th April (Garry Kasparov's 34th birthday, and also the day I completed my first chess 'world tour' of Scotland) in this International Year of Sport, a 21-year-old golfer, Tiger Woods, played like a tiger at the US Masters and gave a brilliant demonstration of what can be achieved through bold **attacking** play combined with sustained yet calm concentration. The record books got a new entry of the youngest-ever winner, and with the best score and biggest margin.

Time-warping 91 days further back, there was the birthday of HAL, the chess-playing super-computer from the film *2001: A Space Odyssey*, in which the machine stated 'I am a HAL 9000 computer, production number three. I became operational at the HAL plant in Urbana, Illinois on January 12, 1997'. Four months later in New York, a relative named Deeper Blue, weighing 1.4 tons and calculating up to 300 million positions per second, defeated Kasparov in a mere 19 moves with sacrificial, attacking play in the final game of their match. It is true that the Earth's highest-ranked human chess player made a serious mistake on move seven, but the manner in which the computer capitalized on the error was a perfect advert for the merits of playing in a vigorous fashion. (For a detailed account of the man versus machine challenge, I would refer you to the excellent book *Kasparov v Deeper Blue* by GM Daniel King, but I've no doubt that an immensely more special event in Danny's life was his marriage to Ireland's lovely Mairead O'Siochru in June – many congratulations!)

Tiger Woods and Deeper Blue have, in different ways, shown us the power of an attacking approach backed up with good concentration and accurate calculation. Kasparov had already underlined that at the end of 1996 by the way he played to win the Category 21 six-player double-all-play-all event at Las Palmas, where the average rating was approximately 2757. His play was just as daring in overcoming all the obstacles on a star-strewn path to another first place on 6½/10 at the Category 19 (2719 average rating this time) Novgorod tournament in June. Kasparov's FIDE rating on 1 July 1997 set an all-time-high record (so far!) of 2820. The PCA World Champion's attacking play still contains as much bite as Deeper Blue's computer bytes.

One of the most successful counterattacking weapons in Kasparov's opening repertoire is the Sicilian Najdorf (1 e4 c5 2 ♘f3 d6 3 d4 cxd4 4 ♘xd4 ♘f6 5 ♘c3 a6), named after the great GM Miguel Najdorf (1910-97) who passed away, aged 87, in Spain's city of Malaga on Friday 4 July, half a century after he won the strong 1947 tournament at Mar del Plata with the fantastic score of 14/17, ahead of runners-up Grandmasters Gideon Ståhlberg and Erich Eliskases. The latter, one of Austria's finest-ever players, also died during 1997 at the age of 83 in Argentina's city of Cordoba.

Such stars really deserve far more than a few words here, but I will try to highlight some especially notable points about Najdorf, since I actually met him at several Olympiads. Much earlier he had represented Poland (Najdorf was born in Warsaw) in the Olympiads of 1935, 1937 and 1939, but certain circumstances during the Second World War led to him adopting Argentine nationality in 1944. Afterwards he won the national championship no less than nine times, and played tremendous chess for Argentina at Olympiads from 1950 to 1976 plus the Candidates events of Budapest 1950 and Zurich 1953. As well as having numerous brilliant tournament victories, Najdorf was also amazing in simultaneous displays. He once played 202 games, scoring 182 wins, 12 draws and only 8 losses. As if 93.1% was not good enough, he notched up a 93.2% with a tally of 226 wins, 14 draws and a mere 10 losses from a 'simul' over 250 boards! Another outstanding feat was 39 wins, 4 draws and 2 losses out of 45 games ... played 'blind' without sight of the actual boards! In some ways it is quite fitting that Najdorf's last public appearance, the week before he died, was at Kasparov's simultaneous display in Madrid.

When I was in Sweden during April 1996, Indonesia's Professor Max Wotulo, a good friend of Najdorf, told me a very amusing story which reveals another delightful aspect of the hero's character. Apparently Efim Bogoljubow (1889-1952; World Championship challenger in 1929 and 1934) reckoned that he would need to beat Najdorf in the last round of a tournament in Stockholm in order to win the first prize. So, prior to the game, Bogoljubow bought Najdorf a large bottle of Scotch whisky! The strong stuff had the opposite effect to the desired one: Najdorf won in scintillating style and was awarded the Best Game Prize. His words to Bogoljubow after the game showed typical good humour: 'If you want a point from me, just give me water'! However, with his renowned attacking abilities, Najdorf could down any opponent (and a drink!) when firing on all cylinders.

So although all the chapters of *S.T.A.R. Chess* have their own *special theme and role* (S.T.A.R., again!), I am particularly recommending an attacking style of play with a sound basis. This can often be made even more effective by injecting some originality into the game during the opening phase. Therefore the many battles which I have chosen for this book are packed with interesting ideas covering a wide spectrum of openings that should cater for most players. *H.O.T. Chess* and *C.O.O.L. Chess* are also brimming full with other creative ideas that are keen to burst out onto the chessboard, and IM Jonathan Rowson, who is one of the hottest stars around, made good use of a cool line *en route* to winning the 1997 Aberdeen Open. This friendly Scottish J.R. bought *C.O.O.L. Chess* on the evening of Friday 9th May and digested the contents of game number one as his bedtime reading that night. The following day, J.R. flashed out his newly-acquired opening ideas and defeated GM Dr Colin McNab in only 27 moves. I think you will benefit from and greatly enjoy seeing more examples of such powerful play, so several brilliant J.R. performances feature in *S.T.A.R. Chess*. By the way, I was recently told by 11-year-old Rafe Martyn (another of the talented young people with whom I often discuss chess) that his friend David Atkinson genuinely thought that I am a Grandmartian! This prompted Rafe's mother, Kedrun, to suggest that I ought to dress like one in order to publicize this book, but that is one gambit I'd rather not accept!

Also starring in 1997 was the 1st Mind Games Olympiad at the Royal Festival Hall on London's South Bank from 18th-24th August. This was a global Mind Sports event for card and board games (including Chinese Chess or 'xiang qi'), and a wide assortment of other mental tests such as crosswords, memory, calculation and IQ items. I bet that the 16 schoolchildren who qualified for the Terafinal of the Kasparov/Save The Children UK Chess Challenge loved playing at the same venue, with the atmosphere charged by thousands of brilliant buzzing brains. Don't worry if you couldn't be there ... *S.T.A.R. Chess* contains a great variety of puzzles, problems and tests to keep us sharp, and alert to tactical possibilities in particular. However, the importance of dusting off any cobwebs of tiredness from the mind was emphasized to me on Wednesday 9th April 1997 by my father, who has been a medical doctor in Dundee for the past 32 years. Dad said to me 'Even as you get older, never think that you cannot succeed in playing better chess than you do today. Energy is important, but it can take many forms, and the primary type you need in chess is energy for thinking. Therefore get plenty of rest and sleep so that your brain can function as well as God made it capable of doing.'

My father's good practical advice is another example of S.T.A.R. (sleep tight and rest!), and following it can also help us to defeat the toughest puzzles we will meet. The puzzle aspect of the book should be especially enjoyable and beneficial, since the problems have been designed to improve skills in logical thinking, which, in turn, has spin-offs in chess. In the words of Mikhail Moiseevich Botvinnik (World Champion 1948-57, 1958-60, 1961-3), 'Chess is the art which expresses the beauty of logic'. In the case of compositions, I feel studies train amazing resourcefulness (S.T.A.R. yet again!).

You may, whenever you wish, compare your own puzzle solutions with the ones which I have given in the section near the end of this book (unless I state that the answer appears at some earlier point), but we can learn to increase our patience and determination by not looking up the answers until we have really given each problem our best unhurried shot. One does not have to be a great mathematician in order to solve any of the puzzles in *S.T.A.R. Chess*, no matter how difficult certain ones may seem. Attacking the problems with calm, logical thinking (perhaps using a pencil and paper too) can make them crack in every case. Here is a quick one right now: my first two letters are a man; my first three a woman; my first four a brave man; my whole a brave woman. What am I? The key word does, in a sense, celebrate the fact that this year is the centenary of the first women's international chess tournament, but cover up the next few lines before you see the answer!

OK, congratulations on finding the word 'heroine' relating to girls or women such as England's Harriet Hunt who won the World Under-20 Ladies Championship in Zagan, Poland, in July with a scorching score of $10^1/2/13$ that was as hot as the planet Venus. Incidentally, males are represented on Venus only by James Clerk Maxwell, after whom the planet's Maxwell Mountains are named. All other such features on Venus have female names, including Nightingale, Helen, Guinevere and Xiao Hong (this last one being a Chinese novelist), and indeed Romania's team for the 2nd European Ladies Club Cup finals at Rijeka, Croatia in June 1997 was called Venus.

Back to Earth now, and a little background information about the games in *S.T.A.R. Chess*. I have endeavoured to supply, as far as possible, complete games with detailed analysis and explanations, since I believe that, in general, such material is more instructive than game fragments. Including the 20 'main' games, *S.T.A.R. Chess* contains 73 *complete* games, 48 of which were played in 1997, while about 16% are my own games. I also recommend that, if possible, you use *two chessboards* side by side when playing through the games. Then, whenever you encounter a whole game within the notes to another game, you can pause the main game on board one while enjoying the extra game on the second board.

Many of the players involved are grandmasters or international masters (in certain cases the titles were achieved some time after the games, though that is a point of only very minor importance), but I believe that if a game is annotated fully and with lucidity, then it can benefit most levels of players. You always have the option to skim through only the main moves, but the much fuller accompanying explanations and analysis will always be there in the notes whenever you want to study more closely. Stefaan Six, a Belgian friend, likes to pick any complete game and quickly jot down its moves from the book onto a sheet of paper. He then plays over the game and tries to produce his *own* analysis and notes to it. Afterwards, Stefaan compares his findings to the details given in print. Such an exercise is clearly time-consuming, but the rewards can be great in terms of personal development. By the way, the next time someone asks you 'How far can you see?' in the context of analysing moves, a star reply is 'Oh, around 12 million million million miles!', since that is the distance between our planet and the Andromeda Spiral, the most remote object which can be clearly seen by the naked eye without any external optical aid.

Some people like a deep, accurate, analytical approach, while others prefer ideas put forward using words alone. I have aimed to provide the best of both worlds, and you will find that they sometimes overlap. Marnix van der Zalm, a Dutch friend from Utrecht, likes the fact that, from time to time, my notes bring in anecdotes and other items which (in his words) 'Give the reader welcome, lighter moments of joy to regain energy and become revitalized before continuing with the interesting but more intense and demanding chess moves'.

All of the annotations are my own, except in a few instances where the names of friends who made special contributions are stated, but here I particularly want to thank Nicholas Gross from Brussels and Kevin O'Connell from Ipswich for their help and suggestions. In the cases where I have previously analysed a game for any form of publication, I have now substantially increased and improved the analysis myself. Hopefully we will use the ideas to score many sparkling attacking victories, so the opponents will be knocked out and 'seeing stars'! We, on the other hand, are armed with our inspirational motto from Henry Ford which appeared as a cryptogram several pages ago: *'There is no man living who isn't capable of doing more than he thinks he can do'*. This statement is a direct quotation, but of course I intend it to refer equally to males and females. Also, the star motto is not intended to encourage arrogance. After all, none of us would be capable of doing all that we can do if God had not given us so many wonderful gifts. Instead, the motto should be an encouraging reminder of the achievements that can be accomplished if we use the gifts well. Still, one should be patient and not expect too much instant success. On that note, I laughed when I read a surprise letter on 27 June from Ray Dolan, Secretary of the Staffordshire Chess Association. Ray showed his sense of humour when he wrote to me 'I keep watching the newspapers and teletext to see if you have become World Champion'! Well, I did capture the Under-17 title in 1978/9, but I apologize to Ray for keeping him waiting on the big one! Nevertheless, I'm all in favour of positive thinking.

On the subject of newspapers and teletext, I often spot lovely puzzles in numerous publications and on various TV channels, yet the names of the original composers are not always mentioned beside the diagrams. At least in the teletext case one can (usually) press a button which reveals the solution and the composer's name, but infuriatingly that button on my TV control box was not working for a while! Still, the required information was obtained with the expert help of Holland's Harold van der Heijden, whose computer database (as at 8 July 1997) contained 49,434 endgame studies! Full credit should always go to the ingenious composers, and in all cases in this book I have written their names with the puzzles or solutions. I also wish to thank Eddy van Espen, Marcel van Herck and Fernand Joseph for their invaluable contributions in this area.

Finally, just a few quick words regarding mnemonics and other memory aids in the remaining minutes before lift-off. The key point about acronyms, acrostics and other similar items is that they should be fun. If one enjoys remembering something useful, then one is much more likely to retain and recall it easily, even under pressure in a chess game, for example. *S.T.A.R. Chess* is packed with games, so instead let's allow ourselves here to enjoy a lighter acrostic: **M**y **V**ery **E**ducated **M**other **J**ust **S**erved **U**s **N**ine **P**umpkins, which provides a way of remembering that Mercury, Venus, Earth, Mars, Jupiter, Saturn, Uranus, Neptune, Pluto are, in order of increasing distance from the Sun, the nine planets in our Solar System (and they orbit the Sun in slightly elliptical paths around it). Numbers can also furnish us with fun ways of remembering or working out details. For instance, the late Professor A.C. Aitken (1895-1967) of Edinburgh, Scotland, liked to exercise his mind by doing mental calculations such as 37 times 53 or 44 squared plus 5 squared or 40 squared plus 19 squared, each of which yields the answer 1961, the year when Yuri Gagarin made his pioneer flight into space.

Our star motto (Henry Ford's statement given earlier on) reminds us that we can do a lot more than we might sometimes think we can, but of course some work is required, and 'Practice makes perfect' as the saying goes.

The countdown is complete, so let's now launch into our colourful chess adventure, keeping a smile on our faces and a rainbow in our hearts.

Paul Motwani
Brussels, 25 August 1997

Dedications

I thoroughly enjoyed my six-day chess 'world tour of Scotland' from 8-13 April 1997, and I would like to dedicate *S.T.A.R. Chess* to the following very dear friends for their warm hospitality and all the work they did which made the events in their cities so memorable. It was really encouraging to get requests for more visits, and sometime in 1998 I hope to do an even wider tour ... the Galactic tour of Scotland!?

With special thanks to:
Jim & Jean Chalmers of Dundee
Alec & Alice Collie of Perth
Alex & Fiona Thomson of Stirling
Terry & Alison Purkins, Alan Heavens and Gordon Davies of Edinburgh
John Glendinning of Glasgow
Adrian Boal, Duncan Malcolm, David & Sheila Smith and Len, Phyllis, Natalie & Gary Weir of Ayr & Troon
My wonderful week with you in Scotland could outshine the brightest star.

1 K.I.P.P.I.N.G. with the Dragon

'It's a great game of chess that's being played, all over the world' – Lewis Carroll (the pen-name used by the 19th century author and Oxford professor of Mathematics, Charles Lutwidge Dodgson, who is perhaps best known for writing *Alice in Wonderland* in 1865). In the 32 countries where I have played chess, I always found our Royal Game and its players in general to be as wonderful as in Carroll's wonderland. In 1997, for example, the Staffordshire Centenary International Tournament, organized in the English town of Walsall by FM Lawrence Cooper and David Anderton OBE of the Walsall Kipping Chess Club, was an especially memorable 'Scheveningen-type' event comprising two teams A and B each of nine players in which every person in team A played against every person in team B, and vice-versa. I want to say a bit more about some of the people involved, because the many perfect aspects of the organization created a superb model example for others to emulate in future events.

Five nations were represented, and the existing titles and average ratings within the teams were such that norms towards the titles of Woman Grandmaster, International Master and Grandmaster were all attainable, and happily Ireland's Mark Quinn did achieve his third IM norm. During a celebration meal, IM Robert Bellin (the 1979 British Champion) and his wife, WGM Jana Bellin (British Ladies' Champion on eight occasions), proposed a toast to Mark on behalf of their club. The shamrock (Ireland's clover leaf national emblem) is looking particularly healthy this year because Bryan Kelly, the other Irish player competing at Walsall, made his second IM norm with a round to spare at the Newport International in July. *Comhghairdeachas faoi leith do dha réalt fichille* (pronounced something like: Ko-yayr-deck-uhs Fwee Leh Do Yah Railt Fick-uhl) is Irish Gaelic for '*Many congratulations to two stars*'!

Incidentally, if A=1, B=2, C=3, ..., Z=26, then the total value of the letters in 'star' is 58. So, as a very quick extra, *S.T.A.R. Chess* ought to contain a 58-letter 'word' somewhere in the book! Well, in the Welsh island Anglesey, there is a village called *Llanfairpwllgwyngyllgogerychwyrndrobwllllantysiliogogogoch*. In English, the name means 'The Church of St Mary in the hollow of white hazel near the rapid whirlpool, and the Church of St Tysilio of the red cave'. 'Walsall' is easier, so let's return there now!

Richard Furness (the expert International Chess Arbiter who developed some features of the pairings system that was first used in the 1994 Oakham School Masters Tournament) and the eighteen competitors were accommodated and well-fed at the homes of several very nice families in or around Walsall, and this arrangement added a friendly social side to the event without detracting from the competitive element of the tournament. Each day, well before the afternoon round of play at the Bentley Leisure Pavilion, I and nine others were given the perfect food for thought in the form of lunch cooked by Mrs Ilse Young, the wife of Dr Norman Young, the Walsall Kipping Club President. It turned out that the top prize winner in team B, GM Bogdan Lalić, adores pizza, and I recall that the same was true of FM Holger Grund, a talented German teenager who in 1996 won an all-play-all tournament organized by Sweden's Jan Berglund in the little town of Timrå. I also happen to know a pizzeria in Antwerp called *L'EKO* (although Hungary's 17-year-old GM Peter Leko is more famous!), but unfortunately the correlation between chess superstars and pizza-eaters is not reinforced by IM Jonathan Rowson, since team A's winner favours coco-pops!

My feelings about the Staffordshire Tournament are encapsulated by the acronym S.T.A.F.F.O.R.D.S.H.I.R.E. (Sensational Time And Fantastic Friends/Organization Really Done Superbly/Hope I'll Return Eventually!), but the action really starts with **K.I.P.P.I.N.G.** (Kings In Perpetual Peril/Incredibly Nice Games). There are three facets to this mnemonic:

1) Kipping is an informal word for sleeping, and this reminds us of the importance of trying to go into each game with the mind as fresh as possible. For example, at the six World Chess Olympiads where I have represented Scotland to-date, getting lots of sleep was always a vital part of my pre-game preparation, and the results were good (21 wins, 38 draws and just seven losses out of 66 games played mostly on top board).

2) K.I.P.P.I.N.G. is also a small tribute to Cyril Stanley Kipping (1891-1964), who was a prolific composer of chess problems (particularly the 'mate in three moves' type), and was General Editor of *The Problemist* from 1931 until he passed away. Happily, in 1959 he was awarded the title of International Master of FIDE for Chess Compositions. Mr Kipping was also the Headmaster of Wednesbury Boys High School, and introduced chess into the curriculum there in 1927, as he firmly believed that our Royal Game can teach concentration and reasoning plus a healthy amount of self-reliance, and is a most useful training for the mind.

In 1992 the Walsall Kipping Chess Club had its 50-year jubilee, and part of the celebrations was a special weekend tournament (won by GM Murray Chandler) which was the third strongest event in the UK that year (with only the Lloyds Bank Masters and the British Championship itself being stronger). I also find it quite fitting that the following 'White to play and mate in three' problem (composed by James Quah and published in 1992 in *The Problemist*) won a Kipping Prize, since Mr Kipping loved elegant 'three movers'.

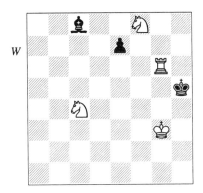

The solution appears before the first game of this chapter.

The Walsall Kipping Club continues to thrive, even more so since the formation of its 'Supporters Club' by Mrs Patricia Payne on 14 October 1996. Chess T-shirts, scarves, hats, and other attractive items are all now available.

3) The third facet of K.I.P.P.I.N.G. is **K**ings **I**n **P**erpetual **P**eril/**I**ncredibly **N**ice **G**ames. Almost every day, I see fresh games in which one or both of the players involved attacks the opponent's king with great energy, so that the enemy monarch is given no time to relax. A king under constant fire is in a state of perpetual peril, and if the aggressor doing the attacking remains alert then chances to play pretty tactical combinations often arise naturally from the flow of the battle. If such opportunities are seized, we can get incredibly nice games.

Walsall's Correspondence Chess GM, Maurice Johnson, who was the British Correspondence Chess Association Champion in 1989/90 and 1990/1, certainly knows how to make the 'Sicilian Dragon' breath out fire. In the following sizzling game from the 1997 Pelikan Memorial Correspondence Tournament, Maurice's energetic counter-attacking play demonstrates why many supporters regard him as a greater star than the famous footballer named Maurice Johnson who played for Celtic but later switched to the arch-rival team, Rangers! Just minutes before we kick off, let's see the answer to the aforementioned Kipping Prize problem.

Solution to earlier puzzle

1 ♘e3! forces checkmate in two more moves as follows:
    a) 1...e5 2 ♘d5 followed by 3 ♘f6#.
    b) 1...e6 2 ♘g4 followed by 3 ♘f6#.

c) 1...♝e6 (countering the knight moves that occurred in variations 'a' and 'b') 2 ♘g2 followed by 3 ♘f4#.

d) 1...♝b7 2 ♘f5 followed by 3 ♘g7#.

Apart from guiding you through many incredibly nice games (the majority of which were played in 1996/7) within the notes to Maurice Johnson's main game, my further aims in this chapter are:

1) To help you to enjoy the Sicilian Dragon as much as I now do.

2) To show that the Dragon is actually a rather logical opening, in spite of its fiery features.

3) To present numerous star ideas that will add to your enjoyment, confidence, knowledge and understanding.

4) To make use of the fact that the Dragon is an ideal opening for illustrating attack and counterattack with lots of tactics cropping up throughout. The Yugoslav Attack (beginning at move seven of the game) has for many years been the principal battleground in the Dragon, and we will see White's strategy of quick attack being met by powerful reactions. The contents of this action-packed chapter will also show how the Dragon handles various other attempts to wound it.

Therefore let's enter the Dragon and start a dazzling new 'purple patch' in our chess. However, there is no point in taking a shallow approach to a complex opening, so our main game featuring the Dragon is going to take us deep into its lair. Do not be afraid, though: 'The longest journey begins with one step' (translation of an ancient Chinese proverb). Prepare yourself now for a far-reaching but exciting trip full of adventures with dragons putting kings in perpetual peril...

Game 1
H. van Kempen – M. Johnson
Pelikan Memorial Correspondence Tournament 1997
Sicilian Defence

1 e4

'Best by test' is how Robert J. Fischer, World Champion 1972-5, liked to describe this move, his favourite of all the 20 possible legal first moves. Certainly, Fischer always played it with great verve, and to make sure our brains too are switching swiftly into a high gear, here is a puzzle that needs piecing together.

Picking pieces

Imagine that Kathleen has a black bag containing the 32 chessmen which make up one complete standard set.

Without looking into the bag, she quickly picks out four chessmen at random, one at a time. Which of the following is more likely to happen:

a) The four chessmen that Kathleen picks out will all be white;

b) You will guess her favourite first move correctly with one guess?

When ready, you can compare your answer with the one given in the solutions section near the end of this book.

1 ...   c5

The Sicilian Defence got its name due to a 17th century player, Pietro Carrera, who lived in Sicily. It won't affect his career now, but since this counter-attacking opening involves the c-pawn, I feel the name Carrera ought to be better-known!

2 ♘f3

I have seen the Morra Gambit, 2 d4, netting a lot of points for White in club matches, but GM Murray Chandler demonstrated a very effective antidote for Black *en route* to winning the 1992 Walsall Kipping Jubilee weekend tournament. N.Down-Chandler continued 2...cxd4 3 c3 (3 ♕xd4?! will cost White valuable time after 3...♘c6, but 3 ♘f3!?, intending 4 ♘xd4, has a good chance of transposing back into a main line of the Sicilian, since the attempt 3...e5 to avoid that by saving the black pawn on d4 allows White to obtain a dangerous lead in development via 4 c3! {4 ♘xe5?? ♕a5+} 4...dxc3? {4...♘c6 is better} 5 ♘xc3, and he is well placed to utilize the outpost at d5 or even d6) 3...dxc3 (there is a saying

'the best way to refute a gambit is to accept it') 4 ♘xc3 e6 5 ♘f3 ♗c5! (5...♘f6? is inappropriate due to 6 e5, but instead Black finds another way to activate his pieces located on the kingside, with a view to getting castled there quickly and safely) 6 ♗c4 d6 (a careful, purposeful move, designed to cut out ideas like e5 followed by ♘e4 by White) 7 0-0 a6 (after 7...♘e7, the reply 8 ♘a4 is irritating for the c5-bishop, so, before continuing with piece development, Black plays the useful little pawn move ...a6, which creates a safe retreat at a7 for his dark-squared bishop while also making queenside expansion with ...b5 a possibility) 8 a3? (being a pawn down, White must strive with every precious move to stay ahead in development and generate some initiative, so 8 ♕e2, intending to exert pressure against the black d-pawn with ♖d1 and ♗f4, is more 'chunky', as IM Jonathan Rowson likes to say) 8...♘e7 9 b4 ♗a7 10 ♕e2 0-0 11 ♗f4 ♘g6 12 ♗g3 ♘c6 13 ♖fd1 e5 14 ♕d2 *(D)*.

14...♗g4! (Black happily leaves his surplus pawn on d6 to be captured because he is concentrating on activating his last minor piece and vacating the c8-square for a rook to land there and exploit the loose situation of White's pieces on the c-file) 15 ♕xd6 ♗xf3 16 gxf3 (White loses material after 16 ♕xd8 ♘xd8! 17 gxf3 ♖c8) 16...♕g5 (the white monarch is now in deadly peril together with his bishop on the g-file, since Black's numerous threats

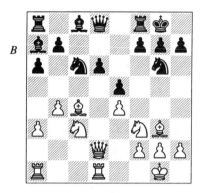

include the advance ...h5, menacing ...h4) 17 ♕d2 ♛xd2 18 ♖xd2 ♘d4 19 ♔g2 (19 ♗e2 loses directly to the fork 19...♘b3 {or first ...♖ac8}, while 19 ♖d3 walks into the short, succulent sequence 19...♖ac8 20 ♗a2 ♖xc3!, ending quickly in another typical, juicy fork tactic with 21 ♖xc3 ♘e2+ then 22...♘xc3) 19...♖ac8 0-1. White's king is down, so we now rejoin the main game with Maurice Johnson about to post off his second move to his correspondence opponent.

2 ...   d6

'Dragon fans' (meaning 'people that love to play the Dragon variation of the Sicilian Defence'; not actors like Scotland's Sean Connery in the film *Dragonheart*!) who adopt another move-order with **2...♘c6** are usually willing to allow White to establish the 'Maroczy Bind', which occurs after **3 d4 cxd4 4 ♘xd4 g6 5 c4**. Then **5...♗g7 6 ♗e3 ♘f6 7 ♘c3**. Now 7...♘g4 8 ♕xg4 (8 ♘xc6?! ♘xe3!) 8...♘xd4 is a plausible continuation. However, a delayed version of the 7...♘g4 trick

backfired badly and cost Black a piece in Korchnoi-Liardet at Baden 1997: **7...d6 8 ♗e2 0-0 9 0-0 ♘g4??** transposes to that game, which finished abruptly after **10 ♗xg4 ♗xg4** *(D)*.

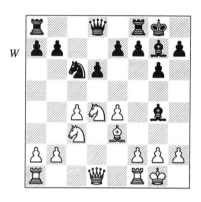

11 ♘xc6! 1-0, in view of 11...bxc6 12 ♕xg4 or 11...♗xd1 12 ♘xd8 ♗xc3 (12...♖fxd8 13 ♖fxd1) 13 ♖fxd1. Curiously, the position resulting from 13 ♖fxd1 actually occurred in the game Åkesson-Heidenfeld at the 1997 European Team Championships in Pula, just one month after Fabrice Liardet's disaster against GM Viktor Korchnoi. Sadly, Ireland's Mark Heidenfeld had to resign at unlucky move number 13, being a piece down without compensation against Sweden's GM Ralf Åkesson. Mark can take some consolation from the fact that I lasted only eight moves longer against Åkesson when he won the 1981 European Junior Championship, but both of our experiences underline yet again the need for remaining as alert as possible to tactical tricks and opportunities.

3	**d4**	**cxd4**
4	**♘xd4**	**♘f6**
5	**♘c3**	**g6**

This is called the Dragon Variation of the Sicilian Defence since Black's pawns are arranged in a similar way to the main stars in the constellation *Draconis*, the Dragon. Garry Kasparov scored two wins and two draws with the Dragon out of the four games in which he employed it against GM Viswanathan Anand during their 1995 PCA World Championship match. That result prompted me to write a little poem expressing equally optimistic hopes for our future (as Black) in the Dragon, a paragon system of attacking play, but White is not feeling so happy against it these days.

A paragon of beasts, one might say
The Dragon feasts on White today
Wise to be Black, clever to attack
Otherwise flak forever flies back
Enough balls of flame to light a
terrible pyre
Rough, always the same, if you fight
the incredible fire
Opponents in a right mess go using
water by the flagon
Exponents enjoy bright chess (no
losing!), hotter with the Dragon.
You'll run far with 5...g6
A cool fun star of lively tricks!

6 ♗e3

As one might expect, players should steer clear of the fiery Dragon unless they know precisely how to handle it.

Therefore I was really surprised to see Simen Agdestein, who is Norway's top grandmaster and an international footballer to boot, getting involved with the Dragon instead of sticking to quieter openings which he knows thoroughly and tends to employ most effectively. In the first round of the 1997 Doeberl Cup competition in Canberra, Australia, the 2600-rated GM got overturned in only 20 moves by the Dragon in the hands of a bright young star named Brian Tindall. Here is how that brief encounter went: **6 ♗g5** (on e3 the bishop would give added protection to the d4-knight, but flying on ambitiously to g5 leaves both the bishop and the knight less secure) **6...♗g7 7 ♕d2** (White should avoid the variation 7 ♗e2 ♕a5 8 ♕d2? ♘xe4! 9 ♘xe4 ♕xd2+ 10 ♔xd2 ♗xd4, because an important pawn drops off, but 8 ♗d2 is playable, and at least his monarch will soon get castled to safety on the kingside) **7...♘c6** (threatening 8...♘xe4! 9 ♘xc6 {9 ♘xe4 ♘xd4 simply leaves White a pawn down without compensation} 9...♘xd2 10 ♘xd8 ♘xf1 11 ♘xf7 ♔xf7 12 ♖xf1 ♗f5 with a superb position for Black, principally due to his powerful bishop pair coupled with having an open c-file for his rooks, factors which allow him to exert tremendous pressure on White's queenside) **8 ♘b3 ♗e6 9 f4?!** (this case of 'f for forward' is too ambitious, and White should instead prefer immediate piece development with ♗e2 followed by 0-0, but Chapter 3 of

C.O.O.L. Chess provides lots of successful examples involving my favourite f-pawn motto) **9...0-0 10 ♗e2** (a similar position was reached in Apicella-Svidler, Erevan Olympiad 1996, except that White had 0-0 instead of ♕d2 while Black had ...a6 instead of ...♗e6, and the continuation led to a novelty by Black at move 14: 10...b5 11 ♗f3 ♗b7 12 ♔h1 ♘d7 13 ♖b1 ♖e8 14 ♘d5 f6! 15 ♗h4 e6 16 ♘e3 g5! 17 ♗g3 gxf4 18 ♗xf4, after which GM Peter Svidler, the young man who later in 1997 became Russian champion for the third time, started to enjoy the outpost at e5 with 18...♘de5 – see game 279 in *Informator 67* for the remaining 23 moves, if you wish) **10...a5!** (gaining space and seizing the initiative) **11 a4 ♖c8 12 ♖a3** (12 0-0? loses a pawn to 12...♕b6+ 13 ♔h1 ♗xb3 14 cxb3 ♕xb3) **12...♘b4!** (threatening both 13...♘xe4! 14 ♘xe4 ♘xc2+ and 13...♖xc3 14 bxc3 ♘xe4) **13 ♗f3 ♕b6** (preventing White from castling) **14 f5?** (he should have tried the manoeuvre ♗h4-f2, but the entire character of the position is probably alien to GM Simen Agdestein {who normally opens with 1 d4 or 1 c4}, and unfortunately one mistake now leads rapidly to other ones and a total collapse of his defences) **14...gxf5 15 ♗e3** (D).

It looks as if Agdestein may have overlooked the neat little tactic which Black now uses to deflect White's queen away from defending the e3-bishop. **15...♘xc2+! 16 ♕xc2 ♕xe3+ 17 ♔d1 ♘xe4 18 ♗xe4 fxe4 19 ♘c1**

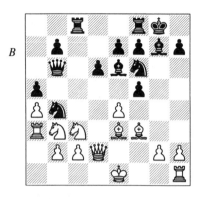

B

♗g4+ 20 ♘1e2 ♕d3+! 0-1, in view of 21 ♕d2 ♗xc3 22 ♖xc3 ♗xe2+, after which Black would be a bishop plus three pawns ahead. The task of winning the game would then be as easy as eating pie, although India's Rajan Mahadevan might prefer memorizing more digits of the never-ending number π (π=3.141592653...), which he has publicly recited as far as the 31,811th digit without a mistake!

6   ...   ♗g7
6...♘g4?? 7 ♗b5+ ♗d7 8 ♕xg4! is a well-known opening trap, but it never does any harm to remind ourselves about important details even at such an early stage in the game. After all, even Garry Kasparov somehow managed to make a serious error in a totally familiar position on move seven of his final game against the computer 'Deeper Blue' in May 1997.

7   f3
This move characterizes the Yugoslav Attack. White rules out ...♘g4 ideas for the moment, while simultaneously supporting his central pawn

on e4 and creating the possibility of making the aggressive advance g2-g4.

An interesting, yet rarely seen alternative is **7 ♗e2!? ♘c6 8 ♕d2** (8 ♘b3 0-0 9 0-0 a5! 10 a4 ♗e6 11 f4 ♗xb3! 12 cxb3 transposes to Motwani-Galanov, Györ 1990, and Smirin-Hodgson, Winnipeg 1997, in which Black scored two victories using ...♘b4 to support the very effective plan of creating a passed d-pawn with ...e6 and ...d5) **8...0-0 9 0-0-0** *(D)* which transposes to the blindfold game Ivanchuk-Anand, Monaco 1997.

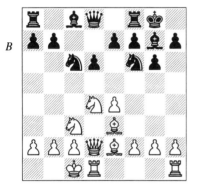

We get the same position as the one we will analyse after 9 0-0-0 in the long note to White's ninth move later, except that the move ♗f1-e2 replaces f2-f3. Is that difference significant? Well, IM Jonathan Rowson and I discussed it in some detail on 1 June 1997, and we think Ivanchuk's set-up merits serious attention. Instead of going all-out for a kingside attack (which Black has been beating off very successfully in practice while simultaneously proceeding

with his own active plans), White adopts a more flexible approach. He can play near the centre with f2-f4, ♖he1, and ♗f3, planning the disruptive advance e4-e5. The space-gaining idea of h3 followed by g4 is also available.

In the aforementioned Ivanchuk-Anand game, Black got no real counterplay after 9...♗d7 10 ♔b1 ♖c8 (in the simultaneous display which I gave at the O.S.K. {Ons Schaakgenoegen Kempen, Flemish for 'Our Chess Pleasure'} club in the Belgian town of Geel on 14 June 1997, Jeff van de Cruys played 10...a5!? against me, with the good follow-up idea of ...a4 and ...♕a5, but after 11 ♘db5, Jeff made a fatal change of course with 11...♘e5?, allowing White to obtain a decisive spatial advantage by 12 f4 ♘eg4 13 ♗g1 h5 14 h3 ♘h6 15 ♗e3, intending 16 f5 ♔h7 17 g4!) 11 f4, so let us consider two alternatives at move nine:

a) **9...♘xd4 10 ♗xd4 ♗e6** and now:

a1) **11 f4 ♕a5 12 a3** (12 ♔b1?? ♘xe4! is a trick worth remembering, and I'm sure one wouldn't forget it if, playing either colour, the finish 13 ♘xe4 ♕xa2+ 14 ♔c1 ♕a1# happened, but it's better to be Black!) 12...♖fc8, followed perhaps by ...♖ab8 and ...b5, is acceptable for Black. However, the forthcoming variation 'a2' is much more of a problem.

a2) **11 ♔b1!** (a key point of this sneaky move is that Black cannot swap queens *with check*, and the importance of that fact will shortly become very

clear) 11...♕c7 (11...♕a5? 12 ♗xf6!
♗xf6 13 ♘d5 ♕xd2 14 ♘xf6+ {a disruptive *intermezzo* which ruins Black's
pawn structure} and then 14...exf6 15
♖xd2 or 14...♔g7 15 ♘h5+! gxh5 16
♖xd2 is a trap that Black should avoid)
12 f4 ♖fc8 is structurally sound for
Black and he threatens 13...♘xe4!! 14
♘xe4 ♗xd4 15 ♕xd4 ♕xc2+ 16 ♔a1
♕xe2, but after simply 13 ♗f3, White
has a firm grip on the position and can
strengthen it with follow-up moves
such as ♖he1, h3 and g4. Also, at the
right moment, ♘d5 could be really
awkward to face, but White can keep
the unpleasant threat of it just hanging
over his opponent – remember the
saying 'the threat is stronger than its
execution'. Therefore, Black should
consider variation 'b', as follows.

b) **9...d5!?** *(D)*.

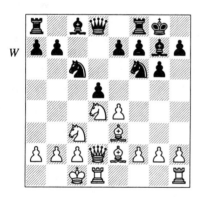

This aggressive reaction in the centre is, in my opinion, a very good
choice when White has played f2-f3
instead of ♗f1-e2, and that view is
confirmed by a lot of analysis in the
long note at move nine. However, it
seems playable here as well. For example:

b1) **10 ♘xc6 bxc6 11 e5** (11 exd5
♘xd5 transposes to 'b2') 11...♘d7!?
12 f4 e6, planning ...c5 and/or ...f6.

b2) **10 exd5 ♘xd5 11 ♘xc6 bxc6
12 ♘xd5 cxd5 13 ♕xd5 ♕c7** branches
into:

b21) **14 ♕xa8 ♗f5 15 ♕xf8+ ♔xf8**
16 ♗d3 ♗e6 (if White's f-pawn were
on f3, then the e3-bishop would be unprotected, and so 16...♕e5! would be
very strong) 17 ♔b1 ♗d5 (17...♕b7 18
♗c1 ♕xg2? 19 ♗e4!! ♕xe4 20 ♖d8#),
intending 18 f3 ♗xb2! 19 ♔xb2 ♕e5+
20 c3 ♕xe3. In effect, White has 2♖ vs
♕ at the end of that line, but the fact
that his king is exposed guarantees
Black excellent chances in this case.

b22) **14 ♕c5 ♕b7!**, simultaneously attacking the pawns on b2 and
g2. Notice that White's g-pawn would
not be *en prise* if the move 7 ♗e2 had
not been played!

7 ...   0-0

It is always good to ask 'Why am I
castling?' rather than automatically
making this move, especially as castling can never be done a second time
by the same player during the same
game. The two most common reasons
for castling are:

1) To transfer the king to a safer location.

2) To bring a rook closer to the
centre or nearer to the opposite wing
(compared to where the rook started
from).

In the case of the move 7...0-0 which Maurice Johnson has just played, it is perfectly normal according to 'theory' and it certainly fulfils point '2'. Point '1' is debatable though, since White can throw his h- and/or g-pawn up the board to attack Black's castled king (but see Morozevich-A.Fedorov within the long note to White's ninth move later, because Black's king turns out to be quite safe on g8, and he also makes excellent use of having a rook on the f-file after castling).

I know that Nikolai Gurtovoi, a very creative correspondence player from Latvia, is fond of winning without castling, and in this line of the Dragon he feels that (at least for the moment) Black's king is safer on e8 than on g8. The game Ozoliņš-Gurtovoi in the semi-final stage of the 1991 Latvian Correspondence Championship is an interesting example of the 'non-castling' approach. The continuation was: **7...♘c6 8 ♕d2 h5!?** (simultaneously stopping plans of ♗h6, g4 or h4-h5 that White may have been brewing) **9 h4 ♗d7 10 ♗c4 a6 11 ♗b3 b5 12 0-0-0** (White does not want to play timidly, so he bravely puts his king on the wing where Black is attacking because in return he immediately gets a rook onto a central file where there are possibilities of opening up lines to attack the opponent's uncastled monarch) **12...♘a5 13 ♔b1 ♖b8 14 ♗g5 ♘c4 15 ♗xc4** (15 ♕e2 e5 leaves the d4-knight

trapped in mid-board!) **15...bxc4 16 b3 ♖b7** (16...♕b6?! allows 17 ♗xf6! followed by ♘d5 after Black recaptures on f6) *(D)*.

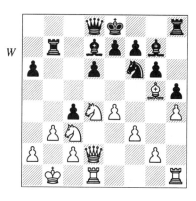

17 e5! (White wants to prise open the d-file to exploit the fact that the lady on d8 is no longer protected by a rook on b8) **17...dxe5 18 ♘c6 ♕b6** (18...♕c7 19 ♘xe7 ♔xe7?? leaves the f6-knight pinned and so White would win by forking Black's king and queen with 20 ♘d5+) **19 ♘xe5?** (I much prefer the more disruptive 19 ♘xe7, because after the tame move played in the game, the balance swings violently in Black's favour) **19...cxb3 20 cxb3 ♗f5+ 21 ♔b2 ♘d7 22 ♘xd7 ♖xd7** (just look at Black's pieces pointing so menacingly towards White's king and queen) **23 ♕e3 ♗d4 24 ♕e1 f6 25 ♗d2 ♔f7!** (the h8-rook will take no more moves than it would on f8 to slide over to the c- or b-file, so why should Black castle and decentralize his king when instead it will be perfectly safe where it now stands?) **26**

♖c1 ♖c8 27 ♕e2 ♗e5 28 ♖hd1 a5
0-1, facing the terrible threat of ...a4,
yet unable to hit back with anything
meaningful. For instance, 29 f4 loses
material to 29...♗g4 if Black wants to
win it, but first 29...♗d4 may be even
more powerful: 'the threat is stronger
than its execution'.

    8 ♕d2   ♘c6
    9 ♗c4

We have reached a major cross-
roads. It currently has three really
massive main routes branching off,
but each of them could single-handedly
absorb us for years because the variations involved are anything but light!
However, let us take a comet-like approach and have at least a fleeting look
at how some stars have been faring recently on the three biggest Dragon
highways. Nevertheless, we should
examine the surface closely enough to
find various gaping holes which were
overlooked by certain previous ana-
lysts. This will occupy us for several
pages, but our tactical vision will be
sharpened through the process, and by
the end I think a good number of you
will want to enter the Dragon again in
your own games after getting a flavour
here of its juicy lines. In the words of
Confucius, the famous Chinese philosopher, 'There are many revolutions
in the Dragon's tail'.

The most popular alternative to 9
♗c4 is:

a) **9 0-0-0** has very often been answered by 9...♘xd4 (which can transpose after 10 ♗xd4 ♗e6 11 g4 to a

position we will consider further on
via the move-order 9 g4 ♗e6 10 0-0-0
♘xd4 11 ♗xd4) or:

a1) **9...d5** is a gambit continuation.
First we consider its acceptance:

a11) **10 exd5 ♘xd5 11 ♘xc6 bxc6
12 ♘xd5** (after 12 ♗d4 masses of established theory exists for the variation 12...e5 13 ♗c5, but less attention
has been given recently to 12...♗xd4
13 ♕xd4 ♕b6!?, when Black is helped
by the facts that a queen exchange on
b6 would bring a2 under attack after
...axb6 and also 14 ♘xd5 cxd5 15
♕xd5 ♗f5 threatens ...♖ac8 or ...♖fd8
with considerable activity for the deficit of one pawn) **12...cxd5 13 ♕xd5
♕c7** and now:

a111) **14 ♕c5** is better than taking
the rook according to *Batsford Chess
Openings 2* for example, but the continuation of the game Rowson-Hodgson, East Kilbride 1996, demonstrates
some lovely tactical ideas for Black:
14...♕b8 15 ♕a3 (15 b3 ♗f5 16 ♗d3
♖c8 17 ♕a5 ♖c3! 18 ♗xf5 ♖xe3 19
♗e4 ♕f4! gave Black good play in
Ivanchuk-Hodgson, Amsterdam 1996,
because White's position was so vulnerable on the dark squares in general,
but I recommend that you study the
complete annotated game in *Informator 67*) and now:

a1111) **15...♕c7!** (IM Jonathan
Rowson thinks that this is objectively
the best move because it enables Black
to play ...♖b8 soon, thereby causing
White a lot of irritation at b2, but since
a repetition of position is possible with

16 ♕c5 ♕b8 17 ♕a3 and so on, I will give a plausible and pretty alternative that I discovered in home analysis – see a1112) 16 ♔b1 ♖b8 17 ♗c1 ♗f5 18 ♗d3 ♖xb2+! 19 ♗xb2 ♖b8 20 ♕b3 ♗e6! 21 c4 ♖xb3 22 axb3 ♗xb2 23 ♔xb2 a5, and, in spite of having the slight material deficit of ♕ vs 2♖, Black was the one pressing for a win because of the exposed situation of White's king, although Jonathan Rowson defended tenaciously and eventually secured a draw.

a1112) **15...♗f5** 16 ♗d3 ♕e5 17 ♗xf5 ♕xf5 18 ♕d3 ♕a5 19 ♕d5? *(D)*.

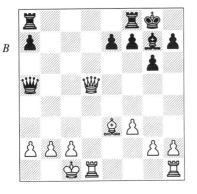

19...♗xb2+!! 20 ♔xb2 ♖ab8+ 21 ♔c1 (21 ♔a1?? ♕c3#) 21...♕a3+ 22 ♔d2 ♖fd8 is a neat illustration of how difficult it is for White to be sure of escaping being burned by the fire from Black's Dragon bishop.

a112) **14 ♕xa8?! ♗f5** (*BCO 2* does not examine the line beyond this point, but there are two reasons why I feel it is useful for us to go a bit

further: a lot of tactics crop up to keep us sharp; Black is down on material by a substantial amount, so one ought at least to question the soundness of his moves rather than just blindly accepting premature assessments) **15 ♕xf8+ ♔xf8** and then:

a1121) **16 c3?** ♗xc3.

a1122) **16 ♗d3?** ♕e5! 17 ♗xf5? ♕xe3+ 18 ♔b1 ♕b6! simultaneously threatens ...gxf5 and ...♕xb2# while averting the ♖d8# finish that would have occurred after the careless move 18...gxf5??.

a1123) **16 ♖d2 ♕b8!** should give Black at least enough initiative to compensate for his material deficit (which is equivalent to having ♕ vs 2♖+♗). A logical reason for this is that White still has a rook and bishop which are currently doing not very much on the first rank. Therefore Black's chances can be good provided he acts quickly before White gets time to coordinate his extra material forces. This general assessment is confirmed by the following variations:

a11231) **17 ♗d4?** ♗h6.

a11232) **17 c4** ♗c3! 18 ♖f2 ♕e5 (or 18...♕b4) 19 ♗h6+ ♔e8 20 ♖e2 *(D)*.

20...♗xb2+! 21 ♖xb2? ♕e1#.

a11233) **17 ♗b5** ♗xb2+ (the alternatives 17...♕xb5?? 18 ♖d8+ or 17...a6 18 ♖hd1 are reminders that White's monarch is not necessarily the only king in danger) 18 ♔xb2 ♕xb5+. Black can soon improve the position of his most precious piece by playing

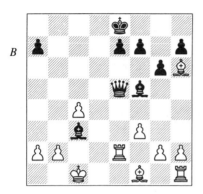

...f6 and ...♔f7 if desired, but White's king is relatively exposed and his isolated queenside pawns are very vulnerable.

After so many rosy variations for Black, you may be wondering why 9...d5 is not *the* answer to 9 0-0-0. Well, two logical replies (other than the capture 10 exd5) have actually been scoring quite highly for White recently:

a12) **10 ♕e1**, to let the d1-rook get at Black's queen on d8, is a favourite line of Russian GM Semion Dvoirys that has really caught on with lots of other players too. Therefore it is difficult to give an accurate and at the same time brief summary concerning details of so many games with 10 ♕e1, but I recommend the 1997 publication *New in Chess Yearbook 42* as one good source of further information. However, since Dvoirys has already caught out two people (namely, Grandmasters Mikhail Brodsky and Oleg Korneev) with a particular trap, I feel others should be alerted here to the

moves involved. They are: **10...e6** (some players prefer the more aggressive 10...e5) **11 h4 ♕c7 12 exd5 ♘xd5 13 ♘xd5 exd5 14 ♕d2 ♖e8 15 h5 ♖xe3 16 ♕xe3** *(D)* and now:

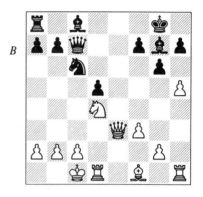

a121) **16...♘xd4?** 17 ♕e8+! (incorrectly given a '?' in game 192 of *Informator 66*) 17...♗f8 18 ♖xd4 ♗f5 19 ♕a4!, and Black does not have sufficient play to compensate for being an exchange down.

a122) Nevertheless, Leko-Hodgson, Groningen 1996 demonstrated an improvement for Black simply by capturing on d4 in a different way, viz. **16...♗xd4!**:

a1221) **17 ♕e8+?** ♔g7 18 h6+ ♔f6 19 ♖xd4 ♘xd4 (19...♗f5!? forces 20 ♕e3, in view of 20 ♕xa8? ♘xd4 21 ♕h8+ ♔g5 and then 22 c3 ♕f4+ 23 ♔d1 ♗c2+ 24 ♔e1 ♕e3+ 25 ♗e2 ♕xe2# or 22 ♔d2 ♕xc2+ 23 ♔e3 ♕c1+! 24 ♔f2 ♕xb2+ 25 ♗e2 {25 ♔g3 ♘e2+ 26 ♗xe2 ♕xh8 27 f4+ ♔f6} 25...♕xe2+ 26 ♔g3 ♕e3 27 ♕d8+ f6 28 ♕xd5 ♘e2+ 29 ♔h2

♕f4+ 30 g3 ♕xg3#, pretty lines where White's king is in perpetual peril) 20 ♕h8+ ♔g5 21 ♕xd4 ♕f4+ is excellent for Black, whose king is playing a very positive, active role in attacking the opponent's far-advanced yet vulnerable h-pawn.

a1222) The game continued **17 ♖xd4** ♘xd4 18 ♕xd4 ♗f5 19 ♗d3 ♗xd3 20 ♕xd3 ♕e5 (the queen's power radiating in many directions is, in general, most apparent when the royal lady is centralized) 21 hxg6 hxg6 22 ♖d1 ♖d8 23 ♕d4 ♕xd4 24 ♖xd4 b6 25 ♔d2 (25 c4 can be answered by 25...♖c8!) 25...♔g7 26 ♔d3 (26 c4 ♔f6 intending ...♔e5 is also fine for Black) 26...♔f6, and Black had almost fully neutralized White's attempts to profit from the fact that the black d-pawn is isolated.

a13) Besides 10 ♕e1, the other most fashionable try for White is IM Leonid Milov's move **10 ♔b1**, with the following ideas in mind:

a131) **10...dxe4??** 11 ♘xc6 ♕xd2 (this capture does *not* give check: a key point behind the move ♔b1) 12 ♘xe7+ (a killing *intermezzo* check) 12...♔h8 13 ♖xd2.

a132) **10...e6** 11 ♗b5! (this idea of Turkish GM Suat Atalik is analysed in some detail in game 280 of *Informator 67*) 11...♗d7 12 exd5, aiming to saddle Black with a weakness at d5.

a133) **10...♘xd4 11 e5!?** *(D)* (it is worth comparing this move with the disruptive e4-e5 thrust detailed on page 114 of *C.O.O.L. Chess*) and now:

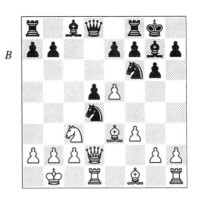

a1331) **11...♘xf3** 12 gxf3 ♘h5 13 ♘xd5 (13 ♕xd5 ♕xd5 14 ♘xd5 ♗xe5 15 ♘xe7+ ♔g7 16 ♖d5! ♗f6 17 ♘xc8 ♖fxc8 18 ♗d3 ♖c7 19 ♗e4 a6 {to prevent ♖b5} 20 ♖g1! {threatening ♖xh5} 20...♔h8 21 ♖gd1 ♖e8 22 a4 ♗h4 23 ♗b6 ♖c6 24 ♗d4+ ♗f6 25 ♖d7 cost Black material in Palac-Hodgson, Erevan Olympiad 1996, and was a powerful demonstration by GM Mladen Palac showing rooks and bishops utilizing open files and diagonals very effectively) 13...e6? (13...♗xe5?? loses to 14 ♘f6+, but the sensible-looking 13...♗e6 14 f4 and 14 ♗c4!? were discussed in game 214 of *Informator 64*) 14 ♘f6+ ♗xf6 15 exf6 ♕xd2 (the line 15...♕xf6 16 ♗c5 ♖e8 17 ♗b5 shows the star bishop-pair at its best) 16 ♖xd2, when Black faces severe difficulties regarding completing his development, and he has the immediate threats of ♗h6 and ♗c5 to contend with.

a1332) **11...♘d7** 12 ♗xd4 ♘xe5 13 ♕e3 ♘c6 14 ♗xg7 ♔xg7 15 ♘xd5 ♕a5 16 b4!! ♕a4 (16...♘xb4?? 17

℅c3+ costs Black a piece) 17 b5 ♖b8 18 ♕b3 (White can opt for other moves such as 18 ♔c1 with the aim of winning material, but instead he chooses a safe, sensible approach that should bring him a clear advantage with precise play) 18...♕xb3+ 19 axb3 e6 20 bxc6 exd5 occurred in the encounter L.Milov-M.Golubev, Biel 1994. White continued with 21 c7, and the game was later drawn after Black managed to round up the far-advanced but weak pawn on c7. However, 21 ♖xd5! bxc6 leaves Black with frail isolated queenside pawns, and White can start attacking the outside one immediately with 22 ♖a5.

a1333) A blitz game Thiel-Golubev at Senden 1996 may rapidly turn out to be the saviour for Black against White's 10 ♔b1 and 11 e5 weapon. The continuation was **11...♘f5 12 exf6 ♗xf6 13 ♘xd5 ♕xd5!?** (D).

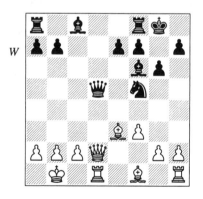

W

This highly imaginative queen sacrifice from IM Golubev (which has also been played by IM Joachim Diaz

of Cuba) represents a big improvement on his earlier play in variation 'a1332', and is a great example of the tremendous creativity that our minds are capable of producing.

On 1 June 1997 at my home in Brussels, IM Jonathan Rowson ('J.R.') and I spent a lot of time analysing the position resulting from **14 ♕xd5 ♘xe3 15 ♕d2 ♘xd1 16 ♕xd1 ♗e6**, and we concluded that Black's position is so solid that White can scarcely make even a small dent on it, in spite of having the material advantage of ♕ vs ♖+♗. Indeed, the further course of the game Thiel-Golubev shows that Black's dark-squared Dragon bishop can create real problems for White's king if he does not tread carefully. The moves were: **17 ♗d3 ♖fd8** (in some cases threatening ...♗f5 followed by ...♗xd3, after which the reply cxd3 would leave White with a weak isolated backward pawn on d3) **18 h4 ♖d4 19 h5 ♖ad8 20 hxg6 hxg6 21 ♕e2 ♖b4 22 b3 ♖b6** (protecting the e6-bishop cuts out any threats of ♗xg6) **23 g4 a5 24 f4 a4 25 f5? axb3! 26 cxb3** (26 fxe6 loses to 26...bxa2+ 27 ♔xa2 ♖a8+) **26...♗xb3! 27 axb3 ♖xb3+ 28 ♔a2**, and now instead of 28...♖b6 29 ♗b5 ♖a8+ 30 ♔b3 in this blitz game, Black would normally have won by playing simply 28...♖dxd3.

In conclusion, J.R. and I reckon that Dvoiris's move 10 ♕e1 (variation 'a12') is really the only worry for Black on the 9 0-0-0 d5 Dragon highway. However, even one headache can make people switch to another treatment, which perhaps explains why within the last few months there has been a resurgence in the popularity of meeting 9 0-0-0 with the logical developing move...

a2) **9...♗d7** *(D)*.

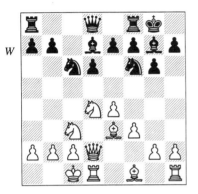

10 g4 (10 ♗c4 transposes to our main game Van Kempen-Johnson, but game three of the Rowson-Hodgson challenge match, Rotherham 1997, went 10 ♔b1 ♖c8 11 h4 ♘e5 12 ♘d5!? ♘h5 13 ♕e1 e6 14 ♘c3 f5, and now Jonathan Rowson reckons he should have played 15 ♘cb5!, subjecting Black's d-pawn, in particular, to terrible pressure) **10...♖c8 11 h4 ♘e5 12 h5 ♕a5 13 ♘b3** (after 13 ♔b1, Black can consider the positional exchange sacrifice 13...♖xc3 14 ♕xc3 ♕xc3 15 bxc3, because he can exert pressure on White's crippled queenside pawns starting with 15...♖c8) **13...♕c7 14 ♗e2 b5! 15 hxg6** (15 ♘xb5? ♗xb5 16 ♗xb5 ♘xf3 is tremendous for Black) **15...fxg6** and now:

a21) **16 g5** is an aggressive move, but as in the next line Black has 16...b4!! because of 17 ♘b5 ♗xb5 18 gxf6 ♗xe2 (18...♗xf6? 19 ♗xb5 ♘xf3 20 ♕e2 gave White a decisive material advantage in Lau-Tiviakov, Montecatini 1994) 19 fxg7 *(D)*.

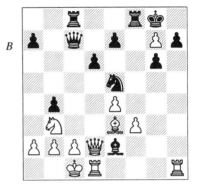

19...♖xf3! 20 ♕xe2 ♖xe3 21 ♕xe3? ♕xc2#.

a22) Morozevich-A.Fedorov, Krasnodar 1997 continued **16 ♔b1** (this is too timid) **16...b4 17 ♘d5 ♘xd5 18 ♕xd5+ e6 19 ♕d2 ♘xf3 20 ♗xf3 ♖xf3 21 ♗h6** (21 ♕h2 loses against 21...♖h3! 22 ♕xh3 ♕xc2+ 23 ♔a1 ♕xb2#) **21...♗xh6 22 ♕xh6 ♗c6 23 ♕xb4 ♗f4! 24 ♔a1** (24 ♘d2 is even worse due to 24...♗xe4! 25 ♘xe4 ♕xc2+ 26 ♔a1 ♕xd1#) **24...♗xe4 25 c3 e5 26 ♕a3** (of course, White cannot capture the black d-pawn because of the weakness of his own back rank with the king hemmed in there: 26 ♕xd6 ♕xd6 27 ♖xd6 ♖f1+, and mate follows in at most two more moves) **26...♖cf8 27 ♘d2 ♗c2 0-1**, in view of

28 ♖c1 ♖a4!, neatly trapping White's queen. For me, the best Dragon wins do not drag on!

Naturally, the main game becomes longer when I include extra games in the notes, but certain games are worth it. In the battle we have just witnessed, we saw Alexander Morozevich, a grandmaster rated 2595 at the time of the game, lose seemingly without a chance, so you may well ask 'Where exactly did White go wrong?'. Well, quite sincerely, I do not like the move 10 g4 (even though it has been played by many others) because it leaves the f3-pawn very weak. Also, after the later decentralizing retreat 13 ♘d4-b3, it is not obvious to me where White can find any meaningful improvements on the actual game. However, the 'J.R.' approach mentioned within the notes to White's 10th move is well-worth studying closely, because GM Julian Hodgson found it really tricky to cope with as Black.

In the actual course of Morozevich-Fedorov, Black quickly took total control after possible inaccuracies by White at moves 10 and 13, although it seems extremely harsh to label either of those moves with a '?'. Nevertheless, the rapid swing of the battle in Black's favour is linked to the topic of a very interesting discussion between J.R. and myself in Walsall on Thursday 27 March 1997. Even our non-chess-playing hosts, Dr John Glennie and his wife Frances, were fascinated when J.R. and I talked about my

feeling that Black may often win games because, on every move, he can try to find the perfect reaction to the move which White has just played. In other words, Black's information is always greater by one move, since any move by him is always preceded by a white move. So Black can respond according to what White does, whereas White must show his hand first. If Black can maintain a *flexible* position, then he will have plenty of options available to himself. That makes it more difficult for White, in choosing his own move, to predict which move Black will respond with.

The small sample of battles we have seen indicate that the 9 0-0-0 Dragon highway is a really long, tough road, yet one that is full of exciting possibilities. I hope you will extract a lot of benefit from the journey we have just made along some important sections of the 9 0-0-0 route, but now it is time to take a look at:

b) **9 g4**, which stops 9...d5 because of 10 g5, and aims to get White's kingside assault started without yet making his own king the usual target on c1 that Black likes to attack. The most common response is **9...♗e6**, with the idea that after 10 ♘xe6 fxe6, Black can play for ...d5, or ...♘e5 to harass the white pawn on f3 that was left unprotected when the g2-g4 advance happened. Notes within game 214 of *Informator 64* claim a slight advantage for White after 11 0-0-0 d5 12 exd5 (after 12 g5 d4! both 13 gxf6 ♗xf6

and 13 ♗xd4 ♘xe4! are nice for Black)
12...♘xd5 13 ♘xd5 exd5 14 ♕xd5+
♕xd5 15 ♖xd5 ♖xf3 16 ♗c4 *(D)*.

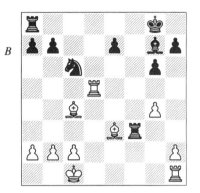

Certainly, 16...♖xe3?? would not
feel like a star move once 17 ♖d8#
lands on the board, but in my home
analysis I was determined to capture
White's dark-squared bishop somehow! It seemed natural to block the
immediate threats from the c4-bishop,
so I came up with 16...e6 17 ♖d3
♘e5!! 18 ♗xe6+ ♔h8 19 ♖b3 ♖xe3!!
20 ♖xe3 ♗h6 (the Dragon bishop
strikes again!) 21 ♖e1 ♖e8 (there is no
hurry to capture the rook on e3 as long
as it remains pinned) 22 ♗d5 ♘xg4,
and Black will emerge shortly with an
extra piece. A moral of this story is
that, although one must hope that most
people really mean what they say, do
or write (otherwise it would be difficult to trust each other), some things
need to be confirmed because anyone
can make a mistake. As Garry Kasparov likes to say, 'Believe it – but check
it!'.

In game 15 of the 1995 PCA World
Championship match, Vishy Anand's
choice at move 10 (after 9 g4 ♗e6)
against Kasparov was **10 0-0-0**, and
the continuation was **10...♘xd4 11
♗xd4 ♕a5 12 ♔b1** (12 a3 is more
popular because then White need not
worry about Black's queen capturing a
pawn on a2 in any variations, so we
will shortly return to move 12 to consider that small but significant pawn-
push) **12...♖fc8 13 a3 ♖ab8 14 ♘d5
♕xd2 15 ♖xd2** (♘xe7+ does not work
here because the reply ...♔f8 is possible, but Black must be especially alert
to such tricks in cases where he still
has a rook on f8) **15...♘xd5 16 ♗xg7
♘e3 ½-½**. I read that the final move
was a novelty (instead of 16...♔xg7)
and the players split the point rather
than battle on with 17 ♗d4 ♘xf1 18
♖xf1, since that gives an opposite-
coloured bishop position, a feature
which often increases the likelihood
of a draw. However, strictly speaking
White would have some advantage
due to possessing more space, and of
course Black *cannot* exchange the
opposite-coloured bishops to reduce
the number of pieces on the board and
make it more difficult for White to
generate threats.

One of my favourite games by GM
Nigel Short saw him converting a spatial advantage into victory after also
developing an initiative on the dark
squares, something which could not
be challenged by his opponent's light-
squared bishop. We shall join the

game Short-Sax, Hastings 1983 after the aforementioned move **12 a3** *(D)*.

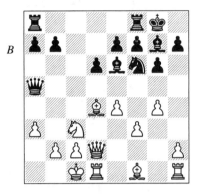

The continuation was: **12...♖fc8 13 h4 ♖ab8 14 ♘d5 ♕xd2+ 15 ♖xd2 ♘xd5** (it is not in the real spirit of the Dragon for Black to opt for a lifeless path where he cannot generate any fire to keep the heat on his opponent, and at this crucial stage I prefer the energetic reaction 15...♗xd5 16 exd5 b5!, intending 17 ♗xa7 ♖a8 18 ♗d4 b4 19 axb4?? ♖a1# or 17 g5 ♘h5 18 ♗xa7 ♖a8 19 ♗d4 b4 20 ♗xg7 ♔xg7 21 ♖d3 ♖a5 {threatening ...♘f4 or ...♖ca8} 22 axb4?? ♖a1+ 23 ♔d2 ♘g3 24 ♖g1 ♘xf1+ 25 ♔e2 ♖xc2+ 26 ♖d2 ♖xd2#) **16 ♗xg7 ♘e3 17 ♗d4 ♘xf1 18 ♖xf1 b6 19 g5!** (increasing White's spatial advantage and preventing Black from freeing his king's position by ...f6 and ...♔f7) **19...h5 20 f4!** (20 gxh6 f6 produces a situation in which White's extra pawn is part of a doubled h-pawn duo that is not particularly useful) **20...♗h3 21 ♖ff2 ♖c6** (21...e6 stops the forthcoming f4-f5 advance, but

after 22 ♗f6 ♖c6 23 ♖f3 ♗g4 24 ♖fd3, the black d-pawn will soon vanish) **22 f5 ♖e8 23 b3!** (White slowly and calmly improves his own position, and effectively says to Black 'I know it's really hard for you to find a constructive plan here when you are so cramped, but I've just moved so now you *must* move') **23...♗g4 24 ♔b2 a6 25 a4 b5 26 axb5 axb5 27 ♗c3!** (the white rook on d2 can now 'see' a potential target at d6, and there is also the possibility of playing ♖d5 to harass the black b-pawn, which cannot advance safely because the reply ♗xb4 is now waiting for it) **27...♖c5 28 f6** *(D)*.

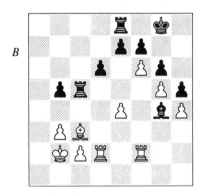

I have never forgotten this method of undermining Black's e7-d6 Sicilian central pawn-chain since it was shown to me in a similar position many years ago by IM Roddy McKay, one of the greatest-ever Scottish chess stars. **28...♖c6?!** (28...exf6 29 ♖xf6 ♖xe4 30 ♖fxd6 ♖e8 is a more tenacious way of defending Black's position because two pairs of pawns get exchanged without granting White the passed b-pawn he gets in the actual game, but the fact that Black's kingside pawn majority remains blocked after 31 ♗f6 for example, still confines him to a life of passivity, as attempts like 31...b4? to immobilize White's queenside majority rapidly lose the b4-pawn to 32 ♖b6, whereas defending with 31...♗e2? fails in view of 32 ♖xe2! ♖xe2 33 ♖d8+ ♔h7 34 ♖h8#, a typical mating configuration exploiting a sensitive back rank) **29 ♖d5 exf6** (after 29...♖c5 30 fxe7 ♖xd5 31 exd5 ♖xe7 32 ♖f6 ♖d7 33 ♗b4, White will win the d6-pawn, thereby obtaining a 3 vs 1 queenside pawn majority) **30 ♗xf6 ♖xe4?** (30...♖b6 offers tougher resistance, and after 31 ♗d4 ♖bb8 32 ♖xd6 ♖xe4 for example, Black's b-pawn lives on to stop White from obtaining any immediate passed pawn) **31 ♖xb5 ♗c8 32 ♖d2!** ♔f8 (32...♖xh4 33 ♖b8 threatens ♖xd6!, but the easiest way for White to win after 33...♔h7 is 34 ♖e2! intending ♖e8, which is much better than going in for 34 ♖xd6? ♖xd6 35 ♖xc8 ♖xf6) **33 c4!** ♔e8 (after 33...♖xh4 34 c5 ♔e8 35 cxd6, White threatens 36 d7+! ♗xd7 37 ♖b8+ ♖c8 38 ♖xc8+ ♗xc8 39 ♖d8#, yet 35...♔d7 still loses on account of 36 ♖e5! ♖xd6 37 ♖e7+ ♔c6 38 ♖c2+, and the c8-bishop will drop off the board unless Black prefers 38...♔d5 39 ♖e5+ ♔d4 40 ♖d2#) **34 ♖bd5 ♖xh4** (34...♖e6 35 c5 ♔d7 36 ♗e5! is equally hopeless for Black) **35 ♖xd6 ♖xd6 36 ♖xd6**

♗d7 37 c5 1-0, in view of the charging c-pawn's imminent advance to c6.

That lovely, flowing game concludes our examination of the second Dragon highway that began with 9 g4. Nigel Short gave a star impersonation of St George, the Dragon-slayer. Incidentally, these days Nigel lives in Greece with his wife Rhea and daughter Kyveli, and, by coincidence, St George's Day (23 April) is celebrated in a special way at Asi Gonia on the Greek island of Crete. All the shepherds in the neighbourhood drive their flocks down to the village for a priest to bless them and wish them fruitfulness and an abundant yield. After the service is over and the priest has sprinkled the flocks with holy water, the animals are milked. The milk is then boiled and shared out by the village girls to the people who came to witness the ceremony, but now we are about to witness some more star moves.

The third Dragon highway features 9 ♗c4, which has already been played against Maurice Johnson (as he is the star of the main game), so let us see how he responds to that move.

    9 ...   ♗d7 (D)
   10 0-0-0   ♖c8

Threatening to win material by 11...♘xd4 12 ♕xd4 ♘g4!.

   11 ♗b3   ♘e5
   12 h4

12 g4 weakens the f3-pawn, and Black can utilize that fact to react energetically with **12...b5!**, planning

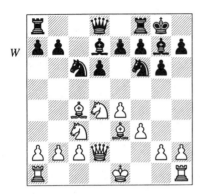

...b4 and/or ...a5-a4, and intending 13 ♘cxb5? ♘xf3! 14 ♘xf3 ♗xb5 15 ♗xa7 ♘xe4 or 15...♘xg4 threatening ...♗h6. In situations like that where White loses his f-pawn, his e- and g-pawns are left critically weak. It is worth comparing this particular case to the one we have already seen in the game Morozevich-Fedorov embedded within the notes to White's ninth move.

After **13 g5** (instead of ♘cxb5), Short-Topalov, Linares 1995 continued 13...♘h5 14 ♘cxb5 ♘c4!?, and Black later won. His h5-knight blocked any hopes White might have had of generating a kingside attack, whereas the open lines on the queenside gave Black good attacking chances there as compensation for his deficit of one pawn. In game 182 of *Informator 63*, Topalov points out that 14...♘xf3 would not have been adequate due to 15 ♘xf3 ♗xb5 16 ♗xa7 (hence his decision to play 14...♘c4). It would be interesting to know if Topalov had already planned 14...♘c4 well in advance

or if he played it out of necessity. Especially if the latter is true, it is worth searching at least one move earlier for alternatives. I did so, and came up with **13...b4!?** *(D)*.

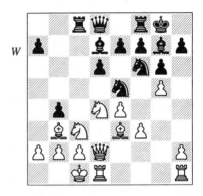

I had great fun working out the following variations:

a) **14 ♘a4** can be answered by 14...♘xe4! 15 fxe4 ♕a5.

b) **14 ♘cb5 ♘h5 15 ♘xa7** (15 ♕xb4 walks into the deadly pin 15...♖b8) **15...♘c4!!** (15...♖b8? 16 f4 ♘g4 17 ♘ac6 lets the knight escape from a7 and deliver a nasty fork during its getaway) branches into:

b1) **16 ♕e2 ♘xe3 17 ♕xe3 ♖c5**, and I would bet that the cornered white knight has less chance of survival than an *Echinarachnius parma* (or 'Sand Dollar') taken out of its sea habitat.

b2) **16 ♗xc4 ♖xc4 17 ♕d3 ♗xd4** (17...♖xd4!? 18 ♗xd4 ♕a5 with many threats, including ...♖a8 and 19...♘f4 20 ♕e3 ♗xd4 with 21 ♕xd4 ♘e2+ or 21 ♖xd4 ♕xa7 to follow) 18 ♗xd4 and then 18...♕c7 or 18...♖xd4 19 ♕xd4 ♕a5 threatening ...♖a8.

c) **14 ♘ce2 ♘h5** leads to:

c1) **15 ♕xb4** a5, intending 16 ♕a3 a4! 17 ♗xa4 ♘c4 or 17 ♗d5 ♕c7 with terrible threats including 18...e6 (trapping the bishop on d5) and 18...♘xf3 19 ♘xf3 ♕xc2#.

c2) **15 ♘g3** a5! (15...♘xg3 is not forced, and indeed it would help White to attack, as is seen by 16 hxg3 planning ♕h2) 16 ♘xh5 gxh5, intending ...a4.

OK, at move 12 in our main game, White pushed his h-pawn (rather than the g-pawn), and I'm itching now to see Maurice Johnson's reply.

12 ... h5

In general, the move ...h5 is not just a prophylactic measure to stop White playing h4-h5, but is 'almost a counter-attack', as it was once described to me by Dundee's Dr David Findlay in a similar position. Black is primarily attacking on the queenside, yet with ...h5 he seizes some space on the opposite wing and invites his opponent to sacrifice at least a pawn by playing g2-g4, after which the reply ...hxg4 creates a passed black g-pawn. When such a situation arises, it almost obliges White to sacrifice more in an all-out attempt to play for mate (otherwise he simply remains down on material), but Black's army is well-developed and coordinated, and it is not uncommon for him to grab a couple of pawns and then later sacrifice back some material in a way which forces exchanges that

lead to a winning endgame. In fact, that Dragon formula for victory is precisely the one employed by Maurice Johnson in our main featured game.

I will just note in passing that Black can play other 12th moves which do not prevent White's plan of h4-h5, but as 12...h5 is looking so healthy nowadays, there is no need to search for alternatives unless you really want to.

13 ♗g5

In game 11 of the Anand-Kasparov 1995 PCA World Championship match, the continuation **13 ♔b1 ♘c4 14 ♗xc4 ♖xc4 15 ♘de2** (bolstering the protection of White's other knight so that Black will be unable to achieve any good exchange sacrifice with ...♖xc3 even if the lady on d2 gets called away later, something which often happens if ♗h6 is played and a bishop-swap occurs) 15...b5 16 ♗h6 ♕a5 17 ♗xg7 (17 ♘d5? ♕xd2 18 ♘xe7+? ♔h7 19 ♗xd2 ♖e8 20 b3 {20 ♘d5?? ♘xd5 21 exd5 ♖xe2} 20...♖c5 {20...♖c7 21 ♗a5! lets White off the hook} 21 ♗b4 ♖xe7 22 ♗xc5 dxc5 results in a position where, in effect, Black has 2♗ vs ♖+♙, and as is most often the case, the mighty bishop pair are a superior force) 17...♔xg7 18 ♘f4 ♖fc8 19 ♘cd5 ♕xd2 20 ♖xd2 ♘xd5 21 ♘xd5 ♔f8 22 ♖e1 gave White a small advantage at this stage, due to the slight pressure he had generated on the central files, but unfortunately a later blunder at move 28 cost him the game.

The very direct move **13 ♗h6** *(D)* has been met in three main ways:

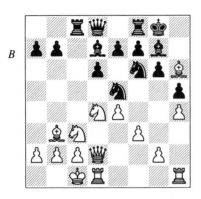

B

a) **13...♗xh6** 14 ♕xh6 ♖xc3 15 bxc3 ♕a5, a speciality some years ago of GM Jonathan Mestel, a star exponent of the Dragon. However, in the last ten years there have been very few examples of Mestel's exchange sacrifice, perhaps for these reasons: 1) Mestel does not play a lot of chess nowadays; 2) the sacrifice may not be fully adequate; 3) the sacrifice is actually not necessary, since Black has (at least) two other reasonable responses to 13 ♗h6, as we shall now see.

b) **13...a5!?** was GM Boris Alterman's novelty, first seen in the encounter Egger-Alterman, Santiago Junior World Ch 1990. Black has ideas of playing ...♖xc3 followed by ...a4 to embarrass the b3-bishop. Therefore 14 ♗xg7 ♔xg7 15 a4 is a logical reply. However, 15...♖c5 16 ♔b1 ♕b6 17 ♘db5 ♖fc8 gave Alterman a very harmonious position in a 1993 game against GM Yehuda Grünfeld. Nevertheless, Alterman may have decided that it is advantageous to be flexible rather than too predictable, because

one year later he answered 13 ♗h6 in another way.

c) The game Apicella-Alterman, Cap d'Agde 1994 went **13...♘c4** 14 ♗xc4 (14 ♕g5?? loses material to 14...♘h7 15 ♕f4 e5) 14...♖xc4 (with the threat 15...♖xd4! 16 ♕xd4 ♗xh6+) 15 ♗xg7 ♔xg7 16 ♖he1 ♕a5 17 ♔b1 ♖fc8 18 ♘b3 ♕a6! (if White had played ♘b3 one move earlier, the reply would have been ...♕c7 to stop the central thrust e4-e5, but since Black now has rooks doubled on the c-file, he can afford to play more aggressively) 19 e5 dxe5 20 ♖xe5 *(D)*

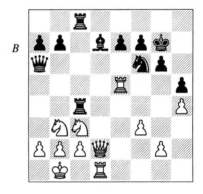

B

20...b5! 21 ♖xe7 b4 22 ♘e4 ♖xc2 23 ♕g5 (23 ♕xc2 ♖xc2 24 ♔xc2 ♕xa2?? 25 ♖a1 is a trap that Black should avoid by means of 24...♗f5, after which his many threats include 25...♘d5! 26 ♖xd5 ♕c4+ followed by 27...♕xd5) 23...♗f5! (intending 24 ♖d6? ♕f1+). Black then had a beautiful, active position which he converted into a win 53 moves later (see *Informator 62*, if you wish).

I do not want to dwell too long at move number 13, so let us rejoin the main game to see the mini-jump which M.J.'s rook now makes on the c-file.

13 ...   ⁺c5

Henry Ford (the famous American automobile manufacturer who also stated the words forming our star motto in the introduction to this book) once said 'Nothing is particularly difficult if you divide it up'. This entire game, for example, is divided into sections with explanations and diagrams at almost every stage to give us a clearer overall picture of the Dragon. We can also split the thinking behind 13...⁺c5 into four main ideas:

1) It supports a ...b7-b5 advance, if Black decides to do that.

2) It allows Black to build up force along the c-file with moves such as ...♛c8 or perhaps ...♛c7 and ...♜fc8.

3) It keeps an eye on the d5-square, where a white knight often lands.

4) Sometimes the c5-rook gets to make the exchange sacrifice ...♜xg5. Potentially, eliminating White's dark-squared bishop can turn the black Dragon bishop into a truly awesome monster and master on the dark squares if there is no counterpart left in the white army to challenge the fiery fianchettoed star piece.

14 g4

In the Anand-Kasparov 1995 PCA World Championship match, the Indian grandmaster generally played very solid, sensible chess (although he is also quite capable of unleashing brilliant attacks and managing tactical storms when in the right mood). The calm move 14 ♔b1 in game 17 of the match was consistent with Vishy's tendency to keep to quieter paths throughout that contest with Kasparov. However, 14...♛a5? would have fallen into a small tactical, yet big positional trap: 15 ♗xf6! ♗xf6 16 ♘d5 ♛xd2 (*not* check: a key point of the earlier ♔b1 move) 17 ♘xf6+ (an important *zwischenzug* before recapturing on d2) 17...exf6 18 ♜xd2, after which Black's weak isolated d-pawn will not live much longer. Kasparov avoided that pitfall by 14...♜e8, but 14...b5 is more of an attempt to attack.

If White wants to adopt an aggressive approach himself, then **14 f4** may seem appropriate, but it hands over the g4-square as an outpost for Black's pieces. That fact was utilized in the continuation of the following wild 1994 correspondence game J.Saskis-M.Johnson: **14...♘c4** (14...♘eg4 15 ♜he1 ♛a5 was very comfortable for Black in Kamsky-Ivanchuk, Buenos Aires 1994, which is annotated as game 238 in *Informator 62*, and since then I have seen no later *Informator* games featuring the move 14 f4) **15 ♛d3** (if White parts with his light-squared bishop in exchange for the c4-knight, then he will soon have to worry about his other bishop being trapped by ...♘g4 and ...f6 because Black's king will no longer experience any difficulties along the a2-g8 diagonal) **15...♘g4!?** (15...♕c8 is a more straightforward approach, but the response to 15 ♕e2 would have been the deadly 15...♗g4 16 ♘f3 ♘xb2! {a typical sacrifice to eliminate White's defenders on the a1-h8 diagonal so that nothing will stand in the way of the Dragon bishop's plans to attack White's king} 17 ♔xb2, and then one of several strong follow-ups is 17...♖xc3 18 ♔xc3 {18 e5 ♕c7 19 exf6 exf6 wins easily for Black} 18...♘xe4++ 19 ♔d3 ♘c5+ 20 ♔e3 ♕b6 21 ♔d2 ♘xb3+ 22 axb3 ♕a5+ 23 ♔e3 {23 ♔c1 ♗c3 seals the fate of the white monarch} 23...♕c5+ 24 ♔d2 ♗c3+ 25 ♔d3 ♗f5+, winning at least White's queen) **16 ♗xc4 ♘f2 17 ♕e2** (17 ♕f1 ♘xh1 18 ♗b3 ♘g3 and then both 19 ♕f3 ♗g4 20 ♕xg3 ♗xd1 21 ♔xd1 ♗xd4 and 19 ♕d3 ♗xd4 20 ♕xd4 ♖xc3! 21 bxc3 ♘e2+ win easily for Black, while 19 ♕e1 ♗g4 20 ♘f3 {20 ♖d3 should lose to 20...♗xd4 21 ♖xd4 ♖xc3! 22 bxc3 ♘e2+, a recurring fork trick that tends to pick up something juicy for Black} 20...♗xc3 21 bxc3 ♔g7, intending ...f6, is similar to the actual game) **17...♘xh1 18 ♗b3** (18 ♖xh1 ♗xd4 keeps Black ahead on material) **18...♗g4 19 ♘f3 ♗xc3 20 bxc3** *(D)*.

20...♔g7 (20...♘g3 can be met by 21 ♕e1, so instead Black prepares to play ...f6) **21 f5 ♘g3 22 ♕e3?** (22 ♕e1 seems more natural to me, but of course the black knight can destroy a couple of White pawns before dying itself) **22...gxf5! 23 ♗h6+ ♔h8 24 e5**

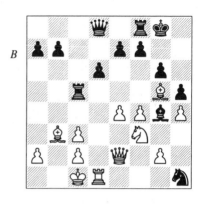

(24 ♗xf8 ♕xf8 simply leaves Black a sound pawn up, so instead White tries to confuse his opponent, but M.J. stays as cool as a mango juice!) **24...♖xc3! 25 ♕xa7** (25 ♕xc3?? ♘e2+) **25...♕a8 26 ♕f2 ♘e4 27 ♕d4 ♕a3+ 28 ♔b1 ♖a8 29 ♖d3** (29 exd6+ e5 30 ♕xe5+ f6 31 ♕d4 ♖xb3+! 32 axb3 ♕a2+ 33 ♔c1 ♕a1+ 34 ♕xa1 ♖xa1+ 35 ♔b2 ♖xd1 puts Black a rook ahead) **29...♕c5 30 ♘g5 ♖xd3 31 ♘xf7+ ♔h7 32 ♕xd3 ♘c3+ 33 ♔b2** *(D)*.

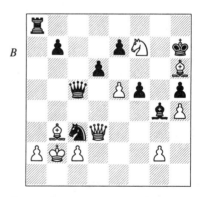

33...♕b4!! 0-1, in view of 34 ♕xc3 ♖xa2+! 35 ♔xa2 ♕xc3. A neat finish from Maurice Johnson, but let's return to the main game now to see his next star move there.

14	...	hxg4
15	f4	♘c4
16	♕e2	♕c8

This increase of force on the c-file not only protects the c4-knight, but also creates the threat of ...♘xb2 and makes ...g3 followed by ...♗g4 possible too.

17 ♗xf6

There are two main ideas behind this capture:

1) White wanted to eliminate the f6-knight so that it could not challenge his own knight when it lands on d5 shortly.

2) White hopes that it will now be easier to make the advance h4-h5, because the reply ...♘xh5 is no longer available to Black.

However, two ultra-aggressive alternatives (to 17 ♗xf6) merit our attention:

a) **17 f5** was played in G.Mohr-Ubilava, Linares 1996. The crisp continuation was **17...♘xb2! 18 ♗xf6 ♗xf6** (18...♘xd1 is analysed in game 239 of *Informator 62*, but as it leads to complications with 19 ♕xg4 {threatening ♕xg6 followed by ♕xg7#}, I prefer GM Elizbar Ubilava's simple capture on f6) **19 ♕xg4 ♔g7 20 ♖hg1** (this threatens ♗xf7, but 20 ♗xf7 ♖xf7 21 ♕xg6+ ♔f8 22 ♖hg1 ♖g7 gives Black a decisive material advantage) **20...♖h8 21 ♗xf7 ♔xf7 22 ♕xg6+ ♔f8 23 ♔xb2 ♖xc3 24 e5**

♗xf5! 0-1, in view of 25 ♘xf5 ♖xc2+ 26 ♔b1 ♕c3! or 25 ♕xf5 ♕xf5 26 ♘xf5 ♗xe5, which completely deadens White's attacking gestures and leaves Black a sound pawn up with the likelihood of picking off the isolated h-pawn shortly too.

b) **17 h5** was a new attempt tried in M.Pavlović-Hodgson, Ubeda 1996. Consistent with the saying 'The best way to refute a gambit is to accept it', GM Julian Hodgson played **17...♘xh5**, putting Black two pawns ahead. Then, in game 287 of *Informator 67*, Pavlović recommends **18 ♗xc4!** (all the instances of '!' for White in this line are given by him, but I think Black is winning, although it's not quite as clear as 18 ♘d5 ♖e8 19 ♘xe7+ ♖xe7 20 ♗xe7 ♘g3 21 ♕h2 ♘xh1 22 ♖xh1 ♖h5 would be) **18...♖xc4 19 ♘d5 ♖e8 20 ♘f5!** (Pavlović) **20...♗xf5 21 exf5** *(D)*.

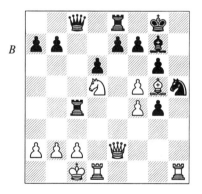

Now there are two possibilities that I like for Black:

b1) **21...e6 22 ♘e7+ ♖xe7 23 ♗xe7 d5** (if 23...♘g3?, then 24 ♕h2

♘xh1 25 ♖xh1 threatens ♕h7#, a line which basically illustrates that a black knight on h5 can sometimes be worth at least a rook if it blocks White's kingside attack) and then:

b11) **24 fxg6 ♘g3 25 ♕h2 ♘xh1 26 ♖xh1 fxg6** with ...♔f7 to follow, an important escape for the black king that was not available in the previous note.

b12) **24 ♖xh5 gxh5 25 f6 ♕c7!**, threatening ...♕xf4+ or first ...♗xf6!, and intending 26 fxg7 ♕xe7.

b2) **21...♘g3 22 ♕h2 ♘xh1 23 ♖xh1 ♕xf5** and now:

b21) **24 ♘xe7+? ♖xe7 25 ♗xe7 ♕xf4+** forces an exchange of queens and wins easily for Black.

b22) **24 ♗xe7? ♖xc2+! 25 ♕xc2 ♕xd5** leaves White with his bishop and rook simultaneously *en prise*.

b23) **24 ♕h7+ ♔f8 25 ♗h6??** ♕xc2#.

b24) **24 ♘e3 ♕e4!?** (24...♖xc2+ is also possible as Black has so many extra pawns) **25 ♘xc4 ♖c8!** (25...♕xc4?? walks into 26 ♕h7+ ♔f8 27 ♗h6, which threatens ♕xg7# or ♕h8#) branching into:

b241) **26 ♕h7+ ♔f8 27 ♕h8+?** (27 ♗h6? ♕xh1+) 27...♗xh8 28 ♖xh8+ ♔g7 29 ♖xc8 ♕e1#.

b242) **26 ♘a3 g3!** 27 ♕h7+ ♔f8, threatening 28...g2 29 ♖g1 ♕e3+.

You may be thinking that so many rosy lines seem too good to be true for Black, and you may wonder more when I tell you that I have never played the Sicilian Dragon in a serious

game (except in the accelerated form 1 e4 c5 2 ♘f3 ♘c6 3 d4 cxd4 4 ♘xd4 g6 on a few occasions in the 1980s)! Well, that was only because I used to carry the misconception that I could not assimilate all the sharp lines in this fiery opening. However, I recently reminded myself of the star motto *'there is no man living who isn't capable of doing more than he thinks he can do'*, and in the course of studying the large number of games **and ideas** included within our main game, I realized several things which gave me the confidence and purpose needed to pursue the Dragon wherever it wanted to take me:

1) Black's pieces tend to get lots of scope and activity in the Dragon, and if one makes them work together in harmony, then beautiful combinative possibilities flow naturally from the position. In particular, when White castles queenside, Black should look out for opportunities to unleash tactics that utilize the open sections of the c- and b-files and/or the power of the Dragon bishop on g7, breathing fire that can be felt at b2 adjacent to White's monarch on c1. In other words, in spite of its reputation for being double-edged, I personally now find the Dragon to be a rather logical creature, and I am no longer afraid to sit beside it as Black. Of course, I am not saying that White's position is devoid of chances, but after spending many many hours in the company of the Dragon, I now trust it.

2) I want to start playing the Dragon, because I have acquired much confidence, knowledge and understanding of it through my work in writing the extensive notes to all the material contained within Maurice Johnson's main game.

3) I think you too will love playing the Dragon and will score lots of points using it, especially if you are willing to invest a few hours to become familiar with some key variations and ideas in this K.I.P.P.I.N.G. chapter. I never encourage people to memorize information without truly understanding it, so in my notes I have endeavoured to give clear explanations to the detailed analysis. It seemed sensible to concentrate on the hottest lines of the Yugoslav Attack (that began with 7 f3), since those paths are followed so often, but some other possibilities are dealt with in the Star Test at the end of this chapter. Obviously deviations are possible at almost every move, but as one gains experience of playing an opening, one's faith, knowledge and understanding increase. Consequently, little sidelines do not cause insurmountable trouble when they crop up. In the words of my father-in-law, Professor Yimin Zeng, 'Let little problems become nothing, and let bigger problems become little'.

For White, though, being a pawn down since his sacrifice at move 14 (that is, 14 g4 hxg4) represents a problem that will only become bigger, unless he can generate real threats to compensate for the material deficit. However, it is not clear that that is possible, as Black has a sound position and a well-developed, harmoniously positioned army. Let us now see Maurice Johnson's 17th move, which involves his star Dragon bishop.

17 ...   ♗xf6 (D)

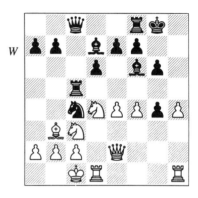

18 ♗xc4

18 ♘d5 looks more obvious, but perhaps White wanted to deny Black the possibility of ...♘b6 or even the exchange sacrifice ...♖xd5.

18 ...   ♖xc4
19 ♘d5

This threatens 20 e5, aiming to push the dark-squared bishop away from protecting the e7-pawn, so Maurice Johnson immediately takes countermeasures.

19 ...   ♖e8
20 ♘xf6+

20 e5 merits consideration, but Black does not necessarily have to retreat his Dragon bishop. Instead,

20...罝c5!? can lead to interesting lines such as:

a) **21 ②xf6+** exf6, and the e5-pawn is under quadruple fire!

b) **21 ②b3 罝xd5!** 22 罝xd5 ②c6, and Black will emerge still at least one pawn ahead but having forced some advantageous exchanges into the bargain. The point is that, in general, swapping off pieces helps a player who is ahead on material to win more easily because as the number of pieces on the board reduces, the chances of the opponent generating any irritating threats also diminishes.

c) **21 exf6 罝xd5** 22 fxe7 豐c5 23 豐e3 罝h5, intending ...d5 or ...②e6 followed by ...罝xe7. It is very common in chess for a player (White in this case) who has embarked on a rather crude attack to find himself saddled later with frail survivors in the form of isolated pawns when his attacking gestures get stopped dead by vigorous yet sound counter-attacking play. Here, the three members of White's kingside and central pawn trio are all virtually blockaded and very vulnerable. Nevertheless, I do wholeheartedly recommend an attacking style of play, but the moves should be soundly-based. Sometimes a violent attacking system scores well for a period because the players on the receiving end panic, but if the attack does not have a sound basis then good lasting antidotes to use against it get discovered quickly. Still, I sympathize with White in his dilemma when

facing the Dragon: if he attacks, the Dragon breathes fire back at him; if he does not attack, Black most certainly will, and quickly too! In short, I know of no easy answer for White against the Dragon. Even super-grandmasters like Michael Adams find it a really difficult beast to handle, for I remember well that in November 1994 at the Moscow Olympiad, Mickey said to me 'What do you do against the Dragon?'.

20   ...   exf6
21   h5 *(D)*

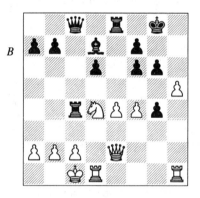

21   ...   g5!

Very sensibly, Black does not allow White to play hxg6 followed by 豐h2. Even dragons are a bit afraid of an open h-file!

22   fxg5

22 f5 is well-answered by 22...d5, exploiting the fact that White's e-pawn is pinned.

22   ...   豐c5!

Maurice Johnson probably spotted far in advance the important detail that

23 ♘b3 would pose him no problems because his queen can capture on g5 *with check*.

23	♕d3	♕xg5+
24	♔b1	d5!

There are several good aspects to this move:

1) It protects the c4-rook and prepares to exchange off the weak isolated d-pawn.

2) After the e4-pawn gets eliminated, Black's f-pawns immediately become passed pawns, and can then support the g-pawn.

25	exd5	♕xd5
26	h6	f5
27	b3	

27 ♘xf5? ♕xd3 28 cxd3 ♗xf5 pins the d3-pawn and consequently makes 29 dxc4 illegal. Alternatively, after 27 h7+, the careless reply 27...♔g7?? allows 28 ♘xf5+ ♕xf5 29 ♕xc4, but simply 27...♔h8 keeps Black in control of the game.

No doubt White would have liked to put up tougher resistance by avoiding an exchange of queens and attacking with as much energy as possible. However, this is difficult to achieve because of tactics based on the weakness of his back rank (where the white king is hemmed in) and the fact that his knight currently requires protection. For example, 27 ♕d2 (threatening ♕g5+) 27...♔h7 28 ♕g5 ♖g8 and then 29 ♕f6 ♖g6 or 29 ♕e3 ♖xd4! 30 ♕xd4 (30 ♖xd4 ♕xh1+) 30...♕xd4 31 ♖xd4 ♗c6 is similar to, but even better for Black than the actual game

continuation because his king is already blockading the white h-pawn and his own rook is ideally placed behind the passed g-pawn to push it through to promotion.

27	...	♖xd4! *(D)*

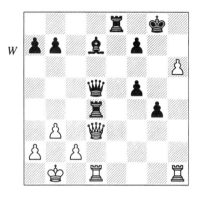

28	♕xd4	♕xd4
29	♖xd4	♗c6?!

There are three main reasons why **29...♗e6!** is better:

1) It simultaneously protects both of Black's passed f-pawns.

2) It does not allow White to achieve the manoeuvre ♖d6 followed by ♖f6.

3) It does not allow White to gain a valuable tempo by attacking the f5-pawn with ♖h5. Time is extremely important in chess, and the precise choice and timing of moves can often make a world of difference between the possible and actual result of a game.

Black is probably still winning after 29...♗c6, but we shall soon see that his opponent could have put up much more stubborn resistance than 29...♗e6 would have allowed. After the latter move, a plausible continuation is **30 h7+** (otherwise Black will play ...♔h7 and ...♖g8) **30...♔g7** (intending ...♖h8) **31 h8♕+** (or 31 ♖d2 ♖h8 32 ♖dh2 ♗d5 33 ♖d1 ♗f3, with a position that is clearly superior for Black to the one he gets after move 31 in the actual game, as here the h-pawn is blockaded not by Black's king, but by a rook which is about to 'eat that pawn', as Arthur Absalom, one of my very young chess pupils, likes to say!) **31...♖xh8 32 ♖xh8 ♔xh8 33 ♔c1 g3 34 ♖d1 f4 35 ♔d2 ♔g7** (35...f3? 36 ♖h1+! ♔g7 37 ♖g1! g2 38 ♔e3 is not what Black wants, because his passed pawns have become blockaded) **36 ♖f1 ♔g6!**, intending 37 ♖xf4 g2, and planning ...♔g5-g4 followed by the calm, controlled, unstoppable advance ...f3-f2.

It's hard to switch into reverse gear after watching pawns charge forward, but we need to go back to see White's 30th move against M.J.

30 ♖h5   ♗e4
31 h7+

White appreciates the importance of preventing ...♔h7 and ...♖g8. If 31 ♖d7, then 31...♔h7! 32 ♖xf7+ ♔g6 gives a nice king-size fork against White's two rooks. A similar tactic arises through **31 ♖d6 ♔h7** (but not 31...♖e6?? 32 h7+ ♔h8 33 ♖d8+) **32 ♖f6 ♖g8!!** (32...♖e7 33 ♖g5!) and now:

a) **33 ♖xf7+ ♔g6 34 h7** loses quickly to 34...♖h8 35 ♖f8 ♖xh7 36 ♖xh7 ♔xh7 followed by the g-pawn

galloping forward, so White must play 34 ♖g7+, although Black still wins with 34...♖xg7 35 hxg7 ♗d5 36 c4 ♗e6 37 ♖h1 (37 ♖h4 g3) 37...♔xg7 38 ♔c1 f4 39 ♔d2 g3 40 ♖f1 ♔g6!, which gives an almost identical position to the one that was reached in the note to move 29.

b) **33 ♖h4** g3 34 ♖xf7+ ♔h8 35 h7 g2! 36 hxg8♕+ ♔xg8 *(D)* and Black wins beautifully.

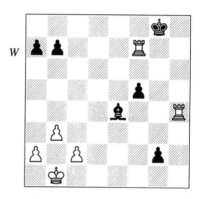

31 ...   ♔h8

After **31...♔g7 32 ♖d6!**, Black has some problems. For instance:

a) **32...♖h8** 33 ♖g5+! ♔xh7 34 ♖h5+ ♔g7 35 ♖g5+, and White has at least a draw after 35...♔h7, whereas 35...♔f8?? walks into the painful skewer 36 ♖d8+.

b) **32...f6?** 33 h8♕+! ♖xh8 34 ♖d7+ ♔g8 35 ♖d8+ costs Black his rook.

32 ♖h4?

After this error, White's rooks have no chance of stopping Black's far-advanced connected passed pawns. 32

♖g5? is also bad, because although 32...♔xh7 33 ♖d2 may be a tempting trick threatening ♖h2#, the simple 33...♔h6 neatly traps the rook on g5. White should have played **32 ♖d6!**, with these ideas:

a) **32...g3** 33 ♖g5 g2 (33...f4 34 ♖f6 shows a key point of the earlier ♖d6 move) 34 ♖d2 planning ♖dxg2, and White has excellent drawing chances.

b) **32...♖c8!** 33 ♖f6 ♖xc2 (after 33...♔g7, 34 ♖d6! threatens 35 h8♕+! ♖xh8 36 ♖g5+, a trick with the same theme as in variation 'a' after M.J.'s 31st move) 34 ♔a1 ♖c7 35 ♖d6 ♖c8 36 ♖f6 ♖f8 (36...♔g7 37 ♖d6 creates the possibility of h8♕+! again) 37 ♖g5 (stopping ...g3) 37...♔xh7 38 ♔b2 ♖c8 (38...♖g8?? 39 ♖xf7+ ♔h8 40 ♖h5# is a funny smothered mate of sorts) 39 ♖xf7+ ♔h6 40 ♖fg7 ♖c6 followed by ...♗d5-f7-g6, and one of White's rooks will be lost. Nevertheless, this variation stemming from 32 ♖d6 represented White's best chance, and it would have made M.J. work harder.

| 32 | ... | g3 |
| 33 | ♖d1 | |

Otherwise ...♗f3 would have prevented this retreat which hopes to stop the g-pawn from promoting.

| 33 | ... | ♖c8 |
| 34 | ♔a1 | |

For thoroughness, let us check a couple of plausible alternatives, although they are not superior to the actual move played:

a) **34 ♖c1** loses more quickly in view of 34...♖xc2! 35 ♖xc2, for example 35...♗xc2+ 36 ♔xc2 g2 or even 35...g2 36 ♖xe4 g1♕+ 37 ♖c1 ♕xc1+ 38 ♔xc1 fxe4.

b) Somewhat better is **34 ♔b2** ♖xc2+ 35 ♔a3 ♖c8 36 ♔b4 g2 (intending to play ...♖e8 and then ...♗d3 followed by ...♗f1 or in some cases ...♖e4+) 37 ♖g1, but Black still wins with 37...♖d8 38 a4 ♗f3 39 ♖h2 f4 (planning ...♗c6 followed by ...f3) 40 ♖gxg2 ♗xg2 41 ♖xg2 ♔xh7, since his king can move forward to support the advance of at least one of the f-pawns, whereas White's king is cut off from the kingside by Black's rook.

After the actual move played in the game, White is perhaps hoping for 34...♖xc2?? 35 ♖d8+ or 34...♗xc2? 35 ♖g1.

34	...	g2
35	c4	♗f3
36	♖e1	♖d8!

Threatening to exchange the e1-rook by 37...♖d1+, after which the g-pawn will soon touch down on g1 and turn into a lovely new queen.

| 37 | ♔b2 | |

The alternatives are no better:

a) **37 ♖h2** f4 (intending ...♗c6 followed by ...f3) 38 ♖g1 ♖d2 39 ♖e1 g1♕ 40 ♖xg1 (40 ♖e8+ would be good if it weren't illegal!) 40...♖xh2.

b) **37 ♖h3** ♖d1+ 38 ♖xd1 ♗xd1 39 ♖g3 ♗f3! 40 c5 f4 41 ♖g5 f6 (41...♗g4 42 ♖xg4 f3 is also sufficient to win, and illustrates a typical situation where two connected passed pawns on or beyond the sixth rank usually defeat a rook's attempts to stop one of them from promoting) 42 ♖g6 ♚xh7, and White's poor rook has run out of squares to flee to on the g-file.

> **37 ...   ♖d2+**
> **38 ♔c3**

If 38 ♔c1, then 38...♖d1+! is the quickest route to victory.

> **38 ...   ♖e2**
> **39 ♖g1   ♖f2** *(D)*

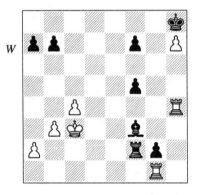

0-1

White resigned because of 40 ♖e1 ♗e2 followed by ...f4, ...f3 and ...♖f1. That was, in my opinion, a near-perfect game by Maurice Johnson, and it is necessary to look at least as far back as move 20 to find any truly worthwhile improvements for White, which is partly why many alternatives were considered early on in the notes.

Exactly one week ago, on the Feast of the Sacred Heart (June 6), I was still buried at the core of the extensive annotations, but later when M.J. was sprinting towards victory around move 35, I felt much joy, also because this part of our S.T.A.R. journey has been completed as I turned 35 today.

We conclude this chapter with several positions (the first three arose from the Sicilian Dragon) and puzzles to keep us sharp. In each case, one of the two sides has a piece in a perilous situation which the opponent can exploit to win, or draw beautifully in the penultimate example. Mostly it is the king who is in mortal danger, but a couple of times there is a different piece having a nightmare. You can compare your answers to the solutions that appear on pages 227-9.

Star Test

1.1

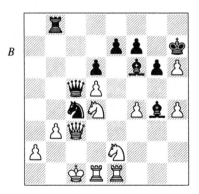

Black to play and win.

1.2

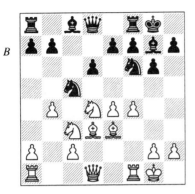

Black to play and win material. Can you identify the previous 10 opening moves which led to the given position?

1.4

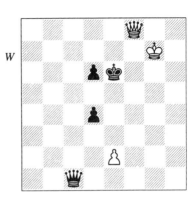

White to play and win.

1.3

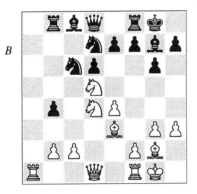

Black to play and win a piece. Also, can you identify the previous 15 opening moves which led to the given position?

1.5

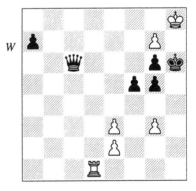

White to play.

a) How can he force a draw by perpetual check?

b) How can he do better and actually win the game?

1.6

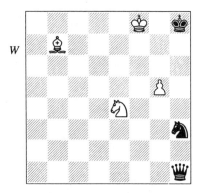

White to play and draw.

Star Challenge no. 1

As a preamble to this puzzle of mine, let us agree that if pieces were sitting on the squares a1, a3, c3, c1 e.g., then we could say that they are arranged in a square, because straight lines drawn from the centres of each of the four little squares to the centres of the two squares nearest by (in the group of four) would form a square.

Now imagine that in a certain game of chess there are only four pieces remaining on the board, and they are arranged in a square. You are told that one piece is on c3, and Black's one and only piece is on a4. You now have sufficient information to discover the locations of the other two pieces, and to help you identify all the pieces, there is the following: if it is Black to move, then the game is a draw, but if it is White to move, then he can immediately give checkmate in a choice of exactly three ways. Can you spot which pieces are on which squares?

2 S.P.O.T. the Star Pieces

On the many occasions when Paul Fitzpatrick, a friend, mentor and former colleague in Scotland, was present before I was due to play an opponent (not necessarily a highly rated one), Paul reminded me of an obvious fact, yet one that is still very helpful and encouraging: 'Remember you are in charge of 16 pieces, the same as your opponent's except for the colour. So if you remain alert, keep an eye on your time consumption, and make full use of the army of star pieces in a more coordinated way than your opponent does, then there is no reason why you cannot win, no matter how high his or her rating is. Of course, the opponent can play that same game too. Therefore never underestimate, and always respect the other person.'

Paul Fitzpatrick's wise advice has inspired numerous pupils to sit down, enjoy being in charge of a 16-piece army, and proceed to work such wonders with it that even highly ranked opponents found the force too much to handle. In a nutshell, the winning formula was: actively use all the star pieces with enjoyment and without fear.

One cannot afford to sit back lazily and wait for lower-rated opponents to make a mistake. Such an unwise, presumptuous approach may work some of the time, but it is hardly a route of self-improvement. To take a tennis analogy, after Sergi Bruguera, the 1993/4 French Open Champion, lost the 1997 final in straight sets to Brazil's unseeded Gustavo Kuerten, he said 'I waited for him to give me the match, but he took the match'. In contrast, Kuerten, who won his first-ever tournament in only the 46th match of his professional career, consistently played lively, attacking tennis, and in total defeated three former French Open champions *en route* to his sensational title win.

Most of the time in tennis, one is primarily concerned with where a single ball is, but in chess the locations of many pieces are important. In general, none of them should be neglected, but some skill is needed to spot which piece should star in the next move. IM Jonathan Rowson (J.R.) says 'Talk to your pieces!'. By that, he means consider each piece in turn and see if it is purposefully placed. As you systematically improve the positions of pieces which are not yet ideally placed to assist with your main strategic plan while simultaneously hindering your opponent's operations, the harmony within your army will increase, and tactical strikes will very often become possible. Consider the following position *(D)*, which arose after Black's 12th move of Rowson-Avrukh, World Junior Ch, Zagan 1997.

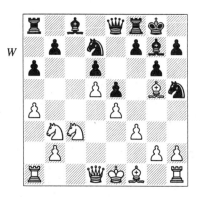

Even if J.R. hadn't already seen Khenkin-Gallagher, Geneva 1996, in which White played **13 ♘d2!** intending ♘c4 and ♘xd6, the 'talk to your pieces' phrase could help him to discover that excellent knight move. It is particularly logical for four reasons:

a) One might think about moving the bishop from f1, but 13 ♗e2 and 13 ♗d3 are quite well-answered by 13...♘f4, a fact which should prompt White to consider moving a different piece.

b) The knight is not doing much on b3, so its position should be improved.

c) The manoeuvre ♘d2-c4 pinpoints the sensitivity of the b6- and d6-squares in the opponent's camp, and actually threatens to trap Black's queen with ♘xd6.

d) The centre is quite closed, so even though White's king has not castled, it is perfectly safe to spend two moves to transfer the knight from b3 to c4. Those two tempi represent a very worthwhile investment of time, as we can see from the benefits mentioned in 'c'.

J.R.'s game continued **13...f6 14 ♗h4 ♘f4** (14...♗h6 15 ♘c4 ♕e7 16 ♕b3 ♖b8 17 ♕a3! ♘c5 18 a5 {White tightens his grip on the position} 18...♘f4 19 ♖d1 ♖d8 20 ♗f2 threatening ♘xd6! was the course of the other battle featuring 13 ♘d2 mentioned above) **15 ♘c4 ♕e7 16 a5 ♖b8 17 ♕b3 ♘c5 18 ♕b6! g5 19 ♗g3** (much better than 19 ♗f2, which allows 19...♘fd3+ followed by ...♘xf2) **19...♖d8 20 0-0-0 ♗f8 21 ♗f2 ♘d7** (a sign that Black cannot find a constructive plan to break out of his cramped position) **22 ♕a7!** (the white queen boldly goes deeper into enemy territory, where it has a paralysing effect on Black's queenside forces since the b8-rook requires constant protection) **22...♖e8 23 g3 ♘g6 24 ♔b1!** (this quiet-looking move is particularly distressing to Black because, in effect, White is saying 'I have all the time in the world to transfer a rook onto the c-file, and in the meantime you have no active plan') **24...♕f7 25 ♗h3 ♕e7 26 ♗e6+ ♔h8 27 ♖c1 ♕g7** (the queen seems to be running around aimlessly like a lost sheep) **28 &Ic2 &e7 29 &e3** (the white knight decides to enjoy fresh pastures on the outpost at f5 where it will land shortly) **29...&f8 30 &f5 &Id8 31 &a4 &e8** *(D)*.

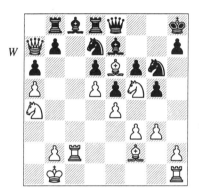

32 &h6! (even before the point where we first leapt into the game at move 12, the star white knight had started its manoeuvre &g1-e2-c1-b3-d2-c4-e3-f5-h6, and two more jumps will see its individual move count reach double figures, after which Black resigns rather than prolonging the nightmare) **32...b5 33 &f7+** (the first check...) **33...&g7 34 &xd8** (...and the first capture {since a pawn exchange at moves 10-11} of this beautifully controlled game by J.R. against an opponent rated 2550) **1-0**.

The 'talk to your pieces' phrase can help one to spot the next move at practically any stage of a battle. For instance, let us take a look at the game Mannion-Rowson, Aberdeen 1997, after White's 38th move *(D)*:

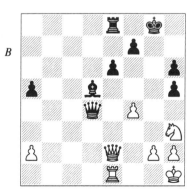

Black's queen and bishop are in excellent centralized locations, but the position of the rook on e8 could be improved to make it perform a strong active function. The g2-square next to White's king is clearly a sensitive spot, so the idea of 38...♔h7 intending ...♖g8 might flash through one's mind. However, 39 ♕xh5 ♖g8? 40 ♘g5+! would virtually force Black to bail out with a draw by 40...♖xg5 41 fxg5 ♕f2 42 ♖g1 (42 ♕e2?? ♗xg2#) 42...♗xg2+ 43 ♖xg2 ♕e1+ 44 ♖g1 ♕e4+ 45 ♖g2 ♕e1+ and so on. Therefore J.R. decided to use his rook to attack the g2 point laterally across White's second rank, and he played 38...♖b8! planning ...♖b2. The game ended 39 ♕xh5 ♕g7 40 ♖g1 (40 ♖e2 ♖b1+ 41 ♘g1 ♕d4 is another way for White to go) 40...♖b2 41 ♘g5 hxg5 42 fxg5 ♖xg2! 0-1. IM Steve Mannion resigned on account of 43 ♖xg2 ♕a1+ 44 ♕d1 ♕xd1#.

A star sign showing that the members of an army are really beginning to gel together with coordinated actions is that events on the board seem to flow powerfully yet almost effortlessly like a cascade of water full of colours, and the opponent will simply be drowned in sacrifices if his forces are less coordinated. That fact is echoed by the following sentence, which can also serve as a memory aid for remembering the names and correct order of the 12 constellations Aries, Taurus, Gemini, Cancer, Leo, Virgo, Libra, Scorpio, Sagittarius, Capricorn, Aquarius, Pisces that make up the star signs of the Zodiac. **A**rmies **T**hat **G**el **Can** **Le**ad **V**ery **Li**vely **Scor**ching **Sa**crificial **Cap**tivating **Aqua**marine **P**lans.

The lovely games and puzzles within this chapter will provide us with hundreds of opportunities to spot the star piece that should best be used to make the next move, but what about the mnemonic **S.P.O.T.**? Well, since it is a universal anagram, it does not matter if someone *opts* to use *pots* or *tops* instead of *spot*. It is the four elements **S**elf, **P**osition, **O**pponent, **T**ime that are important, because that quartet of factors greatly influences the course of a game. Some related key words were described in *H.O.T. Chess*, but since I am constantly refining my approach to (over-the-board or OTB) chess, and trying to make it even more practical and easier to use, S.P.O.T. represents my favourite, newest, simplest and (I think) best checklist for quickly keeping tabs on how the different aspects of a typical over-the-board tussle are progressing. Nevertheless, I was also delighted to hear from many people who play OTB and correspondence chess that they are finding the mnemonics in my two earlier books to be very useful too, as well as all the games and other items.

Let us now consider each element of S.P.O.T. in turn:

1) **Self**: The tussle really begins even before the first move is played, so I always try to take care to get a mixture of sufficient rest and fresh air before any game, so that my body and mind will feel comfortable yet full of energy during the game. Some people like to eat before or during games, but I prefer to separate

food and the start of play by a reasonable time interval (preferably around one hour, otherwise I feel sleepy when blood is diverted from the head to help the stomach digest food). Then I can go for a leisurely stroll outdoors before battle, and augment any earlier preparation by a calm, clear final decision about the opening and style of game I hope to employ against my opponent-to-be. However, in some ways it is an advantage if I have almost no prior knowledge about him or her, because then I tend to relax completely, conserve all my energy for the actual game, and wait patiently until I can form an initial impression when the game begins.

2) **Position**: Right from the first move, it is sensible to aim for positions which one knows and understands well. However, that does not necessarily mean following the latest main line of theory in some opening. Instead, one of *your* favourite pet lines could surprise and trouble even a theoretically well-prepared opponent, especially if the line has not been extensively analysed in many publications. A good example in my case is the Vienna Game (1 e4 e5 2 ♘c3), since I have found that most opponents know much less about it than the Ruy Lopez (1 e4 e5 2 ♘f3 ♘c6 3 ♗b5), for instance. Alternatively, you could employ a well-established opening that you have been studying but have rarely used in practice before, so no opponent could easily predict such a choice when preparing to face you. As your repertoire expands, the task of preparing to play against you becomes more and more difficult for prospective opponents. For instance, GM Nigel Short is an expert in the Ruy Lopez (Spanish Opening), but in 1997 he switched with success to the King's Gambit (1 e4 e5 2 f4) on several occasions. I recall chatting to Nigel about that opening on the Isle of Lewis in July 1995, so it seems his forward planning was looking a long way ahead and included 'f for forward' in a big way! Refreshing attacking play can produce marvellous results.

Another position-related idea that came out of my conversation with Nigel has been extremely useful to me ever since. He was talking about a particular line for White (although it would not matter if it had been a system for Black) and I was suggesting ideas for Black against it. Nigel then said 'Yes, you can, of course, play those moves, but White **is not worse**'. I realized that Nigel had an excellent attitude towards the position: he was content to get one which suited his style while carrying some surprise value if possible, and where his chances were not worse than those of the opponent. If one does not stand significantly worse, then why should one worry, no matter who the opponent is?

I always endeavour to find the best move (and if possible a sound, attacking one), but there may be several very good options to choose from, and sometimes it is necessary to pick one without expecting just too much from the position.

Nigel Short's advice has helped me to be happy if at least I do not stand worse, because one cannot reasonably expect to have a large advantage in the position unless the opponent has made some earlier error.

During a game, I like to sit at the board and remain focused by concentrating on the position for most of the time, but occasionally it is a good idea to get up, walk around, and relax for a few minutes. On returning to the board, I sometimes find it helpful to stand momentarily behind the opponent (without distracting him or her) and take a fresh look at the position from that opposite side of the board. The new perspective often triggers ideas for moves which I had not thought of before. Incidentally, I call this the '180-degree' method, because, in effect, one is turning the board around through a half-turn to view it from the opponent's side. I use this method a lot in preparation. For instance, if I am studying an opening from White's (or Black's) point of view, then I like to look at the board from Black's (or White's) side, since I discover testing ideas that the opponent might play against the opening I am preparing.

3) **Opponent**: Apart from deliberately selecting an opening system and playing in a style which I think the opponent will find awkward to handle, there is another thought which often helps me, even in the full heat of battle: I remind myself that if the game is really complicated and I am finding it difficult, then very likely the opponent is feeling similarly (not counting computers!), so I should try to keep him or her under pressure rather than only being too aware of the pressure I am experiencing. Then the chances of the opponent making an error will increase, and an opportunity to seize victory may well arise. No one is invincible.

4) **Time**: GM William Watson once pointed out the obvious yet very important fact that if one has, say, forty moves to play in two hours, then some self-discipline is needed in order not to take more than three minutes per move, on average. Personally, I still suffer from time-trouble in some games, but I have managed to reduce this problem a bit by noting on the scoresheet the total time I have used after each move, a habit which helps me to be more rigorous in not overstepping the three minutes per move average by too much at any stage. Of course, one learns through experience to recognize critical moments in games, and at such times it may sometimes be necessary to think for a relatively long period, but having done that, one can often speed up afterwards because the difficult decisions and/or calculations have already been done at the earlier critical stage, and they should not be excessively re-checked. Instead, trust oneself and proceed carefully but with a healthy amount of confidence.

So far we have been considering time in the sense of time on the chess-clock, and how it must be used wisely. However, another equally important aspect of time is the idea of making every move really count in a purposeful way, so that no time is wasted. With such an attitude, one will play many beautiful, flowing games of chess.

Sometimes certain non-chess factors in our lives may creep in and negatively affect performance, but the following poem featuring the four elements of S.P.O.T. encourages us to enjoy chess to the full, and put aside any worries while we are playing.

Don't worry or feel taxed by a few pests
No hurry, really relax while you rest
Hey, the mess will wait on the dusty shelf
*Play chess, it's great, and trust one**self**.*
The key components of innovation and attack
*Put the **opponent**'s calculations in a flap*
*For us a bright route to super **positions***
Plus the right boot in, with computer precision!
Stay cool and pressing; every turn counts
That way you'll impress; never burn out
*So we're going far for all **time***
No fear-showing stars in Paul's rhyme!
The core elements, however, are contained in S.P.O.T.
Those four I meant forever to be retained were taught.

We are about to see some truly awesome star games. If we imagine putting ourselves in the shoes of either of the players in any given game, then the foursome of *self, position, opponent, time* can help us to appreciate better what each player experienced during the game. You might also like to try covering up some of the moves with a card to see if you can spot the star piece that will make the next move. I always try to be very clear and at the same time thorough in my notes and analysis, yet I would still encourage you to search for further fantastic possibilities which may sometimes have been missed by myself or the actual players. Apart from the obvious benefits for your chess, you'll feel like a star when you find such sparkling moves!

I hope you don't suffer from astrapophobia (fear of lightning), because White strikes like white lightning no fewer than half a dozen times in the six complete annotated games contained within the forthcoming game, counting that stunning main game itself. Don't be intimidated by the volume of material; it has been included to serve you (among other ways, by giving some powerful related examples of how the opening and middlegame can be conducted very effectively).

Brilliant moves abound in the pages ahead, but because many words have been written since the last puzzle, I think it's time we had another one to solve, just to make sure our brains are buzzing with flashes of inspiration before we set foot inside the game.

King on Edge

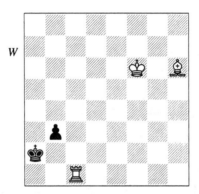

It is White to play and win. You can compare your solution with the one that appears after the first complete game within the notes to the following instructive battle between GM Lev Psakhis and IM Boris Chatalbashev.

Game 2

L. Psakhis – B. Chatalbashev
Benasque 1996
Modern Benoni

1 d4 ♞f6

All forms of the Benoni Defence are characterized by the move ...c5, and Black plays it on his next move in this main game. **1...c5 2 d5** would just transpose after 2...♞f6 3 ♞f3, but **2...e5** gives a position with a very different character, since ...e6 is no longer possible. The Benoni with ...e6 is usually referred to as the 'Modern Benoni',

whereas 2...e5 is called the Semi-Benoni. Let us see how France's Etienne Bacrot, who became the world's youngest ever grandmaster in March 1997 at the age of 14 years 1 month, responded to the Semi-Benoni when he faced it two months later. The game Bacrot-Casagrande, Linz 1997 continued **3 ♞c3** (White anticipates that Black will soon play ...d6, after which his d-pawn supports its neighbours at e5 and c5 but is slightly vulnerable itself, and so rather than play 3 c4, White leaves the c4-square free so that the manoeuvre ♘g1-f3-d2-c4 is possible later to pressurize the d6 point) **3...d6 4 ♘f3** (there is some clever psychology behind this move-order, because by not playing 4 e4, White encourages his opponent to try for ...f5 followed by ...e4, but in reality Black then falls behind in development, the e6-square in his camp becomes very sensitive, and his king soon feels exposed along the h5-e8 diagonal) **4...f5?** (4...♘f6 and 4...♗e7 are more prudent moves) **5 e4** (already 6 ♗b5+ ♗d7 {6...♗f7 7 ♘g5+} 7 exf5 is threatened, and even simply 6 exf5 ♗xf5 7 ♗d3 is positionally very unpleasant for Black, because if his light-squared bishop gets exchanged then the outpost at e6 becomes an extremely vulnerable target for White to exploit by means of the manoeuvre ♘f3-g5-e6) **5...f4** *(D)*.

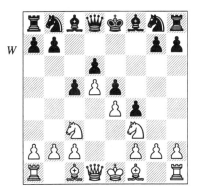

6 ♘xe5!! dxe5 7 ♕h5+ ♔e7 (7...g6? loses a rook to 8 ♕xe5+ ♔e7 9 ♕xh8, whereas 7...♔d7 is met by 8 ♕xe5, threatening 9 ♗b5+ or 9 ♕e6+ ♔c7 10 ♘b5# to mention just a couple of ideas) **8 ♕xe5+ ♔f7 9 ♗xf4** (Bacrot has an attack plus three mobile, connected, powerful pawns in return for his sacrificed knight, while all but one of the pieces in his IM opponent's army are asleep in the back row!) **9...a6** (9...♕e7 10 ♕h5+ g6 11 ♕f3 ♔g7 12 d6 ♕e6 13 ♗c4! ♕xc4 14 ♗e5+ ♔h6 15 h4 {15 ♕xf8+ clearly wins too, but the threat of 16 ♕f4+ ♔h5 17 ♕g5# is even stronger} 15...g5 16 hxg5++ ♔g6 17 ♕h5# is a pretty line) **10 ♗c4 b5 11 d6+! bxc4 12 ♕d5+ ♗e6 13 ♕xa8 g5** (13...♗xd6? loses instantly to the pinning move 14 ♖d1, while the attempt by 13...♕b6 14 0-0-0 ♘c6 to block White's queen's escape-route from the a8-corner fails as 15 d7 forces 15...♘d8, unless Black prefers to bow out with 15...♗e7 16 ♕e8+ ♔f6 17 e5+ ♔f5 18 ♕h5+ g5 {18...♔xf4 19 g3#} 19 ♖he1 ♔xf4 20 ♕f3#, a typical king-hunt variation) **14 ♗e5 ♗g7 15 ♗xg7 ♔xg7 16 0-0-0 ♘f6 17 e5 ♘g4 18 ♕a7+ ♘d7 19 ♘e4 c3** (a desperate lunge to try to land even a single punch on his young opponent, but Bacrot remains cool, calm and completely in control) **20 ♘xc5 cxb2+ 21 ♔b1** (21 ♔xb2?? ♕b8+ 22 ♕xb8 ♖xb8+ 23 ♘b3 ♘xf2 allows Black to turn the tables) **21...♖e8** *(D)*.

   22 ♕c7!! (this threatens 23 ♘xe6+ ♖xe6 24 ♕xd8, and if 22...♕xc7, then

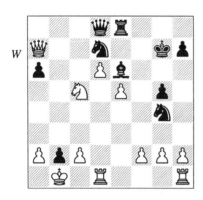

W

23 ♘xe6+ ♖xe6 24 dxc7 ♘b6 25 ♖d6 {25 ♖d8 ♖c6 26 ♖b8 intending 27 ♖xb6! also wins} 25...♖xd6 {25...♔f7 26 ♖xb6! ♖xb6 27 c8♕} 26 exd6 ♘f6 27 ♖e1 ♔f8 28 ♖e7 ♘c8 29 d7! illustrates the enormous power that far-advanced connected passed pawns generally possess} **22...♗f5** (22...♔f7 23 ♘xe6 ♔xe6 24 ♕c4+ ♔f5 25 ♕f7+ ♔xe5 26 ♖d5+ ♔e4 27 ♕f5# is another way for Black to exit) **23 e6!!** (another star move from Bacrot underlines why GM David Norwood, who beat the French prodigy in a quickplay game at the 1995 Intel qualifier in Hastings, recently said 'Now it has dawned on me that those 15 minutes were my taste of stardom'!) **23...♕xc7 24 dxc7** ♘b6 (24...♘xc5 25 ♖d8 and then 25...♗e6 26 ♖xe8, threatening 27 ♖xe6! or 27 c8♕, and 25...♘xe6 26 ♖xe8! ♘xc7 27 ♖e7+ ♔f6 28 ♖xc7 both give White a decisive material advantage, but in the latter variation, note that 26 c8♕ is much less clear in view of 26...♖xd8, after which Black is right back in the game with rook

plus three minor pieces versus White's rook and queen) **25 ♖d8 ♘f6 26 ♖hd1** ♘c8 **27 ♔xb2** (with this capture, White's monarch announces his intention to march up the board and join in the feast of munching the opponent's pieces or pawns, which is sufficient to cause Black to capitulate immediately, since there was little he could do now anyway) **27...♘e7 28 ♖xe8 1-0**, in view of 28...♘xe8 29 ♖d7 ♔f6 30 ♖xe7! ♔xe7 31 c8♕. After that crisp performance by one of the world's brightest new stars, it is time to see the answer to an earlier problem.

Solution to puzzle (posed before Game 2)

In this neat 1928 study composed by the famous Richard Réti, White wins with **1 ♖c3!! b2 2 ♗c1! b1♕ 3 ♖a3#**. Clearly, if Black under-promotes his pawn to a rook or bishop then he still gets checkmated immediately, whereas 2...b1♘ loses quickly to 3 ♖c2+ ♔a1 (3...♔b3 4 ♖b2+) 4 ♔e5 and the knight must give itself up, but of course it could not save the game anyway.

Just before we rejoin the main game at move two, here is another puzzle to keep our tactical vision (which is such a central part of chess) as hot as the Sun's core (which is estimated by scientists to be at a temperature of at least 14,000,000 degrees Celsius, thanks to nuclear fusion).

The Dynamic Duo return!

That title has nothing to do with the new Batman film coming out this year (besides, it's a trio now that Batgirl is around as well as Robin!). Instead, in the following diagram, Black has a dangerous duo of far-advanced passed pawns, and yet White (to move) can use his knight and queen in a dynamic way to win. The solution appears before move four in the main game.

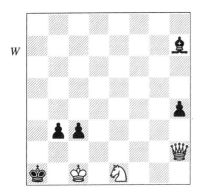

2	♘f3	c5
3	d5	g6

3...e6 4 c4 exd5 (4...d6 5 ♘c3 exd5 6 cxd5 is GM Mihai Suba's preferred subtle move-order as Black, and the reasons will shortly be explained) **5 cxd5 d6** would normally lead to a standard Modern Benoni after the 'automatic' move **6 ♘c3**. However, Suba instead recommends 6 e4! (with the point 6...♘xe4?? 7 ♕a4+) for these main reasons:

a) The c3-knight can become a target for Black's queenside pawns to harass by means of ...a6, ...b5 and then ...b4.

b) The knight would be more ideally placed on c4 to pressurize Black's d6-pawn. Of course, White would probably accompany the manoeuvre ♘b1-d2-c4 by the advance a2-a4 so that the knight could not be bothered by ...b5 after it gets to c4.

However, even with one knight on c3, White can re-route his other horse to c4 via d2. Bosnia's IM Nedeljko Kelečević gave a crushing example of that strategy in a game played against a German FIDE master. **6...g6** transposes to Kelečević-Haist, Baden 1997, which continued 7 ♘d2 ♗g7 8 e4 0-0 9 ♗e2 ♖e8?! (White's chosen system is potentially very dangerous, and Black must combat it with a concrete plan {rather than random moves}, such as 9...♘a6 10 0-0 ♘c7 {supporting the idea of ...b5} 11 a4 b6 12 ♘c4 ♗a6 13 ♗f4 ♗xc4! {eliminating the star piece involved in White's strategy of attacking d6} 14 ♗xc4 ♖e8 15 ♕c2 {15 ♖e1 ♘h5 16 ♗e3? ♗xc3! 17 bxc3 ♖xe4} 15...a6, planning ...♖b8 followed by ...b5) **10 0-0 a6 11 a4 ♘bd7 12 f4 ♖b8 13 ♔h1** (this is not a move that should be played without a definite purpose, but here it is a sensible and useful prophylactic measure which avoids any possibility of ...♗d4+ or other irritations on the a7-g1 diagonal, while also saying to Black 'I don't see a really constructive move for you now, but the ball is back in your court, so please play!') **13...♕e7** (D).

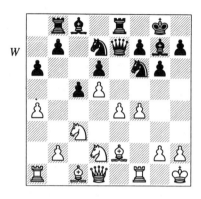

14 e5! (some annotators might say 'this is a thematic pawn sacrifice' and leave it at that, but, apart from his many years of chess experience, I suspect that at least three features resulting from the sacrifice made Kelečević want to play it: 1) after 14...dxe5, White obtains a *passed* d-pawn, which could potentially harass Black's queen and gain a tempo by advancing to d6 later; 2) the h2-b8 diagonal opens up, so White can generate threats based on his opponent having a rook on b8; 3) tactics could arise too on the e-file, where Black's queen and other rook are located) **14...dxe5 15 ♘c4 e4** (15...b5 16 axb5 axb5 17 ♘xe5 ♘xe5 18 fxe5 ♕xe5 19 ♗f4 shows point '2' of the previous note going into action) **16 f5** (this brings back lots of happy memories about the chapter entitled '*f for forward!*' in *C.O.O.L. Chess*, and one specific threat here is ♗f4) **16...b5 17 axb5 axb5 18 ♘a5** (the white knight has spotted an outpost at c6, and it hopes to land a juicy fork there against Black's heavy pieces on e7 and b8)

18...♘e5 19 fxg6 fxg6 (after 19...hxg6 20 ♗g5, White threatens 21 ♘xe4 and Black can never play ...h6 to drive away the powerful enemy bishop that is pinning his f6-knight) **20 ♘xb5 ♘h5** (20...♘fg4 21 ♗f4! {21 h3? ♕h4 is suddenly becoming dangerous for White} and now 21...♕h4 22 ♘d6!? ♘f2+ {22...♖f8 23 ♗g3} 23 ♖xf2 ♕xf2 24 ♗g3 ♕f8 25 ♘xe8 ♕xe8 26 ♘c4 keeps White in firm control of the game, while 21...g5 22 ♘c6! ♘xc6 23 ♗xb8 ♘e3 {23...♘xb8 24 ♗xg4} 24 ♕c1 ♘xf1 25 dxc6 ♗e6 26 ♗d6 ♕f6 27 ♕xf1 puts White a piece ahead) **21 ♘c6 ♘xc6 22 dxc6 ♗e5** (after 22...♕h4, a safe reply is 23 ♕e1, but a more powerful move is 23 ♕d6!, which prevents ...♘g3+ while simultaneously attacking the b8-rook and planning to meet 23...♗e5 by 24 ♗c4+ ♔g7 25 ♖f7+ {25 ♖a7+ is also possible} 25...♔h8 26 ♖f8+ ♔g7 27 ♖g8+ ♖xg8 28 ♕xe5+ and then 28...♕f6 29 ♕xb8 while 28...♘f6 is met by 29 ♗g5 – not 29 ♕xb8?? ♕e1+ 30 ♗f1 ♕xf1#) **23 ♕d5+ ♔h8 24 ♖a7 ♕h4** (D).

25 ♕xe5+! 1-0, 25...♖xe5 26 ♖f8#.

We are about to return to see move four in the main game, but first here is the answer to the problem that appeared before move two.

Solution to puzzle (posed before move two)

In this stunning 1936 study by Paul Keres, White wins with **1 ♘c2+!** and then:

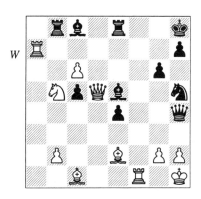

a) **1...♗xc2 2 ♕b8** (threatening 3 ♕a7#; this is also the reply to 1...bxc2) **2...b2+ 3 ♔xc2 b1♕+ 4 ♕xb1#**.

b) **1...♔a2 2 ♘b4++** branching into:

b1) **2...♔a3 3 ♘d3! ♗xd3 4 ♕d6+ ♔a2 5 ♕d5!** (pinning the b-pawn and threatening ♕a5#) **5...♗b5 6 ♕a8+ ♗a4 7 ♕xa4#**.

b2) **2...♔a1** (D).

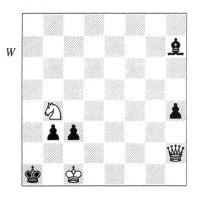

Now **3 ♕a2+!! bxa2 4 ♘c6 h3 5 ♘d4** (intending ♘b3#) **5...♗g8 6 ♘c2#** is a picturesque smothered mate.

4 c4

After **4 ♘c3 ♗g7 5 e4 0-0?!** White has the powerful continuation **6 e5! ♘g4** (after 6...♘e8, a very direct and effective way for White to proceed is 7 h4! {it is worth comparing this approach to a similar line in the Pirc Defence that was analysed on page 23 of *C.O.O.L. Chess*} 7...d6 8 e6! fxe6 9 h5 with a powerful attack, as in Yermolinsky-Khmelnitsky, USA Ch 1995) **7 ♘g5!** (an idea well worth remembering, since 7...♘xe5 8 f4 f6 9 ♘xh7 ♔xh7 10 fxe5 fxe5 11 ♗d3 is fantastic for White, who is then threatening 12 ♕h5+) **7...♘h6 8 h4! f6** (8...♗xe5 9 h5 ♗g7 10 ♘xh7 ♔xh7 11 hxg6+ fxg6 12 ♗xh6, intending 12...♗xh6 13 ♕d2 g5 14 ♕xg5 ♖f6 15 ♗d3+ ♔h8 16 ♖xh6+ ♖xh6 17 ♕xh6+ ♔g8 18 ♕h7+ ♔f8 19 ♗g6 followed by ♕f7# or ♕h8#, is a little illustration of just how powerful White's kingside attack is) **9 ♘ge4!** (it would be unwise and inconsistent for White to let the e-file open up by 9 exf6?! exf6, since his king is still sitting on e1 and so ...♖e8+ could be annoying) and now:

a) The game Khuzman-Minasian, European Team Ch, Pula 1997 continued **9...♘f7 10 h5 f5 11 ♘g5** (threatening 12 ♘xh7 ♔xh7 13 hxg6++ ♔xg6 14 ♕h5#) **11...♘xg5 12 ♗xg5** and then:

a1) **12...h6** loses to 13 hxg6! hxg5 (D) and then:

14 ♖h8+!! ♗xh8 15 ♕h5 ♖f7 16 gxf7+ ♔g7 17 ♕xg5+, and now for example 17...♔xf7 18 ♕xf5+ ♔g8 19

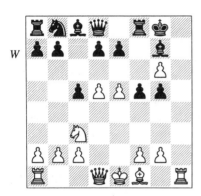

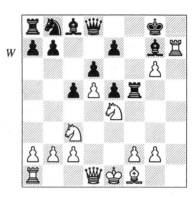

♕g6+ ♗g7 20 d6 e6 21 ♘e4 ♘c6 22 ♘f6+ ♔f8 23 f4, when Black is more tied up than Harry Houdini ever was, and White's myriad threats include 24 0-0-0 followed by ♖d3-g3, and 24 ♘h5 ♗h8 25 ♕h7, winning the only piece that is defending Black's exposed king.

a2) The game continued **12...♗xe5 13 hxg6 hxg6 14 d6! ♗f6** (14...♗xd6? 15 ♗c4+) **15 ♗xf6 ♖xf6 16 ♗c4+ e6** (16...♔g7 17 ♕d2 f4 18 ♘e4 ♖f5 19 g4! ♖f8 20 ♕c3+ is also crushing for White) **17 ♕d2 ♕f8**, and then GM Alexander Khuzman won quickly, elegantly and forcefully, as shown by the solution to position 2.2 in the Star Test at the end of this chapter.

b) J.Horvath-Feher, Elekes Memorial, Budapest 1997 went **9...fxe5 10 h5 d6** (10...♘f5 11 hxg6 hxg6 12 ♕g4 ♕e8 13 ♕h3, threatening 14 ♕h7+ ♔f7 15 ♘g5+ ♔f6 16 ♘ce4#, also gives White a crushing attack) **11 ♗xh6 ♗xh6 12 hxg6 ♗g7 13 ♖xh7 ♖f5** *(D)*.

14 ♕g4 1-0, since Black is a pawn down and in a terrible position, unable

to do much against White's primary threat of 15 ♕h4 or 15 ♕h3 followed by 16 ♖h8+ ♗xh8 17 ♕h7+ ♔f8 18 ♕xh8#.

That game was short even by comparison with most 'miniatures', and yet it provides us with a highly suitable example to put under the spotlight for discussing the four elements of **S.P.O.T.** a bit more.

Self: I imagine you would rather be White than Black in the game we have just seen, so let us pretend to be GM Joszef Horvath for a few minutes. I can tell you that he is a very well-prepared, sound, positional player. From his 14-move win, some people might have formed the impression that he is a wild attacking player. Attacking: yes; wild: no. The point is that his attack was soundly-based and fully justified by features of the **position**. In particular, the **opponent**, IM Gyula Feher, castled too early, first allowing White to gain precious **time** by attacking the black king's knight twice (6 e5 and 7 ♘g5), and when it retreated to h6, it was an extremely logical strategy for Horvath to aim to prise open the h-file in order simultaneously to get at Feher's king and 'dim knight on the rim'.

Joszef Horvath is a quiet, mild-mannered man, so his direct, energetic, attacking approach probably came as a major shock to his opponent, but it was the most efficient and powerful way for him to play. I recommend that we do the same whenever we spot similar opportunities, and plenty of them will arise in the main game, which is coming back into view right now.

4	...	♗g7
5	♘c3	0-0
6	e4	d6
7	h3	

White has more space for manoeuvring than his opponent has, and so the little move h2-h3 carries the prophylactic idea of stopping ...♗g4, with ...♗xf3 possibly to follow, thereby keeping Black somewhat cramped as he cannot exchange pieces. It is also possible that White may later want to play ♗e3 without being harassed by ...♘g4. Furthermore, White's monarch now has a loophole at h2 in case of future problems on the back rank after castling kingside.

| 7 | ... | e6 |
| 8 | ♗d3 | ♘a6 |

Let us consider two related positions here. First, imagine that the a6-knight has already gone to c7, but to keep the number of moves correct, we will suppose that Black has not castled

yet. In fact, that is precisely the situation which arose after eight moves of Azmaiparashvili-Ehlvest, European Team Ch, Pula 1997. Azmaiparashvili continued **9 ♗g5 h6** (9...0-0 transposes to the Psakhis-Chatalbashev game) **10 ♗e3** (it might seem that White lost a tempo in not playing ♗e3 on the previous move, but after 10...0-0 he would actually gain time with 11 ♕d2, attacking Black's h-pawn which was enticed forward to h6 by the move ♗g5) **10...exd5 11 exd5** (this is a more straightforward capture than 11 cxd5, since neither player gets a pawn majority in any area of the board, but White is content to retain his spatial advantage) **11...b5 12 ♕d2!** (this is a frustrating move for Black to face, since White calmly ignores the attempt to stir things up on the queenside, and plays a sensible, strong, developing move that effectively stops 12...0-0 due to 13 ♗xh6) **12...bxc4** (12...b4 13 ♘e2 is tremendous for White because he can follow up with ♘g3, after which most of his pieces will be amassed near, and pointing towards the kingside, but meanwhile the queenside is sealed without any real prospects of counterplay for Black there) **13 ♗xc4 g5** (after 13...h5 14 0-0 0-0, the pin 15 ♗g5, planning ♕f4 and a timely ♘e4, is highly uncomfortable for Black) **14 h4! g4 15 ♘g1** (a case of 'reculer pour mieux sauter' as the French would say, because the knight retreats in order to make a better jump forward to e2 and then g3 where a comfortable place awaits it, especially since Black is in no position to play ...f5 and ...f4 to dislodge any white piece from the g3-square) **15...♘d7** (Black finds a purposeful retreat too) **16 ♘ge2 ♘e5 17 b3 ♖b8 18 ♘g3 ♗f6** (Black could have tried 18...♘xc4 19 bxc4 ♖b4, intending 20 ♘h5? ♗e5, after which he has generated counter-play by attacking White's weak, backward c-pawn, but 'Azmai' may have planned 20 0-0! and then 20...♖xc4 21 ♕e2!! ♖xc3 22 ♗g5+ to win Ehlvest's queen, or 20...♕xh4 21 ♘ce4!! ♗xa1 22 ♘xd6+ ♔d7 23 ♖xa1 ♔xd6 24 ♗xc5+ ♔xc5 25 ♘e4+ and then 25...♔b6 26 ♕xb4+ ♘b5 {26...♔a6 27 ♘c5#} 27 ♕xb5+ with a totally crushing position; or 25...♔xc4 26 ♖c1+ ♔b5 27 ♖c5+ ♔a4 28 ♕c2+ ♔a3 29 ♖a5+ ♖a4 30 ♖xa4#) **19 ♖c1!** (White virtually removes any chance of an 'accident' on the a1-h8 diagonal, and prepares to give support at c4 if necessary) **19...♗xh4 20 ♘ce4!** (the knight trundles round into a powerful central position from where it threatens to land stunning blows like 21 ♘xd6+ ♕xd6 22 ♖xh4) **20...♗xg3?** *(D)* (Black must have overlooked White's star response, but as GM Mark Hebden often says, 'The position was beginning to creak anyway', although 20...♗e7 was relatively best).

21 ♗g5!! 1-0, in view of 21...hxg5 22 ♖xh8+ or 21...♕d7 22 ♘f6+, winning Black's queen in both cases. Apart from his 20th move, GM Jaan

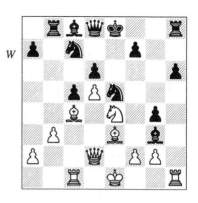

Ehlvest made no glaring errors, a fact which makes White's performance all the more impressive, and also suggests that Black's set-up is perhaps too cramped to offer full equality, especially against a top-class player.

Well, I said that we would consider a second position related to the one arising after Black's eighth move in the main game. However, instead of 8...♘a6, let us take a look at **8...exd5** *(D):*

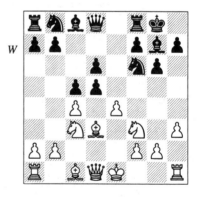

a) **9 cxd5** b5 10 ♘xb5 (10 ♗xb5? ♘xe4! 11 ♘xe4 ♕a5+ 12 ♘c3 ♗xc3+

13 bxc3 ♕xb5 stops 14 0-0 and is excellent for Black) 10...♖e8 11 0-0 ♘xe4 12 ♕a4! ♗d7 13 ♖e1 ♕b6 14 ♖xe4 ♖xe4 15 ♕xe4 ♗xb5 16 a4! ♗d7 (16...♗xd3? loses to 17 ♕e8+ ♗f8 18 ♗h6 ♘d7 19 ♕xa8) 17 a5 was very good for White in Avrukh-Rotshtein, Tel-Aviv 1997, because Black had problems developing his queenside pieces in addition to having a sensitive back rank.

b) The game Danielsen-C.Hansen, Esbjerg 1997 continued **9 exd5** (keeping the pawn structure more balanced) **9...♖e8+ 10 ♗e3 ♗h6 11 0-0 ♗xe3 12 fxe3 ♘bd7** (after 12...♖xe3? 13 ♕d2, 13...♕e7 14 ♘d1! costs Black material, as does 13...♕e8 14 ♖f2 ♘h5 15 ♗e4 ♖xe4 16 ♘xe4 ♕xe4 17 ♖e1 ♕f5 18 ♖e8+ ♔g7 19 ♘g5, Löffler-Haag, Badenweil 1985) **13 ♕d2 ♕e7 14 e4 ♔g7 15 ♖f2 ♘g8?!** (*BCO2* suggests 15...♖f8 followed by ...♘e8, presumably as a way to protect the sensitive f7- and d6-points in Black's camp, but after 16 ♖af1 White still looks to be very much in possession of the initiative) **16 ♖af1 ♖f8 17 ♘b5!** (as well as hitting the d6-pawn, Black's most obvious weak point in the Benoni, White plans to answer 17...a6 by 18 ♕c3+ and then 18...f6? 19 ♘c7 ♖b8 20 ♘e6+ or 18...♘gf6 19 ♘xd6 {alternatively, 19 ♘c7 ♖b8 20 ♘g5 threatens ♘ce6+} 19...♕xd6 20 e5 with a massive attack at no material cost, on account of the fork against d6 and f6) **17...♘h6 18 ♕f4 ♘e5 19 ♘xe5 dxe5** (19...♕xe5 loses a pawn to 20 ♘xd6)

20 ♕g3 (threatening 21 d6, when after 21...♕e6 a very forcing and stronger line for White than 22 ♘c7 ♕xd6 23 ♘xa8 ♗e6 is 22 ♖f6! ♕xf6 23 ♖xf6 ♔xf6 24 ♘c7 ♖b8 25 ♘d5+ and now 25...♔g7 26 ♕xe5+ f6 27 ♘xf6 { or 27 ♕e7+ ♖f7 28 ♕d8 ♖f8 29 ♕c7+} 27...♖xf6 28 d7 ♗xd7 29 ♕xb8 with a decisive material advantage; or 25...♔e6 26 ♕e3 ♘g8 27 ♕xc5 carries many threats, including ♕xa7 followed by c5 and ♗c4) **20...f6 21 d6 ♕d8 22 ♘c7 ♖b8** *(D)*.

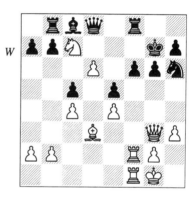

23 ♖xf6!! (I imagine the impact of this stunning star move must have been such that GM Curt Hansen could have mistaken it for 'an asteroid hitting planet Earth', although those words were actually used on 1 May 1997 by Professor Anthony King of the University of Essex to emphasize the magnitude of Tony Blair's landslide victory in becoming Britain's new Prime Minister) **23...♖xf6 24 ♖xf6 ♗xh3** (24...♕xf6 25 ♘e8+ and 24...♔xf6 25 ♕h4+ g5 26 ♕xh6+

♔f7 27 ♕xh7+ ♔f6 28 ♗e2 ♕f8 29 ♘d5+ ♔e6 30 ♗g4+ ♔xd6 31 ♕c7# are also hopeless for Black) **25 ♖e6! 1-0**, in view of 25...♗xe6 26 ♘xe6+ followed by 27 ♘xd8 or 25...♗g4 26 ♕xe5+ ♔f7 (26...♔g8 27 ♖e8+) 27 ♖e7+ ♔f8 28 ♕g7#.

OK, it's time now to see White's ninth move in the main game.

    9   ♗g5!   ♘c7

After 9...h6 10 ♗e3, White will subsequently gain a tempo by attacking the h6-pawn with ♕d2.

    10 ♕d2   exd5
    11 cxd5   b5
    12 0-0   b4

12...c4 13 ♗c2 b4 14 ♘e2 is similar to the actual game continuation except that Black's queenside pawns are looser, and the d4-square is an outpost which could serve as a springboard for one of White's knights to reach the further outpost at c6.

    13 ♘e2   ♕d7
    14 ♘g3

A storm is gathering not far from Black's king.

    14 ...   h5?!

This move weakens the pawn-cover around Black's king, but perhaps lines like 14...♖e8 15 ♕f4! made Chatalbashev want to have the h7-square as a possible retreat for his f6-knight.

    15 ♗h6   ♕e7

The disadvantages of Black's queen being on e7 soon become very apparent, but the f6-knight needed extra protection in view of the threat 16 ♗xg7 ♔xg7 17 ♘f5+! gxf5 18 ♕g5+.

    16 ♗xg7   ♔xg7
    17 ♕g5!

Threatening 18 ♘xh5+ ♘xh5 19 ♕xe7.

    17 ...   ♖e8 *(D)*

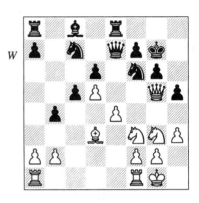

    18 e5!

Opening up a diagonal for White's bishop towards Black's kingside.

    18 ...   dxe5
    19 ♘h4!

Threatening 20 ♘hf5+.

    19 ...   ♔g8
    20 d6!

This deflects Black's queen onto a square from where it cannot help to protect its king laterally along the seventh rank.

    20 ...   ♕xd6
    21 ♗xg6!

Yet another sacrifice crowns a sequence of very powerful moves by Psakhis.

    21 ...   fxg6
    22 ♕xg6+   ♔f8

If 22...♔h8, then 23 ♘xh5 threatens ♘xf6 or ♕g7#.

23	♘gf5	♗xf5
24	♘xf5	♕d7
25	♕xf6+	♕f7
26	♕h8+	♕g8
27	♕h6+	♔f7 (D)

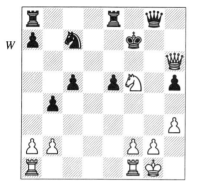

White's clever manoeuvres with his queen have forced the opponent's king and queen into a situation where they can potentially be forked by a knight on h6. This allows Psakhis to reap even more rewards than would be obtained by the other fork, 28 ♘d6+.

28   ♕c6!   1-0

Black threw in the towel, since he could not parry the simultaneous threats of ♕xc7+ and ♘h6+.

Santa's star advice

Are you a fan of attacking play yet, after the many emphatic examples we have had? Is that approach working in your own games? If not, then Santa says **'You can't be— —tackling the right way'**. Then he adds 'I'll give you two identical gifts in place of one'.

'What one?', one might ask. L, of course. Santa's special time is Noël, so we need to have no L in the bold statement. We give up the L in 'tackling', and Santa gives us a double dose of **at** for attack. Our bold statement now reads **'You can't beat attacking the right way'**!

There is an ancient Chinese proverb which (when translated into English) basically says that the hardest part of a problem is often encountered right at the start. The following beautiful puzzle with *White to play and win* was shown to me by a friend eight years ago, and I do feel that the most difficult move to find is the first one. A clue is that if I gave you a clue it would be a give-away!

Good luck mate!

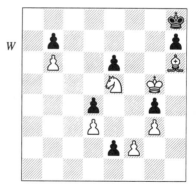

The solution appears after the notes to White's sixth move in the next game, which was perhaps my best one *en route* to winning the 1st Eksakt

Masters ten-player all-play-all tournament with a score of 7/9 at the Cafe de

Roskam in the Dutch town of Tilburg last year.

Game 3
N. McDonald – P. Motwani
Tilburg 1996
Ruy Lopez

1 e4   e5
2 ♘f3   ♘c6
3 ♗b5

The Ruy Lopez (or Spanish Opening) is named after a Spanish priest who analysed the opening in 1561. That is a star year in Spain's history because it was also then that King Philip II declared Madrid to be the national capital city.

3 ...   ♘f6

Four rounds earlier, I had won a good game with a kind of modern Arkhangelsk, 3...a6 4 ♗a4 ♘f6 5 0-0 b5 6 ♗b3 ♗c5, a variation that is especially favoured by GM Alexei Shirov (see page 142 of *H.O.T. Chess*, for example). However, I decided to switch systems against GM Neil McDonald, partly as an attempt to surprise him, and partly because I regard the Berlin Defence (3...♘f6) as a very sound, solid way to tackle a really dangerous opponent who has a fierce attacking style.

4 0-0

If 4 d3, then 4...♘e7!? (planning ...♘g6, ...c6 and perhaps ...d5, but also setting the trap 5 ♘xe5?? c6 6 ♗c4 ♕a5+ 7 ♘c3 ♕xe5) is an interesting

idea that I mentioned on page 170 of *C.O.O.L. Chess*. One month after I wrote that, but two months before the book was actually published, GM Tony Miles showed that he had independently come up with the same ...♘e7 conception, for he used it with success in Vysochin-Miles, Cappelle la Grande 1997. As the famous American statesman, Benjamin Franklin, said, 'An ounce of experience is worth a ton of theory'. Nevertheless, one should enter a battle suitably armed and prepared, which is one of the reasons why I always try in every game to give details that are appropriate to the depth of complexity of the opening variation being discussed.

4 ...   ♘xe4
5 d4

5 ♖e1 ♘d6 6 ♘xe5 ♗e7 7 ♘c3 ♘xe5 8 ♖xe5 ♘b5? (8...0-0 is sensible) 9 ♘d5! 0-0 10 ♘xe7+ ♔h8 11 ♕h5! (threatening 12 ♕xh7+! ♔xh7 13 ♖h5#) 11...g6 12 ♕h6 d6 *(D)*.

13 ♖h5! 1-0 (in view of 13...gxh5 14 ♕f6#) happened in a game Moultrie-Condie which I recall from the 1970s.

5 ...   ♘d6

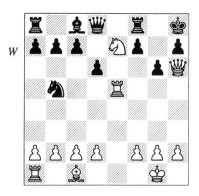

W

This is a key move in Black's defence, since it attacks the 'Spanish bishop' on b5, something which would not be true if the extra moves ...a6 and ♗a4 had been played earlier.

If I had never before seen the position after White's fifth move and was asked to come up with an instant suggestion for Black, then 5...♗e7 (to block the e-file and safeguard the monarch on e8) would probably come to mind. Indeed, the continuation 6 ♕e2 (6 dxe5 0-0 7 ♕d5 ♘c5 8 ♗e3 ♘e6, intending ...f6 or ...f5, is another possibility) 6...♘d6 7 ♗xc6 bxc6 8 dxe5 ♘b7 was quite popular among masters in the 1980s, but it has been out of the limelight since then, so it could be a good surprise weapon if someone decided to reactivate it...

The situation after 8...♘b7 has always struck me as a funny-looking position. However, it is also quite solid, and Black may follow up with ...0-0 and ...♘c5-e6, then react near the centre with ...f6/...f5 or ...d5.

6 ♗xc6

An enterprising alternative is **6 dxe5!? ♘xb5 7 a4** as in Rozentalis-Motwani at Hastings on New Year's Day 1997. That game continued **7...d6 8 axb5 ♘xe5 9 ♖e1 ♗e7** (9...♗e6? is great for Black in the line 10 ♘xe5?! dxe5 11 ♕xd8+ ♔xd8! {11...♖xd8 12 ♖xe5?? allows 12...♖d1+, but 12 ♖xa7 is better} 12 ♖xe5 ♗d6 13 ♖g5? h6! 14 ♖xg7 ♗e5, which traps White's nomadic rook, but unfortunately 10 ♘d4! is strong since it threatens the simple yet deadly advance f4-f5) **10 ♘xe5 dxe5 11 ♕xd8+ ♔xd8** (I rejected 11...♗xd8?! because of 12 ♖xe5+ ♗e6 13 ♖c5!, intending ♗f4 to pressurize the c7-pawn, and GM Eduardas Rozentalis agreed during the post-mortem analysis that 11...♔xd8 is best) **12 ♖xe5 ♗e6 13 ♘c3 ♔c8!** (planning ...b6 followed by ...♔b7 and ...c6 or ...a6, but also making ...♗f6 a more interesting option now that ♗g5 would no longer be a viable response) **14 ♘e4 h6** (a worthwhile prophylactic move which rules out ideas of ♗g5 or ♘g5 by White and currently leaves his e5-rook a bit short of safe squares to shift to if necessary) **15 ♗e3 b6 16 c4 ♖d8** (16...♔b7 is also possible, intending 17 c5 c6 18 bxc6+ ♔xc6 19 cxb6 axb6 20 ♖c1+ ♔b7 21 ♖b5 ♖a6) **17 c5 bxc5 18 ♗xc5** (Eduardas later admitted that he had underestimated Black's next move, but 18 ♘xc5 ♖d5! 19 ♖xd5 ♗xd5 also leaves White without much trace of his earlier temporary initiative, and his queenside pawns are at least as vulnerable as

Black's are, since they can be attacked by ...♗c4 and/or ...♖b8) **18...♗d6! 19 ♖h5 ♗f4! ½-½** *(D)*.

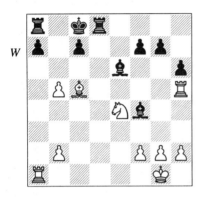

Obviously 20 ♗xa7?? loses after 20...♖xa7 21 ♖xa7 ♖d1#, and Eduardas did not like 20 g3 in view of 20...g6 21 ♖h4 ♗e5, when Black's bishops are looking great. However, I offered a draw for three reasons:

1) Mainly because I felt that 20 ♗e3 is quite satisfactory for White, an assessment with which my opponent concurred.

2) I was already well behind on the clock.

3) I wanted to stabilize my situation in the Premier tournament, especially since (after a previous run of 48 games without defeat) I had just lost three consecutive games to Grandmasters Stuart Conquest, Mark Hebden and Dr John Nunn. I didn't ever remember having four zeros on the trot, and I did not want that kind of novelty. Castling queenside (0-0-0) was bad enough!

Nevertheless, under different circumstances I might well have played on, for these three reasons:

1) One learns more by playing more.

2) Black's position is not worse after 19...♗f4, so there is little to fear in continuing the game.

3) As Denmark's famous GM Bent Larsen once said, 'If Black equalizes, then he is already better'. The second part of this statement might seem like a contradiction of the first part, but I believe Larsen meant that since it is commonly felt that White possesses some advantage in the normal starting position of a game of chess, then he must have lost something if Black later equalizes. At that stage, Black should have a psychological edge, whereas White might feel that the game is gradually slipping away from his grasp.

Personally, I currently feel no less comfortable playing Black than White, and that is because:

1) Opponents who assume that White has an initial advantage (just because he makes the first move) are already under some pressure to prove that superiority, and it is frustrating for them if in practice they are unable to demonstrate an edge for White.

2) With every move as Black, I enjoy trying to find the perfect reaction to the move which White must have just played.

Right now though, just before we return to see my sixth move as Black in the main game, it is time to reveal the answer to the lovely study that was given before Game 3.

Solution to puzzle (posed before Game 3)

In this amazing 1923 study by Leonid Kubbel, White wins with **1 ♘f3!!** (1 ♔f6? fails to 1...e1♕ 2 ♗g7+ ♔g8 3 ♘xg4 h5!, but note that 3...h6? 4 ♔g6! is a neat win ending in twins: ♘f6# or ♘xh6#) **1...gxf3 2 ♔f6 e1♕** (2...♔g8 3 ♗d2 is also hopeless for Black) **3 ♔f7** (threatening ♗g7#) **3...♕e5** *(D)*.

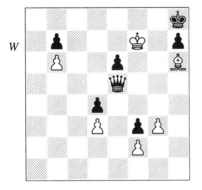

After **4 g4!** Black has no satisfactory move, since checks on f5 or h5 have just been ruled out. Note that the first star move, giving away a knight, was played so that after Black's reply, White would be able to advance g3-g4 later!

6	...	dxc6
7	dxe5	♘f5
8	♕xd8+	

The first time that I can recall having this position in a competitive game was on the morning of Saturday 6 February 1982 in Glasgow, the city where I was born 19 years 7 months 3 weeks and 2 days earlier. I was White against International Master Shaun Taulbut, and I played 8 ♕e2, thinking that 9 ♖d1 was going to be really strong. However, Shaun taught me a trick with 8...♘d4! 9 ♘xd4 ♕xd4 10 ♖d1 ♗g4 (this is the key tactic, since 11 f3 is illegal, but 10...♕g4 is also very playable for Black). Motwani-Taulbut continued 11 ♖xd4 ♗xe2 12 ♗e3 ♗h5 13 ♘d2 ♗g6! (threatening both ...♗xc2 and ...♗c5) 14 ♖c4 0-0-0 with a pleasant position for Black, although the game resulted in a draw 17 moves later.

8	...	♔xd8 *(D)*

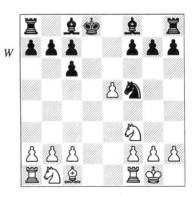

Now and then it's nice to play a move where one does not have to think too hard because no other moves are possible! I have considerable experience of sitting in Black's shoes looking at the same position given in the diagram, and, even against grandmaster opposition, I have only ever lost one game from it (against GM Michael Adams at the 1989 NatWest British Speed Chess Championships), but my results include a draw in 1988 against GM Vishy Anand (see page 41 of *H.O.T. Chess* for the complete game).

Because of the doubled pawns on c6 and c7, Black's queenside pawn majority is not as important as White's useful extra central pawn. However, the e-pawn is on its own in enemy territory and can turn out to be a weakness. Indeed, sometimes Black's king later advances to e6 to threaten the e5-pawn, a fact which confirms that it can actually be quite useful *not* to have castled if queens are absent in the middlegame, because then one's king is likely to be in much less danger. Furthermore, Black has a strong pair of bishops that have plenty of scope. In short, I think that after 8...♚xd8 the future looks safe and sound yet not at all dull.

9 ♘c3

9 c4 is an attempt to seize space before continuing with piece development, but it gives Black a target to attack, and the d3- and d4-squares become potential outposts. The game Kindermann-Z.Almasi, Horgen 1995 continued 9...♝e6 10 b3 a5 11 ♘c3 ♝b4 12 ♘e4 a4 with a very pleasant position for Black.

9 ...   ♚e8

This is a reasonable waiting move that says to White 'I want to see what you're doing next', but experience has taught me that the return to e8 also has constructive points. For instance, if Black later plays ...♝e6 and White is able to respond by moving a knight (usually) to d4, f4 or g5 to make the capture ♘xe6, then after the reply ...fxe6 it is often good to follow up with ...♚f7, protecting the kingside pawns and newly-born e-pawn.

10 h3   a5

This gains some space on the queenside, where Black has his pawn majority.

11 g4?!

This is consistent with White's last move, but there is a tactical drawback which is quite hard to foresee now because it only shows itself clearly several moves later. The notes at move 14 will reveal that I was following a star game by English IM Jonathan Parker which he played *en route* to winning the 1994 Scottish Championship in Edinburgh, where he then resided. I was fortunate to have been the official commentator at that event, and so I was very familiar with some of Jonathan's excellent ideas.

11 ...   ♘e7

Of course the knight was virtually forced now to retreat from f5 to e7, but even when that is not the case, Black often plays the manoeuvre ...♘f5-e7-g6 to pressurize the e5-pawn and allow the light-squared bishop to 'see' beyond e6. It is worth comparing this situation to another case of '*reculer pour mieux sauter*' which cropped up in the notes to White's 15th move of Azmaiparashvili-Ehlvest embedded within Game 2.

12 ♔g2   h5

'h for hunting!' is an attacking motto of my good friend Gorik Cools, one of Belgium's most creative players.

13 ♔g3   ♘g6
14 ♘e4

Without knowing it at the time, GM Neil McDonald produces a novelty at move 14. Other moves:

a) **14 ♗g5 f6!** 15 exf6 ♗d6+ 16 ♔g2 hxg4 17 hxg4 gxf6 18 ♗xf6 ♘f4+ 19 ♔g1 (19 ♔g3 ♖h3#) 19...♗xg4! 20 ♗xh8 ♗xf3 (threatening ...♘h3#) 21 ♖fe1+ ♔f7 can lead to 22 ♗d4 ♖g8+ 23 ♔f1 ♗g2+ 24 ♔g1 ♘h3#, 22 ♗e5 ♗xe5 23 ♖xe5 ♖h8 24 ♖f5+ ♔g6 25 ♖xf4 ♖h1# or 22 ♖e3 ♖g8+ 23 ♔f1 ♖xh8 24 ♖xf3 (24 ♔e1 only prolongs White's agony) 24...♖h1# *(D)*.

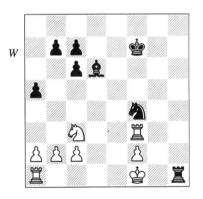

All these lines show Black's pieces exploding on White with great force.

b) The game Rowson-Parker, Scottish Ch 1994, had gone **14 ♗d2 hxg4 15 hxg4 f5! 16 gxf5** (16 exf6 ♗d6+ and 16 g5 f4+! and then 17 ♗xf4 ♖h3+ or 17 ♔g2 ♗h3+ are terrible for White) **16...♗xf5 17 ♖h1** (much more tenacious than 17 ♖ac1 ♖h3+ 18 ♔g2 ♗g4 19 ♘g5 ♘h4+ 20 ♔g1 ♘f3+ 21 ♔g2 ♘xg5! 22 ♗xg5 ♖h5, threatening ...♖xg5 or ...♗h3+) **17...♖xh1 18 ♖xh1 ♗xc2**, and Black managed to convert his extra pawn into a win 32 moves later.

14 ...   ♗e7

I like Black's position, but I made a tactical draw-offer after playing the text-move because, if accepted, then my chances of winning the tournament looked very promising. Neil knew this, and he bravely played on, even though that decision was perhaps not the most objective one.

15 ♗g5   ♗e6

Black continues to develop sensibly, and sometimes ...♗d5 could be annoying for the white knights.

16 ♖fe1   ♖d8

I had to remind myself that the move 16...0-0-0 is illegal (in view of having already moved my king earlier on), but I was happy to seize the open d-file in another way that still means all the members of Black's army are now actively performing useful functions.

17 ♗xe7   ♔xe7
18 ♘c5 *(D)*
18 ...   ♖d5!
19 ♘xe6

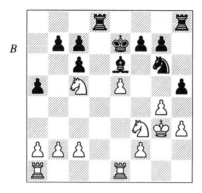

If 19 ♘xb7?, then 19...♖b5 20 ♘d4 ♖xb7 21 ♘xc6+ ♔d7 22 ♘xa5 ♖xb2 wins very comfortably for Black. At first I thought 19...h4+ 20 ♔h2 ♖b8 21 c4 ♖d3 would be even easier, as both of White's knights are *en prise*, but 22 ♘xa5 threatens the fork ♘xc6+. In fact, Black does have a fantastic position after 22...♖xb2 in spite of still being one pawn down, because White's army is so loose and uncoordinated. However, there is an important moral here: if you see a foolproof way to win, then it is generally better to select that route rather than a flashy way which may contain a flaw somewhere down the line. Simple chess is very often the best chess.

19 ...   fxe6

Under slightly different circumstances I might have played ...♔xe6, but allowing ♘g5+ followed by f4 seemed to give White dangerous counterplay unnecessarily. Besides, the capture ...fxe6 lets a black rook enjoy using the f-file soon.

20 ♖ad1   h4+!

This makes the h3-pawn more fixed than the stars in the sky (which do not appreciably change their constellation patterns over periods of many lifetimes, but if we could come back in, say, 50,000 years, then the famous Plough pattern in the Ursa Major constellation would be unrecognizable because two of its stars are moving in a direction opposite to that of the other members).

21 ♔g2   ♖f8
22 ♖xd5

22 c4 ♘f4+ leads to:

a) 23 ♔f1 ♖xd1 24 ♖xd1 ♘xh3, intending 25 ♘xh4 ♖xf2+.

b) 23 ♔h2 ♖d3! (23...♖xd1 24 ♖xd1 ♘xh3 is possible too, because although it is true that after 25 ♘xh4 Black's knight is attacked and White also threatens the fork ♘g6+, there is the resource 25...♘xf2) 24 ♖xd3 (24 ♘g5 c5 {White has almost run out of moves that do not lose material immediately; therefore the calm principle *do not hurry* is particularly appropriate for Black here} 25 b3 b6 26 ♖f1 ♖fd8 27 ♖xd3 ♖xd3 leaves Black in complete control and carrying the threats of ...♖d2 or ...a4 to break up White's queenside pawns) 24...♘xd3 25 ♖e3 ♘xb2 gives Black's knight a tasty bite that shatters White's structure on the queenside.

22 ...   cxd5
23 ♖e3   ♖f4

The rook lands on an outpost in enemy territory and exerts great pressure. The rook's influence is felt not only along the f-file; it can also swing laterally across White's fourth rank.

24 ♔f1 c5

'c for charge!' announces the pawn as it surges forward, seizing more space for Black.

25 ♖b3 *(D)*

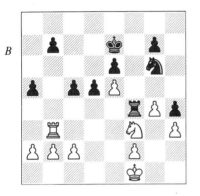

25 ... b5!

Neil McDonald later admitted that, when playing 25 ♖b3 under the increasing pressure, he simply missed that 26 ♖xb5? would leave his knight *en prise*, but of course ...b5 could not have been prevented anyway.

26	♘e1	b4
27	♖e3	a4
28	b3	axb3
29	axb3	c4
30	bxc4	

After 30 ♔e2? d4 31 ♖f3 ♖e4+ 32 ♔d1 ♘xe5 33 bxc4, the rest of the life of White's trapped rook could easily be measured in micro-seconds, but that is even more true for his knight since Black's next two moves would be 33...♖xe1+! followed by ...♘xf3+.

30	...	dxc4
31	♔e2	♔d7

The most precious piece in the entire army has been carefully observing all the events from moves 18 (just after he last moved) to 30, and since the rest of his cohorts are currently very well positioned, he now prepares to join them near the front.

32	♘g2	♖d4
33	♖f3	

White's rook desperately seeks counterplay, having discovered that after 33 c3 b3! 34 cxd4 b2 it cannot prevent the b-pawn from achieving the ultimate stardom of becoming a new queen.

33 ... ♔c6

The king wants a new queen too, so he consistently marches forward to help, and signals to his knight to ignore the e5-pawn for the moment.

34	♖f7	b3
35	cxb3	cxb3
36	♖f3	♖b4
37	♖c3+	♔b5
38	♖c1	b2
39	♖b1	♔a4
40	♘e3	♔b3 *(D)*

Black reached move 40 with less time left on the clock than the opponent, but even all the time in the Universe could not save White now.

41 ♘d1

White plans to meet 41...♔a2 by 42 ♘c3+, but Black's monarch can also invade the seventh rank at c2. However, 41 ♔d2 ♖d4+ 42 ♔e2 ♔a2 is hopeless for White too.

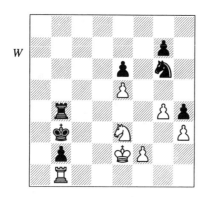

41	...	♔c2
42	♖xb2+	♖xb2
43	♘xb2	♔xb2
44	♔e3	♔c3

From well before move 40, I had calculated the consequences of the sequence which the game is following. It was not my only way to win, but since it is so clear and forcing I decided to go for it. Many years ago, GM Michael Stean wrote an excellent book called *Simple Chess*, and the title made as deep an impression on me as the contents of the book itself did. Therefore I will reiterate what I said at the end of the notes to White's 19th move: *simple chess is very often the best chess.*

45 f4

45 ♔e4 ♔c4 46 f3 ♔c5 47 f4 ♘xf4 48 ♔xf4 ♔d4 is exactly the same as the actual game except that the move number has increased by two.

45 ... ♘xf4! *(D)*

The '!' is given to the move not for flashiness, but for its clarity. Black reduces the number of units on the board, and simplifies the position into a pure ♔+♙ endgame that is definitely winning and not difficult to calculate.

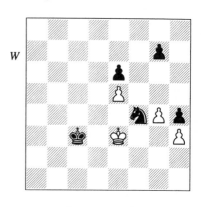

46 ♔xf4 ♔d4
47 ♔f3 *(D)*

The alternatives were:

a) 47 g5 g6 48 ♔g4 ♔xe5 49 ♔xh4 ♔f5 (after 49...♔f4??, White suddenly has half a point more than he should have!) 50 ♔g3 ♔xg5, after which Black will use his e-pawn to divert White's king away from the h-pawn, allowing Black's monarch to eliminate it and then promote the g-pawn.

b) 47 ♔g5 ♔xe5 branches into:

b1) 48 ♔xh4 ♔f4 49 g5 e5 50 ♔h5 e4 51 h4 e3 52 g6 (52 ♔g6 is also much too slow to help White) 52...♔e5 (the e-pawn must not be overly eager to advance, since 52...e2?? produces a stalemate situation) 53 ♔g4 e2, and 54...e1♕ will feel exceptionally good.

b2) 48 ♔g6 ♔f4 49 ♔xg7 ♔g5!, when ♔h6 followed by g5 has been prevented, but Black's star e-pawn cannot be halted, and it will zoom forward towards e1.

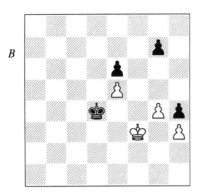

47	...	g5
48	♔f2	♚xe5
49	♔e3	♚d5
50	♔d3	e5
51	♔e3	e4
52	♔e2	♚d4
53	♔d2	e3+
54	♔e1	♚e4

0-1

White resigned in view of 55 ♔e2 ♚f4 followed by the deadly invasion ...♚g3.

Not many tactics arose in the later stages of the game we have just seen, so it's about time we had another puzzle to keep ourselves really alert.

Spot the danger

White is three pawns down, but it is his turn to play. GM David Bronstein, World Championship Challenger in 1951, once said 'The most powerful

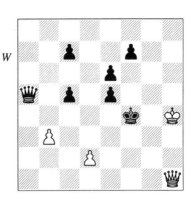

weapon in chess is the next move', so can you find a forcing star continuation which shows that Black's monarch is in terrible danger here? In fact, White can force checkmate or win the opponent's queen. The solution appears after the forthcoming game.

Sweden's GM Ulf Andersson, one of the world's most solid players, has Black. His Latvian opponent, GM Edwin Kengis, many times Champion of that country, spots that (in spite of the deceptively quiet first half-dozen opening moves) White can already put the enemy king in James Bond-type danger starting at move 007. Amazing stuff!

Why not try covering up some of the moves with a card to see how many of them you can predict? Of course, at certain stages one could suggest good moves that differ from those of the actual game but have equal (or brighter!?) star quality. As always, I have endeavoured to expand on such key options at all of the most critical stages of the battle.

Game 4
E. Kengis – U. Andersson
European Team Ch, Pula 1997
English Opening

1	♘f3	♞f6
2	g3	c5

The Polish Defence, 2...b5 (a nice choice with Poland's city of Gdansk celebrating its 1000th birthday in 1997), also seizes space in a highly logical way since Black is then ready to play ...♝b7, countering White's intended fianchetto on the h1-a8 diagonal. Dunnington-Arkell, Walsall 1997 continued 3 ♗g2 ♝b7 4 0-0 e6 5 d3 d5 (this move may obstruct the vision of the b7-bishop, but it does have the advantages of gaining space and hindering the advance e2-e4 by White) 6 ♘bd2 ♞bd7 (D).

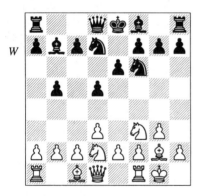

7 e4 (a tactical trick on the next move makes this advance possible, but it leads to several exchanges of material and a really level position in which

Black hasn't much to worry about) 7...dxe4 8 ♘g5 (if Black had the moves ...b6 and ...♝e7 instead of ...b5 and ...♞bd7, then 8 dxe4 would now be strong for White since 8...♞xe4? would lose to 9 ♘e5!, and indeed Black resigned there in the game Kochiev-I.Ivanov, USSR 1976, principally on account of the line 9...♞d6 10 ♗xb7 ♘xb7 11 ♕f3, although more analysis can be found on page 47 of *C.O.O.L. Chess*) 8...♜b8 (a very sensible move from GM Keith Arkell, protecting his loose bishop on b7 and thereby taking the sting out of sequences from White such as ♘dxe4 followed by ♘xf6+, which would otherwise threaten ♗xb7 afterwards) 9 ♘dxe4 h6 10 ♘xf6+ ♞xf6 11 ♘e4 (11 ♗xb7 ♜xb7 12 ♕f3 is answered completely satisfactorily by 12...♕d5 or 12...♜b8, with the latter move intending 13 ♕c6+ ♕d7 14 ♕xd7+ ♘xd7 or 13 ♘e4 ♝e7) 11...♞xe4 12 dxe4 ♕xd1 13 ♜xd1 ♝c5 14 ♗f4 ♜c8! (if 14...♝b6?!, then 15 a4 threatens axb5 or a5, and so Black wisely avoids that line) 15 a4 ½-½. After 15...b4 Black has no serious problems, but a draw is on the cards so the players decided not to prolong the game.

3	♗g2	g6
4	c4	♝g7

We have symmetry again, as existed in the starting position and after move one, but White is about to change that. However, it does not matter whether or not Black can maintain the symmetry. What is important is that he should react accurately and energetically to each of his opponent's moves in such a way that his position retains flexibility and does not become passive.

5 d4   cxd4

Perhaps it is simply a matter of taste, but I would prefer **5...0-0** for several reasons:

1) It maintains the tension in the centre instead of releasing it, whereas after 5...cxd4 6 ♘xd4 the d4-knight is well-centralized and the fianchettoed bishop on g2 enjoys having lots of scope while exerting pressure towards b7.

2) It is a developing move.

Some variations:

a) **6 dxc5 ♕a5+** is very comfortable for Black. Indeed, he even has the lead in terms of piece development, and plans ...♕xc5 to pressurize the white c-pawn.

b) After **6 0-0**, a reply that transposes to what is known as the Yugoslav Variation of the King's Indian Defence is 6...d6, which has a sound reputation. For instance, 7 dxc5 dxc5 8 ♕xd8 ♖xd8 poses Black's king none of the problems that 5...d6 (instead of 5...0-0) 6 dxc5 dxc5? (6...♕a5+ is better) 7 ♕xd8+ ♔xd8 8 ♘e5 would bring.

c) **6 d5** b5!? 7 cxb5 a6 is really a Benko Gambit Accepted in which White has already committed himself to a particular piece-configuration on the kingside, and not one of the more aggressive options that would have been available to him via the 'normal' move-order of the Benko Gambit (1 d4 ♘f6 2 c4 c5 3 d5 b5).

6   ♘xd4 *(D)*

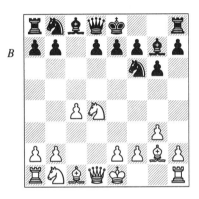

6 ...   d5?!

This meets with a powerful reply. Alternatively, 6...0-0 or 6...♘c6 are both straightforward developing moves that have often been played by other people, but in either case I prefer White after 7 ♘c3. The simple reason is that the c4-pawn gives him a spatial advantage and contributes to his grip on the d5-square, which makes it very difficult for Black to achieve the freeing advance ...d7-d5. Unfortunately, the attempt 6...♕c7? to harass the c-pawn leads in reality to Black's queen becoming exposed, and a highly logical yet forceful exploitation of that fact is 7 ♘b5!, intending 7...♛xc4? 8 ♘1a3 ♛c5 9 ♗e3 ♛e5 10 ♗d4, after which the imminent fork ♘c7+ will net big rewards.

7 ♘c2!

This offer, inviting Black to capture on c4, reminds me of a similar gambit played in Suba-Sax, Baile Herculane Zonal 1982. After **1 c4 e5 2 g3 c6 3 d4 exd4 4 ♛xd4 d5** (4...♘f6 5 ♗g2 ♘a6!?, intending ...♗c5, transposes to the game Züger-Christiansen, Bern 1996, and the entire annotated game can be found on page 143 of *C.O.O.L. Chess*) **5 ♗g2 ♘f6 6 ♘f3**, Black played **6...dxc4** instead of the 'usual' move 6...♗e7. Then, rather than re-capture on c4, GM Mihai Suba continued in gambit fashion with **7 ♛xd8+!**, aiming to profit from his better development and the situation of his opponent's king after **7...♚xd8** *(D)*.

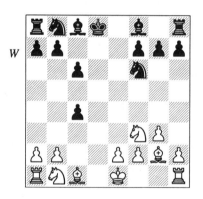

The strongest follow-up is **8 ♘bd2**, intending:

a) **8...b5 9 a4!** (9 ♘e5 ♚e8 is also possible, but White should not then

continue 10 ♘xc6? due to 10...♗b7) 9...♗b7 10 ♘e5 ♚e8 11 axb5 with an overwhelming position for White.

b) **8...♗e6 9 ♘g5 ♗b4 10 0-0** ♗xd2 11 ♘xe6+ fxe6 12 ♗xd2 ♘bd7 13 ♖fc1 ♘b6 14 a4 a5 15 e4 followed in some order by f3, ♗f1 and ♗e3. Black's shaky units on c4 and b6 will then really start to feel the heat from White's powerful bishop pair in an open position.

c) **8...♗b4 9 0-0 c3 10 bxc3 ♗xc3 11 ♖b1** followed by ♘c4 with a colossal initiative carrying further threats like ♖b3, ♖d1+, ♘d6, ♘g5 or ♗a3, to name just five which show Black is barely alive!

A lead in development is often sufficient to bring victory and seal the lid on a game. I cannot stress enough the importance in general of not falling far behind in development, and that is even more crucial in an open position as opposed to a closed one. With that momentous thought in mind right now, it is in a sense quite fitting that in Hong Kong today, Tuesday 1 July 1997, the Chinese President, Jiang Ze Min, said 'July 1st will go down in the annals of history as a day that merits eternal memory' (his Mandarin translated into English). You may or may not share his sentiments, but in our chess context, **L.I.D.** certainly represents something that should never be forgotten.

I should also emphasize that the **quality** of one's development is important too. For instance, after the moves 1 e4 ♘f6 2 e5 ♘d5 3 d4 ♘c6? (3...d6 is much better, to challenge White's spatial advantage) in Alekhine's Defence, Black has two knights in play compared with his opponent's two central pawns, yet White already has a near-decisive advantage because his pawns are about to chase Black's knights to their doom. The continuation might be: 4 c4 ♘b6 (4...♘db4 is the only way to avoid losing a knight, but of course after 5 a3 ♘a6 6 b4 ♘ab8 7 f4, threatening d5, I would not say 'Black is OK'!) 5 d5! ♘xe5 (5...♘b4 6 c5! ♘6xd5 7 a3 also nets White a piece) 6 c5 ♘bc4 *(D)*.

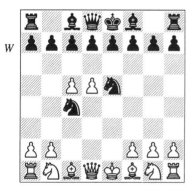

Now 7 f4 e6 may give Black some swindling chances, since ...♗xc5 is in the air and 8 fxe5 runs into 8...♕h4+. Does the early queen move 7 ♕d4! merit attention? Well, although in general we should be careful in the opening phase about bringing the queen out into the open, the answer to the question here is definitely 'Yes!'. In this case, White's queen is powerfully centralized on d4 as it cannot be harassed there. Furthermore, Black will lose a piece due to the trio of terrible threats 8 ♗xc4, 8 b3 and 8 f4.

In conclusion, we can say that **L.I.Q.D.** (**l**ead **i**n **q**uality **d**evelopment) is vital. I find that quite appropriate, because water is a vital **liquid** in our lives. One of the nicest and truest statements I have ever heard about water was spoken by Ross Mackie, a former pupil at Aberdeen Grammar School. He said 'Water does for the body what purpose does for the mind'.

Let's return now to the main Kengis-Andersson game for more L.I.Q.D. in action.

7 ... dxc4

I have no doubt that GM Ulf Andersson realized how dangerous it is to capture on c4 here, but in fact he had little choice in the matter because White was threatening 8 cxd5, and 7...♗e6 would not help due to 8 ♘c3 dxc4? 9 ♕xd8+ ♔xd8 10 ♗xb7.

8 ♕xd8+ ♔xd8

I played 8...♔xd8 too against GM Neil McDonald in Game 3, but the position was very different and my king had few worries there.

9 0-0!

'There's an exclamation mark, but why?' one might ask. The reason is because Kengis's move is a perfect example of the saying 'the threat is stronger than its execution' being put into practice. White could have immediately played moves like ♘ba3 or ♘d2 or ♘e3 in order to win the c4-pawn,

but instead he prepares to activate a
heavier piece with ♖d1+ soon and remains flexible with his other troops,
thereby keeping his opponent guessing and worried about where the white
lightning will strike next.

9   ...   ♘c6
10   ♖d1+   ♔c7
11   ♘ba3

A knight on the rim is not always
dim! Here White plans the simple,
strong capture ♘xc4, and ♘b5+ could
be annoying for Black too.

11   ...   ♗g4 (D)

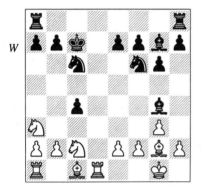

W

12   ♗xc6!

Many players would not consider
parting with their fianchettoed star
bishop, especially one with such a fine
view. However, Kengis is thinking
clearly, and he realizes that either
12...bxc6 13 f3 ♗e6 14 ♘d4 (threatening 15 ♘xe6+ fxe6 16 ♘xc4) leaves
Black with a vastly inferior pawn
structure, or 12...♔xc6 brings his exposed monarch further out into the
open, as happens in the actual game.

12   ...   ♔xc6
13   ♘xc4   ♖ad8

It is not necessary to try to calculate
an absolutely forced win for White after 13...♗xe2, since one can quickly
spot that Black's king is in grave danger:

a) 14 ♘d4+ ♔c5 15 ♘xe2 ♔xc4
16 ♗e3 ♔b5 17 a4+ ♔a6 (17...♔c6?
18 ♖ac1#) 18 b4 b6 19 a5 and then for
example:

a1) 19...♘d5 (hoping to play
...♗xa1) 20 b5+! ♔b7 21 a6+ ♔b8 22
♖ac1 ♘xe3 23 ♖d7 and soon ♖b7#.

a2) 19...b5 20 ♘d4 ♘d5 21 ♘b3!!
threatening ♖xd5 or ♘c5#.

b) 14 ♘e5+ ♔c7 15 ♖e1, after
which White has firmly retained the
initiative and can even win back a
pawn (on f7) if he wants to do so.

As I indicated a few lines ago, it
was clear long before the end of variations 'a1' and 'a2' that Black was in
big trouble. Nevertheless, it keeps us
super-sharp sometimes to analyse a bit
deeper than the position necessarily
demands, and the more we practice
the better and faster we become.
Hopefully the calculations we do in
S.T.A.R. Chess and beyond will help to
extend our current horizons in terms
of how deeply we can analyse.

Still, it is worth reiterating here a
point I made in C.O.O.L. Chess that
many really good moves which we
would like to find fall into one of the
following six simple categories: checks;
captures; moves that threaten something; moves that try to expose the

enemy king; moves seeking *outposts*; moves seeking *sensitive squares*. That set of six guidelines was encapsulated by the following key part of a poem:

Think 'Check, Capture, Threaten, Expose'
Easy to remember, I suppose
Don't forget the other pair
Namely 'Outpost and Sensitive square'.

When one looks at chess in nice, simple ways like that, it very often becomes much easier, as if all haziness had departed, allowing the shining stars to be seen clearly.

14 ♘e5+   ♚b6

After 14...♚c7 15 ♗f4, Black's monarch is facing a trio of deadly 'discovered checks' since White's e5-knight threatens to capture on g4, g6 or f7, each time unveiling a cheeky check from the f4-bishop.

15 ♗e3+   ♚a6
16 ♘b4+   ♚b5 (D)

16...♚a5? loses quickly to the fork 17 ♘bc6+!, although White can first exchange rooks on d8 if he wants to.

17 ♘ed3

The number of different legal positions that are possible on a chessboard has been estimated at 2×10^{43}, which is a '2' followed by 43 zeros (a rather large number!). For me, one of the main pleasures in studying chess is the enjoyment I get from encountering as many of the game's beautiful possibilities as God will let me experience

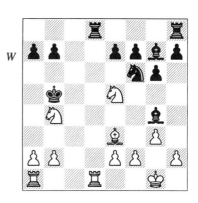

in one lifetime. Today I got a big bonus in an unexpected way. Instead of 17 ♘ed3, I thought that Kengis had played **17 ♘bd3**, and some lovely variations arose when I began to analyse from that starting point. Many of the following lines illustrate the wonderful harmony in White's army, the terrible peril Black's king is in, and lots of star moves that are mostly checks, captures, threatening or exposing moves (four of the six important categories mentioned in the notes at move 13). For example:

a) **17...♗xe2 18 a4+ ♚a6 19 ♘c5+ ♚a5 20 b4+** (even easier than 20 ♘xb7+) and then:

a1) **20...♚xb4 21 ♖db1+ ♚c3** (or 21...♚a5 22 ♘xb7+ ♚a6 23 ♘c5+ ♚a5 24 ♘c6#) **22 ♖b3+ ♚c2 23 ♖a2+ ♚d1 24 ♖b1#.**

a2) **20...♚b6 21 ♘e6+ ♚a6 22 ♘c7#.**

b) **17...b6** is also hopeless, due to **18 a4+ ♚a6 19 ♘xf7 ♗xe2 20 ♘xd8 ♖xd8** (20...♗xd1 21 ♘b4+ ♚a5 22 ♘dc6#) **21 ♘b4+** followed by ♖xd8.

That line is simple and strong for White, so strictly speaking there is no need to consider **19 a5** instead. However, the amazing possibilities arising from 19 a5 made me associate it with a new motto: 'a for attack!'. Here is a small sample:

b1) **19...b5** 20 ♘c5#.

b2) **19...bxa5** 20 ♘c6 attacks d8 and a5 in particular. It would be nice if White could play 20 ♖xa5+ ♔xa5 21 ♖a1+ and announce 'Checkmate!', but unfortunately Black has 21...♔b5. Instead, after the simple, sound and strong move 20 ♘c6, one pretty finish is 20...♔b5 21 ♖xa5+! ♔xc6 22 ♘b4+ ♔c7 23 ♖xa7+ ♔c8 24 ♖c1+ ♔b8 25 ♘a6#, while another is 20...♖c8 21 ♖xa5+ ♔b7 22 ♖xa7+! ♔xc6 23 ♘b4+ ♔b5 24 ♖b7+ ♔c4 25 ♖c1+ ♔b3 26 ♘d3+ ♔a2 27 ♖a7+ ♔b3 28 ♖a3#.

b3) **19...♔b7** 20 ♘xf7 ♗xe2 21 ♘xd8+ ♖xd8 22 ♘c5+ ♔c8 23 ♖xd8+ ♔xd8 24 axb6 axb6 25 ♘e6+ followed by ♘xg7 gives White an enormous material advantage.

b4) **19...♗xe2 20 axb6+ ♔b5 21 ♖dc1!** splits into the following main branches:

b41) **21...axb6 22 ♖c3** (threatening ♖b3#) 22...♖xd3 23 ♘xd3 and White should win.

b42) **21...♗xd3 22 ♖c5+!** ♔b4 (22...♔xb6 23 ♖c3+ and then 23...♔b5 24 ♖b3# or 23...♔b7 24 ♖xa7+ ♔b8 25 ♘c6+ ♔c8 26 ♘xe7++ ♔b8 27 ♖b3+ ♗b5 28 ♖xb5#) 23 ♘c6+ ♔b3 24 ♖a3+ ♔xb2 25 ♗c1+ ♔b1 26 ♖b3+ ♔a2 27 ♖b2+ ♔a1 28 ♖a5# *(D)*.

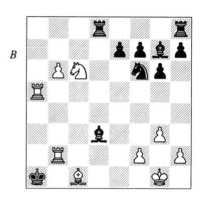

B

After that breathtaking king-hunt it's time to see how Black's monarch is faring in the actual game.

| 17 | ... | ♗xe2 |
| 18 | a4+ | ♔a5 *(D)* |

The alternative was 18...♔c4 19 ♖dc1+ ♔b3 20 ♖c3#.

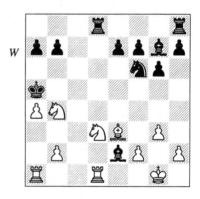

W

| 19 | ♘c6+! | bxc6 |

Now Black's king again suffers.

20	b4+	♔a6
21	♘c5+	♔b6
22	♖xd8	♖xd8
23	♘e6+	♔b7
24	♘xd8+	

White has a decisive material advantage. If this were a swimming race, one could say 'A few more yards of the pool and he'll be home and dry'!

24 ... &c7

25 &e1

Simple, strong chess. Kengis is following the general principle that it is good to exchange pieces when one is ahead on material, since as the number of units remaining on the board decreases, the opponent's chances of creating any threats dwindle, and one's own material advantage almost wins the game by itself, provided complacency does not set in and cause a blunder.

25 ... &xd8

After 25...&c4 26 &c1 &d5, White has the important resource 27 &xc6! to extricate his knight, as 27...&xc6 loses quickly to 28 b5. Another line requiring even less calculation is 25...&f3 26 &xf7.

26 &xe2 &d5

26...a6 27 &d4 is also bleak for Black.

27 &xa7 &xb4

28 &c5 &a6

28...&d5 is no better, due to 29 a5 e6 30 a6 &c8 31 &a2 and now:

a) 31...&b8 32 a7+ &a8 33 &a6 followed by &xc6.

b) 31...&c7 32 &d6 &a8 33 &c2 (33 &b2?? &xb2 – it's easy to miss 'long-range' moves) 33...&d7 34 &d2 &c8 35 &e7 intending &d8+ wraps up the game.

Actually, it is not strictly necessary to give analysis at this stage as White is winning very comfortably. However, I think it is always a good policy to look for a clean, straightforward and efficient route to victory. The given variations fulfil those criteria.

29 &xe7+ &d7

30 &g5 &f8

Even here it is possible to find an attractive finish, but, much more importantly, the following line is also entirely sound: 30...f6 31 &e3 c5 32 &b2 &c6 33 a5 (threatening &b6+) 33...&b4 *(D)*.

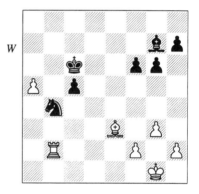

34 &xc5!! and then:

a) **34...&xc5** 35 &xb4 &xb4 36 a6, when the a-pawn cannot be prevented from becoming a new queen on move 38.

b) **34...&d3** (don't worry: that fork was anticipated, and we will not make a meal out of winning with White!) 35 &b6+ (35 &a2 &xc5 36 a6 is also sufficient) 35...&xc5 36 &b7 &f8 37 &f7 &d6 38 a6, and once again the little a-pawn causes havoc in Black's camp. Small things can be most troublesome,

and another example is the poliomye-
litis virus, which has a diameter of only
0.000028 millimetres.

31	♖d2+	♔e6
32	♖d8	♗d6
33	♗f4	1-0

There was no point in Black prolonging his own agony with 33...♗xf4
34 gxf4 c5 35 a5 c4 36 ♖d4 c3 37 ♖c4.

The winners of Game 4 (which we
have just seen) and Game 5 (soon to be
in view) are from Latvia and Aberdeen respectively. Let's take a short
pause in our star chess journey to hear
about an amazing journey from the
Latvian capital of Riga to the Scottish
town of Banchory near Aberdeen.
Howard King (the son of Aberdeen
chess congress organiser Jim King)
married a lovely Latvian girl on 10
May 1997. 39 guests were due to
make the giant 3,000 kilometre step
from Riga to Banchory for the wedding, so travel costs could have become almost astronomical. However,
Howard paid for a coach for his bride's
family and friends. It turns out that the
father of the bride (not actor Steve
Martin!) is a star organist who has
played for such eminent people as the
President of Latvia, the King and Queen
of Sweden, and President Mitterand.
So the Church of Scotland in Banchory got treated to a superb organ re-
cital, and the funds raised added a few
welcome notes! I'll give one more big
one: many sincere congratulations to
the new Mr and Mrs King.

From four to five

Since we are currently somewhere between Game 4 and Game 5, here is a
nice little brainteaser involving the
words 'four' and 'five'. It was thought
up by the famous writer Lewis Carroll,
who featured at the start of Chapter 1.

Change FOUR to FIVE in seven
steps, creating a new word each time
by changing only one letter:

FOUR

_ _ _ _

_ _ _ _

_ _ _ _

_ _ _ _

_ _ _ _

_ _ _ _

F I V E

A solution appears well before
game five.

Solution to puzzle (posed before Game 4)

In this lovely 1929 study by Leonid
Kubbel, White wins with 1 ♕g2 (threatening ♕g4#) 1...f5 (1...♔f5 2 ♕g4+
♔f6 3 ♕g5# or 1...e4 2 ♕g3+ ♔f5 3
♕g5#) 2 ♕e2 (threatening ♕e3#) 2...e4
3 ♕e1!! (planning ♕g3#, and intending 3...♔f3 4 ♕f1#) 3...♔e5 4 d4+ cxd4
5 ♕xa5+. The neat queen moves all
carried deadly threats rather than immediate checks, until the moment when
the white lady eliminated her 'opposite number'. In a game Black could

now resign, since 5...♔d6 6 b4 d3 7 ♕c5+ ♔d7 8 ♔g5 (planning ♔f6, and intending 8...d2 9 ♕d4+ followed by ♕xd2) puts White's victory beyond doubt.

From the starting position of the puzzle, a tempting continuation is 1 ♕f1+ ♔e4 2 ♕c4+ ♔f3 3 ♕d3+ ♔f4 4 ♕e3+ ♔f5 5 ♔h5, planning ♕f3#. However, Black can defend by means of 5...♕b4! (but not 5...♕a8? 6 ♕g5+ ♔e4 7 ♕g2+, a sneaky skewer), and then he even threatens to win by 6...♕g4+ 7 ♔h6 ♕g6#.

Would you like a draw?!

I could imagine myself asking that reasonable question if I were Black in the forthcoming position *(D)*, but you don't have to reply 'I do', even though today (2 July 1997) is my second wedding anniversary! That's another way of saying it's White to play and win, and the beautiful solution appears after Game 5.

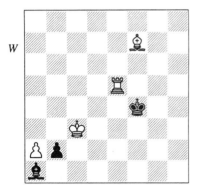

Solution for 'four to five'

One solution is:
FOUR-FOUL-FOOL-FOOD-FORD-FORE-FIRE-FIVE (but congratulations if you found other ones).

L.I.F.E. of a young star

It seems a very short time ago that I first encountered a small boy named Jonathan on a train somewhere in Bonnie Scotland. I could have asked him 'Where are you from?', 'Why are you here?', 'Where are you going from here?'.

International Master Jonathan Rowson ('J.R.') from Aberdeen is now 20 years old, and has developed into a real chess star at a meteoric rate. He frequently asks himself the three aforementioned 'motivation questions' when seeking direction in life and reminding himself always to try his very best at chess or Politics, Philosophy and Economics at Keble College, Oxford University, or whatever else he is doing at any given time.

There are so many opportunities to learn from other people, some older and some younger than ourselves. I, for one, find a lot of inspiration in Jonathan Rowson's love of life and desire to use his talents as well as he can. I know that a multitude of other people also feel excited and stimulated by Jonathan's achievements so far (such as his impressive 4-2 match victory over GM Keith Arkell in Edinburgh during December 1996), and are hoping for even greater things before he turns 21 on 18 April 1998.

J.R.'s favourite chess saying, *'Talk to your pieces'*, was mentioned near the start of this chapter, and I now find it to be extremely useful in my own games for identifying the piece whose location most needs to be improved. That is a simple yet highly rewarding way of planning ahead, and the more one concentrates on finding purposeful placings for the pieces, the greater will be the harmony and flexibility within one's army. When that happens, your main plan has a good chance of succeeding. Furthermore, if you were finding it difficult actually to formulate a concrete plan (or *Strategy*), then I believe that in practice the more 'user-friendly' ideas of **S.A.T.**:

a) seeking sensible squares for (all of) one's pieces while

b) aiming to attack and

c) staying alert to tactics

will generally keep you satisfied and your opponent sitting with a lot of problems to think about.

You might be thinking 'Not another mnemonic!', but remember this: they are intended to be fun, easy, helpful ways of thinking about key aspects of chess. If you don't like a particular mnemonic then don't use it. However, ideas that you enjoy (perhaps new ones created by yourself) should make your thought processes flow comfortably in a very natural way with the minimum of tension.

We can all learn new methods that improve our performance. Then we will flow with greater ease and power, gaining the confidence to expand into other ways of thinking and playing (with our repertoire, for example). That's **L.I.F.E.**!

OK, now it's time to see IM Jonathan Rowson in action *en route* to winning the 1997 Aberdeen Open. J.R.'s opponent in the following game is Alan J. Norris, a very fine player of both over-the-board and correspondence chess. Try to spot as many star moves as possible. I optimistically predict that you will get them *just right (j.r.)*!

Game 5
A. Norris – J. Rowson
Aberdeen 1997
English Opening

1	♘f3	♘f6
2	c4	g6
3	♘c3	♗g7
4	e4	

4 d4 would stop the very interesting reply that J.R. plays, but maybe Alan Norris wanted to deny Black the possibility of transposing to the Grünfeld

Defence by **4...d5**. However, perhaps more players on the white side will almost be inviting Black to opt for that opening path and continue **5 ♗g5** after seeing the following continuation of Piket-I.Sokolov in 'b' below:

a) **5...c5?!** hits at White's centre in typical Grünfeld fashion, but there is a hidden catch:

a1) **6 ♗xf6 ♗xf6 7 ♘xd5** (a timid reply, but 7 cxd5 is well answered by 7...♕b6!, pressurizing White's units on b2 and d4 simultaneously) 7...♗g7 8 e3 ♘c6 9 ♗e2 0-0 10 0-0 e6 11 ♘c3 cxd4 12 exd4 ♘xd4 13 ♘xd4 ♗xd4 brought success for Black in the game Cifuentes-I.Sokolov, Dutch Ch 1996 due to the power of his dark-squared bishop.

a2) **6 dxc5! ♕a5 7 cxd5** (7 ♕a4+?! ♕xa4 8 ♘xa4 ♘e4! 9 cxd5 ♗d7 10 c6 bxc6 gives Black fantastic activity for his pieces) 7...♘xd5 8 ♕xd5 ♗xc3+ 9 ♗d2 is a position known from the line 5 ♗f4 c5 6 dxc5 ♕a5 7 cxd5 ♘xd5 8 ♕xd5 ♗xc3+ 9 ♗d2. Then 9...♗xd2+ 10 ♕xd2! ♕xc5 11 ♖c1 ♕f5 12 ♘d4 ♕d7 13 ♕h6! has been known to be difficult for Black since the game Timman-J.Littlewood, England vs Holland match, London 1969, while 9...♗e6 is the best chance, though still considered better for White by modern theory. I suspect that the realization that this line was available to White was the reason Ivan Sokolov chose not to repeat 5...c5 in 1997.

b) Piket-I.Sokolov, Dutch Ch 1997 went **5...♘e4 6 cxd5** (6 ♘xd5?? loses

a piece to 6...♘xg5 7 ♘xg5 e6, a nightmare for White's knights, but I remember analysing 6 ♕c1!? in 1975 when I was 13 years old, and so it was interesting to see that idea cropping up in the game Z.Basagić-Tukmakov, Ljubljana 1997, where White obtained some initiative and a lead in development after 6...♘xg5 7 ♕xg5 dxc4 8 e4 0-0 9 0-0-0) **6...♘xg5 7 ♘xg5 c6** (after 7...e6, White can choose between 8 ♕d2 exd5 9 ♕e3+, which produces an interesting position after the forced reply 9...♔f8, or he can opt for 8 ♘f3 exd5 9 b4, with the 'queenside minority attack' strategy of later pushing b4-b5 if Black plays ...c6 to support his d-pawn) **8 dxc6 ♘xc6 9 d5** (after 9 e3, Black again has the recurring trick of pushing his e-pawn to create two threats, in this case from d8 towards g5 and from e5 to d4: 9...e5! fits the bill) **9...♘e5 10 e3 0-0 11 ♗e2 e6 12 ♘ge4!?** (possibly a novelty, and certainly an improvement on Ree-De Wit, Amsterdam 1984, where Black had excellent play after 12 ♘f3 exd5 13 ♕xd5 ♗e6! 14 ♕xd8 ♘xf3+ 15 ♗xf3 ♖fxd8 16 0-0 {16 ♗xb7? ♖ab8 gives Black's rooks much more power than White's very temporary extra pawns are worth} 16...♖d2 17 ♖ab1 ♖c8! due to the superb scope that his bishops and rooks obtained on open diagonals, ranks and files) **12...exd5 13 ♕xd5 ♗f5** (threatening 14...♕xd5 15 ♘xd5 ♗xe4) **14 ♖d1! ♕h4 15 0-0 ♖ad8 16 ♕xb7 ♖b8 17 ♕xa7! ♖xb2** (if 17...♗xe4, then 18 g3 deflects Black's queen away from 'covering' the e4-square, so that ♘xe4 will follow shortly) **18 ♘g3 ♘g4 19 ♗xg4 ♗xg4** *(D)*.

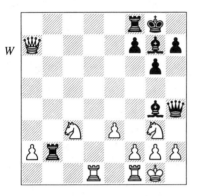

20 ♖d4!! (this dual-purpose star move prevents ...♗xc3 and threatens 21 h3) **20...h5** (after 20...♗xd4 21 ♕xd4, the threat of h2-h3 is renewed, and ♘d5 is on its way too, and then Black will have the further worries of ♕xb2 and ♘f6+ to contend with) **21 h3 ♗e5 22 ♘d1!** (the careless capture 22 hxg4?? would allow 22...♗xg3 23 fxg3 ♕xg3, which leaves White without any satisfactory way of stopping ...♕xg2#) **22...♖xf2** (desperation, in view of 22...♖c2 23 hxg4 and then 23...♗xg3 24 fxg3 ♕xg3 25 ♕b7 with ♕f3 or ♕e4 to follow or 23...hxg4 {hoping for ...♔g7, ...♖h8 and ...♕h2#, but it takes too long} 24 ♕a4!, threatening ♕xc2 and ♖xg4) **23 ♖xf2 ♕xg3 24 hxg4 hxg4 25 ♔f1 ♕h4** (White would welcome the move 25...♗xd4, since after 26 ♕xd4 his material advantage is decisive and Black has too

few pieces left even to begin generating any real threats) **26 ♖e4 ♗g3 27 ♖e8!** (planning 27...♖xe8 28 ♕xf7+ ♔h8 29 ♕xe8+ ♔g7 30 ♕f8+ ♔h7 31 ♖f7#, and otherwise White will exchange off Black's rook anyway, once again producing a simplified position with a decisive material advantage) **27...♕h1+ 28 ♔e2 ♗xf2 29 ♖xf8+ ♔xf8 30 ♕a8+ ♔g7 31 ♘xf2 ♕h5 32 ♘d3 ♕b5 33 ♕e4 ♕b1 34 ♕d4+ ♔g8 35 ♕c4 g3 36 ♔f3 ♕f1+ 37 ♔xg3 ♕e2 38 ♘e5 ♕xe3+ 39 ♘f3 g5 40 ♕c8+ 1-0.** Grandmaster Jeroen Piket reached the time-control at move 40 with less than a minute to spare, but then GM Ivan Sokolov resigned, a piece down and in view of 40...♔g7 41 ♕c7, threatening to swap the queens by ♕e5+.

One might ask 'Where exactly did Black go wrong?'. Well, it is quite possible that 7...c6 is no longer adequate, particularly because of White's key idea at move 12. In that case, the safer alternative 7...e6 should be preferred.

Let's return now to the main game, where J.R. is about to play his noteworthy fourth move.

4 ... e5!? *(D)*

Almost everyone plays 4...d6, and after 5 d4 0-0 we have a position which has featured in thousands if not millions of games in the King's Indian Defence (sometimes abbreviated to 'the K.I.D.'). However, J.R.'s choice has some special points that will soon become apparent.

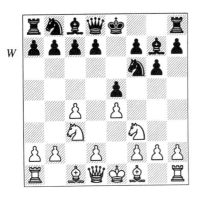

W

It's nice to see someone taking an independent path, and I find that particularly refreshing as I write today, 4 July 1997, since this is Independence Day. Also, at 6:03 p.m. GMT (Greenwich Mean Time), America's NASA (National Aeronautics and Space Administration) Pathfinder space probe was being just as adventurous by landing on the planet Mars after making a journey of 309 million miles that began seven months earlier atop a Delta rocket at Cape Canaveral!

5 d4

If 5 ♘xe5, then 5...♘xe4 6 ♘xe4 (after 6 ♘xf7?? ♕xc3, either 7 ♕f3 ♕e7+ or 7 ♘xd8 ♕xd1 leaves White with a fatal lack of pieces) 6...♗xe5 7 d4 ♗g7 8 ♗g5 f6 9 ♗h4 0-0 gives Black an excellent position. He threatens:

a) 10...g5 11 ♗g3 f5 12 ♘c3 f4, trapping the bishop on g3 and bringing back cool chess memories of 'f for forward!'.

b) 10...♖e8, causing White embarrassment on the e-file, and illustrating the theme 'pin and win'.

c) 10...d5, a relatively minor threat compared with 'a' and 'b', but nevertheless highlighting a positional worry for White that he could easily get saddled with an exposed, isolated d-pawn.

5	...	exd4
6	♘xd4	0-0
7	♗e2	♖e8
8	f3	c6

This is the key idea behind Black's fourth move. J.R. threatens ...d5 on his next turn, and after 9 ♗e3? he would be, in effect, a tempo ahead compared with the well-known line 1 d4 ♘f6 2 c4 g6 3 ♘c3 ♗g7 4 e4 d6 5 ♘f3 0-0 6 ♗e2 e5 7 ♗e3 exd4 8 ♘xd4 ♖e8 9 f3 c6, because his d-pawn is ready to make the leap ...d7-d5 in one move instead of first going to d6. Incidentally, when I was in Walsall on April Fools Day 1997, J.R. said to me at lunch 'You've just lost a tempo'. You can imagine how puzzled I looked, but he was right: without realizing it myself, I had actually dropped a small packet of *Tempo* tissues!

9 ♗g5

White tries to restrain Black's ...d5 idea, but J.R. has a very determined d-pawn!

9 ... ♕b6

9...h6 10 ♗h4 ♘a6 sets the trap 11 ♕d2? ♘xe4!, with 12 ♗xd8 ♘xd2 or 12 ♘xe4 ♕xh4+ to follow, but J.R.'s move has the immediate logical points that it attacks vulnerable units at b2 and d4 in White's camp.

10 ♕d2

10 ♘a4 ♕a5+ 11 ♗d2 ♕d8 is a funny line, since Black's pieces are exactly where they were after move 8, and yet they are now better placed to enforce ...d5 because of the changes in White's camp. Furthermore, 12...♘xe4 13 fxe4 ♗xd4 is threatened.

10 ... d5!

10...♘xe4 11 ♘xe4 ♕xd4 favours White, but we should find the real reason why that is so:

a) The obvious attempt to win material by **12 ♘d6** is tempting in some lines. For example:

a1) **12...♕xb2** 13 ♕xb2 ♗xb2 14 ♘xe8 ♗xa1 15 ♘c7 ♗e5 16 ♘xa8 b6 17 ♗d8 (planning ♗c7) 17...♘a6, when at the very least, White can sacrifice on b6 and still emerge an exchange up.

a2) **12...♖xe2+** 13 ♔xe2! (not 13 ♕xe2? ♕xd6) also puts White an exchange ahead, and his knight sits like a huge boulder on the outpost at d6 from where it stifles Black's development.

However, Black can challenge the enemy knight with:

a3) **12...♖e6!** 13 ♘xc8 ♕xd2+ 14 ♔xd2 ♘a6 15 ♘e7+ ♔f8, and White cannot avoid losing his material advantage because his stranded steed is doomed in view of threats like ...h6, ...f6 and ...♗f6.

b) Nevertheless, White is doing pretty well if he plays **12 ♕xd4 ♗xd4 13 0-0-0** (not 13 ♗f6? ♖xe4! 14 fxe4 ♗xf6). For instance:

b1) **13...♗g7** 14 c5, planning ♗c4 and ♘d6, with a powerful bind on the position.

b2) **13...c5** *(D)*.

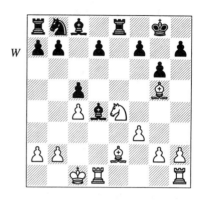

14 ♖xd4! cxd4 15 ♘f6+ ♔f8 and then:

b21) **16 ♗h6+ ♔e7 17 ♘d5+ ♔d6 18 ♔d2** (18 ♗d1!?) threatens ♗f4+ followed by ♘c7, and 18...♔c6 can be met by 19 f4 planning ♗f3.

b22) **16 ♘xe8 ♔xe8 17 c5** (17 ♖e1 d6, intending ...♗e6) threatens ♖e1 and then ♗c4+ followed by ♗h6+ and ♖e8#. Black can stop that, but he is still in a bad state because most of his army is not yet awake!

b3) **13...d5!** is almost forced (in view of Black's severe problems in variations 'b1' and 'b2'), but although Black is hanging on after 14 cxd5 cxd5 15 ♗b5 ♘c6, even 16 ♖xd4 dxe4 (16...♘xd4? loses a piece to 17 ♘f6+ ♔f8 18 ♗xe8) 17 ♗xc6 bxc6 18 ♖xe4 ♖xe4 19 fxe4, intending ♖d1, gives White the better chances since there is still a pair of rooks on the board, and he can aim to attack Black's isolated queenside pawns. The most tenacious defence is probably 19...♗e6 20 a3

(20 b3 a5 planning ...a4) and then 20...f5 or 20...♗b3. However, in the first case, 21 exf5 followed by ♖e1 carries some sting, and in the latter case 21 ♔d2 followed by ♔c3 or ♖c1 leaves Black facing an uphill struggle.

Of course, J.R. has avoided such passivity by reacting vigorously in the centre with ...d5 back at move ten, and we will now see the reply from Alan Norris.

11 exd5

If 11 cxd5, then 11...♘xd5 threatens ...♕xd4 or ...♗xd4 and is excellent for Black.

11 ... cxd5

By leaving his knight on f6, J.R. is inviting his opponent to go in for the line 12 ♗xf6 ♕xf6 13 ♘xd5 ♕xd4 14 ♕xd4 ♗xd4 15 ♘c7, as 15...♗d7 16 ♘xa8 ♖c8! (16...♘a6? 17 ♖d1) 17 ♖d1 ♘c6 followed by ...♖xa8 rounds up the over-ambitious white knight.

12 cxd5 ♘a6

12...♘xd5?? 13 ♘xd5 ♕xd4 14 ♕xd4 ♗xd4 15 ♘c7 costs Black a large amount of material.

13 0-0-0 ♘b4

14 ♗b5?!

This just encourages the e8-rook to shift to a better location. However, I can see why Alan Norris might not have liked 14 ♗xf6 ♗xf6 15 a3: Black could consider 15...a5!?, but the simple retreat 15...♘a6, threatening ...♘c5 followed by ...♗xd4 and ...♘b3+, also gives plenty of compensation for a deficit of one pawn since White's king is in a dangerous position and J.R.'s

very threatening dark-squared bishop is reminiscent of the Dragon bishop that was such a star in Chapter 1.

14 ... ♖d8

15 ♔b1

15 ♗c4 is well met by 15...♕c5.

15 ... ♘bxd5

16 ♗c4 *(D)*

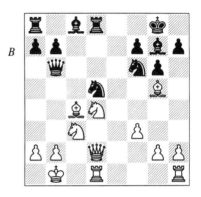

16 ... ♘b4!

The knight has been to b4 before! However, this time the open d-file means that the white knight on d4 is in an unpleasant pin, and little combinations like 17...♗f5+ 18 ♔a1 ♖xd4 19 ♕xd4 ♘c2+ are eager to star in the game.

17 ♘a4

This loses, but it is difficult to suggest any truly worthwhile improvement here.

17 ... ♕a5

18 a3 ♗f5+

19 ♔c1

After 19 ♔a1 either 19...♘c2+ or 19...♖xd4 20 ♕xb4 ♕xb4 21 axb4 ♖xc4 is also 'curtains' for White, and

Black has enough material to make real ones!

19 ...   Ⅱac8

20 ♕c3

Many deadly replies are possible in response to 20 b3, but one of the simplest and best options is 20...♘d3+.

20 ...   Ⅱxc4!

Alan Norris is having to face a man who is playing like Chuck Norris, a six-times World Karate Champion and film star.

21 ♕xc4   Ⅱc8

22 ♕xc8+   ♗xc8

                    0-1

White resigned in view of 23 ♗xf6 ♗xf6 24 ♘c3 ♘a2+ 25 ♘xa2 ♗xd4 for example. Black has the decisive advantage of ♕ + minor piece vs 2Ⅱ, and 26 Ⅱxd4 ♕c5+ nets Black even more juicy rewards.

The ease with which Black got a very nice position from the opening adds further weight to the points I made earlier in the book regarding my feeling that White does not necessarily possess an initial advantage which some people assume comes automatically because of having the first move. England's 23-year-old GM Matthew Sadler also seems particularly to enjoy finding the perfect reactions to each of White's moves. The young star from Chatham scored ten consecutive wins with Black out of a certain ten games at the 1996 Erevan Olympiad and 1997 European Team Championships in Pula, helping his country to a great historic first place in the latter event.

Afterwards, GM Nigel Short said 'I have been waiting for this moment for twenty years'. Incidentally, back in 1977, Chuck Norris (the film star mentioned after Black's 20th move in Game 5) played the lead role in the movie *Good Guys Wear Black*!

Solution to puzzle (posed before Game 5)

The key to this amazing study by I.Mazel is **1 Ⅱe4+!!**, which wins as follows:

a) 1...♔xe4 2 ♗g6+ ♔d5 (2...♔e3 3 ♗b1 ♔e2 4 a4 ♔d1 5 ♔b3 ♔c1 6 ♔a2 keeps the bishop on b1 firmly blocking Black's bishop and pawn, whereas White's a-pawn is hurtling forward like a meteor and its imminent promotion on a8 is unstoppable) 3 ♗b1 ♔c5 4 a4 ♔b6 5 ♔b4 ♔a6 6 a5 ♔a7 7 ♔b5 ♔b7 8 a6+ ♔a7 9 ♔a5 ♔a8 (the alternative 9...♔b8 10 ♔b6 ♔a8 11 ♗e4+ ♔b8 12 a7+ is also hopeless for Black) 10 ♔b6 ♔b8 11 a7+ ♔a8 12 ♗e4#.

b) 1...♔f3 2 ♗h5+! ♔xe4 3 ♗g6+ is identical to line 'a' except that the move number has increased by one.

c) 1...♔f5 2 ♗g6+ ♔xg6 3 ♔c2 ♔f5 4 Ⅱe1 leaves Black's king cut off from the left-hand side of the board, so the a-pawn can again advance virtually unimpeded. With 4...b1♕+ 5 ♔xb1 ♗c3, the bishop prepares to sacrifice itself later for the a-pawn, but afterwards White's simple task will be to checkmate with ♔+Ⅱ vs ♔.

We have almost reached another of my favourite points in our journey: the next Star Test. In all of the first seven positions it is *White to move (except 2.4, where it is Black to play and win)*, and he can achieve victory in each of those six cases, apart from the neat draw in 2.5. The answers appear on pages 229-232.

Each of the six different chess pieces (king, queen, rook, bishop, knight, pawn) gets a chance to star in the first move played (though not necessarily in the same order as the pieces are mentioned in brackets). Enjoy the puzzles, and more opportunities to spot the star pieces.

Star Test

2.1

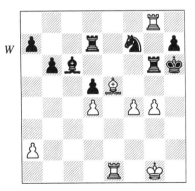

2.2

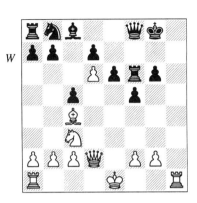

2.3

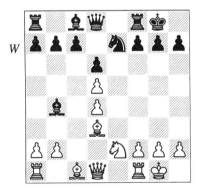

As well as discovering how White wins, can you also identify the ten previous opening moves that led to the given position?

2.4

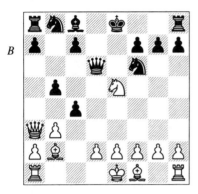

2.6

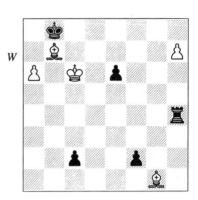

As well as discovering how Black wins, can you also identify the seven and a half previous opening moves that led to the given position?

2.5

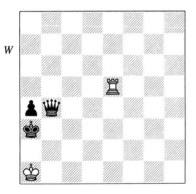

2.7

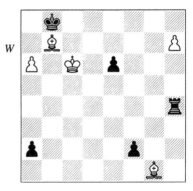

This elegant little study was composed in 1968 by Fernand Joseph, who lives in Sint-Agatha-Berchem near Brussels. Twenty-five years later he created the following lovely 'twin' studies with their elegant twists.

Star Challenge no. 2

Parts 'a' to 'c' inclusive of this star challenge are mine, and part 'd' is based on a tremendous study by Eddy van Espen, a Belgian friend (although Eddy's original example actually began half a move earlier).

In a certain game, the players both have to make 40 moves in two hours each. After two hours and six minutes of play, player X has consumed half an hour more on the clock than his opponent, Y. They each still have *more than six moves* to make to complete 40 moves, but both players have, on average, an exact *whole* number of minutes left on their clocks per move up to and including move 40 (although not the same whole number of minutes for the two players).

a) How much time does each player have left on his clock to reach and complete move 40?

b) How many moves does X still have to make, up to and including move 40? What about Y?

c) Which player has White, which one has Black, and whose turn is it to move?

d) Consider the following position *(D)*:

Imagine that the given position refers to the game described before and during parts 'a' to 'c' inclusive. One of the players, X or Y, can win before move 40 is reached, but which one and how?

That problem combined chess and time, but now it is time for T.I.M.E. in Chapter 3.

3 T.I.M.E. to Move

Time was the fourth element of the mnemonic S.P.O.T. in Chapter 2, but it is so important that we are going to watch it for a second time in this new phase of our star journey. I have suffered a lot through getting into time-trouble and damaging my chances of finding the best moves. Nevertheless, our inspirational star motto (*'There is no man living who isn't capable of doing more than he thinks he can do'*) has helped me to fight my way out of many a tight spot. For instance, in one game at the 1994 Moscow Olympiad, my scoresheet and a digital clock gave the frightening evidence that I had to make 9 moves in 6 seconds: an average of less than 0.67 seconds per move. I reached the time-control with a good position! Even a moment's thought is better than no effort, and in the recent film *Star Trek: First Contact*, the android Mr Data described a period of 0.68 seconds as being 'almost an eternity'. Still, the '0.75 second per move story', as I like to call it, is quite an achievement: in 1931, US master Sidney Bernstein turned up 1 hour 59½ minutes late for a match, but he overcame the obstacle of 40 moves in 30 seconds and drew his game! However, I do not wish to encourage such daring episodes. For a start, one is very likely, if arriving late for a game nowadays, to lose the battle by default after an hour, or even half an hour of time has elapsed on one's clock, with only its ticking to fill the silence of an empty chair.

The real moral of the story is this: manage your time properly so that each move can be given the attention it needs, but if you do get into time-trouble, don't give up or become flustered. Keep calm and fight hard. It can be really unnerving for an opponent to face someone who continues to play good, strong, sensible moves even with very little thinking-time left. In such cases, the opponent often makes the mistake of thinking more about clock times than finding objectively correct moves, and the tables may easily turn on him or her. Here is an amazing example that I witnessed earlier this year *(D)*.

We join B.Lalić-Arakhamia, Walsall 1997, with White about to make his 33rd move. GM Bogdan Lalić had at least 15 minutes left, whereas IM Ketevan Arakhamia-Grant had about 30 seconds in which to make the eight moves until the time-control at move 40. She had been hanging on extremely well in time-trouble for many moves, and Bogdan was getting visibly more and more rattled because Keti had so far survived all his attempts to land a knockout blow. Suddenly there was a chance with **33 ♕a3!**, attacking Black's pieces on b2 and d6 simultaneously and intending 33...♗xa3 34 ♗e5+ ♕f6 35 ♗xf6#, but Bogdan missed it! Instead the game went 33 ♕f2 ♗g7 34 ♕f4 ♘xe4 35 ♗xe4 ♖c4! 36 ♖e1 ♖a4 37

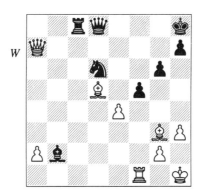

♗c6 ♖xf4 38 ♗xf4 ♗f8 39 ♗e5+ ♚g8 ½-½, as although Black no longer stands worse, her clock flag was teetering on the brink of falling, and Keti was relieved and happy just to get the game finished. Bogdan must have been disappointed about overlooking a clear win, but he accepted the outcome very sportingly.

Lalić is a very strong grandmaster, so the example we have just seen shows that there can be hope for the player in time-trouble, no matter who the opponent is. However, time is invaluable, so it is better to preserve enough of it for when it is really needed. I am trying to do that too! In the words of opera singer Dame Kiri Te Kanawa, 'Time I value above all things. It just gets more and more precious.'

It's now time to introduce **T.I.M.E.** (although if any possible inhabitants of other planets ever read *S.T.A.R. Chess*, they may wish to rearrange the four letters of T.I.M.E. to get I'M E.T.). To carry out the *manoeuvres* associated with a strategy successfully, one not only needs time on the clock, but also time in the sense of taking a realistic number of moves. In other words, the manoeuvres must be done with *efficiency*, where every move really counts. Both players should have a strategy in mind, but the one who possesses the *initiative* is in the 'driving seat', and that person has the better chance of powering through the opposition and achieving planned goals. How does one get the initiative in the first place? Well, it's all about playing with maximum energy, attacking flair, and striving with every move to spot *tactics* that allow one to seize the initiative. When that happens, one can start to dictate the course of the game, rather than always having just to react to what the opponent is doing.

IM Douglas Bryson (the Scottish Champion in 1996 and 1997) often quotes the well-worn maxim 'Chess is ninety-nine percent tactics'. People could debate endlessly about whether the 99% label is too high (or not high enough) to quantify the importance of tactics. However, it is crystal-clear that tactics are absolutely crucial in our Royal Game, and a seized tactical opportunity can end a battle just like a sudden bolt of lightning may topple a tree. That is one of the reasons why my books always provide hundreds of opportunities for sharpening our tactical vision.

Nevertheless, much more often than not, tactics flow logically from the position. If one stays alert and due attention is being paid to the other three T.I.M.E. elements (initiative, manoeuvres, efficiency), then the tactical element will not go out of control of its own accord. Still, it is vital to remember that tactics are practically omnipresent in chess, and no less in the endgame than during the earlier phases. So let's see a star study, composed by M.Dukić in 1981, to nudge our tactical powers up another couple of notches.

Time for promotion

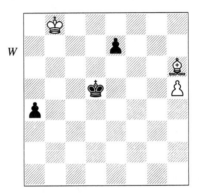

It is White to play and win. The solution appears after the following game from the 1995 Dundee Congress. Jonathan Rowson (J.R.) is a more powerful player now than he was two and a half years ago, but I still consider this game to be one of my best-ever efforts in chess so far. I did not get into time-trouble (miracles do happen!), and all aspects of T.I.M.E. are clearly present in the battle.

Game 6
P. Motwani – J. Rowson
Dundee 1995
Philidor's Defence

1	e4	d6		3	♘c3	e5
2	d4	♘f6		4	♘f3	

Jonathan Rowson and I do not consider 4 dxe5 dxe5 5 ♕xd8+ ♔xd8 6 ♗c4 to be troublesome for Black. After 6...♗e6 7 ♗xe6 fxe6, these points come to mind:

a) Black can follow up with ...♗d6, ...♘c6 and ...♔e7, after which his king is safe and ideally placed for getting quickly to the centre or either wing, especially as the endgame phase draws near.

b) The position is by no means a 'dead draw'. On the contrary, Black enjoys the use of a partly open f-file as a result of having doubled e-pawns, and those useful units on e5 and e6 control, in particular, the important central squares d4 and d5.

4 ...   ♘bd7

The same position can be reached via Philidor's Defence (1 e4 e5 2 ♘f3 d6), since 3 d4 ♘f6 4 ♘c3 ♘bd7 looks very sensible. However, I think that 4 dxe5! ♘xe4 5 ♕d5! ♘c5 6 ♗g5 favours White, but he is denied that possibility by J.R.'s chosen move-order.

Fans of the Philidor might also suggest the traditional move-order **1 e4 e5 2 ♘f3 d6 3 d4 ♘d7** for Black, but again White has something more potent than automatic routine development through 4 ♘c3. This time **4 ♗c4!** pinpoints the vulnerability of the f7-square adjacent to a nervous king *(D)*.

For example:

a) **4...♘gf6?** 5 dxe5 ♘xe5 (the alternative moves 5...♘xe4? 6 ♕d5 and 5...dxe5? 6 ♘g5 are even worse) 6 ♘xe5 dxe5 7 ♗xf7+! ♔xf7 8 ♕xd8

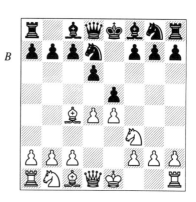

♗b4+ (hoping to play ...♖xd8 next) 9 ♕d2! ♗xd2+ 10 ♘xd2 puts White a sound pawn ahead.

b) **4...♗e7?** 5 dxe5 ♘xe5 (5...dxe5? is at least three times more terrible because of 6 ♕d5! ♘h6 7 ♗xh6) 6 ♘xe5 dxe5 7 ♕h5! nets White a unit on e5 or f7.

c) **4...exd4 5 ♘xd4** (5 ♕xd4 is also excellent as the centralized queen enhances White's development) **5...♗e7?** (better is 5...♘gf6) walks into a blast of gale-force seven at f7 due to **6 ♗xf7+!! ♔xf7 7 ♘e6** and splits into two twisters:

c1) **7...♔xe6** 8 ♕d5+ ♔f6 9 ♕f5#.

c2) **7...♕e8** 8 ♘xc7 ♕d8 9 ♕d5+ ♔f8 10 ♘e6+ ♔e8 11 ♘xg7+ ♔f8 12 ♘e6+ and then 12...♔e8 13 ♕h5# or 12...♔f7 13 ♕h5+! ♔xe6 14 ♕f5#.

5 ♗c4   ♗e7
6 0-0

This time 6 ♗xf7+? only carries White's wishful thinking, which gets blown away by 6...♔xf7 7 ♘g5+ ♔g8 8 ♘e6 ♕e8 9 ♘xc7 ♕g6! (seizing the initiative) 10 ♘xa8 ♕xg2 11 ♖f1 exd4

12 ♕xd4 ♘e5, threatening ...♘f3+ and ...♗h3.

| 6 | ... | 0-0 |
| 7 | a4 | |

This move not only gains some space, but also reacts against the idea of ...c6 and ...b5 even before Black has shown that card.

| 7 | ... | c6 |

Creating possibilities like ...♘xe4 because the response ♘xe4 can be answered by the fork ...d5, a tactical trick which White avoids with his next move.

| 8 | ♗a2 | b6 |

Black is currently more cramped than White, so he correctly continues edging forward in a slow, solid fashion, hoping that there may later be a time and place somewhere on the board where he can react more vigorously.

In Zso.Polgar-I.Eriksson, Erevan wom OL 1996, there was action on the opposite wing with 8...h6. That game went 9 h3 ♕c7?! (this move may look plausible, but 9...♖e8, intending ...♗f8 followed by ...exd4 and ...♘c5 to pressurize White's e-pawn, is a more purposeful, efficient and consistent way to play, especially since Black's previous move ruled out any possibility of 10 ♘g5 to attack f7) 10 ♘h4! (manoeuvring towards f5 or g6, and loaded with the tactical point 10...♘xe4? 11 ♘g6! and then 11...♘xc3 12 ♘xe7+ or 11...♘df6 12 ♘xf8, winning material for White) 10...♖e8 11 ♗e3 b6 (after 11...♘xe4 12 ♕h5 {12 ♗xf7+ first is also strong} 12...d5, White can almost get away with the spectacular 13 ♘xd5 cxd5 14 ♕xf7+ ♔xf7 15 ♗xd5+, intending 15...♔f8? 16 ♘g6#, but since Black has 15...♔f6, White should play more steadily with 13 ♘xe4 ♗xh4 14 ♕xh4) 12 ♘f5 ♗f8 13 ♕f3! (planning ♕g3 followed by ♘xh6+) 13...exd4 14 ♗xd4 ♘e5 (14...♗b7 15 ♘xh6+! gxh6 16 ♗xf6 also wins for White, and so her initiative is already irrepressible) 15 ♗xe5 ♖xe5 16 ♘xh6+ gxh6 17 ♕xf6 ♗g7 18 ♕f3 ♕e7 19 ♕d3 ♕h4 20 f4 (IM Zsofia Polgar utilizes her kingside pawn majority to launch an assault against the enemy monarch, and she avoids the greedy capture 20 ♕xd6?, which would allow Black to play 20...♗xh3!, intending 21 gxh3 ♖g5+ and then 22 ♔h2 ♗e5+ or 22 ♔h1 ♕xh3+ 23 ♕h2 ♕f3+ 24 ♕g2 ♕xg2#) 20...♖e8 21 ♖ae1 ♗f5 22 ♖e3 (of course 22 exf5? allows 22...♖xe1) 22...♕e7 23 ♖g3 ♗d7 (23...♗h7 24 ♕d4! ♕f8 25 f5 ♔h8 26 f6 is a forceful example of my motto 'f for forward!') 24 f5 (this carries the twin threats of f6 and ♖xg7 followed by f6) 24...♕f6 (D).

25 ♖g6! 1-0, because the f7-pawn is pinned, and after 25...♕d4+ 26 ♕xd4, another pin makes the reply 26...♗xd4+ illegal.

| 9 | ♕e2 | a6 |

Two rounds later, the game Motwani-N.Bathie diverged with 9...♕c7 10 ♖d1 h6 (10...♗b7 transposes to Sermek-Summerscale, Cannes 1997,

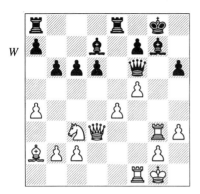

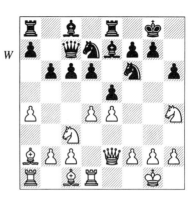

where Sermek continued with 11 ♘h4, but then 11...♖ae8! 12 ♘f5 exd4! 13 ♘xd4 {if 13 ♖xd4, then 13...d5! threatens ...♗c5} 13...d5 planned ...♗d6, with pressure for Black against White's pawns on e4 and h2) **11 ♘h4** (the manoeuvre ♘h4-f5 is particularly logical after ...h6 has been played because Black's h-pawn becomes a target for White to attack, but sometimes ♘h4-g6 is strong too) **11...♖e8?** (this fatally weakens the f7 point, but 11...exd4 12 ♖xd4 ♘c5 13 ♘g6 ♖d8, planning ...♗e6 or ...♘e6, is acceptable for Black and keeps White's initiative within a manageable level) with the following position *(D)*:

12 ♕c4! (12 ♗xf7+ ♔xf7 13 ♕c4+ was tempting too, in view of 13...♔f8? 14 ♘g6#, but 13...d5 14 exd5 ♘f8 15 dxc6+ {or 15 d6+ ♗e6} 15...♗e6 16 d5 ♘xd5 17 ♘xd5 ♗xh4! 18 ♕xh4 ♕xc6 is much less convincing for White than the actual game continuation) **12...d5** (12...♖f8 fails to 13 ♘g6) **13 exd5 exd4 14 ♘b5!** (much stronger than 14 d6 ♗xd6 15 ♕xf7+ ♔h7 16

♗xh6?, which loses to 16...♘e5! 17 ♕xc7 ♗xc7 and White has two pieces simultaneously *en prise*) **14...♕e5 15 dxc6 ♕h5 16 ♖e1** (16 ♕xf7+ ♕xf7 17 ♗xf7+ ♔xf7 18 cxd7, with ♘c7 to follow, also wins for White) **16...♘e5 17 ♖xe5!** (the first move in a short, forced, efficient tactical sequence) **17...♕xe5** (it is very important that 17...♕d1+ can be answered by 18 ♕f1) **18 ♕xf7+ ♔h7 19 ♕g6+ ♔h8** *(D)*.

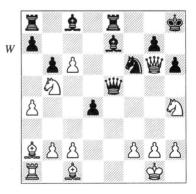

20 ♕xe8+! 1-0, due to 20...♘xe8 21 ♘g6+. In spite of that defeat, my friend Nicol Bathie still believed quite rightly that Black's position could have been playable earlier on, a view which my notes confirm. In a way, the findings in post-game analysis are a kind of victory for Nicol, and I am reminded of some wise words by the character Alfred in the film *Batman and Robin*: 'The victory is in defending what we know is right while we still live'. Now, however, we go straight from the movies to more moves.

10 ♖d1

With the threat 11 dxe5 dxe5 12 ♘xe5.

10 ... ♕e8?!

10...♕c7 seems more natural and less cramped to me, although J.R. was quite right when he once pointed out that what is 'natural' to one person may not necessarily be so to another.

11 ♘h4! *(D)*

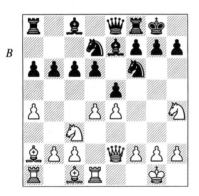

The knight is manoeuvring towards the f5-square, an idea that has cropped up in all of the games contained within the earlier notes of the main game.

11 ... ♗b7

After 11...g6? 12 ♗h6, Black's rook on f8 is trapped, which shows one disadvantage of the move ...♕e8.

12 ♘f5 ♔h8

J.R. had originally intended to play 12...b5, but now he spotted that 13 d5! is very good for White after 13...c5 14 axb5 or 13...b4 14 dxc6.

13 ♗g5

Black is being subjected to increasing pressure, and White's initiative is clear.

13 ... b5

14 dxe5

14 d5 cxd5 15 ♘xe7 ♕xe7 16 ♗xd5 is also very strong for White.

14 ... dxe5

15 ♕f3

This not only allows the c3-knight to manoeuvre to g3 via e2 if Black plays ...b4, but also threatens the tactical sequence 16 ♘xe7 ♕xe7 17 ♖xd7! ♕xd7 18 ♗xf6 gxf6 19 ♕xf6+ ♔g8 20 ♖d1 ♕c7 21 ♖d3 ♖fe8 (21...♖fd8 loses just as quickly to 22 ♖g3+ ♔f8 23 ♖g7 ♖d7 24 ♖xh7 with the terrible threat of ♖h8#) 22 ♖g3+ ♔f8 23 ♕g7+ ♔e7 24 ♕xf7+ ♔d8 25 ♖d3+ ♔c8 26 ♕xe8+ ♕d8 27 ♕xd8#. That line is virtually forced and Black certainly has no truly worthwhile improvements on it, but it is not difficult to follow or calculate, especially if one realizes that all of White's moves there are either checks, captures or moves that carry direct threats.

15 ... ♘c5 *(D)*

16 ♖d6!!

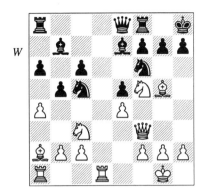

This carries the deadly tactical threat of ♘xe7 or ♘xg7, followed in either case by ♖xf6. The ♖d6 move is actually very clear and logical, because I simply wanted to increase the pressure against Black's f6-knight.

16 ...   ♘g8

16...♗xd6 is met by 17 ♘xg7! intending:

a) 17...♔xg7 18 ♗xf6+ ♔g6 19 ♕f5+ ♔h6 20 ♕g5#.

b) 17...♕d8 18 ♗xf6 ♗e7 19 ♘e6+ ♗xf6 20 ♘xd8 ♗xd8 21 ♖d1, with a decisive advantage for White in terms of both material and superiority of position.

17 ♗xe7!

The f5-knight is about to star in a stunning sacrifice, so White preserves that piece for a moment and instead uses the dark-squared bishop to eliminate its 'opposite number' in Black's army.

Roughly speaking, GM David Bronstein considers that, on a scale of comparative values, a pawn = 1 point; a knight = 3 points; a bishop = 4 points; a rook = 5 points; a queen = 9 points; the king has 'infinite' value. GM Julian Hodgson has another view about bishops, but one which also differs from the conventional idea that a knight and bishop are each worth 3 points. He recently told J.R. that a bishop should be worth about 3½ points, particularly when it is fianchettoed, because it is then that one often sees its longer-range capability in action compared with the knight's L-shaped movements of fixed length.

Of course, Bronstein, Hodgson and other great players only use the 'points' idea as a rough guideline on certain occasions, especially because they understand very well that there are many exceptions in which the conventional values of pieces can take a quantum leap due to special overriding circumstances on the chessboard. Personally, I sometimes find it useful to tally up the points quickly at the end of a calculation, just as a way of double-checking that I am not about to give away an extra-generous quantity of pieces! However, it is not the points, but rather the precise features of any given position that really determine which player is 'ahead'.

Incidentally, since I mentioned Julian Hodgson, did you know that 'the Julian' is the name given to the number of days since 1 January 4713 BC. Therefore the Julian is increasing by 1 with every new day. Someone would have to love counting to work it out! There are extra complications too. For example, Pope Gregory XIII decreed in the year 1582 that, to compensate for previous errors amounting to ten days in the calendar, the day following 4 October 1582 should be 15 October 1582, but certain countries did not adopt the new Gregorian calendar until the year 1918!

Knights are no less tricky than days and nights, as we are about to discover.

| 17 | ... | ♘xe7 *(D)* |

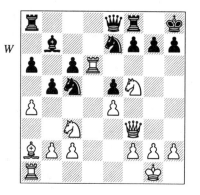

18 ♘xg7!!

Another star move in the efficient and virtually forced sequence that began with 16 ♖d6.

18	...	♔xg7
19	♕f6+	♔g8
20	♕g5+	♘g6

20...♔h8 21 ♕xe5+ ♔g8 22 ♕xc5 leaves Black two pawns down in a hopeless position.

21	♖xg6+!	hxg6
22	♕xg6+	♔h8
23	♕h6+	♔g8
24	♖e1!	

The final piece of heavy artillery is about to be swung over via e3 to g3, where it will start firing directly at Black's exposed monarch. If I had been in time-trouble (for a change I wasn't!), I might have played 24 ♕g6+ ♔h8 25 ♕h6+ ♔g8 26 ♖e1. That is identical to the actual game, except that the move-count is higher and so the time-control at move 40 is not so far away. However, one must be extremely careful to avoid unintentionally allowing a three-fold repetition of position whereby the opponent can suddenly claim a draw. In such situations, even many experienced players have taken home half a point less than should have been achieved, and that includes this writer. For instance, at Groningen in 1990/1, I was a queen for a rook up against GM Vladimir Tukmakov, but that is only half the story, because time-trouble ran away with the other half in a repetition of a familiar disaster.

It occurs to me that lots of nations have flags with stars, but if one wants to be a brighter chess star then avoid flag trouble on the clock!

| 24 | ... | ♕d7 |

J.R. intends ...♕g4, but he has no fully satisfactory way to block the g-file. Another attempt, but a less tenacious one, is 24...♘e6 25 ♖e3 ♘f4 26 ♖g3+ ♘g6 27 ♖xg6#. That simple line illustrates how important it is that the f7-pawn is pinned, a fact which means that Black has no time to play ...f5 to give his king an escape route.

25 ♖e3

A key point, which had to be foreseen not later than the sacrifice at move 18, is that 25...♕d1+ does not cause White any back-rank problems because of 26 ♘xd1. However, since all of my moves from 16 ♖d6 onwards have been checks, captures or carriers of direct threats, the calculations involved were not really too difficult even though the results are aesthetically quite pleasing. In good, strong, simple chess, the variations are often clear, as opposed to being messy or murky. Rather than scrambling around in the dark, simple chess is like proceeding along a brightly-lit path, or following a shining star. Even Batman said 'To succeed, just pick a star and follow it'. Maybe a little robin told him that, but it works!

25	...	♕g4
26	♖g3	♕xg3
27	hxg3	b4

There is little else for Black to do, but at least his b-pawn tries to reach b3 in order temporarily to shut out the bishop on a2 which has been a source of so many headaches for him.

28	♕g6+	♔h8
29	♕h5+	♔g8

After 29...♔g7, White's queen can capture the e5-pawn with check, and then Black's knight on c5 drops off too.

30 ♕g6+

White repeats the position that he had at move 28 and takes another look to decide on the final course of action,

but there will be no further repetition or any draw today.

30	...	♔h8 *(D)*

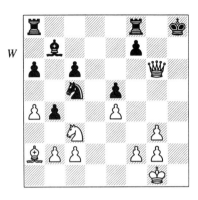

31 ♗xf7!   1-0

J.R. resigned in view of 31...bxc3 32 ♕h6# or 31...♖xf7 32 ♕xf7 bxc3 33 b4!, deflecting his knight from defending the bishop.

Solution to puzzle (posed before Game 6)

In that 1981 endgame study composed by M.Dukić, White wins with **1 ♗f8!!** and now:

a) **1...♔e6** 2 h6 ♔f7 3 h7 followed by 4 h8♕. If White had played 1 ♗g7?, then 3 h7 could be answered by 3...♔xg7, whereas 3 ♗b2 ♔g6 4 ♗c1 a3 5 ♗xa3 ♔xh6 is a typical line in which Black draws by using his passed a-pawn to divert the bishop away from defending the h-pawn.

b) **1...a3** 2 h6 a2 3 ♗g7 e5 4 ♗xe5! ♔xe5 5 h7 a1♕ 6 h8♕+, a neat skewer which wins the queen on the next move.

The Cage

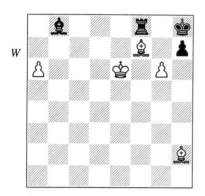

In this stunning 1969 study by B.Pasternak, it is White to play and win. Black's cornered king is almost locked in a *tin cage*, which helps White to win the *game*. As an extra little puzzle of mine, can you make an eight-letter English word using all of the different letters in the three italicized words? The solutions appear after Game 7.

We are now going to time-warp back to Saturday 15 March 1997 and land at Norton Hall, Middlesborough, where the ICI Katalco Quickplay tournament was held on that day. We will arrive at the start of the penultimate round to see Bolton's Jeff Horner about to play a short but extremely interesting game with Black against GM Chris Ward, the reigning British Champion at that time. Nobody there knows yet that Jeff is going to pack an amazing amount of tactics, initiative and efficiency into such a brief encounter. Who could guess that White will scarcely get a chance to complete any manoeuvres?

Maybe it was the following giant-killing performance by Jeff that inspired nine-year-old star Gawain Jones to defeat IM Malcolm Pein in the final round.

Perhaps only GM Michael Adams celebrated more then, with his 5/5 score and top prize. However, let's start the moves now because T.I.M.E. is of the essence, especially in a quickplay event.

Game 7
C. Ward – J. Horner
Middlesborough 1997
Chigorin Queen's Gambit

1	d4	d5
2	c4	

2 ♘f3 ♘c6 transposes to Beaton-Norris, Scottish Ch, Aviemore 1997. Black obtained a very pleasant position after 3 ♗f4 ♗f5 4 e3 e6 5 ♗d3 ♘ge7 6 0-0 h6!?, intending ...g5 and ...♗g7.

2	...	♘c6

Chigorin's Defence is a very reasonable attempt by Black to seize the initiative and already obtain a slight lead in piece development, almost before the chess clock beside him has had a chance to get into its stride of ticking. This counterattacking system also carries some surprise value, since 2...♘c6 is played far less often than the following tried and tested trio:

a) 2...dxc4, the Queen's Gambit Accepted, or QGA for short.

b) 2...e6, the Queen's Gambit Declined (or QGD).

c) 2...c6, the Slav Defence.

The most famous modern exponent of Chigorin's Defence is the young Russian GM Alexander Morozevich.

3 ♘c3

There are three most likely alternatives, and in response Black has a hat full of tricks that we are about to see:

a) **3 cxd5 ♕xd5 4 ♘f3 e5!** (White was threatening ♘c3, but that can now be answered by the pin ...♗b4), and now for example 5 dxe5 ♕xd1+ 6 ♔xd1 ♗g4 7 ♗f4 ♘ge7 8 ♘bd2 ♘g6 9 ♗g3 0-0-0 (threatening ...♗xf3 followed by ...♗b4) 10 ♔c1 ♗b4 planning ...♖he8 with abundant activity, deadly development and high harmony in Black's army. A good deal for one temporarily sacrificed pawn!

b) **3 e3 e5!** (a vigorous reaction, just as at move four in line 'a') 4 dxe5 (4 cxd5 ♕xd5 5 ♘c3 is answered by 5...♗b4) 4...d4 (I prefer this to 4...♗b4+ 5 ♗d2 dxc4, as chosen by Black in Leitao-Vescovi, São Paulo 1997), and now for example, 5 ♘f3 ♗b4+ 6 ♗d2 dxe3 7 fxe3 (7 ♗xb4 exf2+!) 7...♕e7 is fun for Black, whereas White's frail

doubled extra e-pawn will not survive for long.

c) **3 ♘f3 ♗g4 4 cxd5 ♗xf3** (4...♕xd5? 5 ♘c3 ♕a5 6 d5 0-0-0 7 ♗d2 is terrible for Black, so he must be careful not to let his pieces be attacked with too much gain of tempi for White) and then:

c1) **5 gxf3 ♕xd5 6 e3 e5** (6...e6 7 ♘c3 ♕h5 also merits attention, and indeed that path was chosen in Karpov-Miles, Bugojno 1986) 7 ♘c3 ♗b4 8 ♗d2 ♗xc3 9 bxc3 exd4 (9...♘ge7 allows White's pawns to advance with gain of time by 10 c4 ♕d6 11 d5, but 9...♕d6 is a reasonable alternative) 10 cxd4 ♘ge7 produces a situation that is rich in possibilities for both players. White has a bishop pair in an open position, whereas Black has a straight pawn structure plus a lead in development and a sneaky duo of knights whose manoeuvring capabilities can trouble the best of opponents.

c2) **5 dxc6 ♗xc6 6 ♘c3 ♘f6** (6...e6 7 e4 ♗b4 8 f3 ♕h4+!? 9 g3 ♕h5, planning ...0-0-0 and ...f5, lets White have a big pawn centre, but Black's active pieces keep it under pressure in a manner that reminds me of similar strategies which GM Tony Miles has often employed successfully in numerous creative original opening lines) 7 f3 (preparing the central advance e2-e4) 7...e5!? 8 dxe5 ♕xd1+ 9 ♔xd1 0-0-0+ 10 ♔c2 ♘d7 11 e6 (11 ♗f4 ♖e8 {or 11...♗c5 followed by ...♖he8 or ...♗d4} also represents a sensible course for both players, but 11 f4 is met by 11...f6!, for example 12 exf6 ♘xf6 or 12 e6 ♘c5 13 f5 g6 14 b4 ♘e4 15 b5 ♗d5 gives Black too much activity and leaves White's pawns over-extended) 11...fxe6 12 e4 ♗c5 13 ♗c4 ♖de8 (planning ...♖hg8 and ...g5-g4) 14 h4 ♘e5 15 ♗b3 *(D)*.

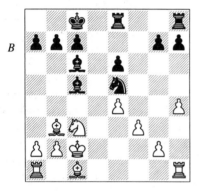

15...♗d7!, intending the manoeu-vre ...♘c6-d4+ illustrates efficiently that the Chigorin Defence can offer Black enormous activity, and certainly more than enough in this case to com-pensate for having an isolated e-pawn.

3   ...   ♘f6
4   cxd5

Once again, there are three most likely alternatives:

a) **4 ♗g5 ♘e4!** 5 ♘xe4 dxe4 6 d5 *(D)*.

6...e6!! (a typically tricky tactic in the Chigorin) 7 ♗xd8 (7 dxc6? ♕xg5 8 cxb7?? ♗b4+ 9 ♕d2 ♕xd2# would no doubt give White quite a fright) 7...♗b4+ 8 ♕d2 ♗xd2+ 9 ♔xd2 ♘xd8 is very comfortable for Black.

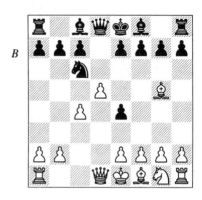

b) **4 e3 ♗f5 5 ♕b3** might look tempting for White because of his threats against the pawns at d5 and b7, but Black will gladly sacrifice the lat-ter unit by 5...e6 6 cxd5 exd5 7 ♕xb7 due to 7...♘b4 8 ♗b5+ ♔e7! 9 ♗a4 ♖b8 10 ♕xa7 ♖a8 11 ♕c5+ (11 ♕b7 is relatively best, although Black can repeat the position by 11...♖b8 12 ♕a7 ♖a8, or go for more with 11...♖xa4 12 ♘xa4 ♘c2+) 11...♗e6 12 ♕b5 ♗d3! 13 ♕b7 ♗a6, neatly trapping White's wandering queen.

c) **4 ♘f3** branches into:

c1) **4...♗g4** 5 cxd5 ♘xd5 6 e4 ♘xc3 7 bxc3 e5 8 d5 ♘b8 9 ♕a4+! ♘d7 (9...♗d7 10 ♕b3 leaves Black with his b- and e-pawns simultane-ously *en prise*) 10 ♘xe5 ♕f6 *(D)*.

I am giving a diagram here because several theoretical manuals convey the impression that Black is OK after 11 f4 ♗d6, but about ten years ago I saw Sweden's IM Pia Cramling playing the star move 11 ♗e2!!, and since then various people have fallen victim to that brilliant discovery. The idea is to

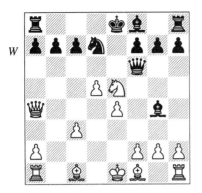

decoy Black's g4-bishop away from defending the knight: 11...♗xe2? 12 ♕xd7#. However, 11...♕xe5 12 ♗xg4 ♕xc3+ 13 ♗d2! ♕xa1+ 14 ♔e2 ♕xh1 15 ♕xd7# does not help Black either, nor does 11...b5 12 ♕xb5 ♕xe5 13 ♗xg4 ♕xe4+ 14 ♕e2, since White forces the exchange of queens and remains a sound pawn up.

In conclusion, I do not like line 'c1' for Black, but it was important to show why. Therefore let's turn our attention now to lines 'c2' and 'c3', especially the latter.

c2) **4...dxc4 5 e4 ♗g4 6 ♗e3 e6 7 ♗xc4 ♗b4 8 ♕c2 0-0** (8...♗xf3 9 gxf3 ♘xd4? 10 ♗xd4 ♕xd4 11 ♕a4+ costs Black his bishop) **9 ♖d1** looks nice for White with his big pawn centre and extra space, although Black eventually won in Van Wely-Morozevich, Amsterdam 1995. GM Alexander Morozevich also seems to enjoy the line that goes 5 d5 ♘a5, but that would not be to my taste with Black because of the knight on the rim and White having the initiative.

c3) **4...♗f5! 5 ♗g5** (5 cxd5 ♘xd5 transposes to our main game) **5...♘e4!** (this is identical to line 'a', except that White has the extra move ♘g1-f3 whereas Black has ...♗c8-f5) and now White can try:

c31) **6 ♘xd5? ♘xg5 7 ♘xg5** *(D)*.

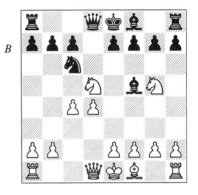

7...e6 leaves White's two knights simultaneously *en prise*, and the tactical ideas here should be compared to those arising at move six in Piket-I.Sokolov within the notes to White's fourth move of Game 5.

c32) **6 cxd5 ♘xc3 7 bxc3 ♕xd5** gives Black a nice, active game.

> **4 ... ♘xd5**
> **5 ♘f3**

5 e4 ♘xc3 6 bxc3 e5 7 d5 ♘e7 8 ♘f3 ♘g6 followed by ...♗c5 or ...♗d6 is fine for Black. Instead of 7 d5 in that line, White can maintain the tension in the centre by playing 7 ♘f3. Then 7...♗g4?! transposes exactly to line 'c1' as in the notes to White's fourth move, but 7...exd4! 8 cxd4 ♗g4 9 d5 ♗b4+ leads to:

a) 10 &d2 &xf3! 11 gxf3 &xd2+ 12 ♕xd2 ♕f6! (gaining a vital tempo by attacking the loose rook on a1) 13 ♖b1, and now 13...♘e5 or 13...♘d4 is crushing. White's moves looked very plausible, and yet they were simply overwhelmed by the tremendous activity of the opponent's pieces. That factor made the initiative and tactics flow in Black's favour with great force.

b) 10 ♔e2 ♕e7!! (10...♘e5? 11 ♕a4+) 11 dxc6 ♕xe4+ 12 ♗e3 ♖d8 (threatening not just ...♖xd1, but also 13...♕c4+ 14 ♕d3 ♕xd3#) 13 ♕b3 (D).

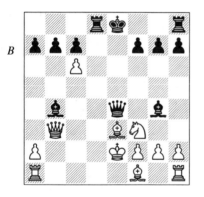

13...♖d2+! (an efficient exploitation of pins!) 14 ♔e1 ♖xa2+ 15 ♔d1 ♖xa1+ and then 16 ♔e2 ♖e1# (using another pin) or 16 ♗c1 ♕e1+ (and again!) 17 ♔c2 ♖xc1+ 18 ♔d3 ♗f5+ 19 ♔d4 ♕e4#. White got drowned in a torrent of tactics beginning at move seven, and most of his moves since then were virtually forced. Meanwhile the power in Black's army increased at

an awesome rate, and the attacking manoeuvres of the pieces exploded on White like a supernova.

5 ...   ♗f5

Designed to stop 6 e4, which can now be answered by 6...♘xc3 7 bxc3 ♗xe4.

6 ♗d2?!

This is already a critical moment because Black has a lead in development, and he can easily translate that into a very dangerous initiative if White plays even one timid, unnecessary move. It is true that 6 g3? loses to 6...♘db4! 7 e4 ♗g4 8 ♗g2 ♘xd4! 9 ♕a4+? (9 0-0 is relatively best, although Black is simply a sound pawn ahead, but 9 ♕xd4? loses immediately to the fork 9...♘c2+) 9...b5! 10 ♘xb5 ♘dc2+ and then 11 ♔e2 ♕d3# or 11 ♔f1 ♕d1+ 12 ♘e1 ♕xe1#.

However, instead of 6 g3?, White should prefer 6 e3, planning ♗d3 or ♗b5. Then 6...♘db4? can be met by 7 e4, intending 7...♗g4 8 a3! and then 8...♗xf3 9 gxf3 (the reason for not playing g3 earlier) or 8...♘xd4 9 axb4 ♘xf3+ 10 gxf3 ♕xd1+ 11 ♘xd1 (11 ♔xd1? is answered by 11...♗xf3+ followed by ...♗xh1) 11...♗xf3 12 ♖g1 e6 13 ♗d2 ♗xe4 14 ♘c3, and in this case White has the initiative and his extra piece is much more important than Black's three surplus pawns, which have hardly begun to advance.

After 6 e3, what should Black do? Certainly not 6...♘cb4? because of 7 e4 ♘xc3 8 bxc3, and the pieces on b4 and f5 are simultaneously *en prise*.

The active-looking move 6...e5 is tempting (hoping for 7 dxe5?! ♘db4! 8 e4 ♕xd1+ 9 ♔xd1 0-0-0+ 10 ♗d2 ♗g4), but 7 ♗b5! is a powerful reply. Instead, 6...e6 is sensible. Then a plausible continuation is 7 ♗d3 ♗b4 8 ♕c2 ♗xd3 9 ♕xd3 ♕f6!? 10 0-0 0-0-0, with an interesting position.

Let's see the actual game continuation now.

6	...	e6
7	g3 *(D)*	

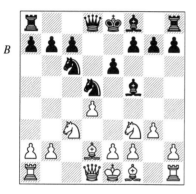

7	...	♘db4!

A quieter option is 7...♗e7, intending 8 ♗g2 0-0 9 0-0 ♗f6 with a well-developed, harmonious position for Black. However, Jeff Horner plays a stronger, more incisive star move.

8 ♖c1

8 e4? loses immediately to 8...♗g4, since White is in triple trouble at f3, d4 and c2.

8	...	♘xd4
9	♕a4+	

9 ♘xd4 ♕xd4 10 ♘b5 is refuted by 10...♘d3+!! 11 exd3 ♕e5+ 12 ♗e2

♕xb5. However, I also had great fun analysing **10...♕e4**. Here are some possibilities:

a) **11 f3?? ♘d3#.**

b) **11 ♘xc7+ ♔e7** (11...♔d7?? walks into the discovered check 12 ♗xb4+) and now:

b1) **12 ♗g2 ♕xg2 13 ♗xb4+ ♔f6 14 ♗c3+** (14 ♕d4+ loses to 14...e5 15 ♘d5+ ♔g6!) 14...♔g6, and Black's king is much safer than White's.

b2) **12 ♗xb4+ ♕xb4+ 13 ♕d2 ♕xd2+ 14 ♔xd2 ♖d8+ 15 ♔e3** (to stop the manoeuvre ...♗e4-c6) 15...♔f6 16 ♗g2 ♗b4!** (an efficient way to develop because ...♗d2+ is threatened) 17 ♖hd1 ♖xd1 (17...♗c5+ also wins) 18 ♖xd1 ♗c5+ 19 ♔f3 h5 (threatening ...♗g4+) 20 h3 *(D)*.

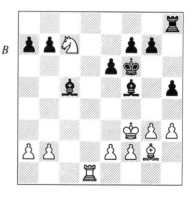

Now 20...♔e5 threatens 21...♗e4#. The much greater harmony in Black's army compared to White's is manifest. Black's pieces are exerting a much stronger influence than White's are.

b3) **12 ♗g5+ f6** branches into:

b31) **13 f3 ♕e5 14 ♗f4 ♕a5** threatening ...♘d3#.

b32) **13 ♘xa8** (threatening to play 14 ♖c7+ ♔e8 15 ♕d7#) **13...fxg5 14 ♖c7+?.** Do not play a check just because it's possible. Here it simply helps Black by making his monarch move to a safer place. Furthermore, the dark-squared bishop will no longer be blocked in by its king. During coaching on 9 July 1997, ten-year-old Geoffrey Absalom (one of my pupils) said 'There should be some strategy behind a check'. Quite an astute comment from such a young player!

After 14 ♖c7+?, a plausible continuation is 14...♔f6 15 f3 (15 ♕d8+ ♔g6 16 ♕e8+ ♔h6) 15...♕e3 16 ♖c3 (to stop ...♘d3+, but it doesn't!) 16...♘d3+! 17 ♖xd3 ♗b4+ 18 ♖d2 ♖d8, and just like in the film *Star Wars*, there will be an 'R to d2'!

9 ... c6
10 ♘xd4 ♕xd4

Black now threatens a stunning queen sacrifice in the following variation: 11...♘c2+! 12 ♔d1 *(D)*.

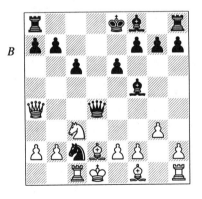

12...♕xd2+!! 13 ♔xd2 0-0-0+ 14 ♘d5 ♗b4+! 15 ♕xb4 ♘xb4, and White will lose at least a piece. Naturally, 12 ♖xc2 (instead of 12 ♔d1) is also hopeless in view of 12...♕xa4 13 ♘xa4 ♗xc2.

11 ♕b3 ♕e5
12 ♗g2 0-0-0

This is much simpler and stronger than 12...♘d3+, since 13 ♔f1 ♘xc1?? runs into 14 ♕xb7, attacking a8 and c6.

13 ♗e3 ♗c5
14 ♘d1

A lovely line is 14 ♗xc5 ♘d3+ 15 ♔f1 ♘xc1 16 ♕a3 ♕xe2+! 17 ♘xe2 ♖d1#.

14 ... ♖xd1+!!

The most efficient path to victory.

15 ♕xd1

The alternatives are no better:

a) 15 ♖xd1 ♘c2+ and then 16 ♔f1 ♗xe3 17 fxe3 ♘xe3+ or 16 ♔d2 ♗xe3+ 17 fxe3 ♘xe3! 18 ♕xe3 ♖d8+.

b) 15 ♔xd1 ♗xe3 and now 16 ♕xe3 ♖d8+ 17 ♔e1 ♘c2+ 18 ♖xc2 ♗xc2! 19 ♕xe5 ♖d1# or 16 fxe3 ♖d8+ 17 ♔e1 ♘d3+!, transposing to the actual game.

15 ... ♗xe3
16 fxe3 ♖d8

The last big gun slides into position for the final salvo.

17 ♕b3 *(D)*
17 ... ♘d3+!

Yet another star move by our hero from Bolton puts the final bolt in White's coffin.

0-1

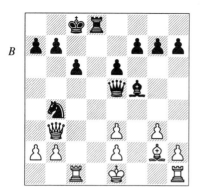

B

White resigned in view of 18 exd3 ♕xe3+ 19 ♔d1 ♗xd3 20 ♖e1 ♗e4+ 21 ♕d5 ♖xd5#. It's very seldom indeed that GM Chris Ward loses games in such drastic fashion, but on this occasion Jeff Horner's mastery of T.I.M.E. was impeccable.

Solution to puzzle (posed before Game 7)

This lovely study has an attractive **magnetic** quality ('magnetic' being the eight-letter word that you were invited to find). White wins with **1 a7!!** (for a fleeting moment, 1 ♗xb8? ♖xb8 2 ♔f6 threatens g7#, but 2...hxg6 ends White's dream of winning, whereas 1 ♔e7? ♗xh2! 2 ♔xf8 ♗d6+ 3 ♔e8 ♗c5 also draws easily for Black as he can simply sacrifice his bishop for the a-pawn if required) **1...♗xh2** (1...♗xa7 2 ♗e5#) **2 ♗e8!!** (this disruptive move plans a promotion, but meanwhile causes a commotion!) **2...♖xe8+ 3 ♔f7** (threatening g7#) **3...♖g8 4 a8♕!** ♖xa8 **5 g7#**. White gave away all his

unnecessary material except for the precious small pawn that really mattered to his king, and in the end he received the ultimate reward.

M. Najdorf's Century

Did you know that there is a new century every Wednesday?! Here is the reason: if A=1, B=2, C=3, ... , Z=26, then the total value of the letters in *'Wednesday'* is exactly 100. The same is true about *'M. Najdorf's'*, which you can check by an addition at *'lightning'* speed.

Grandmaster Miguel Najdorf died in early July 1997. Some details about the great man are given in the introduction to this book, but here I want to say more on the subject of his simultaneous displays because they hold a S.T.A.R. idea suitable for players at most levels. Najdorf frequently notched up far more than a century score in very large 'simuls', yet almost any chess player could give a modest simul against two or more opponents at the same time. It's tremendous fun to do, and *simuls toughen a repertoire* (**S.T.A.R.**) by letting a player try out lots of different ideas against his or her numerous opponents. For example, during my first 'world chess tour of Scotland' from 8-13 April 1997, I played exactly 100 games altogether in simuls at Perth, Stirling, Edinburgh, Ayr and Troon (not counting the coaching in Glasgow or the 'tandem' simul in Dundee where GM Dr Colin

McNab and I played alternate moves against each opponent). I was pleased with my tally of 97 wins, 3 draws and no losses, but the score does not reflect the fact that many opponents produced tricky and interesting ideas that really made me think.

Most players who give simuls tackle opponents with much lower ratings, the difference usually being at least 400 points, and indeed that was the case during my Scottish tour. However, GM and former World Champion Boris Spassky sportingly agreed to let me play in his simul at Glasgow's *Holiday Inn* on Friday 25 September 1987, when his FIDE rating was 2620 and mine was 2425 (since *Tron Marketing* and the *Sunday Mail* newspaper had run a competition, linked to the Glasgow Weekend Congress, in which the winners of each section earned the chance to play in a simul against Spassky). I won in 22 moves, but that did not deter me from recently taking up a challenge similar to the one Spassky had. I accepted an invitation to play many strong opponents simultaneously, providing an extremely tough test of repertoire, concentration and stamina...

High Steaks!

De Lustige Vrijpion (Flemish for 'The Happy Passed Pawn') chess club in the Belgian town of Erps-Kwerps invited me to give a talk followed by a simul on 28 June 1997. Fortunately the heavy downpour on that Saturday morning gave way to sunshine in the afternoon, allowing the planned outdoor chess and barbecue events to go ahead as intended. For me, the stakes were almost as high as the steaks, because I faced tougher opposition than ever before. Of my 23 opponents, two were rated over 2300, a further three over 2200, and six more over 2100, while the standard among the other dozen was generally quite high too. Therefore, as well as enjoying the social side to the day, I found the play to be a most valuable training. I was also very happy to score 14 wins, 8 draws and only 1 loss, but just before we look at one of the best games from the simul against an opponent with a national rating over 2200, let's warm up with some tactics.

Knight Time

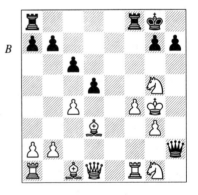

This position is based on a certain brilliant sacrificial game by GM Miguel Najdorf.

There are precisely 19 unoccupied squares on the first four ranks in the white position. The challenge is to place a black knight on one of those squares (excluding the square e4) so that Black can then play and force checkmate in no more (and no less) than two moves.

Che's Chess

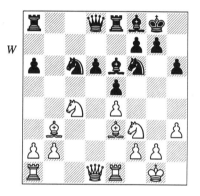

This was the final position in a 1962 simul game Najdorf-Che Guevara, because the players agreed a draw. The legendary Argentine guerrilla leader playing Black is probably one of the few opponents who is more famous than Grandmaster Najdorf himself! Even now, 30 years after the death of Che Guevara, new books are being written about him, and his character will be one of the main figures in an upcoming Warner Brothers film called *Tania*.

Against one of *the* opponents of the 20th century, Najdorf was possibly just being generous in agreeing to a draw. However, can you discover the previous 16 opening moves that led to the given position, and find how White could have won material by force at the end? The solutions appear after the next game, so you will first have plenty of time, and T.I.M.E. too!

Game 8
P. Motwani – R. Houdart
Erps-Kwerps 1997
Modern Defence

1	e4	g6
2	d4	♗g7
3	♘c3	

3 ♘c3 is no more and no less flexible than 3 ♘f3. The latter move denies White the possibility of playing f3 or f4, which are key parts of certain aggressive systems. However, it retains the option of supporting the d4-pawn by playing c3, which is sometimes quite appropriate given the pressure that Black's fianchettoed bishop is exerting towards the centre. Still, if possible I prefer to omit the move c2-c3 and continue instead with piece development at lightning speed, since that is how I very often succeed in seizing the initiative. For instance, 3 ♘f3 c6 4

♘bd2 d5 5 ♗d3! dxe4 6 ♘xe4 (D) is a line with which I have scored 100% as White in numerous games.

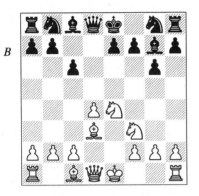

Here are several examples:

a) Motwani-R.Clapham, Dundee 1991 went **6...♗g4 7 0-0!** (lightning development again) **7...♘d7** (7...♕xd4 8 ♘xd4 ♗xd1 9 ♘b5! cxb5 10 ♗xb5+ followed by 11 ♖xd1 is tremendous for White, as is 7...♗xd4 8 ♗c4! ♗xf3 {8...♗g7? 9 ♗xf7+! costs Black his queen, and 8...♗b6? 9 ♗xf7+! ♔xf7 10 ♘fg5+ followed by 11 ♕xg4 is equally disastrous} 9 ♕xf3 ♘f6 10 ♗h6, since the king on e8 is unable to castle and the moves ♖ad1, ♖fe1 and ♕b3 are just three of White's many deadly threats) **8 ♖e1** (threatening ♘d6+) **8...♕c7 9 ♗c4** (threatening 10 ♗xf7+! ♔xf7 11 ♘fg5+ with 12 ♕xg4 to follow) **9...♘gf6 10 ♘eg5 e6** (D).

11 ♘xf7! ♔xf7 12 ♘g5+ ♔g8 (12...♔f8 13 ♕xg4!, planning ♘xe6+, wins for White, whereas 12...♔e7 can be answered in various ways including 13 ♖xe6+!?, intending 13...♗xe6 14

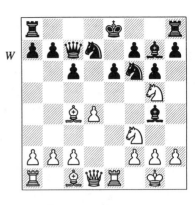

♘xe6 to fork the pieces on c7 and g7) **13 ♘xe6 ♗xe6 14 ♗xe6+ ♔f8 15 ♕f3** (a simple, yet extremely strong threat is the manoeuvre ♗f4-d6+) **15...♔e7** (15...♘b6 16 ♗f4 ♕d8 17 ♕a3+ ♔e8 18 ♗g8+ ♔d7 19 ♕h3+ ♘g4 20 ♕xg4# is a small sample of the firepower behind White's pieces, especially when they control several open diagonals and files) **16 ♗f4 ♕a5 17 b4!** (17...♕b6 18 ♗xd7+ ♔xd7 19 ♕h3+ ♔d8 20 ♕e6 ♖e8 21 ♕d6+ ♔c8 22 ♖xe8+ ♘xe8 23 ♕e6+ ♔d8 24 ♗g5+ ♔c7 {...♕xg5 is no longer possible, which illustrates one point of the deflecting move 17 b4} 25 ♕e7+ ♔c8 26 ♕xe8+ ♔c7 27 ♗f4+ ♗e5 28 ♗xe5# is an almost forced sequence of tactics) **18 ♖ab1 ♕xb1 19 ♕a3+! c5 20 ♖xb1 ♗xe6 21 ♖e1+ 1-0**. Bob Clapham resigned in view of 21...♔f7 22 ♕b3+ ♔f8 (22...♘d5 23 ♕xd5+ demonstrates the significance of White's 19th move, which forced Black's c-pawn to move from c6 so that it could not support ...♘d5 later) 23 ♗d6# or 21...♔f5 22 ♕d3+ ♔xf4

23 ♕g3+ ♔f5 24 ♖e5+ ♘xe5 25 ♕xe5+ ♔g4 26 f3+ ♔h4 27 g3+ ♔h3 28 ♕e6+ ♘g4 29 ♕xg4#, a typical, efficient king-hunt in which the aggressor sacrifices almost all except the pieces needed to deliver checkmate. 'Where exactly did Black go wrong?', one might ask. That is a good question. My honest feeling is that the particular opening system involved simply favours White because he has more space and development. I talked earlier in the book about finding perfect reactions with Black to each of White's moves, but in my opinion the opening we have just seen does not reach the required standard. One major criterion lacking is that it does not hit back at White with sufficient energy, and so Black has little hope of either seizing the initiative or even just equalizing.

b) Returning to the position after White's 6th move, five months after the previous game Motwani-Polei, Aalborg 1991 diverged with **6...♘d7 7 ♕e2** (threatening ♘d6+) **7...♘df6** (7...♕c7 can be answered by 8 g3, planning to harass Black's queen with ♗f4) **8 ♘eg5 ♖h6** (IM Vladimir Polei avoids 8...h6? 9 ♘xf7! ♔xf7 10 ♘e5+ and then 10...♔f8 11 ♘xg6+ followed by ♘xh8 or 10...♔e8 11 ♗xg6+, which is reminiscent of the moves 1 e4 c6 2 d4 d5 3 ♘d2 dxe4 4 ♘xe4 ♘d7 5 ♘g5 ♘gf6 6 ♗d3 e6 7 ♘1f3 h6?! {7...♗d6 is generally thought to be best} 8 ♘xe6! ♕e7 9 0-0 fxe6 10 ♗g6+ ♔d8 11 ♗f4 played in Deep Blue-Kasparov, New

York (6) 1997, since although White does not have an immediate forced winning sequence, the lack of safety of Black's king and the poor coordination in his army fully justifies White's earlier piece sacrifice) **9 0-0 ♗g4 10 ♖e1 e6 11 h3 ♗xf3 12 ♘xf3 ♘f5 13 c3 ♕e7?** (White stood better due to possessing more space and a powerful bishop pair in a fairly open position, but now he has a tactical sequence that wins material by force) **14 ♗xf5 gxf5 15 ♘h4!** (threatening ♘xf5) **15...♘e4 (D).**

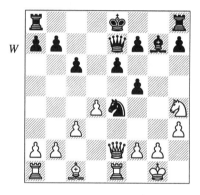

16 ♘xf5! exf5 17 f3 0-0-0 18 fxe4 ♕xe4 (18...fxe4? 19 ♕g4+) **19 ♕xe4 fxe4 20 ♖xe4**, and White converted his extra pawn into a win after another 20 moves.

c) **6...♗xd4 7 ♘xd4 ♕xd4 8 ♗e3** (8 ♗d2!, planning ♗c3, is really strong) and now:

c1) **8...♕xb2 9 ♖b1 ♕xa2 10 0-0** provides Black with three extra pawns but leaves him critically behind in development, one emphatic illustration being **10...♘d7 11 ♖e1 ♘gf6 12 ♘xf6+ ♘xf6 13 ♗c5** and then:

c11) **13...e6 14 ♗d4** is simple chess, although White has other winning moves too.

c12) **13...♗e6 14 ♖xb7 ♘d7 15 ♖xd7! ♗xd7 16 ♖xe7+ ♔d8 17 ♗c4 ♕xc4 18 ♕xd7#**.

c13) **13...♘d5 14 c4 ♘c3** (**14...♕a5** loses to **15 ♗d4 ♘c3 16 ♕d2**) **15 ♖xe7+ ♔d8 16 ♗f5+! ♘xd1 17 ♖xd1+ ♗d7 18 ♖exd7+** and now **18...♔e8 19 ♖e1+ ♕e2 20 ♖xe2#** or **18...♔c8 19 ♖d8++ ♔c7 20 ♖1d7#**.

c14) **13...0-0 14 ♗xe7 ♘d5 15 ♗xf8 ♔xf8** (**15...♘c3 16 ♕d2! ♘xb1 17 ♕h6 ♕b2 18 ♗g7 ♕xg7 19 ♖e8+ ♕f8 20 ♖xf8#**) **16 ♕c1** (threatening ♕h6+) and now **16...♔g7 17 ♖a1** wins Black's nomadic queen, as does **16...♘f6 17 ♖b4** (manoeuvring towards the kingside, but simply **17 ♕f4** is also good) **17...♕a5** (this is not absolutely forced, but Black is clearly in a very bad state anyway) **18 ♖f4** when there is **18...♕c3 19 ♖xf6! ♕xf6 20 ♕h6+ ♕g7 21 ♖e8+** or **18...♔g7**, when the winning combination deserves a diagram *(D)*:

19 ♖xf6! ♔xf6 20 ♕b2+ ♔g5 21 ♖e5+.

c2) Motwani-Van Herck, simultaneous, Geel 1997, against an opponent with a national rating around 2250, continued **8...♕g7 9 ♕d2 f5** (Marcel van Herck lashes out with this move because **9...♘f6?** loses practically by force to **10 ♗h6** and then **10...♘xe4 11 ♗xg7 ♘xd2 12 ♗xh8** or **10...♕g8 11**

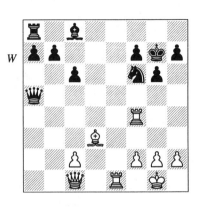

♘xf6+ exf6 12 0-0-0 ♘d7 13 ♖he1+ ♔d8, and now for example **14 ♕a5+ b6 15 ♕c3 ♔c7 16 ♗b5 ♗b7 17 ♖e7 ♖d8 18 ♗f4+ ♔c8 19 ♗xc6 ♗xc6 20 ♕xc6#**, a very forcing and efficient sequence) **10 ♘c3 ♗e6 11 0-0-0 ♘d7 12 ♗c4! ♘f8 13 ♗xe6 ♘xe6 14 ♕d7+ ♔f7 15 ♖he1** (at the time of this game, I intuitively felt that activating the final major piece is even clearer for White than **15 ♕xb7 ♘f6**, and when I see the position again now, I realize that I was still playing to maximize my initiative, something that the ensuing absence of queens diminishes to a certain extent, but as White emerges a sound pawn up the outcome is not really in doubt) **15...♘f6 16 ♕xe6+!** (again, an efficient and forcing route) **16...♔xe6 17 ♗h6+ ♔f7 18 ♗xg7 ♔xg7 19 ♖xe7+ ♔h6 20 ♖xb7**, and White later converted his extra pawn into a win.

3   ...   c6

Some players like to go for ...c6 and ...d5, while others avoid pawn contact for the moment by playing 3...d6. In the latter case, the continuation **4 f4**

②f6 would transpose to game 3 of *C.O.O.L. Chess*.

    4   ♗e3   d5
    5   ♕d2! *(D)*

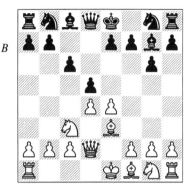

I spotted this move in a newspaper chess column about ten years ago, and I recall that the star playing White was a super-GM of the future, Judit Polgar. Her idea of developing and also keeping the tension in the centre is much stronger than 5 e5, which would allow the manoeuvre ...②h6-f5.

    5 ...   ②f6

5...dxe4 gives up Black's foothold in the centre, and White has a pleasant spatial advantage after 6 ②xe4.

    6 e5

This advance is now well-timed as it gains a tempo by attacking the f6-knight. Continuing to maintain the central tension through supporting the e4-pawn with 6 f3 does not work so smoothly because after 6...dxe4 7 fxe4 Black has the tactical idea 7...e5!, intending 8 dxe5 ♕xd2+ 9 ♗xd2 ②g4 followed by ...②xe5 with a superb

outpost on e5 for Black, and 7...②g4 is also an option.

    6 ...   ②e4

6...②g4 would be straying too far off course. After 7 ♗f4, Black's wandering knight is in a whole lot of trouble, since White threatens to trap it with h3 or f3. 7...f6 could be tried, and indeed 8 ②f3 fxe5 9 dxe5 ②d7 puts White's e-pawn under some pressure. However, simply 8 exf6 ②xf6 9 ②f3 0-0 10 ♗d3 leaves Black with glaring weaknesses at e5, e6 and e7.

    7 ②xe4   dxe4
    8 0-0-0   ♗e6
    9 ②e2!

The knight has the flexibility to manoeuvre to c3 or f4, from where it can harass Black's units at e4 or e6.

    9 ...   a5

9...♗xa2? is only a problem for the owner of the bishop, as 10 b3 followed by ♔b2 or ②c3 shows. However, after the move just played, 10...♗xa2 is almost a threat because of 11 b3 a4 12 ♔b2 (12 ♕c3 is strong too) 12...axb3 13 cxb3? (13 ♖a1 bxc2 and here 14 ♖xa2? ♕b6+ also wins for Black, but 14 ②c1! is a different story) 13...♗xb3! 14 ♔xb3 ♕d5+ 15 ♔c2 ♖a2+ 16 ♔c1 ♖a1+! (much more efficient than automatically grabbing the queen on d2) 17 ♔b2 ♕a2+ 18 ♔c3 ♕a3+ 19 ♔c2 (19 ♔c4 b5#) 19...♖a2+ 20 ♔b1 ♕b3+ 21 ♔c1 ♖a1#.

    10 a3

With this game being just one of 23 games in a simul., I decided to play it safe here.

10	...	b5
11	♘f4	♕c8
12	♗e2	

'The threat is stronger than its execution', so White continues to mobilize the forces in his army rather than capture an enemy bishop that actually has nowhere better to go than its current location. If Black wants to spend valuable time to move his bishop from e6, then White will not object.

| 12 | ... | 0-0 *(D)* |

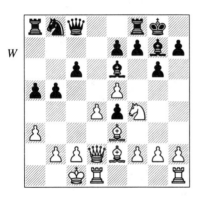

| 13 | f3 | exf3 |
| 14 | ♗xf3 | |

By exchanging off Black's far-advanced e-pawn, White obtains more space in which to manoeuvre around the centre.

| 14 | ... | ♖d8 |
| 15 | ♕f2 | |

White's queen moves onto the freshly opened f-file, not only because Black no longer has a rook protecting the f7 point, but also to avoid tactics involving ...♗xe5.

| 15 | ... | ♖a6 |

A sign that Black was finding it difficult to formulate a constructive plan in his cramped position, although perhaps he was hoping to challenge White's pawn centre by playing ...c5 without allowing ♗xa8.

| 16 | ♖he1 | |

Now, in a chess sense at least, White has total **H.A.P.P.I.N.E.S.S.**: **H**armony **A**chieved, **P**ieces **P**ositioned **I**n **N**ice **E**ntirely **S**ensible **S**quares. That is simply an observation here, as even I would not normally stop to use a nine-letter acronym during a real game with a strict time-limit! Nevertheless, happiness and harmony are highly desirable things in chess and more generally in life, so it is quite appropriate to make a link between them.

| 16 | ... | ♗d5 |

16...c5 can be answered in various very good ways including 17 d5, especially because the e1-rook is ready to give support to White's e-pawn.

| 17 | h4 | b4 |

After 17...♗xf3 18 ♕xf3, White threatens to play h5, and 18...h5 is unsatisfactory for Black as 19 e6! causes his kingside pawn-chain to crumble.

| 18 | a4 | |

It is sensible to keep the position as closed as possible in a region of the board where the opponent is trying to attack.

18	...	b3
19	c3	♕f5 *(D)*
20	♖d2	

White avoids the deadly tactical trap associated with 20 g4?, which is

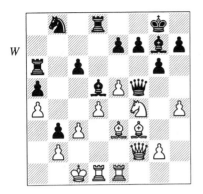

20...♕c2+! 21 ♕xc2 bxc2, and Black would win material on d1 or f3, where pieces are simultaneously *en prise*.

20	**...**	**h5**
21	**♘xd5!**	

White suddenly clarifies the situation because a simple, strong, forcing sequence is available.

21	**...**	**cxd5**
22	**♗d1**	

The dual threats are 23 ♗xb3 and 23 ♕xf5 gxf5 24 ♗xh5, so Black's next move is mandatory.

22	**...**	**♕xf2**
23	**♖xf2**	**♖b6**
24	**g4**	

White's initiative persists, despite the absence of queens.

24	**...**	**hxg4**
25	**♗xg4**	**f5**

Quite understandably, Black does not wish to wait passively for White to play h5.

26 exf6

26 ♗d1 is also very good because White threatens to make the advance h4-h5. That little move is enough to affect Black's fragile g6-f5 pawn chain like a battering ram bashing against it. For instance, 26...♔f7 27 h5 e6 28 hxg6+ ♔xg6 *(D)*.

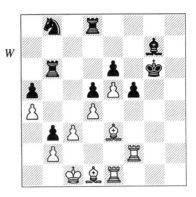

Now 29 ♗h5+!! finishes efficiently as follows:

a) 29...♔xh5 30 ♖g2, threatening ♖h1#.

b) 29...♔h7 30 ♗f7 ♗h6 31 ♗xh6! (even stronger for White than 31 ♖h2 ♔g7) 31...♔xh6 32 ♖g2 followed by 33 ♖h1#.

26	**...**	**♗xf6**
27	**♗g5**	**♔f7**

27...♗xg5+ 28 hxg5 ♘c6 29 ♗e6+ ♔g7 30 ♖f7+ ♔h8 31 ♖h1+ ♔g8 32 ♖fh7+ ♔f8 33 ♖h8+ ♔g7 34 ♖1h7# is another way for Black to go.

28 h5   ♖h8

Black's knight has still not moved from its starting position, but it is too late for 28...♘d7 in view of 29 hxg6+ ♔xg6 30 ♗xf6 and then for example:

a) 30...♘xf6 31 ♗e6 ♔g7 32 ♖g1+ ♔h8 (32...♔f8 33 ♖g8#) 33 ♖h2+ ♘h7 34 ♗f5 followed shortly by mate.

b) 30...exf6 31 ♗e6 ♘f8 32 ♖g1+ ♔h7 33 ♖h2#.

c) 30...♖xf6 31 ♖fe2 ♘b6 32 ♖xe7 ♘xa4 33 ♗d1 ♖b8 (33...♖f2 loses to 34 ♗xb3 ♘xb2 35 ♗c2+) 34 ♖g1+ ♔h6 (34...♔f5 35 ♖e5+ ♔f4 36 ♖g4#) 35 ♖e5 threatening ♖h5#.

29 hxg6+ ♔xg6 (D)

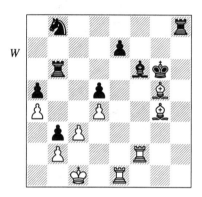

30 ♗f5+! ♔f7

30...♔xg5 31 ♖g1+ ♔h5 32 ♖h2+ ♗h4 33 ♖g4 followed by 34 ♖hxh4# is similar to earlier variations in the notes where Black's king is trapped on the open h-file by a white rook on the g-file and another one next door that gets to deliver checkmate.

31 ♗xf6 exf6

31...♖xf6 32 ♗e6+ ♔f8 33 ♖xf6+ exf6 34 ♗xd5 followed by ♗xb3 picks off two of Black's weak, scattered pawns, while all of White's own pawns remain intact, strong and connected.

32 ♖fe2 1-0

Black resigned in the face of the dual threats of 33 ♗e6+ followed by

♗xd5 and 33 ♖e7+ ♔f8 34 ♖e8+ ♔g7 35 ♖g1+, winning the rook on h8. Robert Houdart also realized that after 32...♖d8, White has 33 ♖e7+ ♔f8 34 ♖h7 (threatening ♖h8+) 34...♖bd6 35 ♖eh1, and there is no satisfactory way to prevent 36 ♖h8+ ♔e7 37 ♖1h7#.

The question 'Where exactly did Black go wrong?' was asked after the Motwani-Clapham game within the notes to White's third move of the main game we have just seen. The same question is very pertinent here too, and once again I feel that the opening system chosen was the big root of Black's growing problems later in the game. He should not advance his d-pawn to d5 (as played on move four) unless it can be maintained there in the centre and/or used to create pressure against White's pawn centre. In the actual game, White's d4-e5 pawn chain drove a wedge into the opponent's position and locked his fianchettoed bishop out of play for almost the entire game from move six onwards. In such cases the defender is virtually reduced to being a helpless spectator, watching his position melt under mounting pressure like a snowman exposed to bombardment by the Sun's rays.

Solutions to puzzles (posed before Game 8)

The square you were seeking for a black knight is **f3**. Then Black forces checkmate in exactly two moves with **1...♘e5+! 2 fxe5 h5#**. In the game

Glücksberg-Najdorf, Warsaw 1935, the knight was actually on g6, and Black added to the earlier sacrifices of three other minor pieces by giving the knight away too with the star move 1...♘e5+!, winning as given before.

The 16 moves of the Najdorf-Che Guevara game are **1 e4 e5 2 ♘f3 ♘c6 3 ♗b5 a6** (the most common response to White's Ruy Lopez or Spanish Opening, but see Game 3 for 3...♘f6) **4 ♗a4** (the justification for 3...a6 is that 4 ♗xc6 dxc6 5 ♘xe5?! can be answered by 5...♕d4 or 5...♕g5, but I have tried 5 0-0, 5 d4 and 5 ♘c3 as White on various occasions, and the third case has even caught strong IMs in encounters that were not close when they fell into the tactical trap 5...f6 6 d4 ♗d6? {6...exd4 is better} 7 dxe5 fxe5? 8 ♘xe5!, planning 8...♗xe5 9 ♕h5+) **4...♘f6 5 0-0 ♗e7 6 ♖e1** (now 7 ♗xc6 followed by ♘xe5 really is a threat) **6...b5 7 ♗b3 d6** (after protecting the e5-pawn, Black 'threatens' ...♘a5 to eliminate the star 'Spanish' bishop on b3, therefore White now plays c3 to create a flight square at c2 for his prized piece and also to support the central advance d2-d4) **8 c3 0-0 9 h3** (9 d4 does not suit all players because of 9...♗g4, although 10 d5 and 10 ♗e3 are both possible, with the latter move carrying the sneaky trick 10...♘xe4? 11 ♗d5) **9...h6** (numerous games have ended in draws by three-fold repetition of position after 9...♖e8 10 ♘g5 ♖f8 11 ♘f3 ♖e8 12 ♘g5 ♖f8

13 ♘f3) **10 d4 ♖e8 11 ♘bd2 ♗f8 12 d5** (alternatively, 12 ♘f1 would continue the standard 'Lopez' manoeuvre ♘b1-d2-f1-g3 of the white queen's knight to the kingside, and 12...exd4 13 cxd4 ♘xe4?? costs Black a knight due to the recurring nightmare ♗d5 that we saw in the notes three moves ago) **12...♘e7** (Black must be very careful about putting a knight on the rim by 12...♘a5, because after the reply 13 ♗c2, White threatens 14 b4 ♘b7 15 a4 with a powerful initiative on the queenside, whereas the black knight on b7 has nowhere to go) **13 c4 bxc4?!** (this lets the d2-knight leap straight into a very strong position, so I would have preferred to maintain the tension at the c4-square by not exchanging pawns there and instead playing 13...c6) **14 ♘xc4 c6 15 dxc6 ♘xc6 16 ♗e3!** (Najdorf homes in on the sensitive b6-square in Guevara's camp, and 16...♘xe4?? would cost Black material for various tactical reasons, the simplest one being 17 ♗b6 ♕d7 18 ♖xe4 d5 19 ♘cxe5) **16...♗e6?** (16...♖b8 17 ♖c1, threatening ♘xd6 followed by ♖xc6, is also extremely difficult for Black, but instead 16...♗b7 is relatively best). The 'simul' game was agreed drawn without further play, but the star move **17 ♗a4!** *(D)* wins material for White.

For example:

a) **17...♗xc4** 18 ♗xc6 puts Black's two rooks simultaneously *en prise*.

b) **17...♖c8** 18 ♘b6 ♖c7 19 ♖c1 ♗d7 20 ♕c2 leaves Black helpless

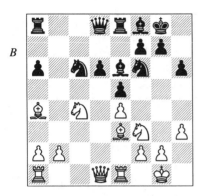

against the threat of ♘xd7 followed by ♗xc6.

c) **17...♗d7 18 ♘b6 ♖b8 19 ♘xd7 ♛xd7 20 ♖c1 ♖ec8** and now:

c1) **21 ♛c2?!** looks tempting, but Black has the resource 21...♘b4!, planning 22 ♗xd7 ♖xc2 or 22 ♛xc8 ♛xc8!.

c2) **21 ♖xc6! ♖xc6 22 ♘xe5! dxe5 23 ♛xd7 ♘xd7 24 ♗xc6** simplifies the situation very efficiently and puts White a sound extra pawn up on the queenside. Since he also has a powerful bishop pair in an open position, the win should only be a matter of time.

Moves speak louder

'Louder than what?' one might ask, and the answer is 'ratings'. Most competitors with high ratings have played very well to achieve them, but I do not want to attach too much importance to figures alone. Although ratings have cropped up elsewhere in this book, we should always remember that almost anyone is capable of producing star moves that are stronger than any rating. Therefore it is always wise to respect an opponent's capabilities, no matter how low his or her rating may be. Also, one should never be intimidated when facing superstars with ratings that might seem astronomical. Instead, approaching each game with the aims of manoeuvring efficiently, seizing the initiative, and then attacking the opponent energetically with a barrage of tactics, should lead to some notable victories. For example, let's join Suba-Turner, Benasque 1997, with IM Matthew Turner about to play his 23rd move against GM Mihai Suba, one of the stars of *C.O.O.L. Chess (D)*.

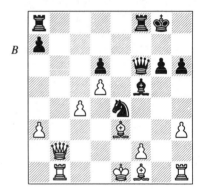

Black employed the King's Indian Defence, one of Kasparov's favourite counterattacking openings, and a variant upon which we saw IM Jonathan Rowson using with deadly effect in Game 5. At move 20, Matthew sacrificed a pawn in order to open up the b- and f-files and seize the initiative. Three moves later, he could now play

23...♘xf2 due to 24 ♕xf6 ♖xf6 25 ♔xf2 ♗xb1+ or 24 ♗d4 ♕e7+ 25 ♔xf2 ♗xb1+. However, Matthew wants to win in the most clear-cut and efficient way that gives White no chance of survival. If only Black's queen could land a devastating check on c3... Perhaps that logical thought helped to find the star move **23...♖ab8!**, which aims to deflect White's queen. The game continued **24 ♕xb8** (24 ♕xf6 loses immediately to the *zwischenzug* 24...♖xb1+ before recapturing on f6, and after 24 ♕c1 ♖xb1 25 ♕xb1 ♕c3+, both 26 ♔d1 ♘xf2+ and 26 ♔e2 ♘g3+ guarantee the win of White's queen by ...♗xb1) **24...♕c3+ 25 ♔e2** (there are some nice manoeuvres in the following line: 25 ♔d1 ♘xf2+! 26 ♗xf2 {26 ♔e2 ♗d3#} 26...♗c2+ 27 ♔e2 {27 ♔c1 ♗b3#} 27...♗d3+ 28 ♔d1 {28 ♔e3 ♗xf1+ 29 ♔e4 gives Black the choice of ...♕d3#, ...♕e5# or ...♗g2#} 28...♕c2+ 29 ♔e1 ♕xf2+ 30 ♔d1 ♕c2+ 31 ♔e1 ♕c3+! {back there again, because although ...♖xf1+ followed by ...♕e2# is desirable, it is unfortunately illegal due to a pin on the eighth rank!} 32 ♔d1 ♗c2+ 33 ♔e2 ♕d3+ 34 ♔e1 ♕e3+ 35 ♗e2 ♕c3#) **25...♘g3+!!** *(D).*

I really like a big check! Black had the possibility to take White's queen or to deliver a check with his own lady, but instead he searched for and found a much more efficient tactical solution. Now 26 ♔d1 ♗c2+ 27 ♔c1 ♗b3# is short and sweet, whereas 26 fxg3 ♗d3+ 27 ♔d1 ♗c2+ 28 ♔e2 (28 ♔c1

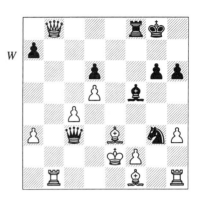

♗b3#) 28...♕d3+ 29 ♔e1 ♕xe3+ 30 ♗e2 ♕c3# is basically the same finish as occurred in the previous note, so instead the actual game went **26 ♔f3 ♘xh1!** (*if* we could remove White's f-pawn from the board, then 26...♗e4++ would win more quickly in view of 27 ♔xg3 ♕xe3+ 28 ♔h2 ♕f2+ 29 ♗g2 ♕xg2# or 27 ♔g4 h5+ 28 ♔h4 ♘f5+ 29 ♔g5 ♕f6+ 30 ♔f4 ♕h4#, but the presence of the pawn on f2 changes things significantly, so Black had to assess the material situation in a cool, objective manner) **27 ♔g2** (if 27 ♕b4, Black can take the rook on b1 with check, yet an even more efficient route to victory would be 27...♗xh3+ and then 28 ♔e2 ♗g4+ 29 f3 ♗xf3# or 28 ♔e4 ♘xf2+ 29 ♗xf2 ♗f5+ 30 ♔f4 g5#, whereas 27 ♕xf8+ ♔xf8 28 ♖b8+ ♔f7 29 ♗g2 ♕xc4 30 ♗xh1 ♕xd5+ is not quite mate but still completely hopeless for White) **27...♗e4+ 28 ♔g1 ♖xb8.** Black sensibly settles for getting a decisive material advantage instead of trying anything flashy. His earlier sacrifices were beautiful and correct, but now it's time to collect the win. That was achieved simply and quickly as follows: **29 ♖xb8+ ♔f7 30 ♖b7+ ♔f6 31 c5** (if White does not want to resign yet, then he could also try 31 ♗xh6 threatening ♗g7+, but Black has 31...♕e1 32 ♗e3 ♘g3! 33 fxg3 ♕xg3+ 34 ♗g2 ♕xg2#) **31...dxc5 32 ♖xa7 ♘g3 33 ♖a6+ ♔f5 34 ♗b5** (perhaps for an instant White might have hoped to play 35 ♗d7+ ♔e5 36 f4+ ♔xd5 37 ♗e6#, but it is Matthew's turn to move...) **34...♕e1+ 35 ♔h2 ♕h1+!** (an elegant finish, with the point 36 ♔xg3 ♕f3+ and then 37 ♔h2 ♕g2# or 37 ♔h4 g5+ 38 ♗xg5 hxg5#, so Mihai Suba throws in the towel, something he does not often have to do because he truly is a star player) **0-1**.

The combined effect of Black's queen and bishop was most striking in many variations of the example which we have just seen. That reminds me of the following statement made by Kasparov during a recent lecture in London: 'Everyone says that the queen and knight are a powerful attacking force, but the queen and bishop can be just as potent.' It is logical that a queen and knight work well together because their movements are totally different, and so complement each other very nicely. Their distinct special abilities do not overlap, but they can, nevertheless, add to produce an awesome force. However, it also makes sense that a queen and bishop can form an

effective team, especially when they are cooperating on adjacent parallel diagonals. In such cases, the queen and bishop possess all the power that two bishops would have, plus a giant extra dose of horizontal and vertical capabilities contained within the queen.

The Suba-Turner example stemmed from a King's Indian Defence (K.I.D.), and the following position is a product of the same aggressive opening.

The K.I.D. strikes again!

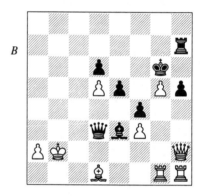

It is Black to play and win, with his queen and bishop starring in a forceful finish that will be revealed after the next game, which is the encounter between IM Erik van den Doel (who finished with 7½/13 in a fine 20th place out of 78 players at the very strong World Junior Championship, Zagan 1997) and GM Gennadi Sosonko at the 1997 Dutch Championship. We are about to see a K.I.D. in reverse, since White plays it with an extra tempo. However, it turns out to be doubly interesting for Black, because instead of castling kingside, he attacks

with ...h5! at move nine. The rest of the game seems smooth and graceful.

Game 9
E. van den Doel – G. Sosonko
Dutch Ch, Rotterdam 1997
Reversed King's Indian

1 ♘f3   c5

It is worth noting that 2 e4 would suddenly produce a Sicilian Defence, which underlines how careful one must be, right from the first move, not to get tricked into an unfamiliar opening. Sosonko is happy in Sicilian territory, but he nevertheless stays alert to sneaky move-order possibilities.

2 g3   d5
3 ♗g2   ♘c6
4 0-0

4 d4 would give White a Grünfeld Defence with an extra move, since the normal version of it for Black is 1 d4 ♘f6 2 c4 g6 3 ♘c3 d5. However, **4...♘f6** is a sensible and adequate response. For example:

a) **5 c4?** dxc4 6 ♕a4 cxd4 7 ♘xd4 ♕xd4 8 ♗xc6+ ♗d7 produces an exact mirror image of the position resulting from White's 9th move in note 'a2' on page 89. That was very difficult for Black so it would be a doubly bad idea to get the position as White!

b) **5 0-0** e6 6 c4 dxc4 7 ♕a4 cxd4 8 ♘xd4 ♕xd4 9 ♗xc6+ ♗d7 10 ♖d1 ♕xd1+! 11 ♕xd1 ♗xc6 is generally regarded as being an ultra-solid line for Black, and he has a full material

equivalent of ♖+♗+♙ to counterbalance White's queen.

4 ...   e5
5 d3   ♗e7
6 e4   ♘f6
7 ♘c3   d4
8 ♘e2   ♘d7

This is a multi-purpose move, and here are some of the ideas behind it:

a) Black may decide to attack on the queenside with ...b5, ...c4 and ...♘c5.

b) If White plays ♘e1 or ♘d2 followed by f4, then the black knight on d7 gives extra support to the e5-pawn, and ...f6 is available too if necessary.

c) There is also the star concept of attacking on the kingside with ...h5 and ...h4, supported by the e7-bishop which can now 'see' the h4-square because it is no longer blocked by the knight that was on f6.

9 ♘d2

This may actually be an error, in view of Black's energetic reaction to it. However, IM Erik van den Doel possibly had the natural thought that White is a tempo ahead compared with Black's normal situation after the standard K.I.D. moves 1 d4 ♘f6 2 c4 g6 3 ♘c3 ♗g7 4 e4 d6 5 ♘f3 0-0 6 ♗e2 e5 7 0-0 ♘c6 8 d5 ♘e7 9 ♘d2 ♘d7 *(D)*.

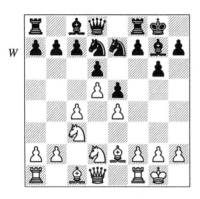

Why is Van den Doel a tempo ahead in the main game compared to the position in the diagram? Well, because Sosonko hasn't castled kingside yet. The problem is, he isn't going to castle there: he plans to attack on the kingside instead! This excellent strategy should be compared to the one employed by Latvia's Nikolai Gurtovoi in Ozolinš-Gurtovoi contained within the notes to Black's seventh move of Game 1. In that example, Black left his king on e8 for many moves because it was perfectly safe there, and meanwhile he launched a ferocious attack against the opponent's castled king.

Before the prize-giving ceremony at the 1989 Edinburgh Weekend Chess Congress, I gave one of my favourite talks, entitled '*Watch that rook's pawn!*'. Well, look out now, because Sosonko's forthcoming star move with

his king's rook's pawn deserves a prize!

9 ...   h5! *(D)*

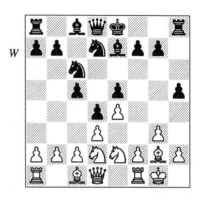

Black seizes the initiative in a manner that reminds me again of my Belgian friend Gorik Cools with his attacking motto 'h for hunting!'.

10 f4

White decides against the idea of trying to stop ...h4 with 10 h4, because after 10...g5 11 hxg5 ♗xg5 and then 12 f4 ♗e7 or 12 ♘f3 ♗e7, Black will achieve the advance ...h5-h4 anyway, and into the bargain he has an opened g-file giving extra attacking chances.

10 ...   h4

11 ♘f3

11 g4 h3 12 ♗f3 exf4 13 ♘xf4 ♘de5 gives Black a dream position, but for White it's like waking up in the middle of a volcanic eruption on Io (a very active satellite that orbits the planet Jupiter), where lava shoots out of hot vents at temperatures around 350 degrees Celsius. The only nice way I can think of to describe such a

fiery red scene is that it looks like a pizza!

11 ... h3!

This forces the fianchettoed bishop to retreat into a corner. It also secures the g4-square as an outpost for Black's pieces to enjoy, since White cannot play h3 himself. In contrast, 11...hxg3 12 ♘xg3 would have allowed White's pieces to become more active than in the actual game.

12 ♗h1 ♘f6

Immediately manoeuvring towards the g4-square, with the little tactical point that after 13 fxe5 ♘g4 14 ♗f4, Black has 14...g5, which means that White's extra e-pawn will vanish quickly. However, even in a bad position when one's life on the board seems to be slipping away, there are almost always some chances of survival if one fights back as energetically as possible. With that thought in mind, 14 e6! (instead of 14 ♗f4 given earlier in the note) 14...♗xe6 15 ♘f4 keeps White alive and kicking, though the poor condition of his bishop on h1 together with Black's control of the e5- and e3-squares in particular gives much cause for concern.

13 ♘d2?

This is simply too passive. White had to hit back more vigorously, as was stressed in the previous note.

13 ... ♘g4
14 ♘b1

The knight retreats because Black was threatening ...♘e3, and 14 ♘c4 is just asking to be attacked by ...♗e6 or

...b5. However, that still looks preferable to the chosen move, which leaves all but one of White's pieces huddled along the first rank.

14 ... g5! *(D)*

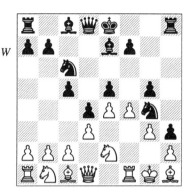

Black's galloping g-pawn threatens to win the game immediately by 15...gxf4 16 gxf4 ♖g8 17 ♘g3 ♗h4 (threatening ...♘xh2) 18 ♖f3 exf4 19 ♗xf4 ♘ce5 20 ♖f1 ♘xh2 (one of several efficient ways to demolish White's defences) 21 ♔xh2 ♘g4+ 22 ♔g1 (22 ♔xh3 ♘f2++ is equally hopeless for White) 22...♗xg3 23 ♗xg3 h2+ 24 ♗xh2 (24 ♔g2 ♘e3+) 24...♘e3+ 25 ♗g2 ♖xg2+ 26 ♔h1 ♕h4 followed by checkmate not later than move 28. Do not be put off by the length of this or any other tactical sequences in *S.T.A.R. Chess* because they actually represent variations in which the moves flow very logically.

15 ♗f3

After 15 f5 ♘h6, Black threatens to complete the imprisonment of White's bishop on h1 by playing ...g4, and then time will seem long and dark to that piece, as it would on the planet Pluto where a 'year' is almost 248 of our Earth years because Pluto takes 247.7 years to complete one orbit around the Sun.

15	...	gxf4
16	gxf4	♖g8
17	♘g3	

If 17 ♔h1, then 17...♗h4 threatens ...♘f2+, and so White is forced to make the capture 18 ♗xg4 as 18 ♘g3? would allow the reply 18...♘xh2 19 ♔xh2 ♗xg3+.

17	...	♗h4
18	♗xg4	

No matter how unappealing this capture is for White, he simply could not allow Black to play ...♘xh2.

18	...	♗xg4
19	♕e1	♕d7
20	a3	

It is clear that White hopes to generate some counterplay by playing b4 as soon as possible, but Black has a star response in mind.

20	...	0-0-0
21	b4 (D)	

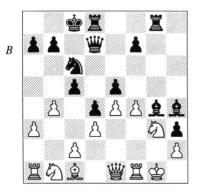

21 ... c4!

Black keeps the queenside almost closed so that White cannot create any attacking chances in that region.

22 ♘d2

White's knight re-emerges before Black can seal it in with ...c3. However, a couple of alternatives merit some attention:

a) 22 dxc4 d3 23 c3 (aiming to stop ...♘d4, but...) 23...♘d4 (the determined knight will not be denied a star role in the action, although 23...♗e2 wins quickly too) 24 cxd4 ♕xd4+ 25 ♕f2 ♕xa1 26 ♗b2 ♕a2 27 ♕c5+ ♔b8 28 ♗xe5+ ♔a8, when White's transient counterplay is finished, whereas Black threatens ...♕g2# and his opponent's problems are compounded by the monster passed d-pawn.

b) 22 b5 ♘e7 23 dxc4 d3 (this is one of many good moves, and it carries several threats including ...♕d4+ and ...dxc2) 24 c3 ♗e2 25 ♖f2 ♗xg3 26 hxg3 ♖xg3+ 27 ♔h2 ♕g4, and White is defenceless against the firepower of Black's heavy pieces, especially since ...♖g8 is coming too.

22	...	exf4
23	♖xf4	♘e5

Black decides not to open the c-file with 23...cxd3 24 cxd3, although he should still win after 24...♘e5 25 ♕f1 ♗xg3 (more incisive than 25...♗g5) 26 hxg3 h2+! and now:

a) 27 ♔h1 ♗h3 28 ♕e2 ♖xg3, and White's defences have caved in.

b) 27 ♔xh2 ♖h8+ 28 ♔g1 ♖dg8 (or 28...♖h3). White is then being bombarded with so many threats that, even in the safety of my home analysis, I cannot help feeling as though I am caught in the middle of an asteroid field. One possible finish is 29 ♘c4 ♘xc4 30 dxc4 ♗e2! (clearing the way for Black's heavier pieces to invade) 31 ♕xe2 ♖xg3+ 32 ♔f2 ♖h2+ 33 ♔xg3 ♕h3#.

24 ♘xc4

If 24 ♕f1, then at the very least Black can transpose to the previous note with 24...cxd3 25 cxd3 ♗xg3, and of course he would have other attractive options too.

24 ...   ♗xg3

25 hxg3

Naturally, it would also be fatal for the white queen to step onto the g-file by 25 ♕xg3 with the king sitting on g1 and a black rook bearing down from g8 towards both of White's royal pieces.

25 ...   ♘f3+

26 ♖xf3 (D)

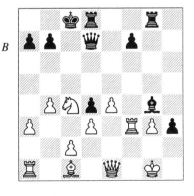

26 ...   h2+!

Black's h-pawn happily offers to sacrifice itself because White's monarch is denied the chance to hide in front of it, as would have happened with 26...♗xf3 27 ♔h2.

27 ♔f2 (D)

After 27 ♔g2 ♗xf3+ 28 ♔xf3 ♕g4+ 29 ♔g2, 29...h1♕+ mirrors the actual game, but a nice alternative is 29...♕xg3+ 30 ♕xg3 ♖xg3+ 31 ♔xh2 (31 ♔xg3 allows 31...h1♕, whereas 31 ♔h1 ♖g1+ 32 ♔xh2 ♖g6 transposes to the main line of this analysis, with the small difference that the move-number has increased by one) 31...♖g6, which leaves White's king without any satisfactory defence against the threat of ...♖h8+. That reminds me strongly of many variations given in the notes to Game 8, except that the black king was the one in perpetual peril there.

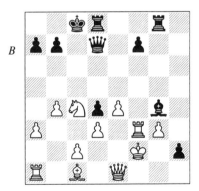

Star Question: If the game had gone 27 ♔xh2 ♗xf3 28 ♘e5, what would have been Black's quickest route to victory? The answer appears after this battle is over.

27	...	♗xf3
28	♔xf3	♕g4+
29	♔g2	h1♕+!

The star h-pawn, which began striding forward 20 moves ago, has succeeded in attaining the ultimate honour by becoming a new queen. That is a happy ending, but 29...♕xg3+ also wins as given in the notes at move 27.

30 ♔xh1

30 ♕xh1 ♕e2+ and then 31 ♔g1 ♖xg3+ 32 ♕g2 ♕xg2# or 31 ♔h3 ♖h8+ 32 ♗h6 ♖xh6# were other ways for White to bow out.

30 ...   ♕h3+

0-1

White resigned in view of 31 ♔g1 ♖xg3+ 32 ♔f2 ♕g2#. That performance by GM Gennadi Sosonko was packed with T.I.M.E., and yet he still managed to save ten percent of his allotted time, because he had 12 minutes left on the clock at the end out of his initial two hours for 40 moves. It's nice to see a really well-played game not being spoiled by time-trouble near the finish.

18-year-old IM Erik van den Doel may have felt like a lost boy after losing to a man three times his own age, but later Erik became a triple star at the Lost Boys tournament in Antwerp during August because:

1) He finished equal second with a super score of 7/9.

2) He was Holland's highest-placed player.

3) He achieved his first GM norm. Many congratulations!

Answer to Star Question (posed at move 27)

It was Black to move in the following position *(D)*:

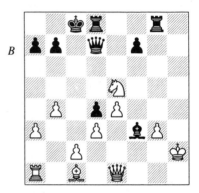

He can deliver checkmate in at most three moves with the stunning queen offer **28...♕h3+!** and then:

a) **29 ♔g1 ♕g2#.**

b) **29 ♔xh3 ♖h8+ 30 ♗h6 ♖xh6#.**

Solution to puzzle (posed before Game 9)

The position you were given arose near the end of Alburt-Mestel, Thessaloniki Olympiad 1984. Grandmaster Jonathan Mestel played 1...e4 (presumably to avoid any problems with ♗c2) and in fact won quickly. However, an efficient and foolproof alternative, in which almost every move by Black is a star check, is **1...♗d4+ 2 ♔c1 ♕a3+!** and now:

a) **3 ♔d2 ♕e3+ 4 ♔c2 ♖c7+ 5 ♔b1 ♖c1#.**

b) **3 ♔c2 ♖c7+** and then **4 ♔b1
♖c1#** or **4 ♔d2 ♕e3#**.

c) **3 ♔b1 ♖b7+ 4 ♗b3** *(D)*.

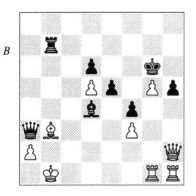

4...♖xb3+! 5 axb3 ♕xb3+ 6 ♔c1
♗e3+ 7 ♕d2 ♕c3+! 8 ♔b1 ♗xd2.
This last move is unfortunately not
check, but capturing a queen is pretty
good too! Another lovely example of
harmony between a queen and bishop
can be found in the rapidly approaching Star Test.

Star Test

In each of the examples (except 3.6) it
is *White to play and win*. Having the
next move often gives very precious
possibilities to seize the initiative, and
in all but one of the following cases
White blends efficient manoeuvres
with star tactics to clinch victory before the opponent has time to retaliate.
The elegant solutions appear on pages
233-5.

3.1

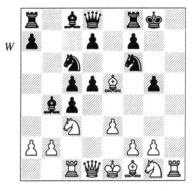

Can you also identify the opening
that led to this position?

3.2

W

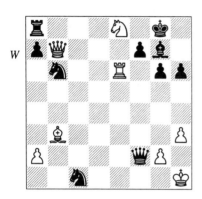

3.4

W

3.3

W

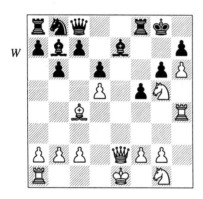

3.5

W

3.6: 'Beam me up Scotty!'

This puzzle of mine celebrates the 30th anniversary of the TV series *Star Trek*, first shown in the USA on 15 September 1967.

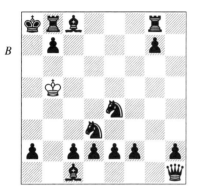

Star Trek is full of wonderful fantasy ideas, so let us allow White's king to say 'Beam me up Scotty' and he will automatically be transported from b5 to any square he chooses where he is not in check. In addition, White's king can select *one* other white piece to be beamed onto a square adjacent to his new position, but the extra piece is not allowed to give check where it lands. It is now Black to move, and as you see he still has his entire army, yet he cannot prevent White winning.

'Please explain', as Captain Kirk so often says to Mr Spock.

Star Challenge no. 3: Thirteen is lucky after all!

Part 'a' of this puzzle is one of my little brainteasers designed to exercise our skills in logic, and part 'b' is a brilliant 1970 creation from the mind of Belgium's Fernand Joseph, who has already treated us to other stunning problems earlier in *S.T.A.R. Chess*.

Mr Price buys 13 chess clocks for a total of £527. The normal price for each clock is a certain whole number of pounds sterling, but after buying a small minimum number of clocks, the man is given £10 discount on *each* further clock.

a) What is the normal price for each chess clock, and how many clocks did Mr Price purchase at the special reduced price? (£1 is worth about 1.6$ US.)

b) To celebrate his bargain buy of 13 clocks, the man decides to compose a 'checkmate in 13 moves' problem *(D)*.

Black threatens to deliver mate in two, but before he has time to say '*Star Wars* is coming', White plays and wins.

4 S.T.A.R. Wars

In this chapter, we will enjoy games loaded with even more action than the American film director George Lucas packed into all 116 minutes of his 1977 blockbuster movie *Star Wars*. However, first let's press the rewind button in order to look back on and summarize what we have seen so far in *S.T.A.R. Chess*. Kings have been in perpetual peril throughout many attacking games, and some of those encounters were also chosen to increase our knowledge and understanding of the fiery Sicilian Dragon that lit up Chapter 1.

Whatever opening one plays, the four factors of self, position, opponent, time will affect the game enormously. So will one's ability to spot the star piece that should best make the next move at each stage. Numerous examples in Chapter 2 were designed to improve our skills in those vitally important areas.

Besides energetic attacking play, the key element of time was an obvious common factor connecting Chapters 2 and 3. However, the latter chapter also linked time to efficient manoeuvres, which can lead to precious opportunities to seize the initiative. At such moments, and indeed at virtually all times in chess, we must be alert to tactical possibilities. So every chapter is overflowing with places where we can sharpen our tactical vision.

In the current **S.T.A.R. Wars** chapter, *tactics* abound more than ever before, and the games continue to feature a variety of openings, which also leads to different types of *strategy*. Nevertheless, *attack* still remains the ultimate goal of the plan in all cases, but of course each player must always try to be ready with a strong *reaction* to counter the opponent's ideas. In another context, Isaac Newton (the brilliant English mathematician and natural philosopher who lived from 1642 to 1727) said 'To every action there is an equal and opposite reaction'. We can apply his law effectively on the chessboard.

Our star motto ('There is no man living who isn't capable of doing more than he thinks he can do') reminds us that no part of S.T.A.R. is beyond our reach, but in this chapter we can sit back and enjoy a sparkling show of strategy, tactics, attack and reaction, bursting forth from numerous really exciting games played by many bright chess stars. All the ideas which we are building up are relevant throughout our adventure together, but at any given stage we will concentrate on the main topic being discussed at that point.

Clear explanatory notes should ensure that there is nothing 'double Dutch' about the forthcoming encounter between Holland's GM John van der Wiel and IM Leon Pliester. However, let's warm up first of all with a dose of hot tactics.

Strike while it's hot

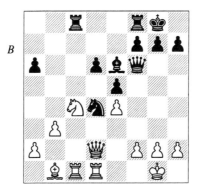

B

This position arose from White's 18th move in De Vreugt-Van der Wiel in the penultimate round of the Vlissingen Open 1997. With one really powerful move, the 1979 European Junior Champion playing Black made his young opponent resign. As you search for the winning move, may the force be with you! The solution can be checked after the first of our star wars, which took place on Monday 7 July 1997, three days before the aforementioned game in the Dutch town of Vlissingen. Does that mean Grandmaster John van der Wiel was not fully fired up yet? No, quite the opposite! Play on and see...

Game 10
J. van der Wiel – L. Pliester
Vlissingen 1997
French Defence

1	e4	e6
2	d4	d5
3	♘d2	♘f6

Chapter 4 in *C.O.O.L. Chess* is called *French Connection*, and there I supported my recommendation for 3...dxe4 with a lot of analysis and explanations.

4 e5

4 ♗d3 is an interesting way for White to maintain the tension between pawns in the centre. A.Grant-G.Nolan, Scottish Ch, Aviemore 1997 continued **4...dxe4** (4...c5 can be met for example by 5 e5 or 5 c3, the latter choice being consistent with the idea of keeping the central tension) **5 ♘xe4 ♘xe4** (5...♕xd4?? loses the queen to 6 ♗b5+, but 5...♘bd7 6 ♘f3 c5 7 dxc5 ♗xc5!? 8 ♘xc5 ♘xc5 transposes to a position that I have seen Russian GM

Alexei Dreev play with success as Black) **6 ♗xe4 ♘d7 7 ♘f3 ♘f6 8 ♗d3 ♗e7** (to me it seems more natural to react in the centre immediately with 8...c5, since Black is slightly cramped so it is logical to try to obtain more space and freedom for manoeuvring, and furthermore if White plays 9 dxc5, then Black can make the recapture 9...♗xc5 without losing a tempo on ...♗e7 first) **9 ♕e2 0-0 10 ♗g5 c5** (10...♘d5?! 11 ♗d2 {11 h4!?} 11...♗f6 12 0-0-0 a5 13 h4 ♘b4? 14 ♗xh7+! produces the same instructive winning 'Greek gift' sacrifice as occurred on page 103 of *H.O.T. Chess*, except that the move number is increased by one here) **11 0-0-0** (11 dxc5 ♕a5+ is an alternative path, but Alan Grant tends to favour a more enterprising approach) **11...♕a5** (after 11...cxd4 12 ♘xd4?! {either 12 ♗c4 or 12 ♔b1 looks much better}, 12...♕a5! makes a lot of sense for Black because White's units on a2 and g5 are attacked simultaneously, but 12...♕xd4 13 ♗xh7+ ♘xh7 14 ♖xd4 ♗xg5+ 15 f4 ♗f6 16 ♖d3 is very double-edged) **12 ♔b1 cxd4 13 ♘e5!** (very interesting play by White: he has sacrificed a pawn, but is now causing Black severe development problems concerning the c8-bishop in particular, as 13...♗d7?? loses a piece to 14 ♗xf6 ♗xf6 15 ♘xd7) **13...♖d8?** *(D).*

14 f4. Alan rejected 14 ♗xf6! here, but to discover his probable reason(s), let's examine both of Black's possible recaptures on f6:

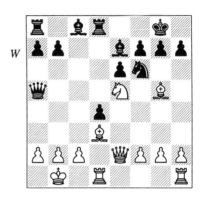

a) 14...gxf6? 15 ♗xh7+! wins for White in a clear fashion as follows:

a1) 15...♔xh7 16 ♕h5+ ♔g7 17 ♕xf7+ ♔h8 (17...♔h6 18 ♕g6#) 18 ♘g6#.

a2) 15...♔h8 16 ♕h5! ♕xe5 17 ♗f5+ ♔g7 18 ♕h7+ ♔f8 19 ♕h8#.

a3) 15...♔f8 16 ♕g4! with the deadly threat of ♕g8#.

a4) 15...♔g7 16 ♕g4+ and now 16...♔xh7 or 16...♔h8 will transpose, apart from the move number, to variations 'a1' or 'a2' respectively, whereas 16...♔h6 17 ♖d3! planning ♖h3# is the end of the road for Black.

b) 14...♗xf6 15 ♗xh7+ leads to the following lines:

b1) 15...♔xh7? 16 ♕h5+ ♔g8 17 ♕xf7+ ♔h7 18 ♖d3! ♗g5 19 ♖h3+ ♗h6 20 ♖xh6+! ♔xh6 21 ♕g6#.

b2) 15...♔f8 16 f4 (16 ♘g4 is also possible) 16...g6 17 h4 ♔g7 traps the bishop on h7, but 18 h5 still gives White an irresistible attack. A plausible finish is 18...♖h8 19 hxg6 fxg6 20 ♗xg6 ♖xh1 21 ♖xh1 ♗xe5 22 ♖h7+ ♔xg6 23 ♕h5+ ♔f6, and White can choose between 24 ♖f7#, 24 ♕f7# and 24 ♕g5#.

b3) 15...♔h8. This move looked unlikely to me at first, but the logic behind it is that White's knight and bishop are *en prise* simultaneously. Play now branches into:

b31) 16 ♕h5? ♕xe5 17 ♕h3 (17 ♗f5+ ♔g8 does not trouble Black either) 17...♕g5, intending ...♕h6, wins easily for Black.

b32) 16 ♘xf7+ ♔xh7 17 ♘xd8 ♕xd8 is not at all convincing for White.

b33) 16 ♘c4! ♕c5 17 ♗d3, and White stands very well. The manoeuvre ♘d2-e4 is available, but most importantly, Black's king is exposed.

It is possible that Alan Grant miscalculated one of the earlier variations, although I find that unlikely because his tactical vision is normally excellent. It seems more probable to me that, after so many moves which gave check in variations 'a1' through to 'b32' inclusive, the strength of a retreat such as 15 ♘c4 in variation 'b33' could easily be overlooked or underestimated. I, for one, did not expect it to be White's best line resulting from correct play by both players after 14 ♗xf6, but I now believe that it is. Nevertheless, Black still has big problems after the move actually played, 14 f4. Indeed, it is possible that Alan deliberately rejected 14 ♗xf6 in favour of 14 f4 because he considered it to preserve all of White's attacking forces and potential, without yet releasing any of

that power through an exchange of material on f6. In any case, Black's position soon caved in under the pressure, as follows: **14...♗d7?** (14...h6 15 h4! is a very worrying line, as shown by little samples like 15...hxg5? 16 hxg5 ♘d5 17 ♖h8+ {or 17 ♕h5} 17...♔xh8 18 ♕h5+ ♔g8 19 ♕h7+ ♔f8 20 ♕h8#; however 15...♔f8 is a much more tenacious defence, but of course it's not always easy to keep cool and calm when one is under heavy attack) **15 ♗xf6 ♗xf6** *(D)*.

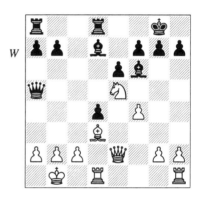

16 ♗xh7+! ♔f8 (16...♔h8 17 ♕h5 gives White a winning attack, and his knight is amply protected {something that was not the case in variation 'b31' of the notes following 14 f4}, whereas 16...♔xh7 17 ♕h5+ finishes Black in much the same way as variation 'b1' went) **17 ♕h5 ♗xe5** (17...♗e8? costs Black his queen to 18 ♘d7+ or 18 ♘g6+, followed in either case by 19 ♕xa5) **18 fxe5 ♗e8 19 ♖hf1 f5 20 ♕g5 ♕xe5 21 ♗xf5! ♗f7 22 ♖de1 ♕b5** (after 22...♕f6, the line 23 ♗xe6

♕xg5 24 ♖xf7+ is very tempting due
to 24...♔g8 25 ♖f5+, but unfortunately 24...♔e8 25 ♗b3+ does not
checkmate Black since he has the resource 25...♕e3, and so White should
simply play 23 ♕xf6 gxf6 24 ♗xe6)
23 a4! (a deflecting move) **23...♕c5
24 ♖xe6! ♖e8 25 ♕h4!** (yet another
star move by Alan Grant persuades
Black to call it a day) **1-0**. Graeme No-
lan resigned facing the threat of ♕h8+,
and also because of 25...♗xe6 26
♗xe6+ ♕f5 27 ♖xf5#.

OK, let's rejoin the main game now
to see Black's fourth move.

4   ...   ♘fd7

4...♘e4 5 ♘xe4 dxe4 6 ♗c4 c5 is a
line that has been tried by some strong
players as Black, but two star games in
particular suggest that **7 d5** is really
powerful for White:

a) The game Onishchuk-Hertneck,
Biel 1997 continued **7...♕b6** (threatening ...♕b4+, whereas after 7...exd5
8 ♗xd5 White threatens 9 ♗xf7+! and
9 ♗xe4) **8 c3** (a calm reaction) **8...♘d7
9 f4 exd5 10 ♕xd5 ♘g6 11 ♘e2 ♗e7**
(Black loses his f-pawn if he captures
on g2, and 11...♘b6 fails due to 12
♗b5+) **12 ♘g3! ♗h4 13 0-0 ♗xg3 14
hxg3 0-0 15 f5 ♕xg3 16 ♗f4!** (deadly
development) **16...♕g4 17 e6 fxe6 18
fxe6 ♘b6** *(D)*.

19 e7+!! (this move destroys the
black position) **19...♘xd5 20 exf8♕+
♔xf8 21 ♗d6++ ♔e8 22 ♗b5+ ♗d7
23 ♖f8#**. Displaying this brilliant
form throughout most of his other nine
games at Biel, Grandmaster Alexander

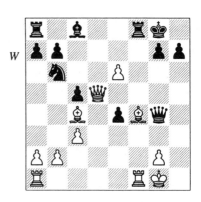

Onishchuk won the tournament with a
massive 8½/10 score, 3½ points ahead
of the three GMs in joint runner-up
spot!

b) The game Kindermann-Dobosz,
Bern 1995 continued **7...♘d7 8 dxe6
fxe6 9 ♘h3!** (this developing move
does not restrict the scope of White's
queen, a fact which is soon shown to
be important) **9...♘xe5 10 ♕h5+ ♘f7**
(after 10...♘g6, White has 11 ♘g5
with a triple attack against black
pawns) **11 ♘g5 g6 12 ♕g4** (White
does not mind being a pawn down
temporarily because his army is well
ahead in terms of mobility and Black's
position is riddled with weaknesses)
12...♘e5 13 ♗b5+ ♔e7 14 ♕h4! (this
move threatens an assortment of deadly
discovered checks) **14...♕a5+ 15 ♗d2
♕xb5 16 ♗c3 ♗g7 17 ♘xe4+ ♔f8 18
0-0-0!** (in effect it is Black rather than
White who is down on material because the pieces scattered along the
eighth rank are in no position to help
their king, who is threatened with 19
♖d8+ ♔f7 20 ♘d6#) **18...♘f7** (after

18...♗d7 19 ♕f4+ ♘f7 20 ♘g5 {easier than 20 ♘d6 ♗h6} 20...♗e8 21 ♗xg7+ ♔xg7 22 ♘xe6+ ♔g8 23 ♕f6, checkmate follows on g7 not later than move 25) **19 ♗xg7+ ♔xg7 20 ♕f6+ ♔g8** *(D)*.

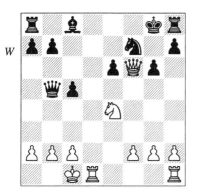

21 ♘g5 1-0. IM Jan Dobosz resigned in anticipation of 21...♕e8 22 ♘xf7 ♕xf7 23 ♖d8+ ♕f8 24 ♖xf8#. GM Stefan Kindermann conducted a typically attacking game, and more similar goodies await us in the main battle.

5 c3

White does not declare yet whether he intends to follow up with ♗d3 or f4. In fact, we will soon see that Van der Wiel favours the system with f4, but even if ♗d3 were his preferred line, I think it is more accurate and flexible to play c3 first. Why? Well, the reason is that Black might play 5...b6 followed by ...♗a6, a pet line of GM Nigel Short. In that case, White can play ♗f1xa6 without losing a tempo on ♗d3 first.

Some players may omit the move c3 in favour of 5 ♘gf3 c5 6 c4, as in Kengis-Farago, Vienna 1991, for example. However, in my opinion the tension in the centre favours Black after 6...♘c6.

5 ... c5
6 f4

After **6 ♗d3 ♘c6 7 ♘e2 cxd4** (7...f6?! 8 ♘f4) **8 cxd4 f6**, let's take a look at three responses for White. The last of them leads to some particularly interesting play, so I'll keep you in suspense for a little while (no cheating and looking ahead now!).

a) **9 ♘f4 ♘xd4 10 ♕h5+ ♔e7 11 ♘g6+ hxg6 12 ♕xh8?** (12 exf6+ ♘xf6 13 ♕xh8 ♔f7 is a sharp theoretical line in which Black is slightly behind on material {basically, ♘+♙ vs ♖} by conventional standards, but his dangerous duo of central pawns can advance and cause White problems) **12...♘xe5 13 ♕h3** *(D)* occurred in a training game Eynon-Nolan, Glasgow 1996.

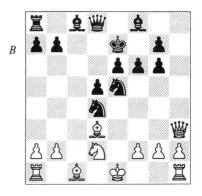

Perhaps it is slightly surprising, but Black could now have won practically by force with **13...♘xd3+! 14 ♕xd3 e5** (threatening ...♗f5) **15 0-0 ♗f5 16 ♕a3+** (16 ♕c3? and 16 ♕g3? lose instantly to the fork 16...♘e2+) **16...♔f7 17 ♕a4 b5 18 ♕d1** (18 ♕a6? ♗c8! traps White's queen) **18...♗c2 19 ♕g4** (19 ♕e1 ♗d3) **19...♗d3 20 ♖e1** (20 ♖d1 ♗e2) **20...♘c2.** After the error at move 12, it is unlikely that White could escape alive.

b) The game Upton-Norris, Aviemore 1997 went **9 exf6** (this option is the one most often played) **9...♕xf6!?** (a rare yet very nice, active, developing move that is a refreshing change from 9...♘xf6) **10 ♘f3 h6** (a prophylactic move to prevent White from harassing Black's queen with ♗g5) **11 0-0** (11 ♘f4 ♗b4+ 12 ♗d2? ♕xf4! costs White a piece) **11...♗d6 12 ♘c3** (I prefer 12 ♘g3 so as to have better defensive and attacking capabilities on the kingside) **12...0-0 13 ♗e3 ♖d8!? 14 ♖c1 ♘f8**, currently intending the manoeuvre ...♗d7-e8-h5. It is not easy for White to generate threats against Black's solid, flexible, improving position, and indeed Alan Norris won a fine game in 32 moves.

c) **9 f4? fxe5 10 fxe5** *(D)* falls into a trap:

10...♘xd4!, but instead of 11 ♘xd4 ♕h4+, the continuation **11 0-0** gives a potentially dangerous lead in development. For example, I have seen two quick wins for White after the plausible-looking move **11...♗c5?!**:

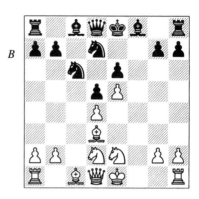

B

c1) Starostits-Jankovskis, Latvian Ch 1997 went **12 ♔h1 ♘xe2** (12...♘xe5 13 ♘xd4 ♘xd3 {after 13...♗xd4 14 ♘b3, 14...♘xd3 15 ♘xd4 transposes into the main line of analysis here, whereas 14...♗b6 loses instantly to 15 ♕h5+} 14 ♘2b3 ♗xd4 15 ♘xd4 ♘xc1 16 ♕h5+ g6 17 ♕e5 is crushing for White since Black's king is exposed, unable to castle, and his pieces are not in a position to defend) **13 ♕xe2 ♘f8 14 ♘b3 ♗b6 15 ♕h5+ g6 16 ♕h6** (threatening ♕g7) **16...♕c7 17 ♗g5 ♖g8** (planning ...♕g7) **18 ♗f6 ♗d7 19 ♖f3 ♗a4 20 ♖af1** (Starostits has amassed an irresistible amount of firepower against Black's disorganized army) **20...♘d7 21 ♗g5 ♕xe5 22 ♕xh7 ♕g7** *(D)*.

23 ♗xg6+! 1-0, due to 23...♕xg6 24 ♕e7#.

c2) Medjedović-Bosković, Yugoslav Ch 1993 was equally devastating: **12 ♘xd4 ♗xd4+ 13 ♔h1 g6** (White was threatening ♕h5+, but notes at move 12 to the game in 'c1' showed that 13...♘xe5 14 ♘b3 ♘xd3 15 ♘xd4 is

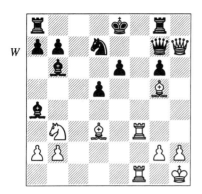

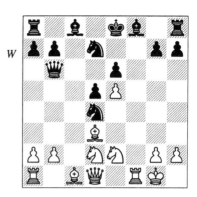

hopeless for Black) **14 ♕g4 ♕b6 15 ♘f3 ♗xe5** (15...♘xe5 16 ♘xe5 ♗xe5 17 ♗g5 puts Black in his recurring nightmare of being unable to castle on either side of the board, and after 17...♗d7 18 ♕f3 there is no satisfactory defence to the threat of ♕f7#) **16 ♗xg6+! ♔e7** (16...hxg6 17 ♕xg6+ ♔e7 18 ♘xe5 ♘xe5 19 ♕f6+ also finishes Black off) **17 ♘xe5 ♘xe5 18 ♕g5+ ♔d6 19 ♗f4 ♕d4 20 ♖ae1 1-0**.

In the games of 'c1' and 'c2', did you notice how much Black missed not having protection on the kingside from his dark-squared bishop? Certain sensitive dark squares collapsed into White's lap as Black no longer had a bishop on f8. Logically then, if it was correct to win a pawn with 10...♘xd4 but wrong to play 11...♗c5, Black's improvement must be waiting to be discovered at move 11. With that thought in mind, I found **11...♕b6!** *(D)*.

It suddenly becomes apparent that 12 ♘xd4 is not an option as 12...♕xd4+ attacks the d3-bishop. Furthermore, after 12 ♔h1 ♘xe5, White is very hard

pushed to demonstrate any real compensation for his two sacrificed central pawns.

Conclusions:

1) Strong moves in defence and counterattack can refute unsound attacking moves, no matter how dangerous certain games may make the attack seem.

2) It is good to learn from lots of games, irrespective of whether the opening lines featured are part of one's normal repertoire or not. However, it is also wise to check other players' ideas for oneself. Often improvements and/or novelties such as 11...♕b6! can be found through personal input, particularly if the big bonus of having a friend's help is being added too.

| **6** | **...** | **cxd4** |

Here, the most common course chosen by Black is **6...♘c6 7 ♘df3 ♕b6** to maintain the central tension and to pressurize White's d-pawn in particular. Let's see two instructive examples:

a) **8 ♘e2** transposes to Dolmatov-Bareev, Russian Ch, Elista 1997, which continued **8...f6 9 g3 cxd4 10 cxd4?!** (this allows Black to develop with gain of time by ...♗b4+, so I prefer 10 ♘exd4, planning to meet 10...fxe5? with 11 ♘xe6 or 11 fxe5 ♘dxe5 12 ♘xe5 ♘xe5 13 ♕h5+ ♘f7 {13...♘g6 14 ♗d3} 14 ♗b5+ ♔e7 15 0-0 with a winning attack for White) **10...fxe5 11 fxe5 ♗b4+ 12 ♘c3** (12 ♔f2? loses a pawn to 12...♘dxe5 13 ♘xe5 ♘xe5, whereas after 12 ♗d2 0-0 13 ♗g2 ♘dxe5!! 14 dxe5 ♘xe5 Black threatens 15...♘xf3+ and 15...♘d3+ 16 ♔f1 ♕f2#, yet 15 ♘xe5? allows 15...♕f2# immediately, while 15 ♘f4 fails to 15...♕e3+ and then 16 ♕e2 ♘xf3+ 17 ♗xf3 ♗xd2+ or 16 ♔f1 ♗xd2 17 ♕xd2 ♕xd2 18 ♘xd2 g5; another pretty variation is 15 ♗xb4 ♕xb4+ 16 ♔f2 ♕e4 17 ♘f4? ♘g4+ 18 ♔g1 ♕e3+ 19 ♔f1 ♕f2#) **12...0-0** (threatening 13...♖xf3! 14 ♕xf3 ♘xd4 15 ♕f2 ♘xe5 and 13...♘dxe5! 14 dxe5 ♘xe5 15 ♗e2 {15 ♘d4 ♕xd4! 16 ♕xd4 ♘f3+ also wins for Black} 15...♘xf3+ 16 ♗xf3 d4 17 a3 dxc3 18 axb4 cxb2 19 ♗xb2 ♕xb4+ 20 ♕d2 ♕xd2+ 21 ♔xd2 ♖xf3 and Black is three pawns ahead) **13 ♗f4 ♗e7!** (threatening ...♕xb2) **14 ♕d2** *(D)*.

14...g5!! 15 ♘xg5 ♗xg5 16 ♗xg5 ♘xd4 (White's central pawns start to dissolve) **17 ♗g2 ♘xe5 18 0-0-0 ♖f2!!** (the force of this star rook move is like that of a castle landing on White's head!) **19 ♕xf2** (19 ♕xd4 ♕xb2#) **19...♘b3+ 20 axb3 ♕xf2 21 ♖d2 ♕f5**

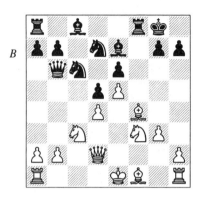

B

22 ♗h6 ♘d3+ 23 ♔d1 ♘f2+ 0-1. GM Sergei Dolmatov resigned, faced with further loss of material. Being able to look back on this brilliant miniature victory must have been some consolation to GM Evgeny Bareev after losing the final of the Russian Championship to St Petersburg's Grandmaster Peter Svidler. That remarkable young man, who celebrated his 21st birthday on Tuesday 17 June 1997, has now won his national championship three times ... so far!

b) Returning to Vlissingen now, two rounds before our main game was played, Van der Wiel-Van Driel saw **8 a3!** *(D)*.

On the evening of that same day (5 July), I drove from The Hague to Vlissingen because I had been invited by one of the principal organizers, Hans Groffen, to commentate on the games of the first round. This was the third time since 1995 that the little Dutch town was hosting a really big tournament, and the friendly atmosphere and excellent conditions are

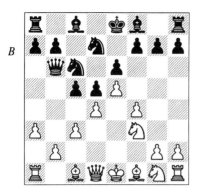

B

such that the many entrants attracted to this year's event included nine grandmasters and ten other titled players. Therefore I knew that as I stood beside a row of demonstration boards talking to an excited audience, star moves would be flying in from all directions. The game we left at the last diagram particularly caught my attention, and a few hours later I said to GM John van der Wiel, 'John, I think the move 8 a3 is very interesting and a bit unusual'. He replied 'It's a bit good too!', and then John told me that he had picked up the little-known idea from seeing some games by GM Alexander Ivanov. We then discussed Dolmatov-Bareev, and agreed that 8 a3 not only stops problems with ...♗b4+, but also threatens b2-b4.

That explains why Erik van Driel played **8...a5**, and the game continued **9 ♘e2 f6** (9...cxd4 10 cxd4 f6 11 ♘c3 {threatening f5 to undermine Black's e6-d5 pawn chain} 11...♗e7 12 ♗e3!? fxe5 {12...♕xb2?? 13 ♘a4 traps the queen that ate the poisoned b-pawn}

13 fxe5 ♘dxe5 14 ♘xe5 ♘xe5 15 ♕h5+ ♘g6 16 ♗b5+ gave White excellent compensation for one sacrificed pawn in a quickplay tie-break game Van der Wiel-Apicella, Linares Zonal 1995, but John pointed out that because his rapid encounter did not get picked up by ChessBase, the move 8 a3 is less well known than it might have otherwise been) **10 g3 cxd4 11 cxd4 ♗e7 12 ♗h3 ♘db8** (12...f5 13 g4 is also nice for White) **13 0-0 0-0 14 ♔h1** (avoiding any problems emanating from Black's queen on the g1-a7 diagonal) **14...♘a6** (this reminds me of the L.I.Q.D. concept that cropped up in the notes to White's seventh move of Game 4, since although Black may not seem to be behind in terms of quantity of development, quality is a big problem since he is cramped, and so his pieces are very short of space in which to manoeuvre and purposeful places to go to) **15 ♘c3** (threatening f5 to break up Black's central pawn chain) **15...♘c7 16 ♗e3!? ♗d7** (16...♕xb2 17 ♘a4 ♕b5 18 ♖b1 ♕a6 19 ♘b6 ♖b8 leaves Black very tied up but with an extra pawn to console himself, although after 20 ♕b3, for example, White has lots of compensation) **17 exf6 ♗xf6?!** (17...♖xf6 is more tenacious because leaving the bishop on e7 enables Black to make the capture ...♗xc5 if White plays the manoeuvre ♘a4-c5) **18 ♘a4 ♕a7 19 ♘c5 ♗c8?!** (19...♖ad8 is relatively best, but Black's cramped position would still be unenviable and without prospects) **20 ♖c1**

♕b6 21 ♕c2 ♖e8 22 ♘e5 (the pressure on Black is mounting to an unbearable level) 22...♘a6 23 ♘a4 ♕a7 24 ♕b3! (this multi-purpose move threatens ♘b6, eyes the enemy king along the a2-g8 diagonal, sets the trap 24...♘xd4? 25 ♕d3, and avoids 24 ♘xc6 bxc6 25 ♕xc6? ♗d7 26 ♕c2 ♗xd4, which would let Black bounce back into the game with some activity) 24...♖b8 25 ♘b6 ♗d8 (D).

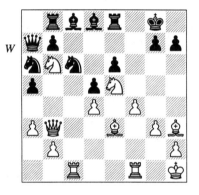

26 ♘xd5!! ♔h8 (the line 26...exd5 27 ♕xd5+ ♔h8 28 ♘f7+ ♔g8 29 ♘h6++ ♔h8 30 ♕g8+! ♖xg8 31 ♘f7# is a typical example illustrating 'smothered mate') 27 ♘f7+ ♔g8 28 ♘d6 1-0. Black resigned on account of 28...♖f8 29 ♘xc8 ♖xc8 30 ♗xe6+ ♔h8 31 ♗xc8.

Being a Gemini myself, I like twins. So after that smooth, controlled performance by John van der Wiel, let's rejoin the main game at move seven for another dose of excellent play by this Dutch star.

7 cxd4 ♘c6

8 ♘df3

This move gives White's other knight the opportunity to support the d-pawn by developing to e2 later, and is therefore much more logical than 8 ♘gf3.

8 ... ♕b6

8...♗b4+ favours White after either 9 ♔f2, planning to gain time with a3, or 9 ♗d2 to exchange dark-squared bishops and leave Black with his very restricted light-squared bishop.

9 a3!

Once again, stopping ...♗b4+ and threatening to expand on the queenside with b2-b4.

9 ... a5
10 ♘e2 ♗e7 (D)

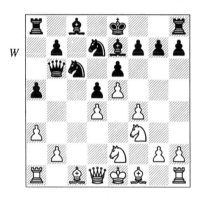

11 f5!?

I am delighted to be able to feature a star example of the cool motto 'f for forward'! White has found a quick way to attack, based on the tactical point that after 11...exf5 12 ♘f4, Black cannot save his d-pawn.

11 ... f6!

A brave reaction from IM Leon Pliester, who is planning 12 fxe6 ♘f8 13 ♘f4 ♗xe6.

12 ♘f4   fxe5!

After 12...♘f8, White is not obliged to make the capture fxe6. Instead, the developing move 13 ♗d3! keeps the black pieces boxed in. It is also an example of putting into practice the saying 'The threat is stronger than its execution' because the possibility of fxe6 still hangs over Black, as well as other unpleasant moves like ♘h5. Of course, in further support of 13 ♗d3, there is the small but important tactical detail 13...♘xd4?? 14 ♘xd4 ♕xd4 15 ♗b5+, winning the black queen on d4.

13 ♘xe6   ♗f6
14 ♘fg5

This attacking move lacks the subtlety of an Alfred Hitchcock movie plot, but the threat of ♕h5+ makes it just as scary! Alternatively, 14 dxe5 ♘dxe5 15 ♕xd5 leads to some fascinating lines. For example, 15...♗xe6!? 16 ♕xe6+ ♔f8 (threatening ...♖e8) 17 ♘xe5 ♗xe5 18 ♗c4 ♗g3+! *(D)* and now:

a) After 19 hxg3 ♖e8, I prefer Black's position.

b) 19 ♔d1? (19 ♔f1?? ♕f2#) 19...♖d8+ 20 ♗d2 (20 ♗d5 ♕b3+!) 20...♖xd2+! 21 ♔xd2 ♕xb2+ branches into:

b1) 22 ♔e3 ♗f2+ 23 ♔e4 (23 ♔d3 ♘e5+ 24 ♔e4 ♕d4#) 23...♕d4+ 24 ♔f3 ♘e5+ 25 ♔e2 ♕b2+ and Black wins.

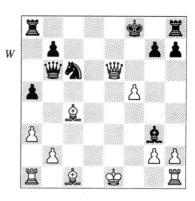

b2) 22 ♔d3 ♘e5+ 23 ♔e3 (23 ♔e4 ♕xg2+) 23...♕f2+ 24 ♔e4 ♕f4+ 25 ♔d5 ♕xc4+ 26 ♔d6 ♕c6#.

Such lines are actually a logical result of the fact that if White plays to win a pawn with 14 dxe5 and 15 ♕xd5, then Black's pieces spring to life quickly and seize the initiative by creating threats against White's two royal pieces in particular. In contrast, the move 14 ♘fg5 fights to keep the initiative. Let's see how Black reacts to it.

14 ...   g6?

14...♘xd4! merits attention. For example, after 15 ♕h5+ ♔e7 16 ♕f7+ ♔d6, I see nothing clear for White. That is especially because 17 ♘xd4 ♕xd4 18 ♕e6+ ♔c7 19 ♘f7 (threatening 20 ♕d6# and 20 ♘xh8) is met by 19...♕e4+, e.g.: 20 ♗e2 ♖a6!; 20 ♔f2 ♕c2+ 21 ♔g3 (21 ♔g1?? ♕c5+ 22 ♗e3 ♕xe3#) 21...♕b3+ 22 ♔f2 (22 ♔g4?? h5#) 22...♕c2+, and the position starts to be repeated, soon leading to a draw; 20 ♔d1 ♕a4+ and then 21 b3 ♕d4+! or 21 ♔d2 ♕d4+ 22

♔c2 ♕e4+ 23 ♗d3? (White should settle for a draw by repeating the position with 23 ♔d1 ♕a4+ and so on) 23...♕xd3+! 24 ♔xd3 ♘c5+ 25 ♔e2 ♗xe6 26 ♘xh8 ♗xf5 27 ♘f7 ♘b3 28 ♖a2 ♗b1, and the rook on a2 is tied up like the Staffordshire knot!

Therefore **15 ♘xd4** should be considered, and then:

a) **15...exd4?** 16 ♕h5+ ♔e7 17 ♕f7+ ♔d6 (17...♔d8 loses to 18 ♘e6+) 18 ♕e6+ ♔c5 (18...♔c7 19 ♗f4+ ♔d8 20 ♘f7#) 19 b4+! axb4 20 ♗f4! (threatening 21 ♖c1# and 21 ♘e4+ dxe4 22 ♕c4#) 20...♕xe6+ 21 ♘xe6+ ♔b6 (21...♔c6 22 ♖c1+) 22 ♗c7+ ♔a7 23 axb4# is one of my favourite lines in this book.

b) **15...♕xd4** 16 ♕xd4 (the line 16 ♕h5+ ♔e7 17 ♕f7+ ♔d6 transposes to earlier analysis which showed that route to be unconvincing for White) 16...exd4 17 ♘e6 ♗e5 18 ♗b5 ♔e7 19 0-0 gives White some initiative as compensation for his deficit of one pawn, but with careful play Black should be fine.

15 fxg6

On his last move, I did not like the option 14 dxe5 for White. However, one must constantly take account of the changes that each move played has made to the position. Here, 15 dxe5 ♘dxe5 16 ♕xd5 looks quite reasonable, largely because the move 14...g6 has left the f6-bishop unprotected, and so 17 ♘e4 is a threat. Still, the actual game continuation is also good for White.

15 ...   hxg6
16 ♕d3!

White chooses this move rather than 16 ♕c2 so that 16...e4 could now be answered by 17 ♕g3, threatening the fork ♘c7+.

16 ...   ♘e7
17 ♕c2!   ♖b8 (D)

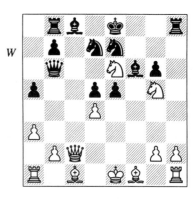

18 ♗b5!

18 ♘c7+ ♔d8?? 19 ♘f7# is possible but not likely (since Black would, of course, choose 18...♔f8), so White plays with more purpose by developing a piece, and he uses the fact that 18...♕xb5?? loses to 19 ♘c7+.

18 ...   ♗xg5

Black does not have time for 18...exd4 in view of 19 ♖f1! (threatening ♖xf6) 19...♗xg5 20 ♘c7+! ♔d8 21 ♗xg5, threatening 22 ♖f7 or 22 ♗xe7+ ♔xe7 23 ♘xd5+.

19 ♘c7+   ♔f7

19...♔d8? 20 ♗xg5 ♕xc7? 21 ♗xe7+ ♔xe7 22 ♕xc7 makes Black's queen vanish like a blip that suddenly goes dead on a radar screen.

20 ♗xg5 ♘f5

20...♕xd4? loses by force to 21 ♖f1+ ♘f5 22 ♖xf5+! gxf5 23 ♕xf5+ ♚g8 24 ♕g6+ ♚f8 25 ♘e6#.

21 0-0-0 ♘xd4

22 ♖xd4! exd4

22...♕xd4 loses to 23 ♖f1+, similar to the previous note.

23 ♖f1+ ♚g7 (D)

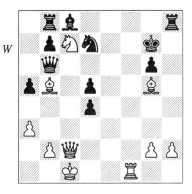

24 ♖e1!

Threatening a deadly invasion on the seventh rank.

24 ... ♖xh2

Other plausible lines are:

a) **24...♖h7** 25 ♘e6+ (25 ♖e6 ♕c5) 25...♚f7 (if 25...♚h8, then 26 ♕xg6 threatens ♕e8+) 26 ♖f1+! ♚xe6 27 ♕xg6+ ♚e5 28 ♗f4#.

b) In my analysis, I found **24...♘f6**, intending ...♗f5, to be a very tough nut to crack. For instance:

b1) At first I wanted to play the spectacular sacrificial line **25 ♖e7+** ♚f8 26 ♕xg6 ♕c5+ 27 ♚b1 ♕xe7 28 ♗xf6, hoping for 28...♕xc7?? 29 ♕e8#, but Black has the resource

28...♕h7! pinning White's queen to the king, and then 29 ♗g7+ is answered by 29...♚g8!.

b2) **25 ♗xf6+ ♕xf6 26 ♘e8+** ♖xe8 27 ♖xe8 and then 27...♗f5?? allows 28 ♕c7+, but Black can improve greatly with 27...♕f4+ 28 ♕d2 ♕c7+! with 29 ♚b1 ♗f5+ or 29 ♚d1 ♗g4+ to follow.

b3) In the end, the recurring problems on the b1-h7 diagonal led me to consider **25 ♗d3!?**, which attacks the black g-pawn and defeats 25...♗f5 by 26 ♗xf5 gxf5 27 ♖e6, whereas 25...♕c6 should lose to 26 ♕xc6 bxc6 27 ♖e7+ ♚f8 28 ♗xf6. Furthermore, 25...♖xh2 goes down instantly to 26 ♗xf6+ and then 26...♕xf6 27 ♘e8+ or 26...♚xf6 27 ♘xd5+.

25 ♗d8

Maybe not the most obvious move, but it does threaten a knight check on e6 or e8 followed by capturing Black's queen, which is very short of safe squares to shift to.

25 ... d3

26 ♕xd3 ♕f2

27 ♘e6+

27 ♕c3+ d4 28 ♘e6+ ♚h6 29 ♘xd4 leaves Black facing a multitude of threats, including 30 ♗c7, 30 ♘f3 intending ♕h8#, and 30 ♘f5+ gxf5 (30...♕xf5 31 ♕h8#) 31 ♕h8+ ♚g6 32 ♖e6+ ♚f7 33 ♖e7+ ♚g6 34 ♖g7#.

27 ... ♚h7

28 ♖f1

The players may well have been in time-trouble here after trying to calculate and assess all the complicated earlier lines, so it is quite understandable if errors creep in. However, any inaccuracies now do not alter the fact that White has been on the verge of victory ever since Black's main mistake at move 14. Nevertheless, for the sake of being as precise as possible, I prefer 28 ♕c3! d4 29 ♘xd4, after which White threatens 30 ♖e7+ ♔h6 (30...♔g8 31 ♗c4+) 31 ♘f5+ ♕xf5 32 ♕h8+ ♔g5 33 ♖xd7+ ♔g4 34 ♖d4+ ♔g3 35 ♗c7+ ♔f2 36 ♖d2+ ♔e1 37 ♗g3+ ♕f2 38 ♗xf2#.

It is very important to keep peace inside oneself and harmony within one's chess army. That is even more vital in time-trouble, otherwise good positions can easily turn horribly wrong at alarming speed. To my mind, 28 ♕c3 is a 'harmony move' because it not only threatens ♕g7#, but also protects the e1-rook and the b2- and c2-squares, where Black's major pieces on his seventh rank might potentially threaten checkmate.

28 ... ♘e5

After 28...♕xg2!, 29 ♖f7+ ♔g8! (not 29...♔h8? 30 ♕d4+) 30 ♖g7+ ♔h8 suddenly confronts White with threats of 31...♖h1+ and 31...♕xb2+. Also, 29 ♕c3 d4! 30 ♘xd4 (of course not 30 ♕xd4?? ♕c2#) 30...♖h1 forces the exchange of White's only rook. Therefore 28...♕xg2 gives Black some counterplay.

29 ♘g5+ ♔g7

It would be over-critical to start appending symbols like '?' to many moves after both players have fought

such a terrific and complex battle, so I will simply point out that 29...♔h6 is preferable since it avoids the pin which follows in the game. After 30 ♖xf2 ♘xd3+ 31 ♗xd3 ♗f5, Black is still very much alive.

30 ♕c3 ♕xg2

Especially if he was very short of time, Black may have missed in earlier calculations that 30...d4 fails due to 31 ♕c7+.

31 ♕xe5+ ♔h6

The alternative was 31...♔g8 32 ♕e8+ ♔g7 33 ♕f8#. For a fleeting moment Black now threatens ...♕c2#, but...

32 ♕h8# *(D)*

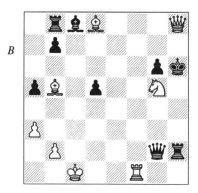

...White gets there first, a bit like an athlete who pips a rival at the end of a hard-fought race by crossing the finishing line some small fraction of a second before the runner-up. In such situations, my very good friend and mentor Paul Fitzpatrick (who was also mentioned at the start of Chapter 2) used to say to me 'Never mind, Paul.

You came in second.' Losses didn't feel too bad then!

Solution to puzzle (posed before Game 10)

In De Vreugt-Van der Wiel, Vlissingen 1997, which I left you to consider some time ago, Black's 18th move **18...♖xc4!!** was extremely powerful. In fact, it was so serious that White resigned in view of 19 bxc4 ♘f3+! 20 gxf3 ♗h3, since he has no satisfactory answer to the dual threats of ...♕g6+ and ...♕xf3, both to be followed by ...♕g2#.

We will find out more about the preceding opening moves when we analyse Game 12 later, but for now let's simply note that 18...♘f3+ is not as strong as the move actually played, as after 19 gxf3 ♗h3, White can fight on with 20 ♘e3, intending 20...♕g5+ 21 ♔h1 (21 ♘g4?? ♕xd2 22 ♖xd2 ♖xc1+ 23 ♖d1 ♖xd1#) 21...♗g2+ 22 ♔g1! and then 22...♗xf3+ 23 ♔f1 or 22...♗h3+ 23 ♔h1. That explains why Black wanted to eliminate the white knight with 18...♖xc4.

Lateral thinking

The Maltese psychologist Edward de Bono is particularly famous for introducing the term 'lateral thinking'. He so named the technique to suggest sideways thought-processes, instead of only moving straight ahead with the development of just one idea. By thinking laterally, a person can create different possible solutions to a given problem, and then select the route that he or she judges to be the best one. In chess, De Bono's concept might, for example, prompt us to consider seeking interesting fresh ways of playing a certain opening, rather than memorizing more theory in one long tunnel-like line. Indeed, a really enthusiastic exponent of lateral thinking will probably feel at home in many different openings, and can then enjoy the benefits that come with being able to switch systems within a flexible repertoire which constantly surprises opponents.

If we acquire more openness to original thinking in general, then it will become easier to be creative in chess and break free from set ways that restrict the mind's ability to generate exciting new ideas. So let's try a puzzle ... in Dutch!

On your guard!

On 6 July 1997, IM Leon Pliester taught me the Dutch words for the first twelve natural numbers:

One = Een; Two = Twee; Three = Drie; Four = Vier; Five = Vijf; Six = Zes; Seven = Zeven; Eight = Acht; Nine = Negen; Ten = Tien; Eleven = Elf; Twelve = Twaalf.

Now imagine a gate to a wonderland of star ideas. An angel guarding the gate will say one word to anyone who approaches. If the person replies with the correct required word, then the gate will be opened to that person. You will hopefully be the fourth person to be allowed in, because three people have already answered correctly as follows.

    Angel: 'Zes'.
    Person 1: 'Drie'.
    Angel: 'Acht'.
    Person 2: 'Vier'.
    Angel: 'Twaalf'.
    Person 3: 'Zes'.

When you approach the gate, the angel says 'Duidelijk', which happens to mean 'clear'. Can you think of the word which will get the stargate opened for you? All will become clear after the following chess puzzle, so you may wish to cover up the next few lines.

A special type of move

If White plays a move of type X, Black **must** respond by moving piece A, but White's move was **not** made using his own pieces A or B. Can you identify the type of move labelled type X, and name the pieces which have been

called A and B? The answers appear after Game 11.

Stargate solution

Each person must respond with the Dutch word that gives the number of letters in the angel's word. Since 'Duidelijk' has nine letters, you needed to say **'Negen'** to get past the gate. Congratulations if you answered correctly. You must be on 'cloud nine' now! Up at those dizzy heights, lots more star moves are about to come into view.

The average rating of the six participants in the super-strong double-all-play-all tournament at Novgorod in June was an awesome 2719. Therefore a score of 4/10, which 'tail-enders' GM Veselin Topalov and GM Boris Gelfand attained, was still more than sufficient for those two stars each to notch up another grandmaster norm-level performance, and I found the following exciting game from round eight to be no less instructive than any of the other 29 games in the entire competition.

Game 11
V. Topalov – B. Gelfand
Novgorod 1997
English Opening

| 1 | c4 | ♘f6 | 3 | ♘f3 | ♘c6 |
| 2 | ♘c3 | e5 | 4 | g3 | ♗b4 |

I like this classical developing move. In contrast, **4...d6** is a bit passive and restricts the scope of Black's dark-squared bishop. In Blackburn-Teetson, Bedlington Club Ch 1992, White immediately seized the initiative and more space with **5 d4!**, and the game continued **5...e4?** (5...exd4 or 5...♗g4 would be relatively best) **6 ♘g5 ♗f5** (we can say that Black has an inferior version of the line 1 d4 ♘f6 2 c4 d6 3 ♘c3 e5 4 ♘f3 e4 5 ♘g5 ♗f5 since David Blackburn's extra move g2-g3 is worth more to White than ...♘b8-c6 is to Black, since ♗g2 can now be played to attack the very vulnerable e4-pawn) **7 ♗g2 ♕e7 8 f3** (8 ♘d5 is really strong too, as shown by 8...♘xd5 9 cxd5 ♘b8 {9...♘a5?? and 9...♘b4?? both lose instantly to 10 ♕a4+} 10 ♕c2, and the e4-pawn is about to become a thing of the past) **8...exf3** (after 8...e3 9 ♘ge4, the over-adventurous black e-pawn is cut off from the rest of his army and will soon be eliminated by a white piece) **9 ♘xf3 h6** (to stop ♗g5, after which ♘d5 would follow) **10 0-0-0 0-0-0 11 d5 ♘b8** (11...♘e5 12 ♕a4 is also highly uncomfortable for Black, and indeed 12...♘xf3+? would lose at lightning speed to 13 ♖xf3 ♗g4 14 ♖e3 ♕d7 15 ♕xa7) **12 ♕a4 ♘a6 13 b4 ♗d7 14 ♕a3** (14 b5 ♔b8, intending ...♘c5, grants Black's knight on the rim some prospects that it should not have) **14...♔b8 15 ♘d4** (a storm is gathering not far from Black's king, and already 16 ♘c6+! bxc6 17 ♕xa6 is

threatened) **15...♕e5 16 ♘db5 ♘g4** (another possibility is 16...g5 to stop ♗f4, but it leaves Black extremely weak along the f-file and on the a1-h8 diagonal, which means that a logical continuation is 17 ♗b2 {threatening ♘e4} 17...♕e3+ 18 ♔h1 ♗g7 19 ♖f3 ♕e7 20 ♖af1 ♖hf8 21 ♘d1 ♘h5 22 ♗xg7 ♘xg7 23 ♖e3, and White wins whichever piece Black interposes on e6 to save his queen's life) **17 ♗f4 ♕h5 18 h3 ♘e5 19 ♗xe5?** (the bishop that is being voluntarily exchanged was an important guardian of the dark squares, so instead I much prefer 19 g4 ♕h4 {19...♗xg4 20 hxg4 ♘xg4 threatens nothing, but White can play 21 ♖f3 followed by ♖h3 if he wants to be ultra-safe} 20 ♗e3! {not only attacking a7, but also making ♗f2 possible to drive away Black's queen} 20...♘xc4 21 ♗xa7+ ♔a8 22 ♕a4, after which White threatens 23 ♗f2 ♕g5 24 ♘xc7+) **19...♕xe5** (19...dxe5 also merits consideration because it frees the dark-squared bishop and threatens ...♗xb4 or ...♗xh3) **20 ♔h2 ♗e7?** (20...h5! {threatening ...h4} 21 h4 g5 22 hxg5 h4 is terrible for White) **21 ♘xa7! ♘xb4??** (Black's panic reaction opens up the b-file where his own king is located, but perhaps he feared 21...♔xa7 22 b5 h5 23 bxa6 b6 24 ♘b5+ ♗xb5 {24...♔b8 is better, to answer 25 a7+ by 25...♔b7} 25 cxb5, after which the c7-pawn is exposed and weak, and White threatens ♕c1 followed by ♕c6) **22 ♖ab1 ♕d4** *(D)* (22...♘c2 23 ♖xb7+ ♔xb7 24 ♖b1+

♚a8 25 ♕a6 leaves Black helpless against the three threats of mate that he is then facing on the next move).

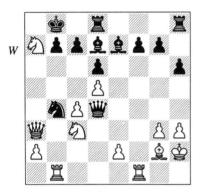

23 ♘c6+! ♘xc6 24 dxc6 1-0. Apart from one inaccuracy at move 19, White played a very powerful, controlled game.

David Blackburn is no doubt missed by many friends in the UK, but he is doing well working in Bulgaria. In fact, during a surprise phone call from David on August 11, he told me that mnemonics are really useful in his management training work. He often reminds people to check that their objectives are **S.M.A.R.T.** (**s**pecific, **m**easurable, **a**chievable, **r**elevant, **t**ime-bounded). Also, **W.E.C.H.A.** (**w**ork experience, **e**ducation, **c**ircumstances, **h**ealth, **a**ims) is frequently used as a guide in interview questioning to cover important categories, but it occurs to me that if I were an interviewee, then I might rearrange the letters and get A.C.H.E.W. to remind myself not to sneeze!

One problem is that Bulgaria uses a Cyrillic alphabet, which challenges David to find smart ways to overcome that obstacle. However, let's return now to the main game, where Bulgaria's number one chess star, GM Veselin Topalov, will soon encounter some huge hurdles.

5 ♗g2   0-0
6 0-0   e4

In Edinburgh 1990, a game J.Grant-Motwani associated with the city's Café Royal Oyster Bar team tournament, went **6...♖e8 7 d3 ♗xc3 8 bxc3 e4 9 ♘d4 h6** (played to stop ♗g5, but 9...exd3 10 exd3 h6 11 ♖b1 ♘xd4 12 cxd4 d5 13 ♗f4 c6 14 ♕d2 b6 15 a4 ♗f5 16 c5 ♘d7! 17 ♖fc1 ♕f6 18 ♖b4 ♖e6, intending ...♖ae8, also gave Black a fine position in a rapid super-GM encounter Karpov-Anand, Frankfurt 1997) **10 dxe4 ♘xe4 11 ♕c2 d5 12 ♖d1** (the drawback to this move is that it weakens White at f2) **12...♘xd4 13 ♖xd4** (13 cxd4 is answered strongly by 13...♗f5, intending after 14 f3 to play 14...♘d6!, which is clearer for Black than 14...♘xg3 15 e4 or 14...♘f2 15 ♕xf5 ♘xd1 16 ♕d3; otherwise after 14 ♕b3 dxc4 15 ♕xc4 {15 ♕xb7 ♖b8 16 ♕xa7 ♘c3 is also fantastic for Black} 15...♘d6! White's queen cannot save the e2-pawn) **13...♕f6 14 f3** (14 ♗xe4 dxe4 15 ♖xe4 can be met in various good ways including 15...♗f5 16 ♖xe8+ ♖xe8 17 ♕b2 ♗h3, threatening 18...♕f3! 19 exf3 ♖e1# and planning 18 ♕xb7? ♖e2 or 18 ♗e3? ♕c6! 19 f3 ♖xe3, a line which illustrates that White's king's situation is much less secure after parting with the fianchettoed bishop) **14...c5 15 ♖xd5 ♕xc3!** (much clearer for Black than 15...♘xc3 16 ♗b2) **16 ♕xc3 ♘xc3 17 ♖xc5 b6 18 ♖c7 ♘xe2+ 19 ♔f2 ♘d4!** (threatening ...♘e6 or ...♖e2+ and planning to meet 20 ♗e3? with 20...♘c2 or 20...♖xe3 21 ♔xe3 ♘c2+) **20 f4 ♖b8 21 ♖xa7 ♖e2+ 22 ♔f1 ♗e6** (developing with a threat to the c-pawn) **23 ♖c7 ♖e8** (this carries the deadly threat of 24...♗h3! 25 ♗xh3 ♖e1+ 26 ♔g2 ♖8e2#) **24 ♗a3 ♗g4** (the harmony in Black's army is now decisive, and the numerous threats include 25...♘c2 and 25...♖xg2! 26 ♔xg2 ♖e2+ 27 ♔g1 {27 ♔h1 ♘f3 or 27 ♔f1 ♗h3+ 28 ♔g1 ♘f3+ 29 ♔h1 ♖xh2#} 27...♘f3+ 28 ♔f1 ♖xh2 followed shortly by ...♗h3#) **25 ♗d5 ♖xh2 26 ♗xf7+** (if 26 ♖e7, then a pretty line is 26...♖d8 27 ♔g1 ♖xd5!! 28 ♔xh2 {28 cxd5 ♘f3+ 29 ♔f1 ♗h3#} 28...♘f3+ 29 ♔g2 ♖d2+ with 30 ♔f1 ♗h3# or 30 ♔h1 ♖h2# to follow) **26...♔h7 27 ♗xe8** *(D)*.

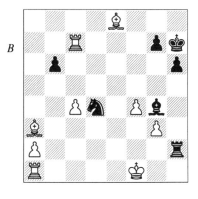

B

27...♗e2+! 0-1, because 28 ♔g1 and 28 ♔e1 are both answered by 28...♘f3#.

7	**♘g5**	**♗xc3**
8	**bxc3**	**♖e8**

Black has given up one of his bishops for a knight, but in return he now has a superior pawn structure and a lead in development.

9	**f3**	**e3**

9...exf3 is also possible, but Gelfand opts to keep the f-file closed by sacrificing a pawn and inflicting further damage on White's pawn structure.

10	**dxe3**	

10 d3 d5 gave Black a very fine position in Hodgson-Masserey, Horgen 1995, although GM Julian Hodgson eventually won that game.

10	**...**	**b6!**

Black currently intends to play ...♗a6 soon, thereby pressurizing the c4-pawn, which is the most exposed unit in White's assortment of weak isolated and doubled pawns situated towards the queenside.

11	**e4**	**h6!**

One hallmark of great players is that they can interrupt the main plan in order to take necessary and effective measures that counter the opponent's operations. Gelfand spotted that after 11...♗a6, Topalov could play 12 f4, intending dangerous variations like 12...♗xc4 13 e5 or 12...h6 13 ♘xf7! ♔xf7 14 e5 ♘g8 (14...♘h7 loses quickly to 15 ♗d5+ ♔f8 16 ♕d3) 15 ♗d5+ ♔f8 16 ♕d3 ♘ge7 17 ♕h7 (17

♗a3 d6) 17...♘xd5 18 cxd5 ♘e7 19 f5 ♘xd5 20 f6 gxf6 21 ♗xh6#.

12 ♘xf7?!

Veselin Topalov makes a bold but incorrect sacrifice rather than have the passive retreat 12 ♘h3 answered by 12...♗a6.

12	...	♔xf7
13	f4	♔g8

13...♘xe4? loses to 14 ♕d5+.

14	e5	♘h7
15	♗a3	♗b7
16	♗e4	♔h8
17	♗c2 *(D)*	

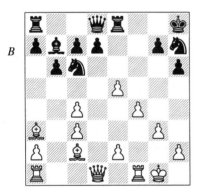

White threatens ♕d3 followed by ♕xh7#.

17 ... ♘xe5!!

This star reaction is perfectly timed. Black returns his surplus material in order to nullify White's attacking attempts and seize the initiative himself.

18	fxe5	♖xe5
19	♗xh7	

19 ♕d3 ♗e4 20 ♕d4 ♕e8 is also excellent for Black.

| 19 | ... | ♔xh7 |

It is not too early to say that Black has a winning position, because his strategy of saddling the opponent with permanently weak pawns has triumphed over White's sacrificial attacking gestures.

20 c5

20 ♖f8 ♕g5 21 ♖xa8 ♗xa8 22 ♕xd7 ♕e3+ 23 ♔f1 ♕xe2+ 24 ♔g1 ♕g2# is another way for White to bow out.

20 ... ♕e8!

Black remains calmly in control but still alert to tactics, and so he avoids 20...bxc5 21 ♗xc5 ♖xc5 22 ♕b1+, which would give White some activity and drawing chances.

21	♕d3+	♗e4
22	♕d2	♕e6

Rather than make the capture ...bxc5 immediately, Black improves the position of his queen and gives White an opportunity to lose quickly with 23 cxb6 axb6 24 ♗b2 (24 ♗b4? c5) 24...♕h3 25 ♖f2 ♖f8! and then:

a) 26 ♖xf8 ♕g2#.

b) 26 ♕d4 ♖xf2 27 ♕xf2 ♖f5 28 ♕d4 ♕g2#.

c) 26 ♖af1 ♖ef5 (with the threat 27...♕g2+! 28 ♖xg2 ♖xf1#) 27 ♕e1 *(D)*.

Now 27...♖h5! leaves White helpless against the threat of 28...♕xg3+! 29 hxg3 ♖h1#.

23	♖f2	bxc5
24	♖af1	♖e8
25	c4	

Desperately hoping to create some counterplay with ♗b2 and ♖f7.

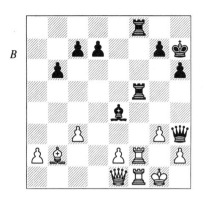

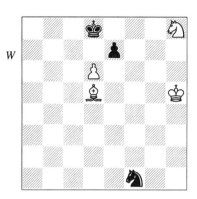

| 25 | ... | ♕h3 |
| 26 | ♗b2 | ♖g5 |

Threatening 27...♖xg3+ 28 hxg3 ♕h1#.

27	♕c3	♖e6
28	♕e3	♖g4
29	♖c1	h5

0-1

White resigned since he could not satisfactorily counter the threat of 30...h4.

Solution to puzzle (posed before Game 11)

The type X move is a **double check**. It cannot be made with a king or queen, but the opponent must respond by moving his king. Therefore in the puzzle, piece **A is the king and B is a queen**.

Drama in open air

Some people might abandon this position as a 'dead draw', since although White has an extra bishop, his only pawn is about to be eliminated, and the black king looks relatively safe out in the open, well away from any possibility of being checkmated in a cramped corner location. However, drama is destined to develop in open air, because it is White to play and win. The beautiful solution to this 1982 star study by M.Travasoni appears after Game 12, but now another dramatic episode involving air is waiting in the wings to open out before you.

When no buses were running from Liechtenstein at suitable times on a certain Sunday in 1996, IM Jonathan Rowson (J.R.) found himself in the position of having to win his last-round battle in an open tournament in order to gain enough prize money to afford a taxi to Switzerland's Zurich Airport ... otherwise walking back to Scotland would have been replacing flying home! The task was plain but not simple, and it seemed to add a new dimension to the term 'Swiss system' of pairings! Just before we see how J.R. fared against FIDE Master Friedrich

Norbert of Germany, I have another curious airport tale to tell. When my wife Jenny and I visited Ivo Timmermans in Vlissingen recently, Ivo told us that he heard the following clear announcement twice when he was waiting for a friend at Terminal 3 of London's Heathrow Airport on Thursday 26 June. The repeated message through the Tannoy system was: 'Would Paul Motwani please come to the meeting point. Claire Motwani is waiting for him'. Ivo started looking around for me, but not surprisingly he could not spot me as far off as Brussels!

It's true that my star sign is Gemini, but I didn't expect to hear about this kind of twin. Maybe some day we'll meet, and then I'll ask if 'Claire' is really 'Clare' ... one 'I' too many can make a big difference!

Game 12
J. Rowson – F. Norbert
Liechtenstein 1996
Sicilian Defence

1	e4	c5
2	♘f3	♘c6
3	d4	

Pages 116-120 of *C.O.O.L. Chess* contained several nice games featuring 3 ♗b5, the Rossolimo Variation.

| 3 | ... | cxd4 |
| 4 | ♘xd4 | e5 |

4...♘f6 5 ♘c3 d6 transposes to Motwani-Parkin, Stirling 1997, which was one of my best attacking efforts from the six simultaneous displays that formed part of my first chess 'world tour of Scotland'. The game went **6 g3 ♗g4 7 f3 ♘xd4?!** (7...♗d7 is better) **8 ♕xd4! ♗xf3 9 ♗b5+ ♘d7 10 0-0** (a large lead in piece development and use of the opened f-file gives White lots of play in return for the pawn sacrificed on f3; I was following my own recommendation stated on page 122 of *C.O.O.L. Chess*, but later I realized that 10 ♖f1! is stronger because after 10...♗h5 11 ♕d5, Black has no queen check on b6 when my king is still on e1) **10...♗h5 11 ♗e3** (here 11 ♕d5 could be answered by 11...♕b6+) **11...e6 12 e5 d5** *(D)* (Black might understandably have feared the line 12...a6 13 exd6!? axb5 14 ♘xb5, after which he is in a very cramped position and facing the terrible threat of ♘c7+).

13 ♘xd5! exd5? (a panic reaction; it is true that after 13...a6 14 ♘f4, 14...♗g6? 15 ♘xg6 hxg6 16 ♗xd7+ ♕xd7 17 ♕xd7+ ♔xd7 18 ♖xf7+ is also bleak for Black, but he could try 14...♗g4) **14 ♕xd5 ♕e7** (14...a6 15 e6! fxe6 16 ♕xh5+ g6 17 ♕e5! wins neatly for White) **15 e6! ♕xe6 16 ♗xd7+ ♕xd7 17 ♕xh5 ♗d6 18 ♖ad1**

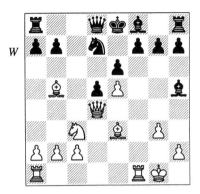

W

(with the simple but deadly threat of ♗f4) **18...♕c7 19 ♕b5+ ♔f8 20 ♖xd6 1-0**. James Parkin resigned because 20...♕xd6 can be answered by 21 ♕xb7 or 21 ♗c5, pinning and winning his queen. Two days later I met James again at a coaching day in Glasgow, where his answers to questions which I asked during a talk were so good that he won several prizes!

5 ♘b5 d6

Alan Norris (who was joint runner-up with 6½/9 in the 1997 Scottish Championship) is an expert on the Löwenthal Variation, **5...a6**, in which Black aims for really rapid development, as shown by the normal path **6 ♘d6+ ♗xd6 7 ♕xd6 ♕f6**. I do not propose to spend the rest of our S.T.A.R. journey on an exhaustive analysis of this Sicilian system, but hopefully the following three quick games will provide some flavour of a tasty counterattacking weapon and pitfalls to avoid, and so whet your appetite sufficiently to create a desire for further investigation.

a) Eynon-Norris, Glenrothes 1997 continued **8 ♕d1** (this popular move may well have to be regarded as an error if my assessment in the notes at move 13 holds up for Black in future, since White has no better alternatives at moves 9-12) **8...♕g6 9 ♘c3 d5! 10 ♘xd5** (10 exd5? ♘d4 11 ♗d3 ♕xg2 is terrible for White, and 10 ♕xd5? ♗e6 11 ♕d3 ♖d8 12 ♕g3 ♘b4 also leaves him struggling badly behind in development) **10...♕xe4+ 11 ♗e3 ♘d4 12 ♘c7+ ♔e7 13 ♘xa8** (Alan Norris, Alan Minnican {another Scottish friend of mine} and I have found independently that 13 ♖c1 ♗g4 14 ♕d3 ♕xd3 15 ♗xd3 ♖d8 is not nearly as good for White as certain books suggest, the principal reason being that Black can cause problems for the c7-knight, with 16...♔d6 being an immediate threat) **13...♘xc2+ 14 ♔d2 ♘xe3 15 fxe3** (a pretty variation is 15 ♕f3 ♕b4+! 16 ♔xe3 ♕d4+ 17 ♔e2 ♗g4, and Black wins) **15...♘f6** (threatening ...♖d8+) **16 ♕f3?** (White must try 16 ♕b3 to prevent ...♕b4+ and threaten ♕a3+, but 16...♖d8+ 17 ♔e1 ♘g4 creates threats of ...♘xe3 or ...♕f5-f2#, and 18 ♕a3+ can be met calmly by 18...♔f6, whereas 18 ♖d1 ♖xd1+ 19 ♕xd1 {19 ♔xd1? ♘f2+} 19...♕xe3+ guarantees Black at least a draw in spite of his opponent having an extra rook) **16...♕b4+ 17 ♔c2 ♗g4 18 ♕f2** (D).

18...♖c8+ 19 ♔b1 0-1. David Eynon resigned without waiting for 19...♗f5+!, which carries the little tactical point 20 ♕xf5 ♕e1#.

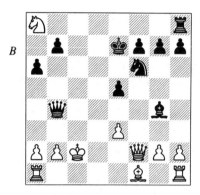

b) The attacking miniature that we have just witnessed may have caused White to seek quieter waters in Bryson-Norris, Scottish Ch, Aviemore 1997, because he deviated at move 8 with **8 ♕xf6**, a more peaceful option than 8 ♕c7. The continuation was **8...♘xf6 9 ♘c3 ♘b4** (9...d5?! 10 exd5 ♘b4 11 ♗d3 leaves Black with the unpleasant choice of 11...♘fxd5 12 ♘xd5 ♘xd5, when White has the advantage of possessing a bishop pair in an open position where he is not behind in development, and 11...♘xd3+ 12 cxd3 h6 {to stop ♗g5} 13 0-0 ♗f5 14 ♖e1, as in Kotronias-Mouroutis, Korinthos 1997, which ended abruptly with 14...0-0-0 15 ♖xe5 ♗xd3 16 ♗f4 g5 17 ♖c1! {threatening ♘e4+} 17...♘d7 18 ♖xg5!! hxg5 19 ♘a4+! ♘c5 20 ♘b6# - a lovely finish by GM Vasilios Kotronias) **10 ♔d2 d6** (certain players have experienced difficulties as Black after 10...d5?! 11 a3 d4 12 axb4 dxc3+ 13 ♔c3!, as 13...cxb2 14 ♗xb2 ♘d7 and then 15 b5 or 15 ♗c4 shows White utilizing open files and diagonals to

good effect to generate strong pressure) **11 a3 ♘c6 12 ♗d3 ♗e6 13 f3 0-0** (13...0-0-0 and 13...d5 merit attention too, because Black's development is very good whereas the white king is not ideally placed on the d-file) **14 ♔e2 d5 15 exd5 ♘d4+ 16 ♔f2 ♘xd5 17 ♘xd5 ♗xd5 ½-½**, in a fairly balanced position.

However, let's return to the main game to see how J.R., going all-out for a win, responds at move six to Black's Kalashnikov Variation, 5...d6.

6 c4

This move exerts a clamp on the d5-square, and there is the same strategy behind the interesting alternative **6 g3**, planning ♗g2. In that case Black should probably react very vigorously with 6...h5!, because the quieter route **6...♗e7** did not bring enough activity in Motwani-R.McKay, Grangemouth 1989: **7 ♗g2 ♗e6 8 ♘1c3 a6 9 ♘a3 h6** (avoiding 9...♘f6 10 ♗g5) **10 0-0 ♘f6 11 ♘d5 0-0 12 ♘c4 ♗xd5 13 exd5 ♘b8 14 a4 ♕c7 15 b3 ♘bd7 16 a5 ♖fe8 17 ♗e3 ♗f8 18 ♖a4! ♘c5 19 ♖b4 ♖ab8 20 ♘b6 ♘fd7 21 ♕g4** (threatening ♗xh6) **21...♘xb6 22 axb6 ♕c8 23 ♕xc8 ♖bxc8 24 ♗h3 ♖a8 25 ♖c4!** (threatening b4) **25...a5 26 ♖a1** and now:

a) **26...♖a6 27 b4! axb4 28 ♖xa6** wins almost by force for White as follows: 28...bxa6 29 ♖xb4 ♖b8 30 b7! a5 (30...♘xb7? 31 ♗a7 or 30...♖xb7? 31 ♗xc5) 31 ♖b6 ♗e7 (31...♘xb7 loses to 32 ♗d7 followed by ♗c6) 32 ♗c8 ♔f8 33 ♗xc5 dxc5 34 d6 ♗d8 35

♖a6 followed by ♖a8; or 28...♞xa6 29 ♖c7! *(D)*.

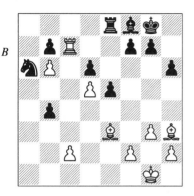

Now 29...♖e7 30 ♖c8 leaves Black really tied up and 30...h5, for example, loses to 31 ♗g5 f6 32 ♗e6+ ♖xe6 33 dxe6 fxg5 34 e7, but meanwhile an actual threat is 31 ♗f1! f5 32 ♗xa6 bxa6 33 ♖c7 planning b7-b8♕, and White's passed b-pawn is unstoppable.

b) The actual game continued **26...g6 27 ♗d2 f5** (IM Roddy McKay desperately seeks counterplay here) **28 ♖xa5 ♞e4 29 ♗b4 ♖xa5 30 ♗xa5 ♖a8 31 b4 ♞f6 32 ♖c7 ♖b8 33 ♗f1 ♚h8** (33...♞xd5? walks into the pin 34 ♗c4) **34 c4 ♞e8 35 c5! dxc5** (35...♞xc7 36 bxc7 ♖c8 37 c6 bxc6 38 ♗a6 is also hopeless for Black, and is another illustration of the power of passed pawns) **36 bxc5 ♖a8 37 d6 1-0.** Black lost on time, although after 37...♖xa5 he could resign following 38 ♖c8 or 38 d7 ♖a8 39 ♖c8.

6	...	♗e6
7	♞1c3	a6
8	♞a3	♗e7 *(D)*

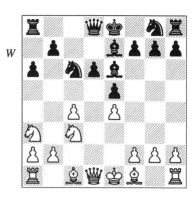

9 ♞c2!

J.R. is a man with a prophylactic plan! He does not intend to allow his opponent to land a knight on the outpost at d4. Instead, De Vreugt-Van der Wiel, Vlissingen 1997 continued **9 ♗d3 ♗g5 10 0-0 ♗xc1 11 ♖xc1 ♞f6 12 ♕d2 0-0 13 ♖fd1 ♖c8 14 ♗b1?** (14 ♞c2 is more purposeful) **14...♞d4 15 b3 b5! 16 ♞d5** (16 cxb5 ♕a5! plans 17 ♕b2 ♖xc3! 18 ♖xc3 ♕xc3, a deadly tactical trick based on the fact that after 19 ♕xc3 there is the fork 19...♞e2+ followed by 20...♞xc3) **16...bxc4 17 ♞xf6+?** (17 bxc4 gives White a poor pawn structure, but it is necessary on account of tactical reasons that are about to become clear) **17...♕xf6 18 ♞xc4** (18 bxc4 also comes too late in view of 18...♞f3+! 19 gxf3 ♗h3, and White has no satisfactory defence against the dual threats of 20...♕g6+ and 20...♕xf3 followed by ...♕g2#) **18...♖xc4!! 0-1.** White resigned for reasons given in the puzzle solution after Game 10.

9	...	♗g5

10 &d3

10 &xg5 ♕xg5 11 ♕xd6?? ♖d8 12 ♕c5 ♕d2# is a quick way to lose.

10 ...   &xc1
11 ♖xc1   ♘f6

Planes were in the air before we started this game, and in fact it was on an aeroplane returning from the Erevan Olympiad on 2 October 1996 that J.R. wrote (practically all of) the following lucid notes: 'With hindsight, 11...♘ge7 may be an improvement, but White still has a very comfortable edge. For example, 12 0-0 0-0 13 ♕d2 ♘g6 14 g3! restricts the g6-knight, and Black can scarcely try for counterplay with 14...f5, because after 15 exf5 &xf5 16 &xf5 ♖xf5 his static pawn centre is an exposed target that White can attack easily.'

It occurs to me (P.M.) that since White has the superior pawn structure, Black must react extremely energetically if he hopes to achieve meaningful play. With that thought in mind, I suggest 11...♘ge7 12 0-0 ♘g6, planning to answer 13 g3 by 13...h5! *(D)*.

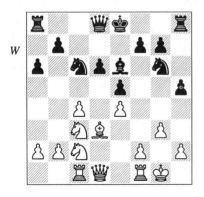

This should also remind us of an important point which has cropped up on several earlier occasions in *S.T.A.R. Chess*: do not castle automatically, but rather consider whether it will really improve one's position. If the answer is 'No', then look for a more purposeful move.

12 0-0   0-0
13 ♕d2   ♖c8

J.R. prefers 13...♕b6. Of course 14...♕xb2 is not a threat since White would trap Black's queen by 15 ♖b1. However, his very sensible idea is to play ...♖ad8 to defend the sensitive d-pawn. You might say 'What's wrong with the alternative plan of putting Black's rooks on c8 and d8?'. Well, J.R. points out that White is quite secure on the c-file, and so a black rook would lack true purpose on c8. Therefore it makes sense to aim for ...♖ad8 and keep the other rook on f8. Eventually Black may be able to try for ...f5 after preliminary manoeuvres such as ...g6, ...♔g7 and ...♘g8-e7, although this reinforces the earlier suggestion that 11...♘ge7 is an improvement over 11...♘f6.

14 ♖fd1   ♕b6
15 &f1!   &g4

15...♕xb2?? makes a White Christmas with 16 ♖b1.

16 ♖e1

After 16 &e2 &xe2 17 ♕xe2, Black should still avoid 17...♕xb2? due to 18 ♘a4! ♕xa2 (18...♘d4 19 ♘xd4 ♕b4 20 ♘f5 ♕xa4 21 ♘e7+ also wins material for White) 19 ♖a1

♕b3 and then 20 ♖db1 or 20 ♖a3 ♘d4 21 ♖xd4!.

16	...	♖fd8
17	b3	h6
18	h3	♗e6
19	♖cd1	

White does not need a rook at c1, so instead he shifts it onto a partly open file where it performs a more positive function.

| 19 | ... | ♕c7 (D) |

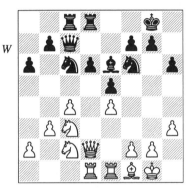

20 ♖e3!

The rook has lateral thinking in mind! It now has the freedom to slide anywhere from d3 to g3.

| 20 | ... | ♘a7 |

Hoping to play ...b5 to achieve some activity.

21 ♖g3

Threatening ♕xh6 and encouraging the opponent to play the decentralizing move 21...♘h5, after which he would no longer have the possibility of giving extra protection to the d6-pawn with ...♘e8. However, after 22 ♖d3 Black has 22...b5!, intending 23

cxb5 ♘f4!. Therefore I would prefer to answer 21...♘h5 by 22 ♖f3, planning 22...b5 23 ♘e3. Then ♘ed5 is an unpleasant threat, and 23...♘f6? 24 ♖xf6! gxf6 25 ♘ed5 ♕b7 26 ♕xh6 wins for White, as does 23...♘f4 24 g3! ♘xh3+? 25 ♗xh3 ♗xh3 26 g4!, neatly trapping the black bishop.

| 21 | ... | ♔f8 |

J.R. points out that 21...♔h8 22 ♖f3 (threatening 23 ♖xf6! gxf6 24 ♕xh6+ ♔g8 25 ♖d3 followed by ♖g3+) 22...♕e7 23 a4 increases White's spatial advantage and leaves Black with little counterplay.

22 ♖f3

Threatening 23 ♖xf6! gxf6 24 ♕xh6+ ♔e7 25 ♘e3 followed by ♘cd5+.

| 22 | ... | ♕e7?! |

22...♘e8!? is passive but quite solid, and although 23 ♘e3 ♘c6 24 ♘cd5 ♗xd5 25 ♘xd5 ♕b8 is cramped for Black at the moment, he at least has the possibility of some counterplay with ...♘d4. Of course White need not hurry to move his knight from c2. Instead of 23 ♘e3 (which relinquishes some control of the d4-square), 23 a4 seizes more space. 23...♕b6 is then quite logical, despite the fact that ...♕xb3 is not a threat due to the reply ♖b1. Nevertheless, Black is very much alive, and the big question is 'Can White significantly strengthen his own position?'. In the actual game, IM Jonathan Rowson does so with great skill.

23 ♖e1!

This move is a far-sighted example of the fact that a rook 'facing' an opponent's queen tends to lead to interesting possibilities. In this particular case, J.R. plans to play ♘d5, which he expects will be answered by ...♗xd5. Then after replying exd5, White can follow up with ♘d4 since ...exd4 would allow ♖xe7.

23 ... ♖b8
24 ♕e3!

Attacking the a7-knight and encouraging Black to defend it laterally with his queen by playing 24...b5. However, White then has the star sacrifice 25 ♖xf6!! *(D)*:

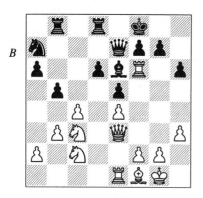

a) 25...♕xf6 26 ♕xa7.

b) 25...gxf6 26 ♕xh6+ ♔e8 27 ♘e3, planning ♘cd5 with a massive attack.

24 ... ♖a8

24...♘c6? loses quickly to 25 ♘d5 ♗xd5 26 exd5 ♘a5 27 ♕b6.

25 a4

J.R. further tightens his grip on the position and in effect says to Black 'I know it's really difficult to find constructive moves in a cramped position, but I've just played so now you *must* move'.

25 ... ♖dc8
26 ♕d2

This 'quiet' move is actually very disconcerting for Black because it not only prods the d-pawn (which is less well defended after the last move), but White also threatens to play a5 followed by the knight manoeuvre ♘a4-b6.

26 ... ♘c6?

This in fact adds power to White's next move although Black's position was already in a critical state.

27 ♘d5! ♗xd5
28 exd5 ♘b8
29 ♘d4!

Threatening the deadly 30 ♘f5 ♕d8 31 ♘xh6!.

29 ... ♘e8
30 ♘f5 ♕g5

After 30...♕d8, J.R. planned to play the star move 31 ♖xe5!! *(D)*.

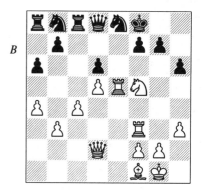

After 31...dxe5 32 ♕b4+ ♔g8 33 ♘e7+:

a) 33...♔h7 34 ♗d3+ ♔h8 35 ♘xc8 ♕xc8 36 ♕f8#.

b) 33...♔h8 34 ♘xc8 (not the only move, but certainly a very safe and sure route to victory) 34...♕xc8 (after 34...♘d7 35 ♘d6, White is simply a pawn up with an overwhelming position, while 34...e4 allows the pretty finish 35 ♕f8+ ♔h7 36 ♘e7 exf3 37 ♕g8#) 35 ♕f8+ ♔h7 36 ♗d3+ g6 37 ♖xf7+ ♘g7 38 ♖xg7#.

31 ♕b4

Creating a deadly simultaneous attack against the pawns on b7 and d6.

31 ... a5
32 ♕xb7 1-0

Black had no wish to see 32...♘a6 33 ♘xh6! ♕xh6 34 ♕xf7#.

So, happily, J.R. reached a score of 6½/9 and won enough prize money to get a taxi to Zurich Airport. We now go from one happy finish to another one...

Solution to puzzle (posed before Game 12)

White wins with 1 ♘f7+ ♔d7 (1...♔e8 2 ♗c6+! ♔xf7 3 d7 makes the d-pawn's promotion unstoppable) **2 ♗c4!** (2 ♗c6+? only draws due to 2...♔xc6 3 dxe7 ♔d7) **2...♘g3+ 3 ♔g4 ♘e4 4 ♗b5+ ♔e6 5 d7 ♘f6+ 6 ♔g5! ♘xd7 7 ♗c4#** *(D)*.

Seeing beautiful checkmates such as this one can increase a player's

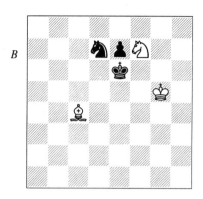

B

awareness of the magical possibilities that can happen on a chessboard, even when at the outset the opponent's king looks relatively safe by not being trapped in a corner. To reinforce this point, here is another example with a similar theme.

No escape

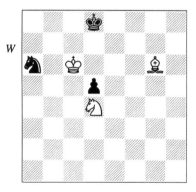

W

This game-like position with White to play and win occurred near the end of a 1934 study composed by V.A. Bron. The solution awaits you before Game 13.

Some people say that the masses of theory published nowadays makes one's head spin. My use of **S.P.I.N.** pins the problem down and nips it in the bud. I happily select any opening that I feel suits my style; practice playing it in simuls, rapid and friendly games to gain experience of the chosen opening before employing it in a more important encounter; improve my knowledge and understanding by letting the new weapon star in a 'big' game as soon as the first opportunity arises; note down (or first memorize for the mental exercise) any relevant games in the opening that I spot being played 'live', or in sources such as newspapers, teletext, magazines and books, so that I build up a useful stock of examples to refer to whenever I want to refresh myself on the topic of the selected opening. However, there are lots of almost identical twin games, in which a player wins in much the same way as someone else has already done. So it makes sense to collect just a modest number of really instructive games, with some overlap (but not too much) for the purposes of comparison and reinforcement.

In a nutshell, this is a fun, fearless approach to the openings, which for me makes them a joyful, exciting part of chess rather than a chore. At the heart of S.P.I.N. there is the truth that if you want to play an opening then you can. Remember our inspirational star motto, and enjoy playing the openings you really want to. Then that fresh feeling will pour over like a powerful wave into your chess in later phases of the game, and drown (in the friendliest sense!) many an opponent. Only a truly awesome event could stop the planets from spinning, and similarly you will be a force to be reckoned with when armed with S.P.I.N. The following poem captures some of that feeling:

*The one you **select** today*
It'll be fun, so elect to play
***Practice** the lines, you'll **improve** and go far*
As an actress shines, a cool movie star.
***Note** new games, spinning around*
Not a few the same, twinning I've found
So concentrate on getting to the heart of spin
It's great, I'm betting you start to win!

For a little change, the following puzzle has absolutely no chess content, but the logical deductive thinking that can be used to solve it has spin-offs in chess.

Some sum!

SPIN
PINS
———
NIPS
———

This 'sum' may be an addition or a subtraction (that is, the top two rows either add or subtract to give the bottom row). Can you discover which one it is, and replace each different letter by a new digit so that the sum works? Once you have determined the numbers that the letters S, P, I, N, represent, try to find a special connection between PINS and another four-digit number, SNIP, apart from the fact that their digits are reversed. The solutions appear on pages 235-6.

Solution to puzzle (posed after Game 12)

White wins with **1 ♔b6** and then:

a) **1...♘b4** 2 ♗b1! stops ...♘a2 and picks up Black's knight with 3 ♔b5 followed by munching!

b) **1...♘b8** 2 ♔b7 ♘d7 3 ♘c6# is a lovely checkmate.

c) **1...♘c7** 2 ♗f5! ♘e8 (2...♘a8+ 3 ♔b7 ♘c7 4 ♘c6+ again wins the black knight, after which White must be able to use his extra ♘+♗ to force checkmate) 3 ♘c6# is another picturesque finish.

Holland's IM Manuel Bosboom is an excellent example of a player who loves to be creative as early as possible in his games. He recently told me that by gaining experience of many different types of positions, his understanding of chess has improved enormously. It is very pleasing when one's efforts are rewarded, and Manuel had his best result to date in the AKN Open at Haarlem in June 1997. His equal first place on 5½/6 represented an overall

tournament performance rating (TPR) of 2771, which included three wins and one draw against GMs Igor Khenkin, Attila Groszpeter, Mikhail Ivanov, and Mikhail Gurevich respectively. Manuel and I both agree that too much significance is often attached to ratings, but he was understandably pleased with his star TPR!

In total, Manuel sacrifices a rook in the sparkling gem that we are about to see, and his GM opponent is thrown off balance like a spinning top starting to spiral downwards. Just before we press the play button for Game 13, here is a lovely 1929 study by Henri Rinck, one of the greatest-ever chess composers. Like Manuel Bosboom, he finds a way for White to play and win despite being a rook down. The solution is waiting for you at a safe place beyond all the explosions coming up in the next hyper-attacking dose of S.T.A.R. Wars.

The Lone R

OK, we now fire ahead into the game as if the Lone Ranger had said to his friend Tonto 'On to Toronto pronto Tonto!'.

Game 13
M. Bosboom – I. Khenkin
Haarlem 1997
Slav Defence

1 d4

Manuel often opens with 1 e4, particularly when he thinks he's going to get to play the King's Gambit (1...e5 2 f4). However, GM Igor Khenkin almost invariably answers 1 e4 with the Caro-Kann Defence, 1...c6. So Manuel spins the wheel knowing the ball will land on the choice 1 d4 today.

1 ...   d5
2 c4   c6

This is the Slav Defence, whereas back in Game 7 we saw lots of very interesting play resulting from 2...♘c6.

3 ♘c3   dxc4

Black is in the mood to grab material at the cost of time and development, while White's mind is in sacrificial gambit mode. A double-edged battle is already taking shape.

4 ♘f3   b5

It may be a bit harsh to label this move as an error, but if I were Black here, I would prefer to hold back with ideas of ...b5-b4 until I was sure that White's knight on c3 could not jump into e4 under good circumstances. For example, **4...e6** transposes to the line known alternatively as the Abrahams Variation, due to its successful use in numerous games by England's Gerald Abrahams, or as the Noteboom Variation, after the great exponent Daniël Noteboom, a talented Dutch player who died in 1932 at the very young age of 21. The 4...e6 line constitutes a superb counterattacking weapon that more often arises via the move-order 1 d4 d5 2 c4 e6 3 ♘f3 c6 4 ♘c3 dxc4. That is the normal route taken in *Play the Noteboom*, which is a 1996 book by Holland's IM Mark van der Werf and FM Teun van der Vorm, and the following fairly recent win by their fellow-countryman IM Marinus Kuijf merits inclusion in any sequel book. The game De Haan-Kuijf, Dutch Interclubs League 1996 went **5 a4 ♝b4 6 e3 b5 7 ♝d2 a5** (well-timed pushing of the queenside pawns is Black's star strategy in the Noteboom Variation) **8 axb5 ♝xc3 9 ♝xc3 cxb5 10 b3 ♝b7** (this precise move defends the a8-rook, whereas 10...b4? 11 ♝xb4 or 10...♘f6?! 11 bxc4 b4? 12 ♝xb4 would be embarrassing for Black) **11 d5 ♘f6 12 bxc4 b4 13 ♝xf6** (13 ♝b2? exd5) **13...♛xf6 14 ♛a4+ ♘d7 15 ♘d4** (stopping ...♛c3+) **15...e5** (*Question: why does Black not play 15...exd5? – the answer* *appears at the end of this game)* **16 ♘b3 ♔e7! 17 ♗e2** (after 17 ♘xa5? ♕b6 White's knight is in a fatal pin, and 17 ♕b5 ♗a6! 18 ♕xa5 ♖hb8, threatening ...♗xc4!, also shows that Black's a-pawn is poisoned) **17...♖hc8 18 0-0 ♘c5 19 ♘xc5 ♖xc5 20 ♖ad1 ♕d6** (in Tilburg on 30 June 1996, I chatted about this position with Maarten Strijbos, another Noteboom expert who reckons that Black is doing very well here because his outside passed pawns on the queenside are far away from White's king, and when the pawns start to run nothing will stop them) **21 f4 e4 22 ♕a1 ♔f8 23 ♕e5** (this works out badly, but there is no obvious alternative way for White to attempt to generate chances for himself) **23...♕xe5 24 fxe5 a4** ('a for acceleration!') **25 ♖f4** (a line like 25 e6 f6 26 d6 a3, with 27 d7 ♔e7 or 27 e7+ ♔f7 to follow, highlights a huge difference between the players' passed pawns: Black's king has the white pawns under control, but the white king is light-years away from the charging black pawns) **25...a3 26 ♖df1** *(D)*.

26...f6! (a cool and necessary reaction to the threat against f7 because 26...a2? 27 ♖xf7+ ♔g8 28 ♖xb7 a1♕ 29 ♖xa1 ♖xa1+ 30 ♔f2 leaves Black with only a memory of his former glorious queenside pawns, while White's central passed pawns suddenly look enormous) **27 exf6 g6 28 ♖h4** (28 ♖xe4 a2 29 ♖a1 b3 is also hopeless for White) **28...a2 29 ♖xh7 a1♕ 30 ♖xa1**

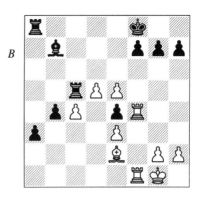

♖xa1+ 31 ♔f2 ♗c8 32 d6 b3 33 d7 0-1. Eric de Haan resigned without waiting for 33...♗xd7 34 ♖xd7 b2 followed by ...b1♕, giving Black his third queen of the game.

Answer to question posed at move 15: Black does not play 15...exd5? on account of 16 c5!, threatening c6 or ♗b5.

5	**a4!**	**b4**
6	**♘e4**	**♕d5**
7	**♘eg5!?**	

Threatening e2-e4, and planning to answer 7...♘f6 by 8 ♘e5!.

7	**...**	**f6**

7...h6 8 e4 ♕a5 9 ♘xf7! ♔xf7 10 ♘e5+ gives White a winning attack. For example:

a) 10...♔e8 11 ♕h5+ ♔d8 12 ♘f7+ ♔c7 13 ♕xa5+ ♔b7 14 ♘d8#.

b) 10...♔f6 11 ♕f3+ ♔e6 12 ♕f5+ ♔d6 13 ♘f7+ ♔c7 14 ♕xa5+ ♔b7 15 ♘d8# gives the same pretty final position as happened in variation 'a'.

c) 10...♔e6 11 ♕g4+ ♔d6 12 ♕xc8 threatens ♘xc4# or ♘f7#.

8	**e4**	**♕a5** *(D)*

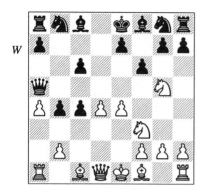

9 ♗xc4!?

IM Manuel Bosboom continues in typically creative fashion.

9	...	fxg5
10	♘xg5	♘h6
11	0-0	♗a6
12	♗e6 (D)	

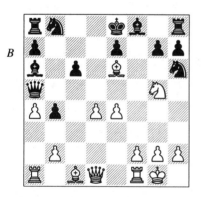

This position really deserves a diagram too because it emphasizes the power of White's light-squared bishop, which right now matters more than the rook on f1.

12	...	♗xf1
13	♕xf1	

A purely counting method might suggest that White only has one pawn for a deficit of one rook, but Black is not well placed to use the extra material. In fact, it is extremely difficult for him to complete the development of his pieces.

13	...	♕a6
14	♕d1	♘d7
15	♗f4	g6

After 15...0-0-0 16 ♖c1 (threatening d5) 16...♔b7, White has the further spectacular rook sacrifice 17 ♖xc6!!, planning:

a) 17...♔xc6 18 ♕c2+ ♔b7 19 ♗d5+ ♔b6 20 ♗c7#.

b) 17...♕xc6 18 ♗d5 ♕xd5 19 exd5 and then:

b1) 19...♘b6 20 ♕f3 and now the play branches into:

b11) 20...♖xd5 21 a5, winning for White.

b12) 20...♘xd5 21 ♘e6 ♖d7 22 ♘c5+ ♔c8 23 ♘xd7 ♘xf4 24 ♕c6+ ♔d8 25 ♘c5 followed by ♘b7# or ♕d7#.

b13) 20...♔c8 21 ♘e6 ♖xd5 22 a5 ♖xa5 23 ♕c6#.

b14) 20...♔a6 21 ♕d3+ ♔b7 22 a5 ♘xd5 23 ♕b5+ ♘b6 (23...♔a8 24 ♕c6#) 24 a6+ and 25 ♕c6#.

b2) 19...♘f6 (the knight wants to avoid being hit by the push a4-a5 that constantly bothered it when placed on b6 throughout all lines stemming from 'b1', but White's knight can cause lots of trouble too) 20 ♘e6 ♖xd5 21 ♕c2 ♖d7 (21...♘e8 22 ♕c4 ♖f5 23 ♘d8+ ♔b6 24 ♕c6+ ♔a5 25 ♘b7# is also nice, at least for one player!) 22 ♘d8+!! *(D)*.

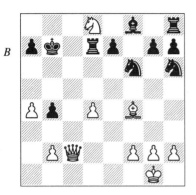

This is stronger than 22 ♘c5+, and Black now gets finished by force as follows:

b21) 22...♖xd8 23 ♕c7+ ♔a6 (23...♔a8 24 ♕c6#) 24 ♕c6+ ♔a5 25 ♕b5# or 25 ♗c7#.

b22) 22...♔b6 23 ♕c6+ ♔a5 24 ♕b5#.

Apart from their beauty, another striking feature of all the variations from 'a' right through to 'b22' is the fact that Black's pieces on the kingside cannot move, not only because they are so restricted in scope, but also because White keeps the threats coming faster than a speeding bullet, and his opponent scarcely has time to react to each one.

  16 ♖c1   ♗g7
  17 ♗c4! *(D)*

White's bishop that has enjoyed a stay on the outpost at e6 moves away with gain of time and makes space for the knight to invade.

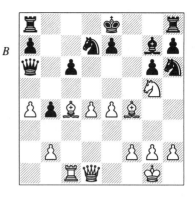

  17 ...   ♕a5
  18 ♘e6

The knight leaps in with great verve.

  18 ...   ♔f7
  19 ♕f3 *(D)*

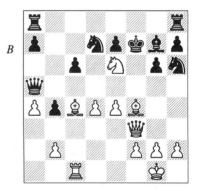

Instead of shifting the knight again, White moves his queen into an attacking position facing the opponent's king, and now threatens a deadly assortment of discovered checks.

  19 ...   ♕h5
  20 ♗xh6+   ♕xf3
  21 ♘xg7+

A killing *zwischenzug* before re-capturing on f3.

| 21 | ... | e6 |

21...♔f6 22 e5+ would be mate if Black didn't have a knight which he can sacrifice on e5, but of course that option is even worse for him than the actual game continuation.

| 22 | ♗xe6+ | ♔e7 |
| 23 | gxf3 | |

White has gone from previously being a rook down for one pawn to now, in effect, having two bishops and two pawns that vastly outweigh Black's extra rook!

23	...	♖ac8
24	e5	♖c7
25	♗b3	♘b6
26	♗g5+	♔d7

26...♔f8 27 ♘e6+ followed by ♘xc7+ sees the extra black rook vanish.

| 27 | ♗e6# | *(D)* |

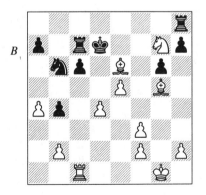

For the third time in the game,

White's star light-squared bishop lands at e6 ... and on this occasion it makes a really big boom!

Solution to puzzle (posed before Game 13)

1 a7? allows Black to defend by 1...♖g8, but instead White wins with **1 h7! ♖h1 2 a7 ♖a1 3 ♖d1!!** and then:

a) **3...♖axd1** 4 a8♕+ ♔f2 5 h8♕ ♖xh8 6 ♕xh8 produces a position that just requires some relatively straight-forward technique before the result 1-0 appears on the scoreboard.

b) **3...♖hxd1** 4 h8♕ ♖xa7 5 ♕h5+ (this skewer is an important tactical detail of the solution) and 6 ♕xd1 leads quickly to a win for White too.

c) **3...♖xa7** (3...♖xh7 loses similarly) 4 ♖xh1 ♖xh7 5 ♖xh7 b5 6 ♖b7 stops Black's pawn in its tracks, like a sprinting athlete that has made a false start, but in this case the b-pawn will not survive to run again.

As we near the end of this S.T.A.R. Wars chapter, it seems appropriate to conclude with several nice examples of checkmate. That is the greatest result of an attack following on from a successful strategy. Normally the opponent will try to react as strongly as possible against one's attempts to 'kill' the king, so we need to spot any tactics that can help to achieve and enforce the ultimate checkmate finish.

Star Test

4.1

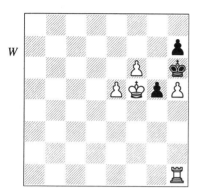

In this little puzzle, it is White to play and checkmate in one move.

4.3

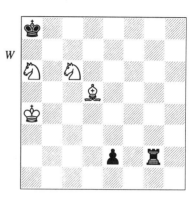

This beautiful 1911 problem with White to play and mate in three moves was composed by the great C.S. Kipping, who featured in Chapter 1.

4.2

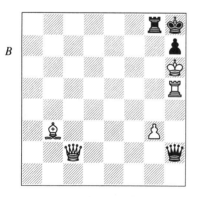

An offering from this author: Black plays and mates in two moves.

4.4

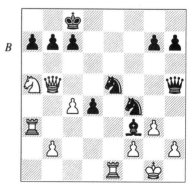

In Emmrich-Moritz, Bad Oeynhausen 1922, it was Black to play and mate in four moves.

4.5

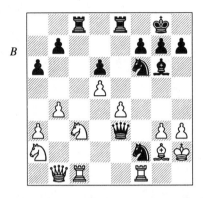

This is based on Karl-Sher, Liechtenstein 1997, but I have adjusted it by transferring the white knight from e2 to a2. In the given position, Black can give an absolutely forced mate in five moves.

4.6

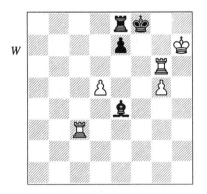

I once saw almost the same position in a study, except that Black had a bishop on e7. With a wave of a magic wand the bishop has now become a

pawn, and White can force mate in six moves.

4.7

This position closely resembles one that occurred 100 years ago in Schiffers-Chigorin, St Petersburg 1897. It is Black to play and mate in seven moves.

Star Challenge no. 4

Part 'a' of this puzzle is from me, while part 'b' is a fascinating example from M.Stosić composed in 1973, the year my brother Joe taught me the rules of chess.

Imagine that in the future there is a sophisticated space station on the Moon, and some people are based there. In the year 2069, the LCF (Lunar Chess Federation) decides to organize a tournament to celebrate the 100 years since Neil Armstrong's lunar landing in Apollo 11. The entry fee is 74 lunes for LCF members and

111 lunes for chessplayers not affiliated to the LCF. The organisers intend to use one third of the fees *from the non-members only* to cover administration costs. All the rest of the money from fees makes up the prize fund, and the total turns out to be between 4700 and 4800 lunes.

a) What is the *exact* total prize fund, and altogether how many players entered the tournament?

b) The tournament winner turns out to be a player who stays particularly alert tactically by solving lots of chess studies and problems, including the following distinctly unusual one *(D)*:

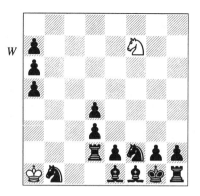

It is White to play and force checkmate in 42 moves!

All the solutions to this Star Test appear on pages 236-7, but before that we have galaxies of exciting ideas...

5 Galaxies of Ideas

One of the most interesting cosmological phenomena are 'black holes', generally formed when a huge star collapses under its own gravity to a single point. Even though they cannot be seen directly, black holes betray their presence and the immense amount of energy they represent by the gravitational pull that they exert on neighbouring bodies and passing light. An analogy with our Royal Game is that many exciting and energetic possibilities exist, but a good deal of creativity may be needed to detect them. So let's switch our minds into ultra-creative mode and go on an original trip around some galaxies in search of interesting ideas.

The Galaxy, of which our Solar System is just a tiny part, is slightly similar in shape to two fried eggs clapped together back to back. The yokes pointing upwards and downwards contain millions of stars, while the main white plane in between is roughly where the Earth is, although far from the centre of the plane. However, to me, having a diet consisting only of fried eggs is like playing the same opening too often, and seems neither appealing nor healthy. So how about considering other galaxies too?

We can think of different galaxies as representing distinct openings. Solar systems within a galaxy are like variations within an opening. Planets in each system can represent lines associated with a variation, and the moons that orbit each planet symbolize the subvariations. However, the shining stars are the brilliant objects that brighten up our lives and also play the role of dazzling novelties, waiting to burst forth onto the chessboard. Just as new stars, moons, planets and even galaxies are frequently discovered, the same can be true of novelties, lines, variations and openings. Such discoveries may come in a flash of inspiration, or sometimes simply because someone is willing to look for them.

Great finds are not made only by established experts. For example, Ganymede, the largest moon or satellite orbiting the planet Jupiter, was first recorded in the year 364 BC by Gan De, a Chinese star-gazer who observed it with his naked eye and no external optical aids. This reminds me of a dramatic chess discovery made at the board on 23 April 1994 by Douglas Smith of Troon. In a 'simul' that I was giving at James Thin bookshop in Glasgow, Douglas found such a strong idea for Black at move ten against one of my favourite lines that he became the first person to beat me in a simul since 1979! Our game began **1 e4 e5 2 ♘c3 ♘c6 3 f4** (I had previously used this variation to win many attacking games, most notably one in only 25 moves against GM Antonio Antunes at the 1992

Manila Olympiad) **3...exf4 4 ♘f3** (4 d4 occurred on page 73 of *C.O.O.L. Chess*) **4...g5! 5 d4 g4!** ('g for go for it!' is a courageous motto, and here it gets well-rewarded) **6 ♗c4 gxf3 7 0-0** *(D).*

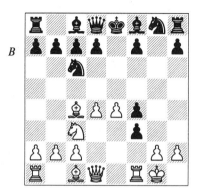

7...♘xd4! (I already knew about this move and its neat tactical point that after 8 ♕xd4? ♕g5 Black threatens ...♕xg2# or ...♗c5) **8 ♗xf4 ♗c5 9 ♔h1 d6!** (much safer than opening the f-file by 9...fxg2+ 10 ♔xg2, after which ♗xf7+ is a big threat) **10 ♗e3** *(D).*

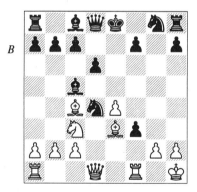

Douglas Smith now found **10...♗e6!**, which he rightly considered to be very logical because it aims to eliminate the white bishop on c4, a dangerous attacking piece. The same idea was played in a game Mi.Tseitlin-Marciano, but Douglas discovered it quite independently. After 11 ♗xd4 ♗xc4 12 ♗xh8 fxg2+ 13 ♔xg2 ♕g5+ 14 ♔h1 ♗xf1 15 ♕xf1 Black is only a pawn up, but he has deadened White's attacking ideas and can soon start to generate a counterattack with manoeuvres like ...♕h5 and ...♘h6-g4. I never again played the gambit variation with 3 f4 after 2...♘c6.

On an amusing note, considering our analogies between astronomy and chess, Douglas Smith is the perfect person to have discovered a really strong star novelty because he once wanted to be an astronaut, although his parents David and Sheila are glad that he found a more 'down to Earth' job involving research in Physics!

Nowadays new ideas are often discovered by players in their analysis at home. Preparation can give one an edge, but it is necessary to check it thoroughly because we are not always as alert and fired up at home as we can be during a tense over-the-board battle in a competitive match. For instance, Magem-Ponomariov, Pamplona 1996/7 started **1 e4 c5 2 ♘f3 ♘c6 3 d4 cxd4 4 ♘xd4 ♘f6 5 ♘c3 g6** (this is a known variation that I used to employ myself more than ten years ago, but in my opinion it is better to play ...d6 before ...♘f6 and then ...g6, as in standard Sicilian Dragon that we discussed in Chapter 1) **6 ♘xc6 bxc6 7 e5 ♘g8 8 ♗c4 ♗g7 9 ♗f4 ♕a5 10 ♕f3! ♗xe5 11 ♗xf7+! ♔xf7 12 ♗xe5+** with an excellent position for White. Young IM Ruslan Ponomariov (currently rated 2555) must have been regarding **10...f6** as his 'improvement' because he played it in Macieja-Ponomariov, World Junior Ch, Zagan 1997. However, his Polish opponent refuted the move effortlessly as follows: **11 e6! d5** *(D)*.

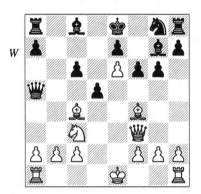

12 ♗b5!! (a star sacrifice that is reminiscent of the great Paul Morphy's play, and a nice way to celebrate the 150th anniversary of the year when the American genius learned the rules of chess in 1847) **12...cxb5** (12...♗b7 13 ♕xd5! is also hopeless for Black after 13...♕xb5 14 ♕d7+ ♔f8 15 ♘xb5 or 13...♕b6 14 ♕d7+ ♔f8 15 ♗e3 c5 16 ♘a4 ♕a5+ 17 ♗d2) **13 ♕xd5 ♕b6** (13...♖b8 14 ♗xb8 is a simple but important tactical point behind White's earlier sacrifice) **14 ♕xa8**

♕xe6+ **15** ♗e3 (White has a decisive material advantage) **15...**♘h6 **16 0-0 0-0 17** ♗xh6 (simple chess is the best route to victory here) **17...**♗xh6 **18** ♖fe1 ♕f5 **19** ♘d5 ♕xc2 **20** ♘xe7+ ♔h8 **21** ♘xc8 ♖xc8 **22** ♖e8+ ♖xe8 **23** ♕xe8+ ♔g7 **24** ♕d7+ ♔g8 **25** ♕xb5 ♕d2 **26** ♕b3+ **1-0**. Ponomariov resigned in view of being too far behind on material and also because ♖d1 was coming next, followed by a decisive infiltration of White's queen and rook into Black's camp. Still, I have no doubt that the very young Ukrainian star will produce lots of successful new ideas in the future.

Chess brainwaves do not occur only in the opening phase. Often an ingenious idea later in the game can help to net an extra half or whole point more than one might expect from a very quick assessment of the position. Therefore, before resigning or agreeing to a draw, it is well-worth having another calm look at the position to see if there are any hidden resources that could bring more points. Since there is no charge for playing on, my motto is, even if you think you're losing, don't resign unless you're completely certain. The following fantastic 1982 study by M. Travasoni shows White to move and draw in a position where many a player might contemplate resignation.

Don't resign!

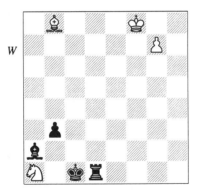

The solution appears after Game 14, which was one of the most interesting encounters at the 1997 Smith and Williamson British Championship.

Game 14
J. Parker – A.D. Martin
British Ch, Hove 1997
Modern Defence

1	d4	g6
2	c4	♗g7
3	e4	d6
4	♘c3	♘c6

4...♘d7 transposes to Game 1 of *C.O.O.L. Chess*.

5	d5	♘d4
6	♗e3	c5
7	♘ge2	

The line beginning with 4...♘c6 has not been played much recently, at least partly because the move 7 ♘ge2 is supposed to give White an advantage according to various theoretical sources. However, I recall GM Mihai Suba telling me in 1990 that he felt the situation is not so clear. Nevertheless, he reckoned that White could obtain an advantage in an uncomplicated way with the simple-chess approach of 7 dxc6. His idea is that after 7...♘xc6 8 ♕d2, White has a kind of Maroczy Bind (which in fact refers to a line of the Sicilian Accelerated Dragon, namely 1 e4 c5 2 ♘f3 ♘c6 3 d4 cxd4 4 ♘xd4 g6 5 c4). Mihai felt that White's extra space and his grip on the d5-square given by the pawns on c4 and e4 mean that Black's position must be considered somewhat worse, although of course he can aim to fight hard.

7	...	♕b6
8	♘xd4?!	

This move has been employed by various fine players in the past, but Black's powerful play in the current game casts a shadow over White's choice. Another, more promising line is 8 ♘a4! ♕a5+ (8...♕b4+? 9 ♗d2 ♕xc4 10 ♖c1 ♕xa2 11 ♘xd4 ♗xd4 12 ♗c4 costs Black his queen) 9 ♗d2 ♕a6 (9...♕c7?! 10 ♗c3! is awkward for Black) and then for example:

a) 10 ♗c3?! ♗d7! 11 b3 ♗xa4 12 bxa4 ♘f6! (12...♕xc4? 13 ♖c1! ♘xe2 14 ♗xg7 ♕xc1 15 ♗xe2 ♕xd1+ 16 ♔xd1 f6 17 ♗xh8 ♔f7 18 g4, with 18...♘h6 19 g5! or 18...g5 19 h4 to follow, is bad for Black) 13 ♘xd4? *(D)*.

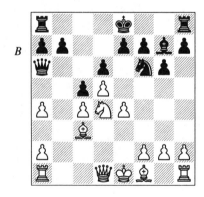

Now 13...♘xe4! 14 ♗b2 ♕a5+ 15 ♔e2 cxd4 gives Black a winning position.

b) **10 ♘xd4! ♗xd4** (10...cxd4?? 11 c5 b5 12 cxb6 wins for White) branches into:

b1) **11 ♗c3? ♗d7!** (the same noteworthy idea cropped up in line 'a') 12 ♗xd4 ♗xa4 13 b3 cxd4 14 ♕xd4 ♕a5+ 15 ♔e2 ♘f6 16 bxa4 ♕xa4 is excellent for Black.

b2) **11 ♘c3!**, intending ♘b5 followed by ♘c7+ or ♘xd4, looks preferable for White.

It is interesting that lines 'a' and 'b1', in which White attempts to win material with ♗c3, are both extremely good for Black. That fact may have led GM Mihai Suba to conclude that the 7 ♘ge2 route is not convincing for White. However, the calm, controlled approach in line 'b2' is very appealing to me. In contrast, the main game, to which we are returning now, is full of fireworks, but they are all exploding under White's feet.

8 ...   **cxd4**
9 ♘a4   **♕a5+**

The fascinating sacrifice 9...dxe3?! 10 ♘xb6 exf2+ 11 ♔xf2 axb6 has been played before, and Black obtains two minor pieces together with dark-square control in return for his queen. However, Andrew Martin's convincing play in the actual game shows that he does not need to opt for a speculative continuation.

10 ♗d2   **♕c7**
11 c5   **♘f6!**

Andrew quite rightly continues with piece development instead of spending precious time to grab material by

11...dxc5, because **12 ♗b5+** is very good for White, as the following sample lines show:

a) **12...♗d7 13 ♗xd7+** and now:

a1) **13...♔xd7 14 ♕b3 b6 15 ♖c1** leaves Black facing the terrible threats of 16 ♕b5+ and 16 ♘xc5+! bxc5 17 ♕b5+ ♔d6 (17...♔d8 18 ♗a5) 18 ♖xc5! ♕xc5 19 ♗f4+ e5 20 dxe6+ ♗e5 21 ♕d7# *(D)*.

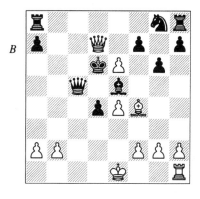

a2) **13...♕xd7 14 ♘xc5 ♕b5 15** b4! followed by a4 is horrible for Black.

b) After **12...♔f8 13 ♖c1 b6 14 b4 ♕e5**, I would be tempted to castle as White because he has such a big lead in development that Black's queen can scarcely afford the time to capture on e4. For instance, 15 0-0 ♕xe4 16 ♗c6 ♖b8 17 ♖e1 ♕f5 18 bxc5 b5 19 ♕b3 intending ♕g3 is overwhelming for White.

12 f3

If Jonathan Parker considered 12 ♗b5+ ♗d7 13 c6 bxc6 14 dxc6, then he might have rejected it because of

14...♗e6! (not 14...♗xc6?? 15 ♖c1), and Black threatens ...a6 or ...♘xe4.

| 12 | ... | 0-0 |
| 13 | ♖c1 | e6! |

This move really caught my attention when I first saw this game. Consider:

1) Black has a lead in development.

2) His pawn on d4 denies White's knight any safe retreat.

3) The black e-pawn threatens to prise open the e-file and expose the king on e1 before White can castle.

14	♗b4	exd5
15	cxd6	♕d8
16	e5	

White could win a small amount of material with 16 d7 ♗xd7 17 ♗xf8, but after 17...♕xf8 Black has a decisive lead in development and he threatens ...♕b4+ to win the white knight on a4.

| 16 | ... | ♖e8 |
| 17 | f4 | |

Black has various very strong continuations after 17 ♕xd4, one example being 17...♘g4 *(D)* and then:

a) 18 fxg4 ♖xe5+ 19 ♔d1 ♖e1+ 20 ♔xe1 ♗xd4, and White's position is hopeless.

b) 18 f4 ♘xe5! 19 fxe5 ♖xe5+ 20 ♔d1 ♖e1+ wins for Black in similar fashion.

| 17 | ... | ♘e4 |

The black knight lands on its powerful outpost with as much weight as the wallet of Texan James Johnson: it is more than 60 metres long when

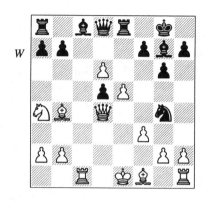

fully open, and contains 2,573 credit cards!

| 18 | ♕xd4 | |

Of course Jonathan Parker saw that Black is threatening ...♕h4+, but 18 ♕f3 loses to 18...f6 or 18...g5. In either case White's pawn centre collapses, and the latter choice by Black carries an extra point: 19 g3 gxf4 20 gxf4 ♕h4+ 21 ♔d1 ♗g4, winning White's queen.

18	...	♕h4+
19	g3	♘xg3
20	hxg3	

20 ♕f2 loses to the destructive sacrifice 20...♗xe5!:

a) 21 fxe5 ♕xb4+.

b) 21 ♕xg3 ♗xf4+ followed by ...♗xg3.

c) 21 hxg3 ♕xh1 (simple, clear and strong) 22 fxe5 ♕e4+, winning the loose bishop on b4.

| 20 | ... | ♕xh1 |
| 21 | ♔f2 | h5! |

Andrew Martin keeps playing energetically with every move, and so the white king gets no peace.

22 ℤc3

If the rook had not been unprotected on c1, then White could have won with 22 ♗g2 ♛h2 23 ℤh1, but that was a big 'if' at the start of this sentence.

| 22 | ... | h4 |
| 23 | ♗g2 | ♛h2 |

Threatening ...h3.

| 24 | gxh4 | ♛xh4+ |
| 25 | ♔e3 | (D) |

25 ♔g1 loses to 25...♗xe5 (or 25...ℤxe5) 26 ♛xd5 (26 fxe5 ♛xd4+) and then for example 26...♗xf4 27 d7 ℤe1+ 28 ♗f1 ♛h2#.

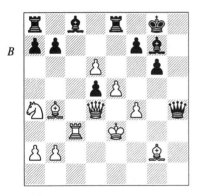

| 25 | ... | ℤxe5+!! |

This star sacrifice ends White's resistance.

26	fxe5	♗h6+
27	♔d3	♗f5+
28	♗e4	♗xe4+
29	♔e2	♗f3+!
30	♔d3	♗e2+

0-1

White's king is finally forced to part from his queen, so he resigns

rather than play on with 31 ♔xe2 ♛xd4.

Solution to puzzle (posed before Game 14)

White draws with **1 ♗f4+ ♔b1** (1...♔b2 2 g8♛ ℤd8+ 3 ♔g7 ℤxg8+ 4 ♔xg8 ℤxa1 5 ♗e5+ b2+ 6 ♔f8 followed by 7 ♗xb2 also draws) **2 g8♛ ℤd8+ 3 ♔g7 ℤxg8+ 4 ♔xg8 b2+** (4...ℤxa1 5 ♗e5+ b2+ 6 ♔f8 followed by 7 ♗xb2 transposes to a line given already) **5 ♔f8! bxa1♛ 6 ♗e5! ♛xe5 stalemate**.

Fast pawn makes it drawn!

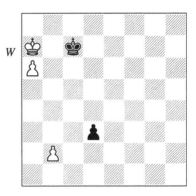

Almost all of the studies in this book start with game-like positions, and so the galaxy of beautiful ideas in the solutions can help to make us more alert to possible resources that could bring us more points in our own encounters. The above 1980 star study composed by S. Mariani shows White to play and draw, with a lovely point at the end of the solution which appears after Game 15.

Extra question: could White still draw if he only had the a-pawn, and not the b-pawn?

I enjoyed visiting the 1997 *Lost Boys* chess tournament in Antwerp, where the galaxy of stars competing included the indefatigable 66-year-old former World Championship challenger, Viktor Korchnoi. He finished runner-up in the eight-player all-play-all Grandmaster group with an excellent score of 5/7, half a point behind a man one third of his own age, Bulgaria's world number four, Veselin Topalov.

Korchnoi notched up emphatic victories against Holland's Paul van der Sterren and Loek van Wely, and also Igor Novikov and Ye Rongguang from the Ukraine and China respectively. Since Korchnoi is at least 25 years older than any of those opponents whom he defeated, they may have felt like lost boys! These younger men were eclipsed by Korchnoi's experience, ingenuity and creativity.

Back in the 1980s, at a tournament in Manchester, Korchnoi stated that he had not yet played his best game. He may still feel the same way after the following tremendous encounter from round three in Antwerp, because it displays all the energy of a star that intends to shine for a lot longer.

Game 15
V. Korchnoi – Ye Rongguang
Antwerp 1997
Caro-Kann Defence

1 c4	**c6**
2 e4	

White transposes to a line against the Caro-Kann Defence, which could also have arisen via the move-order 1 e4 c6 2 c4.

2 ...	**d5**
3 cxd5	**cxd5**
4 exd5	**♘f6**

Some people have tried 4...♕xd5, but the simple, logical developing move 5 ♘c3 favours White as it gains a valuable tempo by attacking Black's queen.

5 ♗b5+	

5 ♕a4+!? *(D)* is a very interesting alternative.

B.Lalić-J.Grant, Walsall 1997 continued **5...♘bd7** (5...♗d7 6 ♕b3 puts Black's b-pawn *en prise*) **6 ♘c3 a6 7 d4 g6** (7...b5? is bad due to 8 ♗xb5 axb5 9 ♕xa8, so if Black cannot advance ...b7-b5, then it seems even more purposeful to play ...g6 at move six and develop as quickly as possible) **8 g3 ♗g7 9 ♗g2 0-0 10 ♘ge2 ♘b6** (if 10...b5, 11 ♘xb5? allows 11...♘b6!,

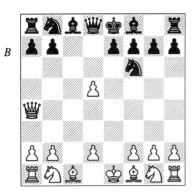

B

winning for Black, but of course White should play 11 ♕b3) **11 ♕b3 ♗g4 12 ♘f4 ♘e8 13 h3 ♗f5 14 ♗e3** (14 g4 ♗d7 leaves White's kingside pawns maybe a little over-extended) **14...♘d6 15 0-0 ♘bc4**, and Jonathan Grant had a playable and fairly active position in which it was not easy for White to make use of having an extra doubled d-pawn.

5	...	♘bd7
6	♘c3	a6

A popular alternative is 6...g6, planning ...♗g7 followed by ...0-0, ...♘b6 and ...♘bxd5 to recover a pawn after achieving more development of pieces. Perhaps Ye Rongguang does not like the line 7 d4 ♗g7 8 d6 exd6 9 ♕e2+ ♕e7 10 ♗f4 for Black, though 10...♕xe2+ followed by ...♔e7, intending ...♘b6 and ...♗e6, has a reasonable reputation.

7 ♗e2!?

I had seen 7 ♕a4 before, but Korchnoi's move was new to me, although I later found out that he played it against GM Vlastimil Hort back in 1970. White lets his opponent win back a pawn on d5 over the next two moves, yet while Black is spending two tempi to recover a pawn, Korchnoi races on with development.

7	...	♘b6
8	♘f3	♘bxd5
9	0-0	e6

After 9...g6, 10 ♕b3 ♗g7 11 ♗c4 or 10 ♕a4+!? ♗d7 (10...♕d7? 11 ♗b5! axb5 12 ♕xa8) 11 ♕b3 ♗c6 12 ♘e5 is unpleasant for Black.

10	d4	♗b4

10...♗e7 11 ♘e5 0-0 12 ♗f3 shows White generating some pressure towards the queenside, and Black has difficulties finding active development for his light-squared bishop as 12...b5 runs into 13 ♘c6 ♕d6 14 ♘xe7+ ♕xe7 15 ♗g5, with at least an edge for White after 15...♘xc3 16 bxc3 ♗b7 17 ♗xf6 gxf6 (17...♕xf6?? 18 ♗xb7 or 17...♗xf3?? 18 ♗xe7) 18 ♗xb7 ♕xb7 19 ♕g4+ ♔h8 20 ♕h4 followed by ♖ae1 and ♖e3 or perhaps f4-f5. However, in such a situation it is important to keep playing energetically, since otherwise Black could start to harass the pawns on a2 and c3 in particular.

11 ♕b3

Seeing the queen on b3 reminds me of the line **1 e4 c6 2 c4 d5 3 cxd5 cxd5 4 exd5 ♘f6 5 ♘c3 ♘xd5 6 ♘f3 e6 7 d4 ♗b4 8 ♕b3** which used to be a favourite of mine, and GM Judit Polgar played it a few times too. Curiously, just as with the story of Douglas Smith that was told earlier in this chapter, there was another simultaneous game that put me off this line some years ago. My opponent was a player rated around 1600 in Edinburgh, but I sincerely apologize for forgetting his name. That is probably because his moves dazed me, and not all names are as distinctive as Douglas Smith! Anyway, the mystery man continued against me with **8...♘c6 9 ♗d3 ♕b6!** *(D)*.

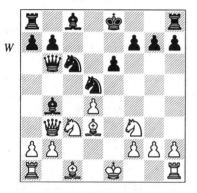

The impact was immediate and awesome. I remember feeling stunned and thinking 'My goodness, that move is *strong*!'. In fact, much later the same year it appeared in *Informator* as a novelty ... by GM Vasily Smyslov. Perhaps someone in Scotland's capital city communicated the ...♕b6 star idea telepathically to the 1957-8 World Champion!

I gave up the line (with 8 ♕b3) after just managing to scrape a draw, but basically White is in trouble once 9...♕b6 lands on the board because Black has the dual threats of 10...♘xd4 and

10...♗xc3+ 11 bxc3 ♕xb3 12 axb3 ♘xc3 winning a pawn in either case, and 10 ♕c4, though possible, is a very clumsy attempt to hold things together. Korchnoi has no such problems in the main game.

11	**...**	**0-0**
12	**♗g5**	**♕a5?!**

12...♗e7 looks more natural to me, although after 13 ♘e5 h6 14 ♗xf6!? (14 ♗h4?! ♘f4! is suddenly nice for Black) and then either 14...♘xf6 15 ♖fd1 (planning to follow up with ♖ac1 and ♗f3) or 14...♗xf6 15 ♖fd1 ♘xc3 16 ♕xc3, I prefer White's position even with its isolated queen's pawn (IQP) because Black still has problems stemming from his restricted light-squared bishop.

13	**♖fc1**	**h6**

If 13...♗d7?, then 14 ♘xd5 ♘xd5 15 a3 ♗d6 16 ♕xb7, when 16...♗a4 17 b4 is good for White, and 16...♗b5 17 b4 ♕a4?? (17...♕b6 is necessary) 18 ♗d1! neatly traps Black's queen.

14	**♗d2!**	

In a sense the bishop is now pointing towards Black's queen, and such a situation tends to produce tactical opportunities.

14	**...**	**♗d7?**

Black appears to have overlooked the sequence with which Korchnoi now wins material. Relatively best is 14...♗e7 or 14...♕b6.

15	**♘xd5!**	**♘xd5**

15...♗xd2 16 ♖c5 b5 17 ♘xf6+ gxf6 18 ♕d3 is also horrible for Black, especially with the pawn-cover in front of his king having been breached. For example:

a) 18...♗f4 19 ♕e4 ♗d6 20 ♖h5 ♔g7 21 ♕g4+ ♔h7 22 ♗d3+ (22 ♕h4 wins too) 22...f5 23 ♕g5 followed shortly by ♖xh6#.

b) 18...♗b4 19 ♖h5 ♔g7 20 ♘e5! fxe5 and now:

b1) I had great fun analysing 21 ♕g3+ ♔f6 (21...♔h7? 22 ♕g5) 22 ♕h4+ ♔g7 and then 23 ♖g5+!? or 23 ♖xh6 ♖g8 24 ♖h7+ ♔f8 25 ♕f6 ♗e8, but this is unnecessary, because the path with 21 dxe5 (the next line, 'b2') is simple, clear and strong.

b2) 21 dxe5 threatens 22 ♕xd7 and 22 ♕g3+. A plausible and pretty finish is 21...♖fd8 22 ♕g3+ ♔f8 23 ♖xh6 and then:

b21) 23...♔e8 24 ♕g8+ ♔e7 (the alternative 24...♗f8 loses really quickly to 25 ♖h7) 25 ♕g5+ ♔e8 26 ♖h7 ♗c6 27 ♖xf7! ♔xf7 28 ♗h5+ ♔f8 29 ♕f6+ ♔g8 30 ♗f7+ ♔f8 (30...♔h7 31 ♕g6+ ♔h8 32 ♕h6#) 31 ♗e6+ ♔e8 32 ♕f7#.

b22) 23...♗c6 24 ♖h7 (threatening 25 ♕g7+) 24...♔e7 (D).

25 ♖xf7+! ♔xf7 26 ♗h5+ (White's queen and bishop now force mate by combining their powers very nicely, a theme which cropped up on several occasions in Chapter 3) 26...♔f8 (if 26...♔e7, then 27 ♕g7#) 27 ♕f4+ ♔g8 28 ♗f7+ ♔h7 29 ♕h4+ ♔g7 30 ♕f6+ ♔h7 31 ♕g6+ ♔h8 32 ♕h6#.

Let's rejoin the actual game, where Korchnoi is about to deliver a knock-out.

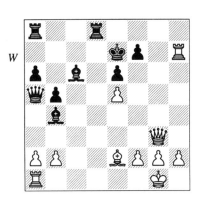

16 ♖c5!! *(D)*

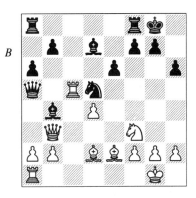

A truly star move by Korchnoi.

16 ...   ♗xd2

The alternatives are bleak too:

a) 16...♗xc5 17 ♗xa5.

b) 16...♕b6 17 ♖xd5! wins.

c) 16...b5 17 ♖xd5! and now either 17...♗xd2 18 ♖xd7 or 17...exd5 18 ♗xb4.

d) 16...♕a4 should also lose to 17 ♖xd5!, although 17...♗xd2 18 ♖xd7 ♕xd7 19 ♘xd2 ♕xd4 gives Black, in effect, ♖+♙ versus ♘+♗ so he can fight on.

e) 16...♗b5 17 ♗xb5! (this is much clearer for White than 17 ♖xd5 ♗xd2) and now:

e1) 17...♗xd2 18 ♗c4 wins material for White.

e2) Even worse for Black is 17...axb5 18 ♖xd5! and then 18...exd5 19 ♗xb4 or 18...♗xd2 19 ♖xb5.

| 17 | ♖xa5 | ♗xa5 |
| 18 | ♘e5! | |

If 18 ♕xb7, then 18...♗a4! threatens 19...♖fb8, and 19 ♘e5 can be met by 19...♗b6! threatening 20...♖a7 and 20...♗xd4.

18	...	♗c8
19	♗f3	♖d8
20	♖c1	♗b6
21	♘xf7!	

21 ♗xd5 is less clear because of 21...♗xd4!, when White has two pieces attacked.

| 21 | ... | ♔xf7 |
| 22 | ♗xd5 | ♗xd4 |

22...♖xd5 23 ♕xb6 wins easily for White.

23	♖xc8!	♖axc8
24	♗xe6+	♔f8
25	♗xc8	♖xc8
26	g3	

A wise precaution, avoiding any possibility of ...♖c1+ being checkmate.

| 26 | ... | b6 |
| 27 | ♕d5 | |

The powerfully centralized queen attacks Black's bishop and also threatens ♕f5+ followed by ♕xc8.

| 27 | ... | ♖c1+ |
| 28 | ♔g2 | ♗c5 |

| 29 | ♕d8+ | ♔f7 |
| 30 | ♕c7+! | 1-0 |

Black resigned in view of 30...♔g8 31 b4 with 31...♗xb4 32 ♕xc1 or 31...♗e3 32 ♕d8+ ♔f7 33 fxe3 to follow. A scorching game by Viktor Korchnoi.

Solution to puzzle (posed before Game 15)

White draws with **1 b4 d2 2 b5 d1♕ 3 b6+ ♔c6 4 b7 ♕d7 5 ♔a8 ♔b6! 6 b8♕+ ♔xa6 7 ♕d6+!** (but not 7 ♕c7? ♕e8+! 8 ♕b8 ♕c6+ 9 ♕b7+ ♕xb7#) **7...♕xd6 stalemate**.

If White only has the a-pawn and not the b-pawn at the start of the puzzle, then Black wins as follows: 1 ♔a8 d2 2 a7 ♗b6! (2...d1♕?? produces stalemate) 3 ♔b8 d1♕ 4 a8♕ ♕d8#.

Take two ... or mate in five!

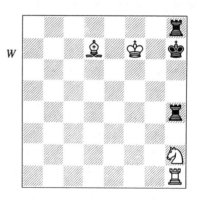

This position relates to part of a 1938 study by T.B. Gorgiev. Your task as White, to play, is to force checkmate in five moves or win both of Black's rooks. The solution awaits you after Game 16, which occurred last year in a ten-player all-play-all event organized in the little Swedish town of Timrå by Jan Berglund of the Karpov Chess School, located at the neighbouring town of Härnösand.

Game 16
A. Hellström – P. Motwani
Timrå 1996
Queen's Pawn Game

1	d4	♘f6
2	♘f3	d5
3	♗g5	

It may be a bit severe to label 3 ♗g5 with a '?!', but I must admit that I have always enjoyed playing Black against this system because it is, in effect, a Trompowsky Attack (1 d4 ♘f6 2 ♗g5) in which I get the extra move ...d5 while White gets ♘g1-f3. The consequence is that ...♘e4 cannot easily be answered by f2-f3, and so Black practically gains an outpost at the e4-square.

A related system is 3 ♗f4, and then De Waal-Wells, Antwerp 1997 continued 3...c5 4 c3 ♘c6 (I would prefer 4...♕b6 because after the move actually chosen White has the option 5 dxc5!?, which basically means that he is then playing the variation 1 d4 d5 2 c4 c6 3 ♘f3 ♘f6 4 ♘c3 dxc4 of the Slav Defence as Black but with an extra tempo due to already having ♗c1-f4) 5 e3 ♕b6 6 ♕b3 c4 7 ♕xb6 (if 7 ♕c2, then a trick worth remembering is 7...♗f5!, intending 8 ♕xf5? ♕xb2 9 ♗e2 e6! {9...♕xa1? 10 ♕c2 puts

Black's queen in trouble} 10 ♕h3 ♕xa1) 7...axb6 *(D)*.

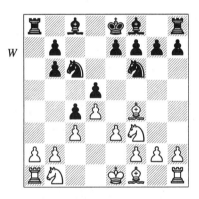

8 ♘bd2 (8 ♘a3 e5! is excellent for Black due to 9 ♘b5 ♖a5! or 9 dxe5 ♗xa3 10 bxa3 ♘e4, and White's ruined queenside structure looks as if it has been hit by one of the tornadoes from the film *Twister*) 8...b5 9 ♗e2 (9 a3 b4! 10 cxb4 ♘xb4 is very nice for Black) 9...b4 10 0-0 e6 11 ♘e5 ♘xe5 12 ♗xe5 ♘d7 13 e4?! (White should consider 13 ♗c7 because 13 ♗g3 allows the strong manoeuvre ...♘b6-a4) 13...♘xe5 14 dxe5 bxc3 15 bxc3 ♖a3! 16 ♗f3? (16 ♘b1 ♖a5 is too

passive for White, and 16 exd5 exd5 17 &f3 &xc3 18 &xd5?? falls into the trap 18...&d3!, winning a piece for Black, but 16 &fc1 is more tenacious) **16...&xc3 17 &b1** (17 exd5 exd5 18 &xd5?? &d3! reiterates an important tactical point) **17...&d3**, and GM Peter Wells converted his extra pawn into a win after a further twenty moves.

    3   ...   &Nf6e4

    4 &Bf4

An alternative is **4 &h4 c5 5 e3 &b6!**:

a) Pete Wells showed me a lovely trick after **6 &c1 cxd4 7 exd4**. Black's g-pawn makes the giant jump **7...g5!!** *(D)* which made me say 'Gosh!' and leads to great lines such as:

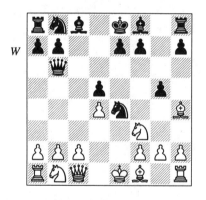

a1) **8 &xg5 &xg5** and then 9 &xg5 &xd4 or 9 &xg5? &xb2.

a2) **8 &xg5 &h6!!** (this threatens 9...&xh4 and 9...f6; it is even stronger for Black than 8...&h6 9 f4) 9 &f4 f6 10 &h3 (10 &c7 &c6 11 &xe4 dxe4 12 &g3 &c1+ 13 &e2 &xd4# is a neat finish) 10...&xh3 11 &xh6 &xh6 12

gxh3 &c1!, which is embarrassing for the rook on a1.

a3) **8 &g3 &c6 9 c3 h5! 10 h4 g4 11 &fd2 &xg3 12 fxg3 e5 13 dxe5 &e3+** with a crushing position for Black.

b) Donk-Wells, Antwerp 1997 continued **6 &bd2 &xd2 7 &xd2 &xb2 8 &d1 e6 9 &e2 c4** (after 9...cxd4 10 exd4?? Black wins immediately with the pin 10...&b4, so instead White would have to go for the gambit route 10 0-0, and then at least he has a lead in development in an open position, which explains why Pete wanted to keep the position more closed with 9...c4) **10 c3** (10 0-0 &b4 is even worse for White) **10...&xd2+ 11 &xd2 &d7**, intending ...&b6-a4, and again Black went on to win with his extra pawn.

    4   ...   c5

    5 e3   &Nc6

    6 c3   &Qb6

    7 &Qc1   &Bf5

When analysing at home after the game, I found the stronger move **7...f6!** *(D)*.

Black's main threat is 8...g5 9 &g3 h5 10 h4 g4 11 &fd2 (11 &g1 is also unsatisfactory) 11...&xg3 12 fxg3, and then 12...&h6, 12...e5 and 12...&c7 are all disastrous for White. However, after the safe-looking reply 8 h3 (in response to 7...f6), we see another star idea behind the little push of the f-pawn, viz. **8...cxd4**:

a) 9 cxd4 &f5 followed by ...&c8 to harass White's queen on the freshly opened c-file.

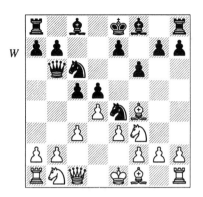

W

b) 9 exd4 e5! (this is the key point) 10 ♗e3 (10 dxe5? ♕xf2+) 10...exd4 11 ♘xd4 ♗c5! with a superb harmonious and active position for Black.

The developing move 7...♗f5 which I actually played is not bad of course, but 7...f6! shows that a small pawn can sometimes pack a bigger punch than a larger piece. Nice examples of my motto 'f for forward' never stop appearing!

| 8 | ♘bd2 | f6 |

'Better late than never!', as the saying goes.

9	h3	cxd4
10	exd4	e5
11	♗e3	♘xd2

For Black, the problem with the continuation 11...exd4 12 ♘xd4 ♘xd4 13 ♗xd4 ♗c5 is that White has the good reply 14 ♘b3!.

| 12 | ♕xd2 | e4 |
| 13 | ♘h4 | ♗d7 |

Threatening ...g5, trapping White's knight on the rim.

| 14 | g3 | ♘a5 |
| 15 | ♖b1 | |

White wants to play ♕d1 and ♕h5+ without leaving his b-pawn *en prise*.

| 15 | ... | ♖c8 |

Star Question: *What is Black threatening? The answer appears after the game.*

16	♕d1	g6
17	♘g2	♗d6
18	♗h6	♔f7
19	h4	♕c6

Defending the d5-pawn against possible harassment by ♘e3, for example, and preparing a 'minority attack' with ...b5-b4.

20	♗f4	♗e7
21	♗e2	b5
22	a3	♘c4

Because of the particular configuration that White's queenside pawns have, it is difficult to play b2-b3, and so Black's knight in effect has an outpost to enjoy at c4.

| 23 | 0-0 | h6! |

Especially after White's monarch has castled on the kingside, Black may want to play ...g5 at some moment. Indeed, it turns out to be the winning stroke eleven moves from now!

| 24 | f3 | |

It is not easy to suggest another active idea for White.

| 24 | ... | exf3 |
| 25 | ♗xf3 (D) | |

After 25 ♖xf3 ♗f5 26 ♗d3, the white rook on the f-file gets pinned by 26...♗g4.

25	...	♗f5
26	♖a1	♘xb2
27	♕b3	♘c4

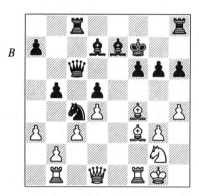

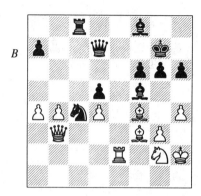

I preferred to maintain a really solid, sound position rather than capturing on c3 and losing my pawns on d5 and then b5.

28 a4   b4!

After 28...a6 29 axb5 axb5 (or 29...♛xb5 30 ♛xb5 axb5 31 ♗xd5+) 30 ♖a7, White has much more activity than he gets in the actual game when Black returns his surplus pawn to keep the a- and b-files closed.

29 cxb4   ♔g7

It makes sense for Black's king to move off the a2-g8 diagonal when White's queen is on it and there is also a bishop pointing towards d5.

30 ♔h2

While White's king was on g1 he had to consider the threat of ...♛b6, after which ♗xd5 would have been met by ...♛xd4+, and the little '+' symbol makes a huge impact.

30	**...**	**♛d7**
31	**♖fe1**	**♖he8**
32	**♖a2**	**♗f8**
33	**♖ae2**	**♖xe2**
34	**♖xe2?** *(D)*	

White overlooked the forthcoming winning sequence. 34 ♗xe2 was necessary, although Black still stands better then because his pieces are more actively placed than those of the opponent, and there is always the possibility of a kingside 'pawn break' with ...g5.

34	**...**	**g5!**
35	**hxg5**	**hxg5**
36	**g4**	

If 36 ♗c1, then 36...g4 traps White's light-squared bishop.

36	**...**	**♗xg4**
37	**♗g3**	**♗d6**

This creates the terrible threat of ...♖h8+.

38	**♗xg4**	**♛xg4**
39	**♗xd6**	**0-1**

White lost on time before I could capture his rook.

Answer to Star Question (posed at move 15)

Back there, it was my rook on c8 that was threatening to make the star capture **16...♖xc3!**, in view of 17 bxc3 ♕xb1+ or 17 ♕xc3 ♗b4, a winning pin.

Solution to puzzle (posed before Game 16)

White wins with **1 ♘g4!!** ♖f8+ (or 1...♖xh1 2 ♗f5#) **2 ♔xf8 ♖xh1** (otherwise White will take Black's second rook) **3 ♗f5+ ♔h8 4 ♘e5** (threatening ♘f7#) **4...♖h7 5 ♘g6#**, a very neat finish.

Look at the rook!

In this 1929 study composed by Leonid Kubbel, Black is a pawn ahead in the endgame but his rook is rather restricted, and so it is White to play and win. The solution awaits you after Game 17.

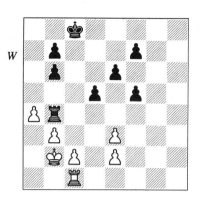

The move c2-c4 very early in the opening may not have a reputation for leading to exciting play, but the fireworks in Games 5 and 11, together with the galaxy of interesting ideas contained in the following GM clash from the 1997 European Team Championship, should help to correct any misconceptions about the English Opening lacking lustre.

Game 17
B. Alterman – J. Magem
European Team Ch, Pula 1997
English Opening

| **1 c4** | **c5** |
| **2 ♘f3** | |

After **2 g3**, a really interesting possibility is **2...d5!?**. Suba-Stefanov, Bucharest 1980 then continued **3 cxd5 ♕xd5 4 ♘f3 ♘c6 5 ♗g2** (the alternative 5 ♘c3 ♕d7 6 ♗g2 e5, to be followed by ...♗d6, ...♘ge7, ...b6 and ...♗b7, gives Black a highly harmonious position and a strong grip on the

d4-square) **5...♗g4**, but 5...e5! 6 ♘c3 ♕d7 would have transposed to the previous note, which is very pleasant for Black.

Instead of 2...d5, GM Chris Ward preferred the symmetrical route **2...g6** in Bezold-Ward, Hastings 1996/7. That game proceeded with **3 ♗g2 ♗g7 4 ♘c3 ♘c6 5 d3 e6** (Black breaks the symmetry to unbalance the position

and White's reply adds another twist)
6 ♗xc6!? *(D).*

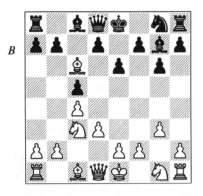

6...bxc6 (after the game, Chris said to me that if 6...dxc6 then he was concerned about 7 ♕d2, with the idea of b3 and ♗b2) **7 f4!** (White improves his central and dark-square control, so if Black trades his fianchettoed bishop for the c3-knight then he will be very vulnerable on the dark squares in general) **7...d6 8 ♘f3 ♘h6 9 e4** (perfectly timed before Black can play ...♘f5) **9...f5 10 e5 dxe5 11 ♘xe5 ♘f7 12 ♕e2!** (12 ♘xc6? ♕c7 is exactly what Black wants because not only will he recover a pawn almost immediately, but his light-squared bishop will get fianchettoed and enjoy a bright future on the h1-a8 diagonal) **12...♗xe5 13 fxe5 ♕d4** (one idea behind not playing ...♘xe5 at move 12 is that 14 ♗f4 can now be met by 14...g5, but instead White has planned a strong temporary pawn sacrifice) **14 ♗e3! ♕xe5 15 0-0-0 0-0 16 ♕f2 ♕c7 17 ♗xc5** (the most striking feature of the position is the

superiority of White's bishop over its black counterpart) **17...♖e8 18 d4** (Chris reckoned that 18 g4! is even stronger because White attacks immediately, and 18...fxg4 19 ♘e4 is terrible for Black) **18...a5**, planning ...♗a6. Black still stood significantly worse, but he managed to hold a draw after a further 38 moves.

2	**...**	**♘f6**
3	**♘c3**	**d5**
4	**cxd5**	**♘xd5**
5	**g3**	

5 e4 was considered on page 178 of *C.O.O.L. Chess.*

5	**...**	**♘c6**
6	**♗g2**	**♘c7**

6...e5? loses a pawn to 7 ♘xe5! ♘xc3 (7...♘xe5 8 ♗xd5) 8 ♘xc6 ♘xd1 9 ♘xd8.

After five moves of Banikas-Macieja, World Junior Ch, Zagan 1997, there was the same position as we have in the main game after 6...♘c7 except that Black's other knight was still at home on b8 and White's king's knight had not yet moved from g1. That battle continued **6 ♕a4+!** *(D).*

6...♕d7 (6...♘d7 is rather passive and 6...♗d7? 7 ♕b3 puts Black's b-pawn *en prise* to two of White's pieces, with 7...♘c6 8 ♕xb7 ♖b8? being a trick that fails to trap the white queen in view of 9 ♕xc6! ♗xc6 10 ♗xc6+) **7 ♕xd7+ ♘xd7 8 ♘f3 e5 9 d3 b6 10 ♗h3!** (threatening 11 ♗xd7+ followed by ♘xe5, but 10 ♘xe5? ♘xe5 11 ♗xa8 ♘xa8 is simply bad for White) **10...f6** (10...♗d6 walks into 11

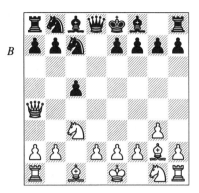

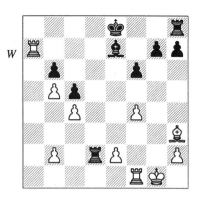

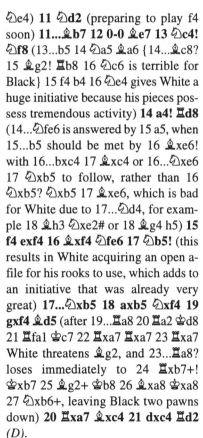

♘e4) **11 ♘d2** (preparing to play f4 soon) **11...♗b7 12 0-0 ♗e7 13 ♘c4!** ♘f8 (13...b5 14 ♘a5 ♗a6 {14...♗c8? 15 ♗g2! ♖b8 16 ♘c6 is terrible for Black} 15 f4 b4 16 ♘e4 gives White a huge initiative because his pieces possess tremendous activity) **14 a4! ♖d8** (14...♘fe6 is answered by 15 a5, when 15...b5 should be met by 16 ♗xe6! with 16...bxc4 17 ♗xc4 or 16...♘xe6 17 ♘xb5 to follow, rather than 16 ♘xb5? ♘xb5 17 ♗xe6, which is bad for White due to 17...♘d4, for example 18 ♗h3 ♘xe2# or 18 ♗g4 h5) **15 f4 exf4 16 ♗xf4 ♘fe6 17 ♘b5!** (this results in White acquiring an open a-file for his rooks to use, which adds to an initiative that was already very great) **17...♘xb5 18 axb5 ♘xf4 19 gxf4 ♗d5** (after 19...♖a8 20 ♖a2 ♔d8 21 ♖fa1 ♔c7 22 ♖xa7 ♖xa7 23 ♖xa7 White threatens ♗g2, and 23...♖a8? loses immediately to 24 ♖xb7+! ♔xb7 25 ♗g2+ ♔b8 26 ♗xa8 ♔xa8 27 ♘xb6+, leaving Black two pawns down) **20 ♖xa7 ♗xc4 21 dxc4 ♖d2** *(D)*.

22 ♖f3!! (another star move from White, and this time the threat is ♖e3, but 22...♖xe2 fails due to 23 ♖a8+ ♗d8 24 ♖d3 ♔e7 25 ♖d7+, while 22...♔f7 23 ♖e3 ♖e8 24 ♗d7 ♖d8 25 ♗c6 is also hopeless for Black) **22...f5** (desperation) **23 ♖e3 ♖d7 24 ♖a8+ ♖d8 25 ♖a6 ♖d6 26 ♗g2!** (White quite rightly wants to win as easily as possible, and his threat of 27 ♖a7 ♖d7 28 ♗c6 is even stronger than making the capture 26 ♗xf5, also because 26...♔f7 now loses to 27 ♖a7 ♖e8 28 ♗c6, whereas if the white bishop were on f5 then Black could attack it and fight on with ...♔f7-f6) **26...♔f8 27 ♗d5** (threatening 28 ♖a7 ♗f6 29 ♖f7+ ♔g8 30 ♖e8#) **27...♖d7 28 ♖a8+ ♗d8 29 ♔g2** (this 'quiet' but deadly move threatens 30 ♗c6 ♖d6 31 ♖e8+ without allowing Black any rook check on d1) **29...♖d6 30 ♖a7 1-0**. Black resigned facing the threat 31 ♖f7+ ♔g8 32 ♖e8#, and due to 30...♖f6 31 ♖d7.

The main game is no less convincing for White, so let's rejoin it now to see his seventh move.

7 a3   g6
7...e5 8 b4 ♗d6 (8...cxb4 9 axb4
♗xb4 10 ♘xe5! is excellent for White
after 10...♗xc3 11 ♘xc6 or 10...♘xe5
11 ♕a4+ ♘c6 12 ♗xc6+ bxc6 13
♕xb4) **9 bxc5 ♗xc5 10 ♗b2 0-0 11
0-0 ♗f5 12 d3 ♕e7** gave Black a very
satisfactory position in the game Va-
ganian-J.Claesen, Antwerp 1997, but
GM Rafael Vaganian eventually defeated Jeroen Claesen in 48 moves.
8 h4!?   h6
9 d3   ♗g7
10 ♗e3   b6? *(D)*
This lets White use a tactical trick
to exploit the fact that the c6-knight is
no longer protected, so Black should
have played 10...♘e6 or 10...♘d4.

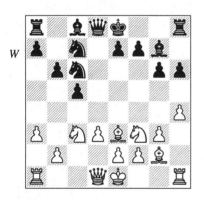

11 h5!
Planning to answer 11...g5? with 12
♘xg5!, threatening ♗xc6+.
11 ...   gxh5
11...♗b7 12 hxg6 fxg6 13 ♘h4!
practically wins for White. For instance, **13...♕d6 14 ♗e4!** (14 ♘e4
♕e6) **14...g5 15 ♘f5 ♕f6 16 ♕a4**

(threatening 17 ♘xg7+ ♕xg7 18
♗xc6+, but 16 ♘xg7+! ♕xg7 17 ♕a4
is also extremely strong and forceful
because 17...♕f6 loses to 18 ♗xg5!
hxg5 19 ♖xh8+ ♕xh8 20 ♗xc6+
♗xc6 21 ♕xc6+) and now:
a) **16...0-0 17 ♗xc6 ♗xc6 18
♕xc6!** and then 18...♕xc6 19 ♘xe7+
followed by 20 ♘xc6 leaves Black a
piece down, as does 18...♕xf5 19
♕xc7.
b) **16...♗f8 17 ♗xg5!** hxg5 18
♖xh8 ♕xh8 19 ♗xc6+ ♗xc6 20
♕xc6+ brings White out a pawn up
with an overwhelming position.
c) **16...♔f7** is more tenacious, but
still very bad for Black.
12 ♖xh5   ♗b7
13 ♕a4
Threatening to play 14 ♘e5! ♗xe5
15 ♗xc6+ ♗xc6 16 ♕xc6+ ♕d7 17
♕xd7+ ♔xd7 18 ♖xe5, and White
emerges from the sequence with an
extra bishop.
13 ...   ♕d7
14 ♖c1   0-0-0 *(D)*

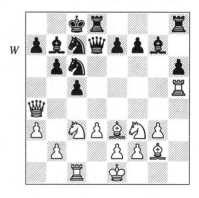

15 ♗xc5!!

A star sacrificial offer by GM Boris Alterman.

15 ... ♔b8

If **15...bxc5**, then 16 ♖xc5 ♔b8 is not completely convincing for White. However, **16 ♘e4!** (threatening ♘xc5 even more than ♖hxc5) **16...♘d4 17 ♕xa7 ♗xe4 18 ♖hxc5!** (but not 18 dxe4? ♘xf3+ 19 ♗xf3 {19 ♔f1 ♕d1+! 20 ♖xd1 ♖xd1#} 19...♕d2+ 20 ♔f1 ♕xc1+ and Black wins) leads to:

a) **18...♘b5** 19 ♖xb5!, threatening ♖b8# and intending 19...♕xb5 20 ♕xc7#.

b) **18...♘c6 19 ♕a4**, and White's attack is irresistible in spite of being two pieces down. Here are a couple of sample variations illustrating how helpless Black's king really is without pawns for protection:

b1) **19...♗d5** 20 ♖xc6 ♗xc6 21 ♖xc6 (threatening 22 ♕a8#) 21...♕d5 22 ♘h4 ♕e5 23 ♕a7, threatening 24 f4 or 24 ♘f3 to deflect the black queen away from defending the c7-knight.

b2) **19...♗xb2** 20 ♖xc6 ♗xc6 21 ♖xc6 ♕d5 22 ♘h4 ♕e5 23 f4 ♕e3 24 ♖xc7+! ♔xc7 25 ♕c6+ ♔b8 26 ♕b7#.

c) **18...♘e6 19 ♘e5!** (stronger for White than 19 ♖xc7+ ♘xc7 20 dxe4 ♕d6) branching into lovely lines such as:

c1) **19...♗xe5** 20 ♗xe4 ♘xc5 (20...♕d6 21 ♕a8+ ♔d7 22 ♗c6+ ♕xc6 23 ♕xc6+ also wins for White) 21 ♗b7+! ♘xb7 22 ♕a8# *(D)*.

c2) **19...♘xc5** 20 ♘xd7 (threatening ♘b6#, but 20 ♗xe4! ♗xe5 21

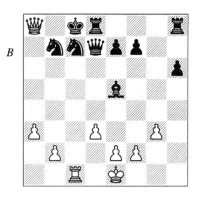

♗b7+! ♘xb7 22 ♕a8# mirrors line 'c1') 20...♖xd7 21 ♖xc5 (21 ♗xe4 wins too) 21...♗xg2 22 f3, and Black has no proper defence against the threat of 23 ♕a8# since 22...♔d8 is met by 23 ♕b8#.

c3) **19...♗xg2** 20 ♘xd7 ♔xd7 (20...♖xd7 21 f3! ♘xc5 22 ♖xc5 transposes to 'c2') 21 ♖xc7+ ♘xc7 22 ♖xc7+ soon forces Black's exposed king to surrender.

These forceful variations explain why GM Jordi Magem did not accept White's offer of a bishop on c5, but as the game goes Black is simply a pawn down without any compensation.

16 ♗e3 f5
17 ♘h4 e6
18 ♘g6 ♖hg8
19 ♘f4 ♘e8
20 ♘b5!

Moving in for the final attack.

20 ... ♘f6

20...a6 21 ♗xc6! ♗xc6 22 ♕xa6! ♗xb5 23 ♕xb6+ ♔a8 (23...♕b7 24 ♕xd8+ ♕c8 25 ♕xc8#) 24 ♖c5 ♖b8 (24...♘d6 loses to 25 ♖c7) 25 ♕a5+

♕a7 26 ♕xa7+ ♔xa7 27 ♖c7++!
forces 28 ♖a7#.

    21 ♖h4   **♘g4** (D)

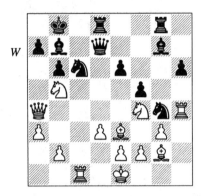

    22 ♖xg4!

White eliminates the knight that wanted to take his dark-squared bishop since that star piece is destined soon to reach the f4-square, with devastating effect against Black's king.

    22 ...   **fxg4**
    23 ♘xe6!   **♗e5**

23...♕xe6 allows the pretty finish 24 ♖xc6! ♗xc6 25 ♕xa7+ ♔c8 26 ♕c7#.

    24 ♘xd8   **♖xd8**
    25 ♗f4   **1-0**

Black resigned in view of being two pawns down in a hopeless position.

Solution to puzzle (posed before Game 17)

White wins with **1 c4!!** (planning ♔c3 to take Black's trapped rook) **1...dxc4 2 ♔c3! ♖xb3+ 3 ♔xc4** with the variations:

a) **3...♖a3 4 ♔b4+** wins the black rook.

b) **3...♖xe3 4 ♔d4+** is similar to line 'a'.

c) **3...♖b2 4 ♔c3! ♖xe2** (or 4...♖a2 5 ♔b3+) **5 ♔d3+** reiterates the idea of a deadly discovered check by White.

Mission Impossible?

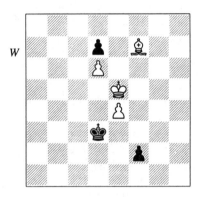

With Black having an unstoppable f-pawn which is about to promote, White's task of trying to save the game may at first sight seem like an impossible mission. However, in this study by R. Alexandrov it is White to play and draw, and the elegant solution awaits you after Game 18.

Chess U.F.O.s!

On 16 August 1997 there were so many lights in the sky near Brussels's huge *Kinepolis* cinema complex that one might have thought a batch of U.F.O.s were about to land. Thousands of people were jumping up and down with the excitement ... of *Abba in concert!* The group of Swedish pop stars provided sensational entertainment and attracted a great deal of interest ... as the Scandinavian Defence (1 e4 d5) has been doing recently!

The Scandinavian is a counterattacking response by Black, but for a long time many people did not take it very seriously, perhaps since it was regarded as being something of a U.F.O. (**unusual fun opening!**). However, it seems to me that the Scandinavian

really started to receive a respected position on the international chess stage after India's Viswanathan Anand employed it against Garry Kasparov in game 14 of their 1995 PCA World Championship match, and got a great position from the opening phase. The following miniature from the 1997 Liechtenstein Open must have been disconcerting for White, but IM Richard Forster's play as Black shows that he is well in tune with the ideas behind the Scandinavian.

Game 18
H. Grabher – R. Forster
Liechtenstein 1997
Scandinavian Defence

| 1 | e4 | d5 |
| 2 | exd5 | |

My Scottish friend Alex Thomson from Tullibody enjoys playing 2 d4 after reading the 1995 book *Blackmar-Diemer Gambit* by IM Gary Lane, although the usual move-order in that opening is 1 d4 d5 2 e4.

| 2 | ... | ♘f6 |
| 3 | d4 | |

3 c4 can lead to very interesting play. For example:

a) **3...c6 4 d4** (4 dxc6?! ♘xc6 gives Black far more than enough development in compensation for his one-pawn deficit, and leaves White's light-squared bishop restricted by the c4-pawn, which has also created serious weaknesses at the d3- and d4-squares)

4...cxd5 5 ♘c3 transposes to the Panov-Botvinnik Attack against the Caro-Kann Defence, which is more often reached via the move-order 1 e4 c6 2 d4 d5 3 exd5 cxd5 4 c4 ♘f6 5 ♘c3. Motwani-W.Rutherford from my simultaneous at Edinburgh's Pentland Hills Chess Club on 11 April 1997 continued **5...e6 6 ♘f3 ♗b4 7 cxd5 ♘xd5 8 ♕c2** (8 ♕b3 ♘c6 9 ♗d3 ♕b6! was mentioned within the notes to White's 11th move of Game 15) **8...♘d7** (top astronomer Terry Purkins, who works at Edinburgh's Royal Observatory, played 8...♘c6 against me in the simul., and we had a long, hard-fought draw) **9 ♗d3 ♘7f6 10 0-0 0-0 11 ♘e5 ♗d7?** *(D)* (there is a tactical flaw in this natural-looking developing move, whereas 11...♗e7 intending ...♘b4 is OK for Black).

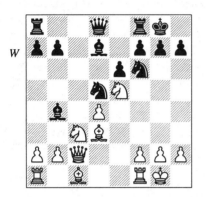

12 ♘xd5! exd5 (not 12...♘xd5? 13 ♗xh7+) **13 ♗g5**, with the dual threats of 14 ♗xf6 (because of 14...♕xf6? 15 ♘xd7) and 14 ♗xh7+. White won this game in 34 moves, but now let's consider another response for Black after 3 c4.

b) **3...e6!?** (this is often referred to as the 'Icelandic Gambit', and it certainly produces some cool games!) **4 dxe6 ♗xe6 5 d4 ♕e7!?** *(D).*

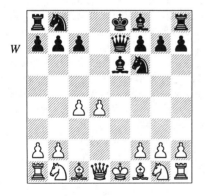

This position occurred in Izsak-Galyas, Elekes Memorial IM tournament, Budapest 1997. Black threatens 6...♗xc4+, and 6 ♗e3 ♕b4+ 7 ♕d2 ♗xc4! is fine for him because after 8 ♕xb4 he recaptures on b4 with check, but 7 ♘d2! is more testing. Also, 6 ♕e2 can be answered with further rapid development by 6...♘c6!, planning to meet 7 d5? with 7...♘d4. However, it is hard to imagine anything worse than what actually happened to IM Gyula Izsak: **6 ♕a4+?? ♗d7+ 0-1**. This just goes to show how easy it is to overlook retreating moves.

3 ... ♕xd5!?

Instead of 3...♘xd5, Black develops another piece. It happens to be his precious queen, but that does not automatically rule it out from the thoughts of creative players who enjoy experimenting as early as possible in the opening. Alternatively, 3...♗g4!? 4 f3 (4 ♘f3 ♕xd5 transposes to the main game) 4...♗f5 5 c4 (5 ♗b5+ c6 6 dxc6 ♕a5+ 7 ♘c3 ♘xc6, intending ...0-0-0 followed by ...e5, caused White problems in Upton-Bryson, Scottish Ch, Aviemore 1997) 5...e6 6 dxe6 ♘c6!? gave Black lots of activity and a big lead in development as compensation for two sacrificed pawns in Bologan-Shirov, Dresden 1997.

4 ♘f3?!

I am being rather strict in appending a '?!' to a move so early in the game, but I feel that 4 ♘f3 lacks punch and allows Black to seize the initiative. 4 ♘c3 looks more natural to me because it immediately gains a tempo by attacking Black's queen. Then 4...♕a5 gives a position that is usually reached via the move-order **1 e4 d5 2 exd5 ♕xd5 3 ♘c3 ♕a5** and then **4 d4 ♘f6**, but instead of playing d2-d4, I like to go for rapid piece development as White with **4 ♘f3** *(D)*.

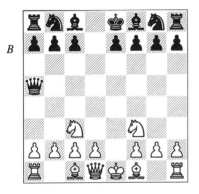

For example, in a simultaneous at Troon in July 1992, I won the following game in 13 moves against an opponent rated around 2000: **4...♘f6 5 ♗c4 c6** (after 5...♗f5, an interesting possibility which was discovered independently by myself and GM Andrei Kharlov, is 6 b4!? ♕xb4 7 ♘e5, threatening 8 ♗xf7+ and 8 ♖b1) **6 ♕e2 ♗f5** (6...♗g4? loses to 7 ♗xf7+! ♔xf7 8 ♘e5+) **7 d3** (limiting the scope of Black's light-squared bishop, and leaving the d4-square free for White to play ♘d4) **7...e6 8 ♗d2 ♗b4 9 a3 ♘bd7?** (9...0-0 was relatively best, so that Black's king would not have to face White's queen along the e-file, a factor which soon proves to be deadly)

10 ♘d4! (not only attacking the f5-bishop, but also threatening ♘b3 to protect the a1-rook and make axb4 possible) **10...♗xc3?** (10...♗e7 was necessary) **11 ♗xc3 ♕e5 12 ♕xe5 ♘xe5 13 ♘xf5 1-0**, due to 13...exf5 14 ♗xe5 or 13...♘xc4 14 ♘xg7+.

Black does not get into any such problems in the main game.

4	...	♗g4
5	♗e2	♘c6
6	c4	

An example featuring 6 0-0 appears on page 113 of *H.O.T. Chess*.

6 ... ♕h5

Let's consider some possibilities after **6...♕f5!?**:

a) **7 d5 0-0-0!** (7...♘b4?? 8 ♕a4+) **8 ♗d3 ♕d7** (planning ...♘d4 or ...♗xf3 and ...♘e5) **9 dxc6 ♕xd3 10 cxb7+ ♔xb7 11 ♕xd3 ♖xd3** is fine for Black, but it is important that 12 ♘e5 is not possible due to 12...♖d1#.

b) **7 h3 ♗xf3** (7...♕h5?? 8 g4) **8 ♗xf3 0-0-0 9 ♗xc6 ♕e6+! 10 ♕e2 ♕xc6** leaves White facing the dual threats of 11...♖xd4 and 11...♕xg2, and 11 d5 fails to 11...♘xd5! 12 cxd5 ♕xc1+.

7 ♘c3

7 h3 0-0-0 8 0-0 *(D)* is met by a star move:

8...♘xd4!! and now:

a) **9 ♘xd4 ♗xe2 10 ♕xe2 ♖xd4**, and Black has won a pawn.

b) **9 hxg4 ♘xg4!** (9...♘xf3+? 10 ♗xf3 ♖xd1 11 gxh5 wins for White) and there is no satisfactory defence to the threat of 10...♘xf3+ followed by

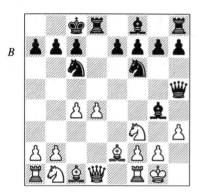

...♕h2# or ...♖xd1. For example, 10 ♘h4 ♘xe2+! (10...♘f3+?! 11 ♘xf3 ♖xd1 12 ♖xd1 gives White a lot of material in return for his queen) 11 ♕xe2 ♕xh4 puts Black a pawn ahead and threatening ...♕h2# again.

7 ... 0-0-0

Intending ...e5, but also threatening 8...♘xd4 9 ♘xd4 ♗xe2 10 ♘cxe2 (10 ♕xe2 ♖xd4) 10...e5, and then for example 11 ♕a4 exd4 12 ♕xa7 ♗b4+ 13 ♔f1 d3 14 ♕a8+ (14 ♘c3 ♗xc3 15 bxc3 ♕d1#) 14...♔d7 15 ♕a4+ b5! 16 ♕xb4 (16 ♕xb5+ ♕xb5 17 cxb5 dxe2+ is also hopeless for White) 16...♕xe2+ 17 ♔g1 ♕d1+ 18 ♕e1 ♕xe1#. That line is a logical, powerful, flowing illustration of what is possible when one player possesses a lead in development. It is also a good advert for the Scandinavian in action.

8 ♗e3 e5
9 d5 e4
10 ♘d4 ♘e5!

Threatening 11...♘xc4 and also eyeing the outpost at d3.

11 ♗xg4+ ♘fxg4

12 ♕a4 ♘d3+
13 ♔d2

13 ♔f1 ♗c5 is terrible for White, and a possible finish is 14 ♘xe4 ♘xe3+ 15 fxe3 ♗xd4 16 ♘g3 (16 exd4 ♕f5+ wins the white knight) 16...♕g5 17 exd4 ♕f4+ 18 ♔e2 ♘xb2 19 ♕xa7 ♖he8+ 20 ♘e4 ♖xe4#.

13 ... ♘xb2
14 ♕b5?

14 ♕b3 fails to 14...♘e5! because 15 ♕xb2 loses to the fork 15...♘xc4+. White had to try 14 ♕xa7 ♘xc4+ 15 ♔e1, threatening 16 ♕a8+ ♔d7 17 ♕a4+, which is why Black cannot play 15...♗b4.

14 ... ♘e5! (D)

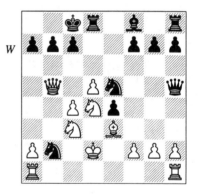

15 ♖ab1 ♘exc4+
16 ♔e1

White loses his queen after 16 ♔c2 ♘a3+ or 16 ♔c1 ♘d3+ 17 ♔c2 ♘a3+.

16 ... ♗b4!
17 ♘c6

A desperate lunge, since 17 ♕xb4 ♘d3+ costs White his queen, as does 17 ♘e2 ♖xd5.

17	...	♗xc3+
18	♔f1	♖d6
19	♘xa7+	♔b8
20	♕c5	

20 ♘c6+ loses to 20...♖xc6! 21 dxc6 ♕xb5, a nice piece of lateral thinking by Black's queen!

20	...	♘xe3+
21	fxe3	♖f6+

0-1

White resigned in view of 22 ♔g1 ♕e2 23 h3 ♕f2+ 24 ♔h2 ♗e5#.

Solution to puzzle (posed before Game 18)

White draws beautifully with **1 ♗e6!!** (intending ♗h3) and then:

a) **1...f1♕** 2 ♗c4+! ♔xc4 stalemate.

b) **1...dxe6?** 2 d7 f1♕ 3 d8♕+, and Black stands worse in the ♕+♙ endgame.

Never a dull moment

That title is actually the name of a very interesting book written by my friend Ron Thompson of Dundee, and includes lots of stories from his many eventful years working for Grampian television. On the chessboard, positions with opposite-coloured bishops have a reputation for often leading to dull draws. However, exciting action is about to erupt in the following study composed by T. Gorgiev and A. Herbstman *(D)*:

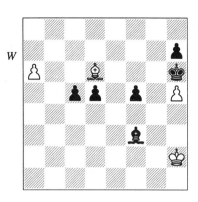

It is White to play and win using some star ideas which appear in the solution after Game 19.

Nearly sixteen years after Croatian grandmaster Ognjen Cvitan won the World Junior Championship in Mexico City in 1981, his enormous talent and appetite for chess remain undiminished. Whenever he is not engaged in an official tournament game, you will almost always find Cvitan flashing out hundreds of brilliant moves in blitz chess. For small stakes which heighten the excitement and tension, this charismatic entertainer takes on anyone who has the courage to challenge him.

Out of 157 competitors at the ever-popular Open event in Biel recently, a Swiss FIDE Master was the unlucky man who had to play Cvitan in the first round. The rapid debacle which followed suggests to me that someone was in a hurry to get back to his favourite and even faster blitz games!

Game 19
O. Cvitan – N. Giertz
Biel 1997
Queen's Gambit Accepted

1	d4	d5
2	c4	dxc4

This is the Queen's Gambit Accepted (QGA), but see Games 7 and 13 for 2...♞c6 and 2...c6 respectively.

3 ♞f3

Two rounds later at Biel, GM Valentin Arbakov (a frequent blitz partner of Cvitan) played **3 e4** against GM Ildar Ibragimov, the eventual tournament winner. Arbakov-Ibragimov continued **3...♞c6 4 ♞f3 ♝g4 5 ♝e3 ♝xf3 6 gxf3** (6 ♕xf3? ♞xd4) **6...e6 7 ♝xc4** *(D)*.

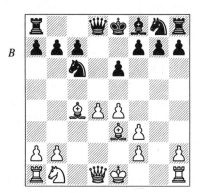

7...♕f6!, planning ...♝b4+, ...♞ge7 and ...0-0-0 with a highly harmonious position for Black in which he will exert lots of pressure against the white d-pawn. In fact, 8 e5? ♕h4 would add to White's problems, because not only

is 9...♞xe5! 10 dxe5 ♕xc4 a threat (lateral thinking again!), but the f5-square has become an outpost for a black piece and later the manoeuvre ...♞ge7-f5 will make the d4-pawn feel much more embarrassed than I was on 27 January 1997 when I ended up dressed in complete emperor's regalia while sitting on a camel at one of the highest points of the Great Wall of China! It only seemed possible in some fantastic Arabian adventure film, yet it happened. I came back down to earth, and relative tranquillity, at the home of my wife's parents on the island of Hainan in the South China Sea. On the last evening there, I was interested to see a one-hour TV programme devoted to Chinese chess or *xiang qi*, which has a lot in common with the international form of modern chess. With such quality educational and recreational features being broadcast regularly, it is no wonder that rapidly increasing numbers of Chinese players are becoming strong as an ox in this Year of the Ox.

3	...	♞f6
4	e3	e6

After 4...b5 5 a4 c6 6 b3, White will soon recover a pawn.

5	♝xc4	c5
6	0-0	a6

Even though I have had pretty good results myself with the QGA, whenever I sat contemplating the position after 6...a6 (a situation which has occurred frequently in my own games), I always had an intuitive feeling that White might well stand better there. After all, he does have a lead in development, and Cvitan's powerful pawn offer further on at move 11 is a highly logical way to try to open up the centre and expose Black's king when he is still sitting on the e-file.

7 ♗b3

A lot of analysis followed the move 7 ♕e2 on page 68 of *H.O.T. Chess*. Another alternative is 7 a4 to prevent ...b5, but Cvitan actually encourages his opponent to make that advance as he wants to attack Black's queenside pawns with a2-a4 after ...b7-b5 has been played.

7 ...   b5

In the fifth round at Biel, Cvitan-Pikula continued 7...♘c6 8 ♕e2 cxd4 9 ♖d1 ♗e7 (9...♗c5? 10 exd4 ♘xd4? costs Black material on account of 11 ♘xd4 ♗xd4 12 ♗e3) 10 ♘c3 0-0 11 exd4 ♘a5 12 ♗c2 b5 13 ♘e4 (threatening 14 ♘xf6+ followed by ♕e4 with the threats of ♕xh7# and ♕xa8) 13...♗b7 14 ♘c5 ♗d5 15 ♘e5 ♘c6 16 ♗g5! (the trick 16 ♘xc6 ♗xc6 17 ♘xe6? backfires on White because of 17...fxe6! {17...♕d5? 18 ♘f4 shows Black 'snatching defeat from the jaws of victory!'} 18 ♕xe6+ ♔h8 19 ♕xc6 ♖c8, and Black wins some material on the c-file, with a plausible finish being

20 ♕xa6 ♖xc2 21 ♕xb5 ♘g4 22 f3 ♗d6! 23 fxg4 ♕h4 24 ♕h5 ♕f2+ 25 ♔h1 ♕xg2#) and after 16...♘xe5 17 dxe5 White had some advantage. So **16...♘xd4** (D) is more critical:

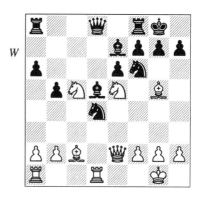

Now the position after **17 ♖xd4 ♗xc5 18 ♗xh7+ ♔xh7** merits serious attention. For example:

a) *Die Schachwoche* magazine of 14 August 1997 gives **19 ♕c2+ ♔g8 20 ♕xc5** (20 ♖h4! transposes to my line 'b') 20...♘e4!, and I agree that 21 ♗xd8 (or 21 ♖xe4 ♕xg5) 21...♘xc5 22 ♗e7 ♖fc8 is absolutely fine for Black.

b) However, after **19 ♖h4+ ♔g8 20 ♕c2** (20 ♗xf6?? ♕xf6 21 ♕h5 threatens ♕h7# or ♕h8#, but Black gets there first with 21...♕xf2+ 22 ♔h1 ♕xg2#) White threatens ♗xf6 followed by ♕xh7#, and it is not easy to find a fully satisfactory response for Black. For instance:

b1) **20...g6?** fatally weakens the f6-knight, and 21 ♕xc5 ♘e4 22 ♗xd8 ♘xc5 23 ♗f6 is followed by 24 ♖h8#.

b2) **20...罝c8** 21 急xf6 急xf2+ 22 豐xf2 豐xf6 23 豐xf6 gxf6 24 ②d7! (24 罝g4+ 當h8 does not worry Black after 25 罝h4+ 當g7 or 25 ②d7 罝g8) 24...罝fd8 25 罝g4+ 當h7 (after 25...當h8 26 ②xf6 it is extremely difficult to dislodge the white knight; *can you see why the attempt 26...罝c4 27 罝g3 罝f4 fails?* – the answer appears at the end of this note) 26 ②xf6+ puts Black's king in an unhappy position.

b3) **20...罝e8** 21 急xf6 急xf2+ (the continuation 21...豐xf6? 22 豐h7+ 當f8 23 ②d7+ costs Black his queen, and 21...gxf6?? is worse due to 22 豐h7+ 當f8 23 豐xf7#) 22 豐xf2! (22 當h1?! 急xh4! 23 急xd8 急xd8 prevents 豐c7 and in effect gives Black a really solid position with 罝+2急+急 versus 豐+②) 22...豐xf6 23 豐xf6 gxf6 24 ②d7! 當g7 25 罝g4+ is very similar to line 'b2', but maybe Black could consider sacrificing an exchange with 24...f5 25 ②f6+ 當g7 26 ②xe8+ 罝xe8.

Answer to question in 'b2'
White would win a rook with 28 罝h3+ 當g7 29 ②h5+ followed by 30 ②xf4.

It is an excellent training for one's patience, self-discipline, and analytical abilities to examine lines such as the ones we have just seen. Despite their lengthy appearance they actually flow very logically, and so we should never be afraid or put off by variations which have to be detailed in order to look at certain positions properly.

8   a4   b4

8...c4 9 急c2 just helps White to achieve the central advance e3-e4, and 9...b4? (threatening ...b3) 10 ②bd2 b3 11 急b1 leaves Black's queenside pawns very over-extended, like a wire that has been permanently damaged by stretching it beyond its elastic limit so that it can never be restored to its original healthy and flexible state.

9   a5!
There are several nice points to this move:

a) White may later be able to utilize the outpost at b6 by manoeuvring there, with ②b1-d2-c4-b6 for example.

b) 急a4+ can be very annoying for Black in some positions.

c) Black cannot play ...a5 to support his far-advanced b-pawn.

9   ...   急b7
9...②c6 10 ②e5! looks good for White. For example:

a) 10...②xa5? 11 急a4+ ②d7 12 dxc5 急xc5 13 ②xd7 急xd7 14 豐xd7+ 豐xd7 15 急xd7+ 當xd7 16 罝xa5, and White has emerged with an extra piece.

b) 10...②xe5 11 dxe5 豐xd1 12 罝xd1 ②d7 13 急a4, planning the aforementioned manoeuvre ②b1-d2-c4-b6.

c) 10...急b7 11 急a4 豐c7 12 豐f3 罝c8 13 e4!! (this star move frees the dark-squared bishop, which is keen to get at Black's queen on c7) 13...cxd4 14 急f4 急d6 15 ②xc6 急xc6 (after 15...急xf4 16 ②e5+!, White wins the f4-bishop) 16 急xd6 (16 罝c1 急xf4 17 罝xc6 also wins for White) 16...豐xd6 *(D)*.

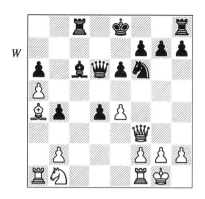

17 e5! ♕xe5 (Black would love to play 17...♗xf3, but it's illegal and rules are rules!) 18 ♗xc6+ puts White a piece ahead.

10 ♘bd2 ♘bd7
11 e4!

11 ♗a4 ♗e7 12 dxc5 ♗xc5 13 ♘b3 0-0 gave Black a playable position in Piket-Lautier, match (2), Monaco 1996.

11 ... ♘xe4?

This capture opens up the e-file when Black's king is still located on it. 11...♗e7 looks relatively best because the alternative **11...cxd4 12 e5!** gives White a strong initiative. Here are some lovely illustrative lines:

a) **12...♘g4 13 ♘c4** (threatening h3) **13...♗xf3 14 ♕xf3 ♘gxe5 15 ♘xe5 ♘xe5 16 ♗a4+** (a recurring headache troubling Black) **16...♘d7** (16...♔e7 17 ♗g5+, with 17...f6 18 ♕b7+ or 17...♔d6 18 ♕f4 to follow, is also terrible for Black) **17 ♗f4 ♖a7** (to stop ♕b7) **18 ♖fd1 ♗c5 19 ♖ac1** (threatening ♖xc5 or first ♗xd7+) **19...♕xa5 20 ♗xd7+ ♔xd7** (20...♖xd7 21 ♕a8+ ♖d8 22 ♕c6+ wins the black

bishop) **21 ♖xd4+!** (a typical sacrifice to expose Black's king when White is well ahead in development) **21...♗xd4** (21...♔e7 22 ♕c6 ♗xd4 23 ♕d6+ transposes to line 'a1') **22 ♕c6+** and then:

a1) **22...♔e7 23 ♕d6+ ♔f6 24 ♕xd4+** (attacking the a7-rook) 24...e5 25 ♖c6+ ♔f5 26 g4+ ♔xg4 27 ♗xe5+ ♔h5 28 ♕d1+ ♔g5 29 ♕d2+ ♔h5 30 ♕e2+ ♔g5 31 ♕e3+ ♔h5 32 ♕h3+ ♔g5 33 f4#. A computer might well find a quicker win, but that is not important. I gave this virtually forced variation to reiterate the point that with very simple, logical moves one can flow along a line for a really long way without experiencing much difficulty.

a2) **22...♔d8 23 ♕d6+ ♖d7 24 ♖c8+! ♔xc8 25 ♕b8#** (D).

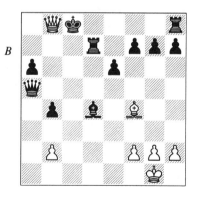

b) **12...♘d5 13 ♘e4 ♗e7 14 ♗g5** and now for example:

b1) **14...♗xg5 15 ♘d6+ ♔f8 16 ♘xb7 ♕c7 17 ♘xg5 ♕xb7 18 ♕f3 ♘c5** (18...♘xe5 also loses after 19

♘xe6+) 19 ♘xe6+! ♘xe6 20 ♗xd5 wins for White.

b2) **14...f6** 15 exf6 gxf6 16 ♘xd4!, intending to meet 16...fxg5 with 17 ♘xe6, threatening 18 ♘xd8 and 18 ♕h5#.

b3) **14...0-0** 15 ♕xd4 is very good for White, particularly because Black is so sensitive on the dark squares b4, c5 and d6.

Star Exercise

Instead of 15 ♕xd4 in line 'b3', I was really attracted by the forthcoming beautiful variations, and I do not want to deny you the enjoyment of playing over them. However, as a good exercise in objectivity, can you find a vital improvement for Black very soon after move 15? The answer appears at the end of the variations.

15 ♘d6 ♗c6 16 ♗xe7 ♕xe7 17 ♖c1 ♗b5 18 ♖e1 ♕d8 (18...♘xe5? 19 ♘xb5 ♘xf3+ 20 ♕xf3 axb5 21 ♗xd5 costs Black a piece) 19 ♘xd4 ♕xa5 20 ♘xe6!! fxe6 21 ♗xd5 exd5 22 ♕xd5+ ♔h8 23 ♘f7+ ♖xf7 (23...♔g8 24 ♘h6++ ♔h8 25 ♕g8+! ♖xg8 26 ♘f7# is a smothered mate) 24 ♕xa8+ ♖f8 (24...♘f8 loses to 25 e6 ♖f6 26 e7) 25 ♖c8 ♔g8 26 ♕d5+ ♔h8 27 ♕xd7! ♗xd7 28 ♖xf8# *(D)*.

Answer to Star Exercise

16...♘xe7! is a big improvement for Black because he threatens ...♗xf3 and ...♘xe5 in either order. Also, 17

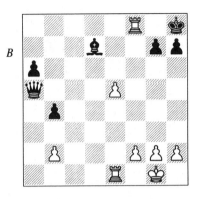

♕xd4 ♗xf3 18 gxf3 ♘c6! shows that White cannot afford to become slack in his play and unwisely ignore the fact that an opponent who fights hard is likely to find tenacious, resourceful defensive moves ... and counterattacking ones too.

12	♘xe4	♗xe4
13	♘g5	♗d5? *(D)*

This loses quickly, although Cvitan's opening play has been extremely strong because 13...♗g6 14 d5 e5 15 ♗a4 ♗e7 16 ♘e6! is also very good for White.

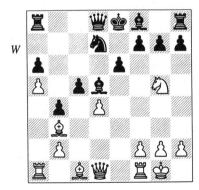

14	♗xd5	exd5
15	♖e1+	♗e7
16	♕h5	g6
17	♕h6	♘f6
18	♕g7	♔d7

18...♖f8 19 ♕xf6 is equally disastrous for Black.

19	♕xf7	1-0

The myriad overwhelming threats included 20 ♘e6 followed by ♘xc5+ and 20 ♕e6+ ♔e8 21 ♕xf6, so Black decided to call it a day.

Solution to puzzle (posed before Game 19)

White wins by 1 ♔g3 ♗e4 (1...♗xh5? is met by 2 a7 followed by a8♕) 2 ♔h4! (threatening ♗f8#) 2...♔g7 3 ♗e5+ ♔f7 4 ♗d4!! cxd4 5 a7 and 6 a8♕.

The final chapter is approaching fast, but first we can enjoy a healthy dose of puzzles to prepare our minds for the forthcoming encounter with E.T. ...

Star Test

It is *White to move* in each of the following seven positions. The first four relate to openings, while the last two take us into the endgame phase, and a middlegame position stars in the other diagram. The solutions contain galaxies of ideas and appear on pages 237-9.

5.1

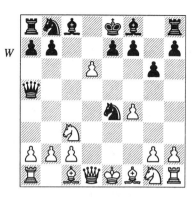

Can you identify the previous six moves which led to this position, and find White's most convincing way to win now?

5.2

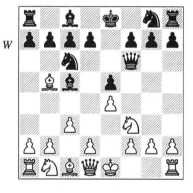

Many people will recognize the famous Ruy Lopez opening here, but on move four the GM in Black's shoes has just played ...♕d8-f6 with the idea of stopping 5 d4. Does his strategy work?

5.3

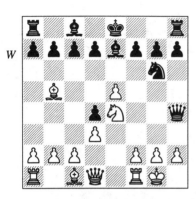

5.4

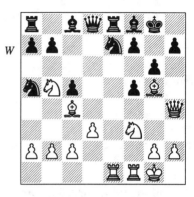

This position also arose from a Ruy Lopez (or Spanish Opening) in the game McShane-Costagliola, London 1997. Luke McShane, the 13-year-old boy with the white pieces, had already become a hero in March by achieving all the requirements for the title of International Master, a fantastic follow-up to winning the 1992 World Under-10 Championship at the age of eight. I certainly share the feelings of Britain's youngest-ever IM (born 7 January 1984), as Luke once summed up our Royal Game with the phrase 'Chess is fun'. He was definitely having fun in the diagram position, since his last move, 9 ♘d2-e4, practically forced the retreat 9...♗c5-e7 to stop 10 ♗g5.

Can you identify the nine opening moves that led to this position, and find Luke's powerful retreat at move ten which quickly won the game for White?

From one English prodigy to another one! Eleven-year-old Rafe Martyn (one of my chess pupils living in Brussels) is excited about going for matches in the Ukraine in February 1998. Besides talent, it is Rafe's hard work at chess and love of the game that have got the young star a place in England's junior squad. He should do well if he can repeat the sort of form which gave him a crushing position after only 15 moves against an opponent rated around 2000 in Belgium.

Can you find Rafe's devastating next move?

5.5

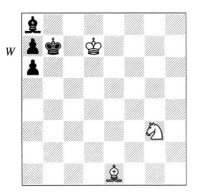

It is White to play and force checkmate in only four moves in this neat 1979 study by E.L. Pogosiants.

5.6

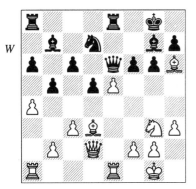

One might say that we have here a close encounter of the third kind! The position is our third case of the Ruy Lopez in the Star Test, and this game, Hraček-Gabriel, Bad Homburg 1997, features two closely matched grandmasters.

Can you find a winning continuation for GM Zbynek Hraček?

Star Challenge no. 5

Part 'a' is an offering from myself, while part 'b' is an elegant study by L. Prokeš.

a) Try tracing the movements of a knight that carries out the manoeuvre ♘e1-d3-b4-d5-e7-f5-h4-f3-e1. After finding a nice 4-pointed star, now try the manoeuvre ♘g2-e3-c2-d4-b5-d6-c8-e7-g8-f6-h5-f4-g2. The 6-pointed star is attractive too, but can you now use a knight to trace out a 10-pointed star on a chessboard?

b) Consider this position *(D)*:

Believe it or not, a knight is the star

piece in this position with White to play and win. While you discover the solution, I'm moving on to the next page because I can't wait to meet E.T. ...

6 Smashing the Mind Barriers

On Saturday 31 May 1997, J.R. (Jonathan Rowson), my wife Jenny and I all went for a very pleasant boat-trip along a canal in the beautiful Belgian town of Bruges. The commentator indicated a nearby house reputed to have the smallest window in the world. It occurred to me that, in a sense, a journey in chess or life is like flowing along a fascinating course, but one can see more by letting the window of the mind become bigger. I am talking about smashing the mind barriers.

Instead of becoming too set and restricted in my thoughts, I enjoy creative, original and lateral thinking. For instance, solving (and also attempting to compose) beautiful studies helps me to look for surprising, resourceful ideas in my real chess games. In other words, that sort of training process which we have experienced together in *S.T.A.R. Chess* encourages our minds to become more open and willing to consider fresh ideas. Then the window of the mind expands and smashes through previous barriers.

Albert Einstein, the brilliant theoretical physicist who lived from 14 March 1879 to 18 April 1955, said that, in general, people use not more than ten percent of their mental capacity, leaving at least ninety percent waiting to be tapped. However, with an open spirit, Einstein himself developed really important theories (which have so far stood the test of time) by giving his mind the freedom to explore new paths. For example, after letting his imagination travel with a beam of light through space, Einstein produced his *special theory of relativity*, which described the effects of moving at very high speeds close to that of light (about 300,000,000 metres per second).

Having gained inspiration from our star motto ('There is no man living who isn't capable of doing more than he thinks he can do') and numerous examples of creative thinking by people, I decided to let my imagination bring an Extra-Terrestrial (E.T.) from another part of the galaxy to have a chat about chess and related topics with P.M. (no prizes for guessing whose name those letters represent!). Here is what happened:

P.M.: 'Welcome to Earth, E.T. You have travelled a long way.'

E.T.: 'Thank you. My journey from Star T was precisely 112359550561797752809 metres long, but playing chess on the way made it seem shorter!'

P.M.: 'Tell me about Star T, please.'

E.T.: 'My people name it Star T because that is where we *start* our journey in life, but in chess I like to think of it as standing for strategy, tactics, attack and reaction, with extra emphasis on tactics.'

P.M.: 'Have you played a lot of chess?'

E.T.: 'Yes. It's a beautiful game that has been known on Star T since long before it started on Earth, and I decided to study, on average, a new chess position for every centimetre of my journey. Life is like a ruler: you have a certain measure of it, and every centimetre is precious.'

P.M.: 'Since your journey was 11235955056179775280900 centimetres long, that astronomical number is also the number of chess positions you have studied.'

E.T.: 'That's correct, but chess is so fascinating that I always enjoy it. In fact, since the number of different possible legal positions is somewhere around 2×10^{43}, I have only studied a little more than the square root! However, throughout my long, happy life I have been letting the window of my mind become a lot bigger, so I can now consider more possibilities, and faster too. For example, I can calculate that 99 times the distance I travelled gives the same number as the distance, but with an extra digit 1 at each end. I mean
$99 \times 11235955056179775280900 = 1112359550561797752809091$.'

P.M.: 'Gosh! How many chess positions can you examine per second?'

E.T.: 'I will give you a little mental exercise to work it out. Let me tell you that the average speed of my space-ship throughout my journey was one percent of the speed of light.'

P.M.: 'That's fast! Still, Einstein's Theory of Relativity would not have affected you much if your speed was just one hundredth of the speed of light. Let me think. Light travels at 300,000,000 metres per second, so you were doing 3,000,000 metres per second, which is equivalent to 300 million centimetres per second. Since you studied one chess position for every centimetre, that means you can analyse at least 300 million positions per second. That's better than Deeper Blue! What chance do I have of ever equalling that?'

E.T.: 'Don't worry. You must realize that I am much more than one million years old, since even travelling at high speeds it took about 1,190,000 years for me to journey from Star T to Earth. It was actually a few millennia less than that, but basically I have had lots of time and experiences through which to improve myself. In fact, I set myself targets for making the window of my mind bigger. During the first one hundred years of my journey, I increased my mind window by a factor of 11. That could be a realistic target for you over a normal lifetime on Earth. Einstein would be pleased to see you using your brain more fully, instead of less than ten percent. I can assure you that I used a lot less than that initially, which meant that I really needed to improve. However, my desire to make progress was, and still is, great. I know from tests which I tried on board the spaceship that I later improved by further factors of 41, 271 and 9091, but I had more than one million years to do it. The important thing is to enjoy trying to do your best in whatever time you are given.'

P.M.: 'Thanks for the good advice. I will keep trying to improve, and although you're a hard act to follow, I am inspired by your fantastic personal improvement. Overall that was $11 \times 41 \times 271 \times 9091$, which means you eventually improved your starting mind window by a factor of 1111111111. Grandmaster Miguel Najdorf once said "Chess is a combination of ten games". Your improvement makes me want to get ten wins!'

E.T.: 'That's OK, but you must be patient and accept ups and downs, like my space-ship getting jostled passing through a field of asteroids! Patience is a star virtue.'

P.M.: 'Yes, that's true. Still, I bet you enjoy being able to analyse 300 million positions per second instead of taking three to four seconds for one position, as you must have needed initially.'

E.T.: 'I am pleased, but let's concentrate on *your* intended improvement. Ruminate while I illuminate the possibilities! I suggest that you play a game against yourself. You will be White and the "new inspired you" will be Black. Sit with two chessboards side by side. The first board will have its white pieces nearest your chair; the second board will have the black pieces nearest. So you play the first move as White on board one, and copy the move onto board two. The "new you" then responds as Black on board two and also copies the move onto board one. You then answer with White's second move on board one, copy it onto board two, and so on. Use a chess clock and play a rapid game, say five minutes for you and four minutes for the "new you". That will give you a chance!'

P.M.: 'How can I suddenly be different as Black?'

E.T.: 'You're already feeling inspired, and you love playing Black because you can find the perfect reaction to each of White's moves.'

P.M.: 'Are you saying that Black must win?'

E.T.: 'Not necessarily, but I feel that the "balance" is tipped in Black's favour. White plays first and is under pressure to try to demonstrate an advantage, when in fact Black has more information and can react according to whatever his opponent does. White must show his hand first. He can try to seize the initiative due to having the first move, but if Black remains flexible then he should always have an excellent reaction available against each of White's possible moves. Of course, in practice that often does not happen because errors creep into the game.'

P.M.: 'What name shall I write down for the "new me"?!'

E.T.: 'OK, he's going to be good, but as with any player there will always be plenty of room for improvement. Nevertheless, I optimistically predict that in your excited inspired state, the "new you" up on cloud nine will be nine times stronger than you. I also know that your star sign is Gemini, the Twins. So I will rename the "new you" as **T.W.I.N. A.M.P.O.**, which stands for the window increased nine-fold, a mega power output. He also bears some resemblance to you because T.W.I.N. A.M.P.O. is an anagram of P. Motwani. You can start your game now.'

P.M.: 'Thanks E.T. I've really enjoyed our chat. Will we meet again someday, maybe at your home?'

E.T.: 'If we both keep wanting and trying to improve, then I'm sure we will. Perhaps not on Star T, because even the stars do not shine forever. However, there is a kingdom where the light never dies. Let's meet there.'

Game 20
P. Motwani – T.W.I.N. A.M.P.O.
Planet Earth 1997
Reversed Modern

1 g3	e5
2 ♗g2	d5
3 a3	

A hyper-modern approach against a hyper-modern opponent!

3 ...	♘f6

A sensible developing move, flashed out at lightning speed.

4 d3	

With the clock ticking again and eating away at my 5 vs 4 advantage in minutes, I already felt uncomfortable and did not like the look of 4 b4 a5 for White.

4 ...	a5

Seizing space and some initiative.

5 ♘f3	♘c6
6 0-0	♗e7

7 a4	

I had the plan of playing c3, ♕c2 and e4, but 7 c3 a4! makes a hole in White's camp at b3 and gives Black a potential outpost there.

7 ...	0-0
8 c3	♖e8
9 ♕c2 *(D)*	
9 ...	e4!

This powerful move gives me E.T. (extra trouble!).

10 dxe4	♘xe4

Threatening ...♗f5 followed by tactical ideas like ...♘xg3, with a discovered attack against White's queen.

11 ♘a3	

After 11 ♖d1 ♗f5 12 ♕b3 ♘c5 13 ♕xd5, Black simply plays 13...♕xd5

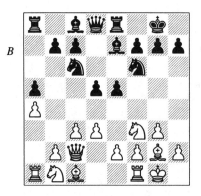

14 ♖xd5 ♗e6 15 ♖d1 ♘b3, a knock-out blow that would leave me 'seeing double'!

11   ...   ♗f5

12   ♕d1

12 ♕b3 ♘c5 13 ♕b5? loses after 13...♘a7! 14 ♕xa5 ♘c6 15 ♕b5 ♖a5, when Black neatly traps White's harassed queen.

12   ...   ♗xa3

Making White's queen's rook recapture on a3, where it is rather misplaced.

13   ♖xa3   ♕d7

Played with the twin strategic ideas of ...♗h3, to swap the fianchettoed defender of White's king, and simply improving the quantity and quality of Black's development.

14   ♖e1

We see how efficient Black's last move was if White plays 14 ♘h4, because 14...♗h3! follows and there is no need to defend the d-pawn. The point is that after 15 ♗xh3 ♕xh3 16 ♕xd5 ♖ad8, Black has a harmonious and fully mobilized army. A plausible

line would be 17 ♕f5 ♕xf5 18 ♘xf5 ♘d2 19 ♗xd2 (19 ♖d1? and 19 ♖e1? both lose to 19...♘f3+) 19...♖xd2 20 ♖b3 b6 21 e3 ♘e5, and Black has lots of pressure in return for his deficit of one pawn. Furthermore, White is passively placed and in no position to make use of his extra e-pawn.

14   ...   ♖ad8

15   ♕b3   b6

16   ♘d4? (D)

16 ♗e3 is more tenacious.

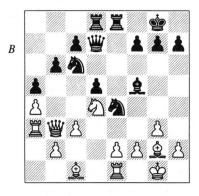

16   ...   ♘e5!

A strong and logical reaction, intending to manoeuvre to the c4-square. It immediately takes advantage of the fact that White can no longer play ♘xe5. Furthermore, his 14th move left the f2-point weakened, and so 17 ♘xf5 ♕xf5 is attractive for Black, as the game continuation demonstrates.

17   ♘xf5   ♕xf5

18   ♗f4

18 ♖f1 ♘c4 19 ♖a2 costs White material due to the fork 19...♘ed2.

18	...	♘c4
19	♖a2	g5!

The attack begins.

20	♗xe4	♖xe4
21	♗c1	

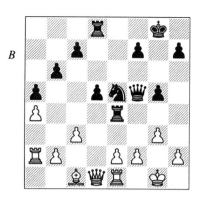

B

21 ♗xc7 gets White's bishop stranded in enemy territory and loses for various reasons including **21...♖c8 22 f3** (planning g4 and ♗g3, whereas if 22 ♗xb6 then the pin 22...♖b8 is painful) **22...♖xc7 23 fxe4 ♕xe4** (threatening ...♘e3 and ...♕g2#) and now for example:

a) **24 e3 ♘xe3 25 ♖e2** (25 ♔f2 ♘g4+ 26 ♔f1 ♕f3+ 27 ♔g1 ♕f2+ 28 ♔h1 ♕xh2#) 25...♕b1+ 26 ♔f2 ♕f1+! 27 ♔xe3 ♖e7+ 28 ♔d4 ♕xe2 29 ♕xd5 ♕d1+ 30 ♔c4 ♖c7+ 31 ♔b5 ♕xd5+ 32 ♔xb6 ♕c5+ 33 ♔a6 ♖a7#.

b) **24 ♖f1 ♘e3 25 ♖f3** (25 ♖f2 ♕b1+) 25...g4 26 ♕xb6 ♕b1+ 27 ♔f2 ♘d1+ 28 ♔g1 gxf3 29 ♕xc7 ♘e3+! 30 ♔f2 ♘g4+! 31 ♔xf3 ♕e4#.

c) **24 ♖aa1 ♘e3 25 ♔f2 ♖e7** (threatening ...♕g2#) 26 ♖g1 ♘g4+ 27 ♔e1 ♕xe2#.

Black's knight is a really dominating star piece throughout those lines, and White's king is in perpetual peril.

21	...	♘e5!
22	♕d1 *(D)*	
22	...	♖e8!

Did you spot Black's last two star moves? The first threatened ...♘f3+, and the second one renewed that threat. White has no time to react properly. For instance, 23 ♖f1 loses to 23...♖xe2! 24 ♕xe2 ♘f3+, winning the queen.

23	♗e3	♘g4!

The knight is leaping around, unable to contain the galaxy of tactical ideas which are emanating from it ... and unfortunately exploding on me!

24	♗d4	

24 f3 loses to 24...♘xe3 25 fxe4 ♕xe4, with the twin threats of ...♘xd1 or ...♕g2#.

24	...	♖xd4!

This efficient finish has more than ample force to crash through White's barriers.

25	♕xd4	c5
	0-1	

I resigned in view of 26 ♕d2 ♕xf2+ 27 ♔h1 ♕xh2#. I think I enjoy playing my other better half more: I mean, with all due respect to my wife Jenny, she's not as tough as T.W.I.N. A.M.P.O.!

As I write today, it is exactly twenty years since the Voyager 2 space-craft was launched from Earth on 20 August 1977, programmed to pass by Jupiter, Saturn, Uranus and Neptune in that order. Just like our journey together, everything went well, and the rendezvous with Neptune took place in 1989 within two minutes of the scheduled time ... no time-trouble problems such as I have experienced! However, I once arrived three *days* ahead of schedule to meet my parents. That was on 13 June 1962, but my mother was not expecting me to be born until the 16th! Curiously, that would have given me the same birthday as my wife Jenny has. By coincidence, she is from Canton in China, and my parents tell me that I was conceived on a boat called *The Canton*. Astrologers tend to love that sort of stuff, while many people prefer a more scientific topic. Now, near the end of this star journey, I think it can be fun for us to enjoy a nice mixture of different topics, including another good dose of chess.

The chart on the following page shows the correct order of the 12 star signs of the Zodiac, and the names of some celebrities whose birthdays make links with particular star signs. I noticed that various newspapers, magazines and books give several different versions of the dates for the periods that relate to the star signs. However, going by the dates listed in the table, all the chess and film stars are matched to the correct signs.

Instead of sharing a table or quarters with at least four stars near to you out of the 48 given ones, you might prefer to be associated with a genius like Albert Einstein, especially since we have been smashing the mind barriers (something that he did so well). OK, let's show that you're on the same wavelength as Einstein by answering all of the forthcoming Star Test questions correctly. At the end of the set of questions, you can check the answers (which appear earlier than usual) to confirm that you have scored 100%, but first there is a preamble to set the scene.

I'm a knight!

In February last year, J.R. asked me the surprising question 'If you were a chess piece, which one would you be!?'. I chose the knight because it can jump over obstacles as it manoeuvres to reach any square on the board, and its short L-shaped movements require it to be patient. Its ultimate reward is to give checkmate, as in the following puzzle position I composed on 20 July 1997 *(D)*:

Star Test

6.1 In the diagram on page 222, White has just given N consecutive checks, the final one being checkmate. N represents a certain number which you have to find. However, you are told that the first of the N checks was **not** made with a bishop or knight, yet neither Black nor White has made any captures since the N checks began. Furthermore, all of Black's moves

No.	Star Sign	Period	Chess Stars	Film Stars
1	Aries (The Ram)	21 Mar - 20 Apr	Garry Kasparov	Marlon Brando
			Zsuzsa Polgar	Doris Day
2	Taurus (The Bull)	21 Apr - 21 May	Matthew Sadler	Al Pacino
			Pia Cramling	Audrey Hepburn
3	Gemini (The Twins)	22 May - 22 Jun	Anatoly Karpov	John Wayne
			Irina Levitina	Marilyn Monroe
4	Cancer (The Crab)	23 Jun - 23 Jul	Vladimir Kramnik	Harrison Ford
			Judit Polgar	Ginger Rogers
5	Leo (The Lion)	24 Jul - 23 Aug	Mikhail Botvinnik	Dustin Hoffman
			Elina Danielian	Maureen O'Hara
6	Virgo (The Virgin)	24 Aug - 23 Sept	Peter Leko	Sean Connery
			Ketino Kachiani-Gersinska	Ingrid Bergman
7	Libra (The Balance)	24 Sept - 23 Oct	Jonathan Speelman	Charlton Heston
			Susan Lalić	Julie Andrews
8	Scorpio (The Scorpion)	24 Oct - 22 Nov	Michael Adams	Richard Burton
			Xie Jun	Grace Kelly
9	Sagittarius (The Archer)	23 Nov - 21 Dec	Viswanathan Anand	Woody Allen
			Wang Pin	Jane Fonda
10	Capricorn (The Sea-Goat)	22 Dec - 20 Jan	Paul Keres	Elvis Presley
			Maia Chiburdanidze	Sissy Spacek
11	Aquarius (The Water-Bearer)	21 Jan - 19 Feb	David Bronstein	Humphrey Bogart
			Nana Ioseliani	Ida Lupino
12	Pisces (The Fishes)	20 Feb - 20 Mar	Veselin Topalov	Michael Caine
			Zhu Chen	Elizabeth Taylor

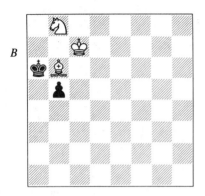

have been absolutely forced since the N checks started.

What was the position just before the start of the N checks, and what number does N represent? That number, and all the other ones in this Star Test, will be needed later for linking up with Einstein.

6.2 A much easier question without tricks: what number does **S** represent if **S** equals the number of planets orbiting the Sun in our Solar System?

6.3 A bit harder than 6.2: what number does **P** represent if **P** equals the number of different positions which can occur on chessboards one **complete** move after the usual starting position? Remember, White gets a move and so does Black.

6.4 In the 1997 hit film *Evita*, there was a song called '*On this Night of a ——— Stars*'. The missing eight-letter word spells a common four-digit number. Simply add 1 to it and you'll have the next whole number **I**, which is sometimes loosely regarded as a kind of 'finite infinity'.

6.5 This one is about **you** ... provided you were born sometime **between 1901 and 1996 inclusive**! If that is not the case, you can work with me, if you like, since I was born on 13 June 1962. **A** equals your age (in years) at your birthday **in 1997**. **Y** equals the number given by the last two right-hand digits of the year in which you were born. **D** equals the difference obtained by subtracting **A** from **Y** if **Y** is the bigger number; otherwise subtract **Y** from **A**. Write down your values for **D, A, Y** (or try my case and make my **DAY**!).

6.6 Time-warp back to the first page of this chapter. Find a vital piece of information, then return here at the speed of light (or let's say, 'relatively fast'!) and write down the value of **E**, which is the symbol I am using for Einstein's star sign number, according to the earlier Star Chart.

Solutions to Star Test 6 (up to 6.6)

6.1 This is an original example of retro-analysis, which basically means working backwards to find out information about what happened previously. The only solution which fits **all** the criteria you were given is *(D)*:

Then the game finished with 1 b7+ ♚a7 2 ♝b6+ ♚a6 3 b8♘#, a neat under-promotion. **N = 3**. That should please C.S.Kipping: he loved and composed many 'mate in three' problems.

6.2 Remember the acrostic **My Very Educated Mother Just Served Us**

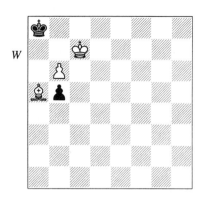

Nine Pumpkins, which provides a way of remembering that Mercury, Venus, Earth, Mars, Jupiter, Saturn, Uranus, Neptune and Pluto are, in order of increasing average distance from the Sun, the nine planets in our Solar System. **S = 9**.

6.3 To each of White's 20 possible first moves, Black has 20 possible replies. So the total number of possibilities resulting from one complete move is 20×20. **P = 400**.

6.4 The song is called *'On this Night of a Thousand Stars'*. **I = 1001**.

6.5 This one is personal! However, just to check that we're thinking on the same wavelength, for **my case** Y = 62, A = 35 (my age in years **in 1997**), D = 62-35 = 27.

6.6 Since Albert Einstein was born on 14 March 1879, his star sign is Pisces. **E = 12**.

Star Challenge no. 6

Introduction: After Game 12 in Chapter 4, we encountered one of my favourite acronyms, S.P.I.N. The planets all spin, but at the same time all of them have different characteristics which make each planet unique. Similarly, all of us who have made this star journey love chess. We have been given different abilities for the game (and special talents in other areas too), but in God's mind we are all unique yet equally important.

You're as special as Einstein!

We are now going to use our previous Star Test common values for **S, P, I, N** and our own different personal answers for **D, A, Y** to discover that we have a special link with Einstein. This will be shown by my forthcoming **SPIN DAY Expression**. However, to emphasize the importance of time and the fact that we should make the most of it, not only in chess but also within a finite number of years on Earth as we are now, the expression only applies if **D, A, Y** relate to a year between 1901 and 1996 inclusive (and if that is not the case, then we can use the **D, A, Y** values of a friend or relative for example).

My *SPIN DAY* Expression

Your star challenge is to calculate the value of the following expression:

$$\frac{[(I \times S) + P - D^2] \times N}{A \times Y}$$

I'm betting that, although most of us have different values for **D, A, Y,** we will nevertheless find that we have a special link. I got 12 for the final answer to my expression. Did you? How about other friends too? If I'm right, we all get the same answer ... and its value is equal to **E** (the answer to problem 6.6 about Einstein).

Example: I×S = 1001×9 = 9009. Adding P then gives 9409. For me, D = 27 (see answer to problem 6.5), so D^2 = 27×27 = 729. Then 9409-729 = 8680. N = 3, so 8680×3 = 26040. For me, A×Y = 35×62 = 2170. Finally, 26040 divided by 2170 equals **12**.

E.T.'s extra treat

E.T.: 'Today, Thursday 21 August 1997, is one of the World Youth Days. I've seen Pope John Paul II visiting Paris to celebrate with more than half a million rejoicing people, and I'm feeling as young as ever!'

P.M.: 'What a wonderful surprise. I didn't expect to see you again so soon.'

E.T.: 'I forgot to say "I'll be back!".' Actually, I wanted to see how you are getting on with smashing the mind barriers.'

P.M.: 'I'm making progress. My third book, *S.T.A.R. Chess*, is almost completed.'

E.T.: 'Good. Then you can relax for a moment while I tell you a joke. How many ears did Captain Kirk have?'

P.M.: 'I'm all ears! Tell me.'

E.T.: 'The answer is three: the left ear, right ear and space, the final frontier! However, this book is not your final frontier.'

P.M.: 'What do you have in mind?'

E.T.: 'You can rest until next Friday. I judge that that should be long enough. After all, in the film *Terminator 2*, Judgement Day was precisely 29 August 1997! After that, I want you to start work on your next **two** books.'

P.M.: 'That makes sense: you did create the idea of a twin for me.'

E.T.: 'It's all arranged. First there will be *Chess Under the Microscope*. Then soon afterwards, *The Most Instructive Chess Games of the Young Grandmasters*.'

P.M.: 'I promise to make them full of new colourful ideas.'

E.T.: 'Good. I've got a multi-coloured puzzle for your readers right now. On Star T, the chess pieces almost seem to come to life. For example, the tops of white pawns glow with different colours depending on which rank the pawn is on. The top starts off as red, but is green before an *en passant* capture and blue afterwards. What colour is the top of a white pawn on Star T as it reaches promotion?'

P.M.: 'E.T., can you type the answer for me in the usual solutions section? I feel a "snack attack" coming on.'

E.T.: 'Certainly, but what's a "snack attack"?'

P.M.: 'Well, when Fré Hoogendoorn, who does the layout for the Dutch *Schaaknieuws* magazine, saw *H.O.T. Chess*, he invented S.N.A.C.K.S. to mean simple **new a**cronym-based chess knowledge system. However, a "snack attack" is even more basic: it means I'm hungry for food!'

E.T.: 'Well, hopefully I have whetted the appetite of your readers regarding your next books, but I don't want to give away anything else. A surprise should be like a box of chocolates: "You never know what you're going to get", as a certain Mrs Gump once said. However, since you have all done well in this star journey, may I recommend the following chocolate goodies to overcome your "snack attack": a Mars bar, a Milky Way and a bar of Galaxy milk chocolate?'

P.M.: 'That'll do nicely for now ... until we meet again!'

Solutions to Tests and Puzzles

The cryptogram given in the introduction to the book was:

SJLZL XE RC VDR AXWXRQ PJC XER'S YDIDMAL CT FCXRQ VCZL SJDR JL SJXRNE JL YDR FC.

JLRZH TCZF.

A promising place to start attacking the coded message is the 'word' XER'S because of the prominent apostrophe. We were also told that each letter must be replaced by a *different* one, so the S after the apostrophe will become T, and in fact XER'S becomes **ISN'T** (YOU'D is not possible because the second 'word', XE, would become YO, which is not a proper word; DON'T is also unacceptable because SJXRNE would become **TJDNNO**, which has no hope of turning into a proper word). Looking at the third word, RC, with R becoming N, clearly C needs to be **O**. We can now go through the cryptogram and change every X, E, R, S, C to **I, S, N, T, O** respectively, which gives:

TJLZL IS NO VDN AIWINQ PJO **ISN'T** YDIDMAL **OT** FOINQ VOZL TJDN JL TJINNS JL YDN FO.

JLNZH TOZF.

Inspecting the word FO, there may seem to be several suitable replacements still available for F, but bearing in the mind the effect on the word FOINQ, it is necessary to change F to

D and Q to **G**. Two thirds of the word TJINNS is already decoded, and one can see that this word must be **THINKS** (so J, N become **H, K**; TWINES is no good with J, N becoming W, E because there would be no solution for the word JL). Clearly JL now becomes **HE**. Also, TJDN becomes **THDN**, which, in turn, changes to **THAN** (since neither E nor I are still available). Similarly, PJO becomes **PHO**, which, in turn, changes to **WHO**. So we can again go through the cryptogram, this time changing F, Q, J, N, L, D, P to **D, G, H, K, E, A, W** respectively. This gives:

THEZE IS NO VAN AIWING WHO ISN'T YAIAMAE OT DOING VOZE THAN HE THINKS HE YAN DO.

HENZH TOZD.

We can now quickly spot that **THEZE** becomes **THERE**; **OT** becomes **OF**; **VOZE** changes to **VORE**, which then becomes **MORE** to make sense of the message (and so VAN turns into **MAN**). Similarly, **HENZH TOZD** changes to **HENRH FORD**, which then becomes **HENRY FORD** (HENRI FORD was not possible because the letter I has already been 'used up'). Also, **YAN** becomes **CAN**, and **YAIAMAE** changes to **CAIAMAE**. However, one can see from the sense of the later words in the message (which are now all known) that this word must be **CAPABLE**, and the only remaining word to complete becomes **LIWING** then **LIVING**.

Finally, our inspirational motto reads:

'**THERE IS NO MAN LIVING WHO ISN'T CAPABLE OF DOING MORE THAN HE THINKS HE CAN DO**'.

HENRY FORD.

The route to decoding the message can be compared to probing the most prominent weaknesses in an opponent's position on the chessboard. After each move, even some small changes in the position can give one clues or information about how and where to best strike next, until eventually really big progress is made, often resulting in the win of material and later the game.

Solving the cryptogram took up some space and time, but doing it properly can help us to develop greater thoroughness, patience and determination: qualities which will be very beneficial in chess and in life generally.

Picking pieces

16 of the 32 chessmen are white, so the chance (or probability) of Kathleen picking a white piece (meaning 'piece or pawn' here) first can be expressed by the fraction 16/32 or 1/2. The likelihood of the next piece also being white is then 15/31, considering the pieces still remaining in the bag. Similarly, the chances of the third and fourth pieces being white too are 14/30 (or 7/15) and 13/29 respectively. So the probability that all four pieces will be white is $1/2 \times 15/31 \times 7/15 \times 13/29$ = 91/1798 (simplifying by cancelling the two occurrences of the number 15). 91 divided by 1798 equals 0.0506 approximately. However, given that there are 20 possible first moves, your chance of correctly guessing Kathleen's favourite move (with only one guess) is $1/20 = 0.05$, which is clearly less than the previous decimal. Therefore, Kathleen's chances of picking four white pieces are slightly better than your chances of guessing her first move.

Star Test 1

1.1 Ernst-Alterman, Manila Olympiad 1992 ended 1...♕a3+ 2 ♔b1 ♗f5+ 3 ♔a1 (3 ♘xf5 ♗xc3 4 ♘xc3 ♕b2#) 3...♕xa2+!! 0-1, in view of 4 ♔xa2 ♖a8+ 5 ♕a5 ♖xa5#.

1.2 One possibility for the previous ten moves which led to the given position is 1 e4 c5 2 ♘f3 d6 3 d4 cxd4 4 ♘xd4 ♘f6 5 ♘c3 g6 6 f4 ♘bd7 (if Black had played the Najdorf variation with 5...a6, then a popular continuation is 6 f4 ♘bd7 {to hinder the advance e4-e5}, but here 5...a6 is replaced by the move 5...g6, which is no less useful to Black) 7 ♗d3 (7 ♘f3

♗g7 8 e5 dxe5 9 fxe5 ♘g4 {if 9...♘h5??, then 10 g4 is a typical way to exploit a situation where 'a knight on the rim is dim'} 10 e6 fxe6 11 ♘g5 ♗xc3+ 12 bxc3 ♕a5!, threatening ...♕e5+ or ...♕xc3+, looks good for Black) 7...♗g7 8 ♗e3 0-0 9 0-0 ♘c5 10 b4? (this leads to the diagram you were given in the Chapter 1 Star Test, but in view of the tactical trick which Black now plays, 10 h3 and 10 ♔h1 {to meet ...♘g4 by ♗g1} are more sensible moves, although 10...b6 followed by ...♗b7 is still a very satisfactory way to answer them).

Black now has 10...♘g4! 11 ♕e2 ♘xd3 12 cxd3 (12 ♕xd3 ♘xe3 13 ♕xe3 ♕b6 leaves White attacked simultaneously at b4 and d4, while ...e5 is threatened too) 12...♘xe3 13 ♕xe3 ♕b6, and then:

a) 14 e5 dxe5 15 fxe5 ♖d8 16 ♖f4 ♗h6 17 ♖af1 ♖xd4!! 18 ♕xd4 ♕xd4+ 19 ♖xd4 ♗e3+ 20 ♔h1 ♗xd4 puts Black a piece ahead.

b) 14 ♘ce2 should be answered by 14...♗g4! 15 ♔f2 ♗xe2 16 ♘xe2 ♗xa1, which wins at least an exchange (in this case, a rook for a bishop) for Black, and is stronger than taking the route 14...e5 15 fxe5 dxe5 16 ♘c2.

1.3 One possibility for the previous 15 moves which led to the given position is: 1 e4 c5 2 ♘f3 d6 3 d4 cxd4 4 ♘xd4 ♘f6 5 ♘c3 g6 6 g3 ♘c6 (some players adopt the move-order 6...♗g7 7 ♗g2 ♘c6, but I think this is risky in view of 8 ♘xc6 bxc6 9 e5) 7 ♘de2

(after 7 ♗g2 ♘xd4 8 ♕xd4 ♗g7 9 0-0 0-0 10 ♕b4, an idea of the late GM Mikhail Tal is 10...♘g4!?, intending to harass White's queen with the manoeuvre ...♘e5-c6, a typically ingenious concept by the 'Magician from Riga', which he uncorked against me at the Glenrothes blitz tournament in 1988) 7...♗g7 8 ♗g2 0-0 9 0-0 ♖b8! (I think this is Black's best line against White's 6 g3 system) 10 a4 a6 11 h3 (White wants to play ♗e3 without being bothered by ...♘g4) 11...b5 12 axb5 axb5 13 ♗e3 b4 14 ♘d5 ♘d7! 15 ♘d4?? (this plausible-looking move leads to the diagram you were given in the Chapter 1 Star Test, but it loses a piece to a lovely tactic, and so White should prevent ...♗xb2 in some other way). Black now wins with 15...♗xd4!! (giving up his Dragon bishop, but winning a piece makes it worthwhile!) 16 ♗xd4 e6! 17 ♘e3 e5 18 ♗a7 ♖a8, and White's dark-squared bishop must confess to being trapped. It is worth comparing this trick with one that is described on page 177 of *C.O.O.L. Chess*.

1.4 This was part of a longer 1929 study by Nikolai Grigoriev. Black's own pawns severely restrict his king, which helps White to win with **1 ♕f7+!** (1 ♕f6+? allows Black to play the safe retreat 1...♔d7) **1...♔e5 2 ♕f6+!** and then:

a) **2...♔e4 3 ♕e6+ ♔f4 4 ♕h6+** ensures the capture of a lady by 5 ♕xc1.

b) **2...♔d5 3 ♕f5+ ♔c4/♔c6 4 ♕c8+** is another skewer that wins Black's queen.

1.5 This was an eye-catching fragment of a much longer 1928 study by F. Prokop. Black's king is in a perilous situation, trapped on the h-file.

a) This allows White to force a draw by perpetual check with **1 ♖h1+ ♕xh1 2 g8♘+ ♔h5 3 ♘f6+ ♔h6 4 ♘g8+**, and so on.

b) However, he can win with **1 g4!!** (threatening 2 g8♘#, but 1 g8♕?? loses after 1...♕f6+ 2 ♕g7+ ♕xg7#) **1...fxg4 2 e4!** (White threatens ♖h1#) **2...♕xe4 3 g8♘+!** (a neat, recurring under-promotion) **3...♔h5 4 ♘f6+**, picking up Black's queen by 5 ♘xe4.

I noticed this position, and the previous one, on Dutch teletext (an excellent source of chess items). Incidentally, when I previously lived in Scotland, I always found the teletext pages on Channel 4 to be a great fountain of information. Now in Brussels, I no longer have access through my TV to John Henderson's chess news and games on page 153, but I am delighted to see that Adam Raoof has managed to get Ceefax pages 578-9 on the BBC channels as another wonderful fountain overflowing with useful and interesting chess 'goodies'.

1.6 In this beautiful 1980 study composed by C.M. Bent, White draws with **1 ♘d6 ♕b1** (after 1...♕f1+ 2 ♘f7+, 2...♕xf7+ 3 ♔xf7 ♘xg5+ is

also a clear draw, but not 2...♔h7?? 3 ♗e4+ ♕f5 4 ♗xf5#) **2 g6!! ♕xg6 3 ♘f7+ ♔h7 4 ♗e4! ♕xe4 5 ♘g5+ ♘xg5** with a **draw** by stalemate.

Star Challenge no. 1

The four pieces are arranged in a square having c3 and a4 as two of its corners, so the other corners must be **b6 and d5**. An easy way to see this is the fact that, in this particular example, each corner is a knight's move away from any adjacent corner. However, c3, a4, c5, e4 are not acceptable because then the pieces would be arranged in a rhombus (diamond), not a square.

We were told that Black's one and only piece is on **a4**, so that square must be where his **king** is located. We also know that if it is Black to move, then the game is a draw, which can only arise here if his lone king is stalemated. This is because if it is White to move, then checkmate is immediately possible. However, we must choose pieces for White on c3, b6 and d5 such that checkmate can be delivered in exactly three ways. Trying different arrangements reveals that **White has a king on b6, queen on c3 and bishop on d5**. Then 1 ♕b3#, 1 ♕a5# and 1 ♗c6# are all possible.

Star Test 2

2.1 In this example, the *king* makes the first star move. There is no piece more precious than the king, and I often remind myself that, in each game, one only gets one king, so look after him well. However, the monarch should still play an active role, when it is safe for him to do so.

In R.McKay-M.Condie, Glasgow 1984, White won with 1 ♔f2!! (threatening 2 ♖h1#) 1-0, in view of 1...♖xg8 2 ♖h1+ ♔g6 3 f5+ ♔g5 4 ♔g3 ♘xe5 5 dxe5, and anyone who can stop 6 ♖h5# deserves a medal!

2.2 Here, a *knight* makes the initial big move. The largest chess piece in the world is reputed to be the knight that stands ten metres tall guarding the entrance to the Dubai Trade Centre. That particular giant piece is not yet into his teens, because I saw the proud knight eleven years ago when he was 'born' for the Dubai Olympiad in 1986.

In Khuzman-Minasian, European Team Ch, Pula 1997, White won by letting his daring knight leap into the fray and disrupt Black's position with 1 ♘d5!!, threatening 2 ♘c7, 2 ♘e7+ and 2 ♘xf6+. The finish was 1...exd5 2 ♗xd5+ ♖e6+ (2...♔g7 3 ♕h6# and 2...♖f7 3 ♕g5 ♕xd6 4 ♕d8+ ♕f8 5 ♗xf7+ {5 ♕f6 ♕g7 6 ♗xf7+ also wins} 5...♔xf7 6 ♖h7+ ♔g8 7 ♖h8+ ♔xh8 8 ♕xf8+ ♔h7 9 0-0-0 g5 10 ♖h1+ ♔g6 11 ♖h6# are other lines which illustrate the great firepower of White's army attacking Black's exposed king, whose pieces on the queenside are dormant and too far

away to help) 3 ♗xe6+ dxe6 4 ♕g5 ♗d7 (4...♕f7 5 ♕d8+, with 5...♔g7 6 ♕h8# or 5...♕f8 6 ♖h8+ to follow, brings White victory as quickly as the actual game continuation does) 5 0-0-0! (much better for White than 5 ♕xg6+? ♕g7) 5...♗e8 (after 5...♘c6 6 ♖h6 ♗e8 7 d7 ♗f7 8 ♕h4 ♕g7 9 d8♕+ ♖xd8 10 ♖xd8+ ♘xd8 11 ♕xd8+ ♕f8, a familiar trick that wins instantly is 12 ♖h8+) 6 ♕d8! 1-0, because Black has no satisfactory way of meeting the threat 7 d7 ♗xd7 (7...♘xd7 8 ♕xa8) 8 ♖h8+ ♔xh8 9 ♕xf8+ ♔h7 10 ♖h1#.

2.3 This time the *queen* makes the all-important first move. It is the only piece that cannot give a discovered check, but the queen is so powerful that it often carries the key to other great discoveries on the chessboard.

The introductory opening moves in V.Milov-R.Rodriguez, New York 1997 were 1 d4 ♘f6 2 c4 e6 3 ♘c3 ♗b4 4 e3 0-0 5 ♗d3 d6?! 6 ♘e2 ♘c6 7 0-0 e5 8 ♘d5! (threatening 9 ♕c2 h6 10 a3 ♗a5 11 b4 ♗b6 12 ♘xf6+ ♕xf6 13 c5 dxc5 14 dxc5 e4 15 ♗xe4 ♕xa1 16 ♗b2 {16 ♘c3 also wins} 16...♕a2, and now for example 17 ♗h7+ ♔h8 18 ♗xg7+ ♔xg7 19 ♕xa2 ♔xh7 20 cxb6 gives White a decisive material advantage) 8...exd4? (he had to try 8...♗a5, because after 8...exd4? 9 exd4 in the actual game, White not only threatens a3 followed by b4, but also the painful pin 10 ♗g5, a move that has been made possible as a result of Black's capture on d4) **9 exd4 ♘xd5 10 cxd5 ♘e7**, which produces the position given in the Star Test.

White now won with **11 ♕a4! c5** (11...♘xd5? 12 a3 ♗d7 13 ♕b3 leaves Black with two pieces *en prise*) **12 dxc6 ♘xc6?** (12...♗a5 13 cxb7 ♗xb7 is hardly appealing for Black, but at least it would limit his material deficit to one pawn instead of one piece) **13 d5 ♕a5 14 ♕xa5 ♘xa5 15 ♖b1!** (much clearer for White than 15 a3 ♘b3) **1-0**, since Black has no satisfactory answer to the threat of 16 a3 ♗c5 17 b4.

2.4 *Pawns* star in this example in a big way, which would have made François-André Danican Philidor proud if he had been alive to see it, and it is particularly fitting that the featured game was played exactly 200 years after the famous Frenchman's birth. Philidor (1726-95) was not only the strongest established chess player of the 18th century, but also a distinguished musical composer, although he is immortalized by his unforgettable words 'Pawns are the soul of chess'.

C.Torre-Ed.Lasker, Chicago 1926 began with the moves **1 ♘f3 d5 2 c4 dxc4 3 ♘a3 e5!** (a little-known yet excellent idea) **4 ♘xe5** (4 ♘xc4 e4 forces the retreat 5 ♘g1 since 5 ♘fe5? f6 6 e3 g6! {6...fxe5 runs into complications with 7 ♕h5+} 7 ♘g4 h5 costs White a knight, yet Black has made seven pawn moves!) **4...♗xa3 5 ♕a4+** (5 bxa3? ♕d4) **5...b5** (I have played 5...♘d7!? successfully on several occasions, and some details are provided on page 172 of *C.O.O.L. Chess*) **6 ♕xa3 ♘f6 7 b3 ♕d6 8 ♗b2?**, but 8 ♕xd6 cxd6 9 ♘f3 followed by ♗b2 or ♗a3 would have been fine for White.

Then Edward Lasker's most forward c-pawn caused chaos by moving further forward with **8...c3!**, and White resigned in view of 9 dxc3 ♕xe5, 9 ♗xc3 ♕xa3, or 9 ♕xd6 cxd6 (the trick 9...cxb2?? backfires due to 10 ♕d4), and White has two pieces *en prise* simultaneously.

Incidentally, Edward Lasker (1885-1981) played a telex game lasting nine hours on the Board of Honour in a match New York vs London, and he was ninety years old at that time! As far as I know, this remarkable man was *not* the same Edward Lasker who was the associate producer of the 1952 American film *The Big Sky*, but, especially with such great people, 'The sky's the limit'!

2.5 Four years after Fernand Joseph composed this neat study in which the star is a *rook*, Bobby Fischer became World Chess Champion in 1972 and said 'I want to live the rest of my life in a house built exactly like a rook'! Is that what they call lateral thinking?!

White draws with **1 ♖e3+ ♕b3 2 ♖d3!!** (the key lateral movement, since 2...♕xd3 produces stalemate, but 2 ♖xb3+? axb3 3 ♔b1 b2 4 ♔c2 ♔a2 followed by 5...b1♕ would have brought White nothing) **2...♔b4 3 ♖xb3+ axb3 4 ♔b2** (4 ♔b1 is also adequate) **4...♔c4 5 ♔b1 ♔c3 6 ♔c1 b2+ 7 ♔b1 ♔b3 stalemate.**

2.6 In this study and its lovely twin in 2.7, a pair of outside passed pawns are ably assisted in an open position by the famous *two bishops*.

White wins with **1 ♗h2+!!** (1 a7+? ♔xa7 2 ♗xf2+ gives White a draw, but not more) and now:

a) **1...♖xh2 2 ♔b6** followed by 3 a7#.

b) **1...e5 2 h8♕+!** (under-promotion to a rook is good enough too, but 2 ♗xe5+? loses to 2...♔a7) **2...♖xh8** (2...♔a7 3 ♕a8#) **3 ♗xe5+ ♔a7 4 ♗d4+ ♔b8 5 a7#.**

c) **1...♔a7 2 ♗b8+!!** (one of my favourite moves in the entire book) **2...♔xb8 3 h8♕+ ♖xh8 4 ♔b6** followed by 5 a7#.

2.7 1 a7+? ♔xa7 2 ♗xf2+ ♔b8 3 ♗xh4 a1♕ 4 ♗g3+ ♔a7 (4...e5?? 5 h8♕+) 5 ♗f2+ gives White a draw, but not more. The same is true of 1 ♗xf2?, since although Black loses after 1...a1♕? 2 a7+! ♕xa7 3 ♗g3+ e5 4 ♗xe5#, he has 1...♖c4+! 2 ♔b6 ♖b4+ 3 ♔c6 ♖c4+ and so on.

White wins with **1 h8♕+! ♖xh8 2 ♗xf2** (threatening a7#) and now:

a) **2...a1♕ 3 a7+! ♕xa7 4 ♗g3+ e5 5 ♗xe5#.**

b) **2...♖c8+ 3 ♔b6!!** branches into:

b1) **3...a1♕ 4 ♗g3+ e5 5 ♗xe5+ ♕xe5 6 a7#.**

b2) **3...♖c6+ 4 ♔xc6 a1♕ 5 a7+ ♕xa7 6 ♗g3+ e5 7 ♗xe5#.**

Star Challenge no. 2

a) The two players X and Y have used 126 minutes altogether, but 30 minutes of that is the extra time which X has consumed compared to Y. 126-30 = 96 and 96/2 = 48. So Y has used 48 minutes whereas X has used 48+30 = 78 minutes. Each player started with 120 minutes, so now **X has** 120-78 = **42 minutes left** and **Y has** 120-48 = **72 minutes left**.

b) X's number of moves left (to reach and complete move 40) multiplied by his number of minutes left per move = 42 minutes whereas Y's number of moves left multiplied by his number of minutes left per move = 72 minutes. We were told that the number of moves left is *more than six*, so the following numbers can be considered:

42 = 42x1 or 21x2 or 14x3 or **7x6** and

72 = 72x1 or 36x2 or 24x3 or 18x4 or 12x6 or 9x8 or **8x9**.

The numbers in bold are the only ones which fit the fact that the players must either have the same number of moves left to play **or** Black can have one move more left. Therefore, **X has 7 moves left and Y has 8 moves left**.

c) Furthermore, **X must be White, Y must be Black, and Black is about to play his 33rd move** (8 moves left, up to and including move 40).

d) Even though it is Black to move, **White (player X) forces checkmate inside 7 moves** (that is, not later than move 39) as follows:

1) **1...f3** 2 g3 f2 3 ♗a3 (threatening ♗d6#) 3...d4 4 c4 e3 (4...d3 5 ♗b2#) 5 d3 f4 6 g4 f1♕ 7 ♗d6#.

2) **1...e3** 2 d3 f3 3 g3 f4 (3...e2 4 ♗f4# is another pretty possibility) 4 g4 e2 5 ♗a3 d4 6 c4 e1♕ 7 ♗d6#.

Those lines, and any other ones, are almost identical except that Black can push his pawns in different orders. However, that cannot prevent White's bishop from delivering a cute checkmate. Eddy van Espen, my Belgian friend who composed the problem in part 'd', clearly has an eagle-eye for beauty on the chessboard.

Star Test 3

3.1 Van Herck-H.Cardon, Belgian Interclubs league 1988, began as a **Nimzo-Indian Defence** (1 d4 ♘f6 2 c4 e6 3 ♘c3 ♗b4), and Marcel van Herck employed the Leningrad Variation, 4 ♗g5. The position in the Star Test showed White about to play his 12th move, which was **12 ♖h8+!!** with these points:

a) **12...♔xh8** 13 ♕h5+ ♔g7 14 ♕xg5+ ♔h7 15 ♗xf6 wins Black's queen because of the threat ♕g7#.

b) **12...♔g7 13 ♕h5!** (threatening ♕h6# or ♕h7#) **13...♖xh8 14 ♕xg5+ ♔f8** (14...♔h7 15 ♗xf6 ♕f8 16 ♕h5+! ♕h6 17 ♕xf7+ ♔g7 18 ♕xg7#) **15 ♗xf6 ♕a5 16 ♕g7+ ♔e8**

17 ♕xh8# is the actual game continuation, in which IM Helmut Cardon sportingly allowed checkmate. The tactics in the next example are equally elegant and efficient.

3.2 In Thoeng-Carlier, Belgian Interclubs league 1994, Black has threats of his own, so White must act quickly. FM Paulus Thoeng played **1 ♘f6+!!** and the game concluded **1...♔h8** (1...♔f8 2 ♕e7#, 1...♔xf6 2 ♖xf6 ♗xf6 3 ♕xf7+ and 1...♗xf6 2 ♖e8+! ♖xe8 {2...♔h7 3 ♕xf7+ ♗g7 4 ♕g8#} 3 ♕xf7+ ♔h8 4 ♕xe8+ ♔h7 5 ♕g8# are clearly hopeless for Black too) **2 ♕xa8+!! ♘xa8 3 ♖e8+ ♗f8 4 ♖xf8+ ♔g7 5 ♖xf7+ ♔h8 6 ♖h7#** – IM Bruno Carlier sportingly allows checkmate.

3.3 In this game, Van Herck-Lavrenov, Belgium 1990, White continued with 1 ♕d2? and later drew. However, **1 ♕xe7!!** loses his queen but seizes the initiative and the win after **1...♖e8 2 ♖e4! ♖xe7 3 ♖xe7**, and Black can resign in view of the threat 4 ♖g7+ ♔f8 (4...♔h8 5 ♘f7#) 5 ♘xh7+ ♔e8 6 ♘f6+ ♔f8 7 ♖g8+ ♔f7 8 h7, because the h-pawn will become a new queen.

3.4 This one is part of a 1992 prize-winning problem by Julien Vandiest. White wins with **1 ♕g5+! ♔b6** (1...♔b4 loses immediately to 2 ♕d2+) **2 ♕d8+ ♔a6 3 ♗xb7+ ♔b5 4 ♕d5+ ♔b4** (4...♔a4 5 ♕b3# or 4...♔b6 5 ♕c6#) **5**

♕d4+ ♚b5 (5...♚a3 6 ♕b2+ ♚a4 7 ♕b3#) **6 ♚b3!** (making the king play an active role, and threatening 7 ♕c4+ ♚b6 8 ♕c6#) **6...a6** (6...♚b6 7 ♕b4#) **7 ♕d5+ ♚b6 8 ♕d8+ ♚b5 9 ♗c6+ ♚xc6 10 ♕xa5.**

3.5 In this tremendous 1995 study by Jan Marwitz, 1 ♗xc6+? ♚b8 2 e6 is tempting, but Black then draws with 2...♘e2+ 3 ♚f1 (3 ♚g2 ♘f4+ and 4...♘xe6) 3...g2+! 4 ♗xg2 ♘g3+ 5 ♚f2 ♘f5, and the e-pawn's advance is halted. Similarly, 1 e6? ♘e2+ 2 ♚f1 g2+ 3 ♗xg2 ♘g3+ 4 ♚f2 ♘f5 nets Black an easy half-point because his knight not only stops e6-e7, but is also ready to sacrifice itself for the e-pawn if later called upon to do so. Furthermore, 1 ♗f3? ♚b7 2 e6 ♚c7 does not trouble Black.

The key in White's winning method is to prevent the black knight from emerging in such a way that it halts the e-pawn. So the initial star move is **1 ♗d3!!** which leads to:

a) **1...♘xd3** 2 e6, and the e-pawn is unstoppable.

b) **1...♚b7** (the main line) **2 ♗c4!** (covering all of the knight's escape routes: a simple yet elegant case of a bishop dominating a knight) and now:

b1) **2...♚c7** 3 ♚g2 ♚d7 4 ♚xg3 ♚e7 5 ♚f4 (5 ♚f2? ♘d3+! 6 ♗xd3 ♚e6 lets Black off the hook) 5...c5 6 ♚f5 (the manoeuvre ♚e3-d2 to capture the helpless knight also wins) 6...♚d7 7 ♚f6 ♚e8 8 e6 ♚f8 9 e7+ ♚e8 10 ♗b5#.

b2) **2...♚b6** (the primary path in this study) **3 ♚g2 ♚c5 4 ♚xg3! ♚xc4 5 e6 ♘e2+ 6 ♚h2!!** followed by e7-e8♕ wins for White, but that is the only correct way. 6 ♚f2? ♘c3 7 e7 ♘e4+ 8 ♚e3 ♘d6, 6 ♚g4? ♘c3 7 e7 ♘d5 8 e8♕ ♘f6+ 9 ♚f5 ♘xe8 and 6 ♚h4? ♘f4 7 e7 ♘g6+ 8 ♚g5 ♘xe7 all let Black pocket a win instead of going home empty-handed.

3.6 White gets his king transported to **b6** and a **knight** beamed onto **b5**, adjacent to the king. Then Black is powerless to prevent the smothered mate ♘c7#.

Star Challenge no. 3

The total price (£527) ends with the digit 7. Even if Mr Price had not received £10 discount on some clocks, the total would still have ended in a '7'. So if £P is the normal price for one chess clock, then 13×P must end in a 7. This can only happen if the last digit of P is 9. For example, 13×£39 = £507, but that is less than £527. So P must be at least 49. 13×£49 = £637, which is £110 more than the total price actually paid.

a) Therefore the normal price for a clock is **£49**, and Mr Price received a discount of £10 on each of **11** clocks. Check: (2×£49)+(11×£39) = £527 for 13 clocks. Note that 13×£59 = £767 which is far too big to fit this problem. So £49 is the only possible normal price in this particular example.

b) White sustains the initiative all the way until mate at move 13 with an elegant mix of sacrificial tactics and efficient manoeuvres, particularly by the rook on f4. The star sequence is: **1 ♗xg4+! gxh2 2 ♗f5+ ♔g8** (2...♖xf5 3 ♖h4+ ♖h5 {3...♔g8 4 ♖h8# or 3...♔g6 4 ♖h6#} 4 ♖xh5+ ♔g6 5 ♘f4#) **3 b8♕+!!** (3 ♗h7+? ♔xh7 4 ♖h4+ ♔g6 wins for Black) **3...♘xb8 4 ♖d8+!! ♖xd8 5 ♗h7+!!** (perfect timing, and the only correct moment for this sacrifice) **5...♔xh7 6 ♖h4+ ♔g6 7 ♖h6+ ♔f5 8 ♖h5+** (the black king now begins what is known among study composers as a 'starflight', since the king has four diagonal escape routes, against each of which White has a distinct and unique winning continuation) **8...♔xe6** (or: 8...♔g4 9 ♖g5+ ♔h4 10 g3+ ♔h3 11 ♘f4#; 8...♔g6 9 ♘f4#; 8...♔e4 9 ♖e5#) **9 ♖e5+ ♔d7 10 ♖e7+ ♔c8 11 b7+! ♘xb7 12 ♖c7+!** (the seventh sacrifice since the start of the sequence!) **12...♖xc7 13 ♘b6#.** Smothered mate makes a lovely finish.

'SPIN sum'

The problem was presented like this:

SPIN
PINS
NIPS
‾‾‾‾

Suppose it is an addition sum. Then the most right-hand column shows N and S adding to give S, so N would have to be zero. However, that would make the left-hand digit of NIPS a zero, which is not possible. Therefore the 'sum' must in fact be a **subtraction**. That is, SPIN-PINS = NIPS, so SPIN = NIPS+PINS, which we can write as an addition sum like this:

NIPS
PINS
SPIN
‾‾‾‾

The left-hand column shows that S must be greater than N (or P). So how can two S's add to produce an N in the right-hand column? The answer is that S+S = N+10. So we can deduce that *S equals 6 or more*, and an N gets written down then a '1' is carried over to the next 'tens' column. This means that, in the second column from the right, P+N+1 produces an I. We can now deduce from the left-hand column that N+P = S. No extra '1' is involved there since N+P+1 would give I (not S). We already know that *S = 6, 7, 8 or 9*, the same as N+P, so *I* which results from P+N+1 must be *7, 8, 9 or 0* (not 10, because I is a single digit).

The third column from the right shows I+I. The result must be less than 10, otherwise a '1' would be carried on to the left-hand column, and we have already established that that is not the case. If I+I is less than 10, then *I is less than 5*. However, we already know that I = 7, 8, 9 or 0, and the only one that fits is **I = 0, zero**. So what about I+I producing P? As P cannot be zero too, **P = 1** is forced, and a '1' must have been carried over from the second column on the right to cause that. Here is how the sum looks at this stage:

$$\begin{array}{r} \text{N01S} \\ \underline{\text{10NS}} \\ \text{S10N} \end{array}$$

Remembering that a '1' gets carried over from the right-hand column to the next column, we can deduce that **N = 8** (so that 1+N+'carried 1' = 10, or 0 then carry 1). Finally, the left-hand column shows **S = 9** (8+1). The complete addition sum (with S = 9, P = 1, I = 0, N = 8) is:

$$\begin{array}{r} \text{NIPS}\quad 8019 \\ \underline{\text{PINS}\quad 1089} \\ \text{SPIN}\quad 9108 \end{array}$$

One possible answer to the extra part about PINS = 1089 and SNIP = 9801 is that SNIP = 9×PINS.

Star Test 4

4.1 Black's last move must have been ...g7-g5, and so the solution is **1 hxg6#**.

4.2 The neat finish is **1...♕d2+! 2 ♕xd2** (2 ♖g5 ♕xg5#) **2...♖g6#**.

4.3 The elegant solution is **1 ♔a5!!** and then:

a) **1...e1♕+** 2 ♔b6 and mate next move (for example, 2...♕f2+ 3 ♘d4# or 2...♖g7 3 ♘e7#).

b) **1...♖g8** 2 ♘d4+ ♔a7 3 ♘b5#, which shows why White did not play 1 ♔b5.

c) **1...♖g7** 2 ♘e7+ ♔a7 3 ♘c8#.

d) **1...♔b7** loses exactly as in line 'c'.

4.4 Black wins beautifully with **1...♕xh2+!!** (1...♕h3?? 2 ♕e8#) **2 ♔xh2** (2 ♔f1 ♕h1#) **2...♘g4+ 3 ♔g1 ♘h3+ 4 ♔f1 ♘h2#**.

4.5 Black wins with **1...♘6g4+! 2 hxg4** (2 ♔g1 ♘xh3++ 3 ♔h1 ♕g1+! 4 ♖xg1 ♘hf2# is a smothered mate of sorts) **2...♘xg4+ 3 ♔h3** (3 ♔h1 ♕h6+ 4 ♗h3 ♕xh3+ 5 ♔g1 ♕h2#) **3...♕h6+! 4 ♔xg4 ♗h5+ 5 ♔f5** (5 ♔h3 and 5 ♔h4 are both answered by 5...♗f3#) **5...♕f6#**.

4.6 The lovely solution is **1 ♖f3+!! ♗xf3** (1...♗f5 2 ♖xf5#) **2 ♖g8+ ♔f7 3 ♖g7+ ♔f8 4 g6** (threatening 5 ♖f7# and 5 ♖g8#) **4...♗xd5 5 ♖f7+! ♗xf7 6 g7#**.

4.7 White threatens **♕a8#**, but Black strikes first with **1...♖h8+ 2 ♔g1 ♖h1+!! 3 ♘xh1 ♗h2+! 4 ♔xh2 ♖h8+ 5 ♗h6 ♖xh6+ 6 ♔g3** (6 ♔g1 ♖xh1#) **6...♘f5+ 7 ♔f4** (or 7 ♔g4) **7...♖h4#**.

Star Challenge no. 4

The non-members pay 111 lunes each, but one third of that money is reserved for administration. 111 divided by three equals 37, and then 111-37 = 74. So 74 lunes out of every non-member's fee goes towards the prize fund. Since the LCF members each pay 74 lunes too, we can say that 74 lunes per person goes into prizes. The total prize fund is between 4700 and 4800 lunes. 4700 divided by 74 equals 63.51..., whereas 4800 divided by 74 equals 64.86...

a) The only whole number between those two answers is **64**, which must be the number of players. Also, 64×74 = **4736**, which must therefore be the exact total prize fund (in lunes!).

b) The winning move is **1 ♘g5!**, threatening 2 ♘f3# and planning 2 ♘h3# if Black moves the knight from f2. The longest line until checkmate is: **1...♖a2+ 2 ♔xa2** (2 ♔xb1? ♖a1+! 3 ♔xa1 ♗c3+ followed by 4...e1♘! lets Black turn the tables) **2...♘d2 3 ♔a1!** (3 ♔a3? and 3 ♔b2? both allow 3...♘c4+ followed by 4...♘e5, winning for Black) **3...♘b3+ 4 ♔b1 ♘d2+ 5 ♔a2!** (basically, the rest of the solution involves repeated triangulation with ♔a2-a1-b1-a2, and Black can only delay the inevitable checkmate by advancing his a-pawns and sacrificing them) **5...a4 6 ♔a1 ♘b3+ 7 ♔b1 ♘d2+ 8 ♔a2 a5 9 ♔a1 ♘b3+ 10 ♔b1 ♘d2+ 11 ♔a2 a6 12 ♔a1 ♘b3+ 13 ♔b1 ♘d2+ 14 ♔a2 a3 15 ♔a1 ♘b3+ 16 ♔b1 ♘d2+ 17 ♔a2 a4 18 ♔a1 ♘b3+ 19 ♔b1 ♘d2+ 20 ♔a2 a5 21 ♔a1 ♘b3+ 22 ♔b1 a2+** (the first pawn goes, because 22...♘d2+ is met by 23 ♔a2 and mate next move)

23 ♔xa2 ♘d2 24 ♔a1 ♘b3+ 25 ♔b1 ♘d2+ 26 ♔a2 a3 27 ♔a1 ♘b3+ 28 ♔b1 ♘d2+ 29 ♔a2 a4 30 ♔a1 ♘b3+ 31 ♔b1 a2+ 32 ♔xa2 ♘d2 33 ♔a1 ♘b3+ 34 ♔b1 ♘d2+ 35 ♔a2 a3 36 ♔a1 ♘b3+ 37 ♔b1 a2+ 38 ♔xa2 (no more a-pawns!) **38...♘d2 39 ♔a1 ♘b3+ 40 ♔b1 ♘d2+ 41 ♔a2** and either **42 ♘f3#** or **42 ♘h3#**, depending on which way Black prefers to be checkmated.

Star Test 5

5.1 M.Pavlović-Zollbrecht, Biel 1997 started **1 e4 d6 2 d4 ♘f6 3 ♘c3 g6 4 f4 c5?** (first 4...♗g7 5 ♘f3, and only then 5...c5 6 dxc5 ♕a5, is OK for Black) **5 dxc5 ♕a5** (5...dxc5 6 ♕xd8+ ♔xd8 7 e5 is also very good for White) **6 cxd6! ♘xe4.** White then won with **7 ♕d5!** (this would fail to ...♗xc3+ if Black already had a bishop on g7) **7...♘c5** (7...♕xd5 8 ♘xd5 ♘a6 9 ♗xa6 renews the threat of ♘c7+) **8 ♗b5+ 1-0**, in view of 8...♘cd7 9 ♗xd7+ followed by ♕xa5.

5.2 Borge-Gretarsson, Copenhagen 1997 went **1 e4 e5 2 ♘f3 ♘c6 3 ♗b5 ♗c5 4 c3 ♕f6?! 5 d4! exd4 6 e5! ♕d8** (Black's strategy of trying to prevent d2-d4 has failed, the key tactical point being that 6...♘xe5 loses to the pin 7 ♕e2) **7 cxd4 ♗b4+ 8 ♘c3 ♘ge7 9 d5 ♘b8 10 0-0 0-0 11 d6** ('d for decisive!') **11...cxd6 12 exd6 ♘g6 13 ♘e4 ♗a5 14 ♕d5 ♕e8 15 b4! ♗b6** (15...♗xb4 16 ♗b2 {threatening ♕d4} is also overwhelming for White because most of Black's pieces are confined in a congested way to the back rank, and they cannot help their king against the forthcoming onslaught) **16 Ξe1** (threatening ♘f6+) **16...♕e6 17 ♕h5 f6** (17...h6 loses to 18 ♗xh6! gxh6 19 ♕xh6 ♘h8 20 ♘f6+) **18 ♘eg5! ♕xe1+ 19 ♘xe1 fxg5 20 ♘f3 1-0.**

5.3 McShane-Costagliola, London 1997 went **1 e4 e5 2 ♘f3 ♘c6 3 ♗b5 ♘d4** (Bird's Defence) **4 ♘xd4 exd4 5 0-0 ♕h4?!** (5...♗c5 is better) **6 d3 ♗c5 7 ♘d2 ♘e7 8 e5! ♘g6** (after 8...0-0 9 ♘e4 ♗b6 10 ♗g5, Black's queen is trapped, a severe penalty for venturing out too early) **9 ♘e4 ♗e7.** Now Luke McShane found the star retreating move **10 ♘g3!**, threatening to trap the black queen in a new way with ♘f5. The game ended **10...♘xc5 11 ♘f5 ♕f6 12 ♘xe7! ♔xe7** (if 12...♕xe7, then the fatal pin 13 Ξe1 threatens to win the black knight with f2-f4) **13 Ξe1 ♔d8** (13...♔f8 14 ♕e2) **14 ♕h5!** (threatening ♗g5 or ♕xe5) **14...h6 15 ♕xe5 1-0.**

5.4 Martyn-Choukouhian, Brussels 1997 went **1 ♘c3 c5 2 e4** (the opening has transposed to the Sicilian Defence) **2...d6 3 f4 ♘c6 4 ♘f3 g6 5 ♗c4** (my creative Belgian friend Gorik Cools likes to play 5 g3 ♗g7 6 ♗g2 here, but he normally gets it via the Modern Defence: 1 e4 g6 2 ♘c3 d6 {2...♗g7 3 h4!? h5 4 d4 d6 5 ♗c4 ♘f6

6 ♗b3 followed by ♗g5 is another of Gorik's cool ideas, and Black cannot play ...h6 to drive White's dark-squared bishop away from g5} 3 f4 ♗g7 4 ♘f3 c5 5 g3 ♘c6 6 ♗g2) **5...♗g7 6 d3 e6** (it is better for Black to aim for this set-up with his d-pawn still on d7 because he can later play ...d7-d5 in one move without wasting a tempo on ...d6 first) **7 0-0 ♘ge7 8 ♕e1 0-0 9 f5** (this example of 'f for forward' crops up a lot in this, the Grand Prix Attack) **9...exf5 10 ♕h4! d5?** (if 10...fxe4 then 11 ♘g5 is crushing, and in Martyn-Thierens, Brussels 1997, Black also lost quickly with 10...♘d4 11 ♗g5! {threatening ♗xe7 or ♘d5} 11...♘xf3+ 12 Ξxf3 ♗xc3 13 bxc3 Ξe8 14 ♕h6 {threatening ♗f6 and ♕g7#} 14...f4 15 Ξxf4 1-0, which is even more drastic than the game Van Mechelen-Lavrenov, Geel 1997: 10...♗d7 11 ♗h6 ♘c8 12 ♘g5 ♕f6 13 ♘d5! ♕d4+ 14 ♔h1 ♗xh6 15 ♕xh6 ♕g7 16 ♘f6+! ♔h8 17 ♕h4! {Jan van Mechelen's move here is much stronger for White than 17 ♕xg7+ ♔xg7 18 ♘xd7 Ξd8} 17...h5 18 ♘xd7 f6 19 ♘e6 1-0) **11 exd5 ♘a5 12 ♗g5 Ξe8** (12...f6 loses to 13 d6+) **13 Ξae1 ♗f8 14 d6!** (a nice clearance sacrifice to re-open the a2-g8 diagonal for White's star bishop pointing towards Black's monarch) **14...♕xd6 15 ♘b5 ♕d8.** 11-year-old Rafe Martyn then showed why I say 'No one is safe when playing this Rafe!', because the game ended with **16 ♗xf7+! ♔xf7 17 ♕xh7+ ♗g7 18 ♘e5+ ♔f8 19 ♗h6**

1-0, in view of 19...♗xh6 20 ♕f7#. Rafe also scored 2/2 with the Grand Prix Attack at the 1997 British Under-11 Championship, and he went on to tie for first place on 5½/7 with Kenan Boztas, Krunal Kahar and Lawrence Trent. Many congratulations to four stars who have come to the fore!

5.5 White wins with **1 ♗a5! ♔b8 2 ♗c7+ ♔b7 3 ♘e4 a5 4 ♘c5#.**

5.6 After **1 ♗xg7**, Black in fact resigned due to 1...♔xg7 2 ♗f5!! followed by:

a) 2...♕f7 3 e6.

b) 2...gxf5 3 exf6+ ♕xf6 4 ♘h5+, a deadly fork.

c) 2...♕e7 3 exf6+ ♕xf6 4 ♗xd7, and White has won a piece.

Star Challenge no. 5

a) The knight manoeuvre ♘g1-e2-c1-d3-b2-c4-a3-b5-a7-c6-b8-d7-f8-e6-g7-f5-h6-g4-h2-f3-g1 traces out one example of a 10-pointed star.

b) White wins with **1 ♖f8 ♖aa8 2 g8♘+!** (the knight I spoke of suddenly appears!) **2...♔g7 3 ♖xe8 ♖xe8 4 ♘e7!** followed by c8♕.

E.T.'s Colour Puzzle

On Star T, the top of a promoting white pawn would be the colour **violet**. From the second rank through to the eighth rank, the white pawn gets the seven different colours of the rainbow, or (as discovered by Isaac Newton in 1666) the spectrum of colours that a beam of white light splits into when passed through a triangular glass prism, for example. The magnificent seven colours (in order of decreasing wavelength) are: Red, Orange, Yellow, Green, Blue, Indigo, Violet. For instance, before an *en passant* capture, a white pawn would be on the fifth rank. That corresponds to the colour green, because remember that the first colour, red, corresponds to a pawn at the start on the second rank (not the first rank).

Always remember: keep a smile on your face and a rainbow in your heart. I hope we will meet again soon...

Index of Openings